THE
ZINC
CITY,

Webb City, Missouri

JEANNE NEWBY

NEWMAN SPRINGS PUBLISHING
320 Broad Street
Red Bank, NJ 07701

First originally published by Newman Springs Publishing 2021

ISBN 978-1-63692-524-0 (Paperback)
ISBN 978-1-63881-709-3 (Hardcover)
ISBN 978-1-63692-525-7 (Digital)

Printed in the United States of America

To Bob Foos who allowed me to write for *The Sentinel* for thirty-one years. To my family who had to share my time with research and writing. And to the many citizens who shared stories, photos, and memories. And to my favorite research partner, Don Freeman.

Contents

Introduction

Webb City, Missouri, incorporated December 1876.

Webb City, the town whose history includes lead and zinc mining, industry, Route 66, Jefferson Highway, and the Southwest Missouri Electric Railway Company.

Founded as a city by John C. Webb in 1876, established as a community by many great men and women throughout the years.

Located in Southwest Missouri, in the heart of the Ozarks.

Not to forget the many neighboring towns which helped to make up the great Tri-State Mining District.

The founding of Webb City, Missouri, 1876.

By Jack Dawson
Webb City Artist

John C. Webb

CHAPTER 1

From the Beginning

From the Beginning

Once upon a time, a long time ago—that's how most fairy tales begin. The story you are about to read seems like a fairy tale, but John C. Webb's fairy tale was true life. The story begins in the great state of Tennessee.

John Cornwall Webb

John Cornwall Webb was born March 12, 1826, in Overton County, Tennessee. He was the second child in a large family. His father was Elijah C. Webb.

Elijah C. Webb was an early pioneer to the state of Tennessee. His family was long-time residents of North Carolina. Elijah's father, Benjamin C. Webb, had fought in the Revolutionary War. Born in North Carolina, Benjamin had migrated with his wife to Tennessee and died there in 1825.

Farming was the occupation that Elijah was familiar with, and when he moved his wife, Martha Johnson, to Tennessee in 1826, it was natural for them to continue their farming tradition. The farm life they provided for their family was a good solid foundation. The children were raised in a spiritual home and attended school in a little log schoolhouse with split-log benches. Education was very important to the Webb family.

In 1849, at the age of twenty-three, John C. Webb found the love of his life, Ruth F. Davis, and they were married. They bought a little farm of their own, and life was pretty content for about six years. Then in 1855, Elijah and his brother James C. Webb, with the family pioneer spirit in their blood, decided to make a change in their lives as they uprooted their families and moved west to the new frontier. Missouri was that new frontier, of which they had heard stories.

The two Webb families settled in an area about three miles east of what would later be known as Joplin. They had good land at the head of Turkey Creek. To this day, there is a Webb cemetery called Harmony Grove located on that original homestead land.

A year later, in 1856, John C. and Ruth Webb joined the family in Southwest Missouri. They stayed a short time on the Webb homestead as they contemplated where they wanted to start their own family homestead.

John found a beautiful site to build a home. Any direction you looked, you could see green meadows. The wooded streams carried lots of cool clear water, and the hills of the Ozarks could be seen in the distance. So in 1857, John invested a few hundred dollars and applied for two hundred acres in Center Creek Township, which later changed to Dubuque Township, and then in 1873 changed to the Joplin Township.

The first project after obtaining the land was to build a log cabin. The cabin was made from unhewn logs, the very logs that John cut down to allow for planting on the land. The roof was made from clapboards (thin narrow boards with one end thicker than the other), held in place by heavy boards. Nails were made by hand and only used when absolutely necessary.

One readily available substance was rocks, which, along with mud and sticks, were used to build the chimney. Eventually John uncovered enough beautiful stones to rebuild the chimney using stone and mortar instead of rocks, mud, and sticks.

The inside of the cabin was dark as glass was hard to come by. Glass could be ordered from St. Louis, but it took eight weeks to travel by horseback, and a wagon took even longer. It was not a smooth trip, and glass did not travel well. Many panes of glass would be broken before the end of the journey.

John eventually added to his cabin with a fireplace at both ends to evenly distribute the heat. A sign of being well-off was whether your cabin had a wooden floor or dirt floor. John was able to put in a wooden floor for his family.

John and Ruth felt they had found a piece of heaven. There was plenty of prairie land to farm, timbered land to hunt, trees for building, and streams for fishing. The family was fed on fish, deer, turkey, squirrel, rabbits, and small birds, plus the fruits and vegetables that John harvested. The land was plentiful, and the family did well. As money was obtained from crops, John added to his acreage until he had 320 acres, of which he cultivated about 100 of those acres.

The log cabin of John and Ruth Webb. Located on what would become the northwest corner of Webb and Broadway Streets in Webb City. Two chimneys, only a small window.

The Story Continues

In 1861, as the Civil War was beginning, Governor Jackson encouraged John to volunteer. He served out the war with the Confederate Army. His family had traveled to Texas during the war as it was not safe in Missouri. At the end of the war, he returned home to work his land. And the family returned from Texas.

One bright June morning, in the year 1873, John C. Webb's simple life was about to take a drastic turn. The forty-seven-year-old farmer headed out to plow his land, as he had for the past seventeen years. He left the log cabin (located on the northwest corner of what are now Broadway and Webb Streets) and headed east to a field located between where Webb City and Carterville are today.

Since John C. Webb did not keep a journal, the actual story varies and has become only memories and legend.

One story claims that as the old mule was pulling the plow, the blade got stuck on a huge rock. Another story says that John sat down to rest a spell, and the sun struck on something shining in the dirt. Either way, John picked up that shiny rock and took it home with him at the end of the day.

The 1883 *History of Jasper County* states that the lead was discovered by Mr. Webb while ploughing corn.

According to the 1899 *W.C. Gazette*, he didn't immediately run out and shout about what he had uncovered. He basically had an idea of what it was since there had been much commotion over toward the Granby area, to the southeast and Unionville (Oronogo) to the north, about some ore being discovered. He set the stone aside and didn't give it too much thought until one day, a wandering miner named Murrell stopped by to ask for a meal from John and Ruth. After dinner, while discussing Murrell's adventures in the mines, John showed him the "shines" that he had dug up. Well, needless to say, Murrell became very excited. If there was ore like that at the surface, then there was bound to be more below the ground.

Murrell convinced John that they needed to start mining the area to see what other treasures lay beneath that good farmland. John said they would have to wait until after the harvest as he had crops that needed tending. His farming was his livelihood, and that came first.

The coolness of fall was setting in as Murrell and Webb began their search for lead in the rich farm dirt. Murrell brought nothing but mining experience to this new partnership. John supplied the land and the tools. But alas, the miners had troubles as the shaft kept filling with water. Each morning, they would have to empty out the water before they began their digging. It didn't take long for Murrell to lose interest; after all, he didn't have anything invested but his time. He thought the ore would be close to the surface, and it would be like walking along and gathering the rich rocks. So when W. A. Daugherty, Webb's neighbor, came along and offered Murrell $25 for his interest in the mine, Murrell jumped at the deal, and he was on his way. After all, he usually made a mere dollar a day in the mines, so $25 was a small fortune.

John Webb was showing a little discouragement also, as he continued to battle the water along with Daugherty. They hadn't uncovered anything of importance but did notice a small vein that Daugherty marked with a hatchet.

Granville P. Ashcraft related how fortune looked down on him one day as he was showing his temper. He had just secured a deal in Oronogo (to buy the Oronogo Circle) for $1,500; he got mad over some small incident and sold it for a measly $50, then wandered over toward Webb City to see what Daugherty was doing. It didn't take much to convince Webb to sell his interest in the mine to Ashcraft, but being a very wise man, Webb only leased them the land, allowing him to draw royalty on anything they might find.

Ashcraft asked Daugherty if he had noticed any signs of mineral, and Daugherty told him about the marks he had made. Ashcraft was lowered into the mine. He drilled some holes, set in some powder and a fuse. The fuse was lit, and Ashcraft had scarcely made the thirty-foot climb to the top when the charge exploded. After the smoke cleared, Ashcraft went back down to find that a cave-like pocket had opened up, which showed a solid mass of lead. That was the beginning of the Center Creek Mines and the beginning of a mad rush on Webb City.

According to the *Encyclopedia of the History of Missouri*, vol. 6 "John C. Webb" (1901), E. T. Webb tells the story of the day John C. Webb found that piece of lead. Since it is Webb's son, this article claims to probably be the most accurate story.

E.T. states:

> *While plowing, and on arriving at the end of a field near a branch, he [John C. Webb] found a nugget of lead. About this time, one Murrell, a wandering miner, came along and fully identified the metal. Mr. Webb engaged him in partnership to sink a shaft, but not much progress had been made when it filled with water, and the discouraged miner counseled abandonment of the enterprise. In this strait, Mr. Webb sought an old neighbor and friend, William A. Daugherty, who at his solicitation, bought Murrell's mining outfit—a spade, pick and tamping iron—paying twenty-five dollars therefore, Webb and Daugherty knew nothing of mining, but they prosecuted the work for about a year, doing their own digging and hoisting. Mr. Webb now withdrew, and Daugherty associated with himself and Granville P. Ashcraft, the two leasing land for mining purposes from the former named [Webb]. They were successful in their operations almost from the outset, taking out nearly 20,000 pounds of lead in sinking their shaft, and afterward reaching a cave deposit which yielded much more. The fame of this success spread rapidly, and that summer there was an influx of population from the adjoining country, and the ground became a great mining camp. Mr. Webb, realizing his want of knowledge of practical mining, held aloof from these operations, but opened his ground to all applicants on the most liberal terms, opening the way of fortune to many. In the same summer he platted Webb City upon his land, and a municipal organization was effected December 15th, 1876. With his characteristic modesty, he declined all official positions in the city of his own creation, but aided in every way its material development, disposing of lots upon the most liberal terms and aiding many out of his means in the building of their homes.*

Ashcraft's Story Adds to the True-Life Fairy Tale

Ashcraft made the first sale of lead from Webb City. Ashcraft was reported as saying that many of the events in life that make history for individuals is more "a moment of chance than of design." He said his decision of a moment to go to Webb City to check on Daugherty, instead of heading off prospecting somewhere else, was the decision that caused him to remain in Webb City the rest of his life, except for a few trips out west.

Ashcraft remembered that Thomas N. Davey, from Carthage, had been working on a pump that just might work to "beat the water." The water was drained with the help of Benjamin F. Hatcher. Here are Benjamin's memories.

Benjamin F. Hatcher recalled:

When Ashcraft first came over from Oronogo and undertook to sink the shaft on Center Creek, where there had been the first lead find in this district, I started with him to run the pump. My recollection is that it took a relay of seven horses, working each horse for two to three hours at a time, to keep the pump going, and all we had then was literally "horse power." It wasn't much of a shaft, as we should think now. It was something less than thirty feet deep, and some lead had been taken out, that was in the dump, but none had been sold. It looked very doubtful about getting any more, as the water was so strong it came out of the top of the hole within a few hours whenever the pump stopped. We kept at it until he got enough out to make several sales of lead, but under great difficulty, and when there was high water there was nothing doing.

People didn't know much about pumps in those days, not around here anyway, and I remember that Thomas N. Davey, then and for a long time after in the foundry business at Carthage, devised a new kind of pump that he had hoped would prove adequate to the water proposition, as we should call it now, at Center Creek. But it didn't work; and for years there was little else but discouragement as to continuous work, for when the pump shaft was down, none of the numerous prospectors were able to get in the ground. Among those interested in working this shaft [besides Ashcraft] in the early day were Ben Webb and John C. Webb, on whose land the discovery was made; Thomas N. Davey, W.A. Daugherty, S.R. Corn, of Joplin, and a practical miner named Mike Jones, who came from Oronogo.

Center Creek Mining Company (originally owned by John C. Webb. The location of the first lead and zinc found in the Webb City area), located between Webb City and Carterville. The Missouri-Pacific train and on the other side of the train is the Missouri-Pacific train depot.

Granville P. Ashcraft

New Blood in the Mining Game

Ashcraft had taken about $200,000 worth of lead from that mine shaft in the first nine years and decided he should sell it while he could. It just so happened that Amos D. Hatten had met up with his uncle Alvin Hatten in Nevada, Missouri, and they were heading for Joplin but decided to get off the train when it pulled into the Missouri Pacific Depot, right by the Center Creek Mine(1883). They met with Grant Ashcraft; he made them a proposition that he would sell them the mine for $8,000, with $2,000 down and the rest in payments. Sounds like another one of those "more a moment of chance than of design."

Ashcraft even went so far as to lease Uncle Alvin Hatten his furnished house (northwest corner of Pennsylvania and Daugherty) while Ashcraft journeyed to California. Alvin and A. D. continued to mine the Center Creek Mine until they depleted the vein that Grant had located nine years earlier. The moment had come when they had to determine what to do next. Hatten recalled that the miners out west would start in the wall, going each way to see if they could find a parallel vein, so Alvin and A.D. decided to do the same as those wise miners from out west. A. D. Hatten said, "We opened up the greatest lead and zinc mine that it has ever been my pleasure to see. In a few months, we had made sufficient dividends to pay Mr. Ashcraft the balance we owed him and we paid our stockholders over $100,000 in dividends." Ashcraft said, in almost forty years, he watched over $10 million worth of ore shipped from the Center Creek Mines.

Another mine on the Center Creek Mining Company's land attracted Hatten's attention, and he bought into it with his cousin-in-law Otis J. Raymond, and they made $26,000 in eight months. They invested that income in building a two-story brick building on the northeast corner of Main and Daugherty Streets; the second brick building to be built in Webb City. That building became the home of Humphrey's Department Store, and later Bradbury Bishop Drug Store and IGA Grocery.

The Hatten-Raymond Block, the second brick building in Webb City. This building became the home of the Humphrey's Department Store.

When Ashcraft sold that first load of ore (fifteen thousand pounds) in 1874, the word was out, and the great mining boom of the Webb City area was ushered in, and the Webb City district became known as the richest zinc and lead mining field in the world. The *1883 History of Jasper County* stated, "*The growth of the city* [Webb City], *has been rapid as its mineral wealth has been astonishing in its richness.*"

John C. Webb's simple farm life was over. People began to arrive by horseback, covered wagons, and even walking. Webb knew he was not cut out for mining, so he put his efforts into designing and organizing a town. Businessmen were arriving as quickly as the miners, building stores, hotels, restaurants, and saloons, lots of saloons.

As John laid out the town, he set aside a block of land for a church and a school as this would be important to any community. On July 26, 1874, Webb hired Elijah Lloyd to survey and plot the town of Webbville. Elijah Lloyd took advantage of the situation and purchased a mine as an investment. He struck payload in 1882. Elijah had come to this area from Kentucky in 1867. His occupation consisted of being a civil engineer, and he worked for the railroad doing surveys. He assisted in laying out the new town of Joplin, Missouri, in 1871 and jumped at the chance to plot this new town of Webbville.

Webb started the building of his new home just a few feet north of his log cabin. He had James McNair build a small home at Daugherty and Tom (northeast corner) in which to live in while his brick mansion was being built on Webb Street. The house was built on Webb Street, facing what was then Main Street and is now known as Broadway Street from Webb Street, east toward Allen Street, which is now known as Main Street. James McNair and his wife, Patience, had arrived in the area in 1874, by way of the St. Louis–San Francisco Railroad, and settled in the newly established town of Oronogo but moved to Webb City in 1875 as the town began to grow.

J. C. Webb's home at 112 North Webb Street.

Land Purchases in Early Days

1844—Government survey of the area was completed, and the settlers could finally begin making proper filings to secure title to their lands. The government land office was in Springfield, which was about a seven to ten-hour trip there and back, weather permitting. The price range on the first entries ranged from 25¢–$1.25 per acre. Usually if one of the neighbors was making the trip to Springfield, he would file for his neighbors and bring back the proper release or deed for the rightful owner.

1856—John C. Webb and his wife, Ruth, purchased 200 acres and later purchased an additional 120 acres.

1856—Thomas Webb (cousin to John C. Webb) purchased land to the southwest (where the Mount Hope Cemetery is now located).

1867—Dr. David Whitworth purchase land west of the future Webb City (by the future airport).

1869—Joseph Aylor purchased a hill just east of Thomas Webb's land and west of the Webb City cemetery.

1869—Andrew McCorkle purchased eighty acres south of John C. Webb (First Street south).

1870—W. A. Daugherty purchased 260 acres west of John C. Webb. Later he purchased 320 acres east of John C. Webb from Carter, soon to be the town of Carterville. Eventually Daugherty would own over 4,000 acres of mining and agricultural land in Jasper County.

John C. Webb's first addition was surveyed by Kos Elliott on August 12, 1876, and recorded August 24, 1876, by James Bolen. J. C Webb's second addition was surveyed by Kos Elliott on September 1, 1876, recorded by James Bolen, September 13, 1876.

Andrew McCorkle's addition was surveyed by Kos Elliott on August 30, 1876, recorded by James A. Bolen, October 23, 1876.

Bolen and Beebe's addition was surveyed by John W. Irwin on October 24, 1876, recorded by James A. Bolin, October 30, 1876.

J. C. Webb's third addition was surveyed by J. W. Gray, February 10, 1877, recorded February 15, 1877.

Andrew McCorkle's second addition was surveyed by Kos Elliott on January 31, 1877, and recorded April 7, 1877.

"A City Is Born"

The city of Webbville was officially platted on July 15, 1875, and recorded by James A. Bolen, September 11, 1875.

The original city consisted of twelve blocks: John (Austin), Daugherty, Main (Broadway from Webb Street east to city limits), Church Street, Joplin (Broadway) west from Webb Street all running east and west. The streets going north and south were: Liberty, Webb, Allen, Tom, Hall. They applied to the court when they discovered Webbville would not be accepted as the name. A village is smaller than a city, and Webbville already had a large population as they applied. So with a few changes, the city was incorporated under the Statutes of the State of Missouri on December 11, 1876 as Webb City, Missouri. James McNair was appointed as the first executive officer (mayor) of Webb City. Within a month, McNair was offered the position of postmaster of Webb City, and he resigned as the executive officer. James Smith took over the position of executive officer for a year. Between December 11, and the end of the year, four more additions were platted.

> *According to a Carthage newspaper—January 25, 1877—War in Webb City. A mob takes possession of the town, defies the authorities, and shooting down citizens. A man, Messie by name, had been lodged in the calaboose for disorderly conduct. A number of his friends, full of whisky, were determined to release him. Armed with revolvers and Winchester rifles, firing by the mob began and continued till dark, when the leaders escaped and a number of accomplices were arrested, after several citizens had been wounded.*

With the rapid growth of Webb City, the town was in need of some law and order. Once the city was incorporated, ordinances could be established to maintain hired law officers. This, in turn, drained the struggling city of the already-meager finances. The city was classified on February 28, 1878, as a fourth-class city, and the governing body was allowed to levy a tax to cover city expenses. December 26, 1889, Webb City was classified as a third-class city. Things were changing, and Webb City was growing.

Even with the organization of enforcement officers, the wild and lawless men would venture into town and cause havoc. The Blunt Raid was a tense time for the citizens as a group of men rode in on their horses, traveling up and down Allen Street (now Main Street). They were drinking whiskey, shooting their guns, and everyone headed for cover. The Webb City marshal rode to Oronogo to telegraph the county sheriff in Carthage. Help came, and seven men were arrested and put in the county jail—where they immediately escaped.

The first hotel to be built was the Transit House (1875) at 208 East Main (Broadway). The two-story hotel had seventeen rooms and was built by Smith and Fisborn. In 1878, the Coyne family arrived in Webb City, and Mr. Coyne took over the operations of the Transit House. Nelse Terron arrived in town (1875) to build the first store. Merchants, lawyers, doctors, almost all professions came in large numbers to be a part of the establishment of a new town. The city was on its way.

The Western Hotel was built in 1876. Dr. J. J. Wolf established his office, and J. Van Buskert moved from Joplin to open a grocery store in 1876. Young Lon Ashcraft recalled that his first day of school was upstairs over the Hall Drug Store, northwest corner of Allen (Main) and Main (Broadway) Streets. Hall's Drug Store became the city hall, post office, schoolroom, and was the main building for the city.

Wood-frame buildings started popping up along Allen (Main) Street (1876). The streets in the downtown area were not paved with bricks until 1905. The dirt streets created dust and mud. Horses were left in the streets while folks were shopping or all day while the men were in saloons which created an entirely different mess in the downtown area.

Photo compliments of Norval Matthews>>

Wheatley's Lumber Yard was located at Webb and Broadway (northeast corner). Hall's Drug Store became city hall, schoolroom, post office. The city's main building. Located to the right of the lumberyard in the above picture. The two-story white building on the corner of Allen (Main) and Main (Broadway). In later years the location of the Webb City Bank. 1878.

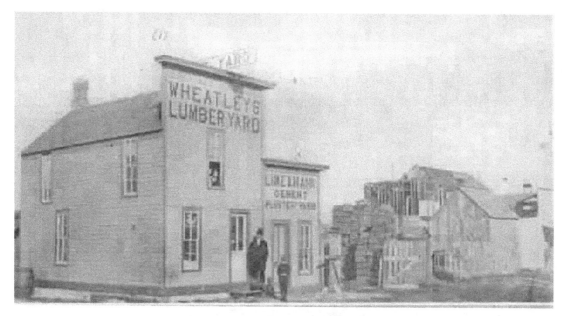

Photo compliments of Norval Matthews

Another view of Wheatley's Lumber Yard (northeast corner of Webb and Main [Broadway]). Catty-corner from the Webb Home 112 North Webb Street.>>

When the new church was being dedicated, John C. Webb was very ill. They ran a telephone wire from the church at Liberty Street and Joplin Street (Broadway Street) to Webb's home at Webb and Main Street (Broadway) so Webb could hear the dedication from his bed. Probably one of the first preaching over the telephone wires.

John Webb set aside a bit of land for a future school and a church. He felt the need for both facilities were important for a growing community. At a later date, he built a Methodist Church at a cost of $5,000 and presented it to the Methodist Church, South.

A friend shared a copy of a book of Webb City from 1894. What a wealth of information. There were pictures of the churches in Webb City in 1894, and it was very interesting as most of these churches were replaced by larger buildings, usually made of brick, block, etc. I thought it would be fun to share these pictures with you. The shapes of the building, as well as the steeples, add such unique architecture of the time. What a fun trip to the past. Church bells, steeples, and stained glass added charm to the city.

M. E. CHURCH SOUTH.

1 ME Church-Liberty and Joplin (Broadway) 1882 started out as
Union Church and became Central Methodist Church

2 First Presbyterian Church built in 1889 at Third and Webb Street. Sold to the Catholic
Church in 1903 for $1,500. Sold in 1940 to the Christian Church.

3 Cumberland Presbyterian Church (1888) corner of Austin and Liberty. Cumberland and First Presbyterian merged in 1906. They gave the church building to the new Carterville Presbyterian Church, and they moved the building to Carterville.

4 The Christian Church (1894) was located at the corner of Joplin (Broadway) and Oronogo Street southeast corner.

5 The First Baptist Church was built in 1886 at North Allen (Main) and Galena Street, $1,600 including the cost of the new bell. The moved the building to the northeast corner of Pennsylvania and Wood Street with ropes, capstan and dollies, and horses. In 1899, they moved the church building *again* to northwest corner of Joplin (Broadway) and Roane Street, and they enlarged and remodeled the building after the move. In 1912, they added a basement and Carthage stone veneer for $21,000. A fire in 1935 ruined the beautiful stained glass windows. The building was

torn down in 1981. What an eventful life in a church building that made it ninety-five years. A special monument was built for the wonderful bell that was purchased in 1886 (info provided by Nola Anderson in 1991).

A four-room wood-frame school, the first school building in the new city of Webb City. Located between Joplin (Broadway) Street and First Street, facing Webb Street, 1877–1893, $2,500. In 1892, four-room wood-frame central school was enlarged to eight rooms.

December 1, 1894—new brick central school was built behind the wood-frame school
building seven months and one week after bond election passed in Webb City.

Getting Control of the City

Many a tale has been told of Webb City during the mining era. The new town of wooden buildings, dirt streets, and no law to speak of brought many a wild night. As the wooden buildings were eventually replaced by brick (to reduce the fire hazards), a pattern emerged. The east side of Allen (Main) Street housed the many saloons, pool halls, and gambling houses. The area from Allen (Main Street) heading east to Carterville on Daugherty Street was referred to as Red Hot Street. Some history trivia says it was Daugherty Street, and others say it was Broadway Street. Since it wasn't an official name in the city, it is hard to prove. But it is noted that originally, Daugherty Street came into Webb City from Carterville and turned left to Broadway a bit further down. That would officially make Daugherty the route into Webb City.

Dolph Shaner noted in his book *The Story of Joplin* that at one time, Carterville was "dry" and Webb City remained "wet," which created quite a bit of foot traffic as miners wandered across Ben's Branch to have some fun. Shaner noted that when the Carterville miners staggered, crawled, and/ or were carried back to Carterville as the Webb City saloons closed at midnight, they woke up the town with their yelling and shooting.

Carterville citizens decided they needed to band together to establish some law and order in their town. Squire Campbell, a deacon of the ME Church South headed the movement. To avoid fatalities, no guns were allowed to be used. The men who were deputized by the marshal carried wooden hammer handles to be used as billy clubs. The miners said they were using pick handles and therefore dubbed the Carterville lawmen the pick-handled police.

The first Saturday night, the organized lawmen caught the miners off guard, and there were some miners who spent the night in jail. The next Saturday night, the miners were prepared and fought off the new lawmen, took their billy clubs, and ended the pick-handled police league.

Webb City's east side of Allen Street continued to flourish as the miners spent all their hard-earned money on the "evils of the devil." Many a rough group from other towns entered Webb City on a Saturday night to have some shooting practice. Citizens were afraid to be out at night, and the wicked seemed to be taking over the town.

Norval Matthews stated in his 1976 commemorative booklet, *City of Webb City*, "*In spite of the efforts of church people and law enforcement officers, Webb City at this adolescent period of her existence at times became a rip-snorting, rioting, mass of lusty humanity.*"

Eventually peace and harmony rested on the streets of Webb City. There were still saloons, pool halls, and gambling, but the law seemed to have control.

According to Marvin VanGilder's book *Jasper County, The First Two Hundred Years*, one of the favorite pastimes from pioneer days into the first quarter of the twentieth century was footracing. A big event in Joplin, it didn't take long for the practice to head over into Webb City. VanGilder told of a Webb Citian named Robert "Buck foot" Boatright who developed foot racing into a fine art. The reputation of Boatright, a saloonkeeper, included his shenanigans as the leader of a band of miners and businessmen who were dubbed the Buckfoot Gang. They had a footracing scam that netted them close to $3 million from unsuspecting gamblers. There was a racetrack in the northeast part of Webb City where the Webb City Athletic Club used to stage their foot races. This group had no shame as they had fixed races, paid off winners with satchels full of newspaper instead of money, or held the money in a wall safe for safekeeping, only to open the safe later and find it empty. Law officials stated that the safe had a false back, and as soon as the money was put in the safe, the men in the next room would remove it.

Boatright eventually opened a commercial gymnasium in the upper rooms over a pool hall on Allen (Main) Street. The building was located on the southeast corner of Daugherty and Allen. There were many stories about the new establishment, but nothing documented. Bets on boxing matches, footraces, and other gambling activities were rumored to have taken place. During a rather questionable footrace scam, Boatright left the area by dark of night, and according to VanGilder, he subsequently died in Kansas City following a workout at a gymnasium.

Decent ladies did not walk on the east side of Allen Street, as it was a sure way to ruin your reputation. When the first opera house of Webb City was built (1883) on the southeast corner of Allen (Main) and Main (Broadway), the Middlewest Building, it was very important that ladies be let out of the buggy directly in front of the opera house or cross the street and enter into the opera house without coming in contact with the activities of the east side of Allen street. The opera house was upstairs, and the downstairs had businesses that also needed to be avoided by the genteel ladies. Originally the two-story Middlewest Opera House faced Main (Broadway) Street. In later years, the building was remodeled, and the building became a three-story building and faced Allen (Main) Street.

By 1937, Webb City had gained the reputation of being a "decidedly church town," according to Ms. Henrietta Crotty, in her book *A History and Economic Survey of Webb City Missouri.* She stated that "*Webb City has twenty active churches which have a morally uplifting effect on the community.*" In her survey, Ms. Crotty doesn't mention how many of those notorious saloons, pool halls, or gambling houses still existed on Main Street.

A 1947 directory lists twenty-three churches, six liquor stores, two pool halls, and only two taverns. Some of the taverns weren't listed but existed!

But the shoot-'em-up days that existed in Webb City's early days soon gave way to civilization. There were still occasional swindlers in the midst, but on the whole, Webb City didn't take too long changing into the wonderful safe community we all remember as kids. Of course, even into the '60s, we (kids) were still forbidden to walk on the east side of Main Street. Old habits die hard!

Building on the left, northeast corner of Daugherty and Allen (Main) Streets, is the second brick building built in Webb City by A. D. Hatten and Otis Raymond, home to the Humphries Department Store. The building on the right is the southeast corner of Daugherty and Allen (Main) Street. This brick building was the home of the Buckfoot Gang and their mischievous gambling.

CHAPTER 2

Time Marches On

Webb City on the Rise

More hotels were being built with the new year of 1877. The Pacific Hotel was built by G. W. Scott at Fifteen South Allen (Main) with twenty rooms, dining room, and parlor. The Pacific Hotel was built to replace the Scott House (101 North Allen [Main] Street) which had burned. The Pacific burned in 1883. The Webb City Hotel was built at 9 South Webb, also known as the Buffalo House.

Hamilton Snodgrass started a grocery business. Charles R. Chinn came to town and opened the largest dry goods store in the city. The C. R. Chinn and Co. Dry Goods was a 17×30-foot building with $3,000 in stock. The year 1877 also brought in the first hardware store, Manker, Hewett, and Co. at 111 South Allen (Main), operated by S. L. and Sarah Manker. They sold groceries and mining supplies.

By 1879, the population within the city limits reached three thousand. The city was alive, and the saloons along the east side of Allen Street did quite a business. Miners were coming into town by horse, buggy, wagon, on foot, stagecoach, and any other way they could travel. There were not enough houses or hotels. Tent cities began to appear close to the many mines. Miners would wait outside of the mines in the event of a miner getting hurt or killed. The miners hoped to be the next one hired to take the place of the unfortunate man.

The north end
of Allen Street
Wonner Bakery

The Buffalo House was located on Webb Street, facing west toward Joplin (Broadway) Street.

The occasion of the photo was the celebration of Columbus Day.

The Webb City Hotel, located on Webb Street facing west down Joplin (Broadway) Street. In the background, you can see the Webb City Hall, which was home to the post office, city hall, Hall Drug Store, the schoolroom, and a local church. The Webb City Hotel became the Buffalo House in 1889, torn down in 1906.

A 1900 write-up about Webb City.

Below is a write-up about Webb City, written in January 1900, for *The Webb City Souvenir*. This was a newspaper-type magazine sent out to promote Webb City, and promote it did! As you are reading, remember, it was written at the turn of the century, the twentieth century:

> I sometimes wonder if our home people fully realize the immensity of our produces and privileges. Think, dear reader, of what you have.
>
> A mild climate and soil on the surface that will produce wheat, corn, oats, potatoes, hay, blue grass pastures and all kinds of fruit that grows in this latitude, equal to any State in the Union.

In addition to all this, dig a hole in the ground and it is not an uncommon occurrence for a forty-acre tract of land to sell for from $20,000 to $100,000 for what it produces under the ground, from the results of that hole, commonly known with us as a "prospect".

We, Webb City people are not at all covetous. There are not enough of us here to mine all the jack and lead in the district if we all live to be 100 years old. We want others to share in our good fortune; therefore we issue this souvenir that a few at least may know of its resources.

Were it possible to have this brief information of our city and its endless resources to reach the thousands of people of the East, where millions of money is lying in bank vaults rusting for employment it would benefit both them and Webb City. Pause for a moment and think of the millions of money that is seeking investment and of the golden opportunities they would have to invest in Webb City and at an enormous profit in most cases.

The young are trained in one of the best public school systems in the state in three handsome and commodious, well lighted, heated, and ventilated buildings; (Central High School on Webb Street, the old Webster School on Allen (Main) Street, and West Side School). Twenty five teachers are employed and there are 1750 school students enrolled.

The article also mentions the Webb City Baptist College as an up-to-date building with its faculty and course of study comparing favorably with eastern institutions.

Webb City Souvenir

The 1900 *Webb City Souvenir* had plenty of information about Webb City; it is interesting that they used the *Souvenir* as a bargaining power to persuade Carterville to join forces with Webb City. Read the following article and see what you think.

The Webb City-Carterville district led Joplin during the week ending February 3, 1900, by 536,670 pounds and by 809,480 pounds for the week ending February 10, 1900. Joplin may boast, and she does, but the cash turning is what counts in estimating the mineral resources of a country. This turn in will be greatly increased this summer and make the Webb City-Carterville district the greatest zinc ore producing district in the world.

Again, the central location of the Twin Cities and large population, if embraced in one corporation as they should be, gives them the lead in population, amount of business transacted, field for investment, manufacturing location, as well as in amount of mineral actually produced and sold for cash.

The facts are, the Twin Cities, as soon as they become one city instead of twins, will take the lead as the most important and populous city in Jasper County and Southwest Missouri. The time is coming. Watch us grow and push to the front. Incorporate as one city and make good streets and sidewalks leading between the two business centers and the place will spring to the front by leaps and bounds, and property values will be tripled almost at once.

It sounds almost like they were saying if Webb City-Carterville had merged as one city back in 1900, that they would have left Joplin behind, and we would have become the metropolitan area of Southwest Missouri.

It's fun to sit and speculate about what if, but it's even more fun to just remember that Webb City and Carterville were the complement to each other to make the Webb City-Carterville district the leading mining district.

The article went on to entice investors to go to the area by stating:

The poor man of today is very often the rich man of to-morrow.

It is impossible to foretell the greatness of the future of the zinc industry of the Webb City-Carterville district, where already more zinc ore is being produced than in any other district in the world.

All the mining heretofore has been done on the southeast, east and north, but within the last two months of 1899, prospectors have developed another large territory adjoining Webb City on the west and southwest. The Daugherty 1,000-acre tract and on the Whitworth land, three shafts are being sunk with good indications of making rich finds in ore. These lands are all owned by Webb City men of wealth and experience in mining and their development will be rapid and thorough and all will be to the great advantage of Webb City.

So, have you heard enough? Are you ready to settle in the great mining district of Webb City-Carterville? Catch the next train and we'll help make you rich!!!

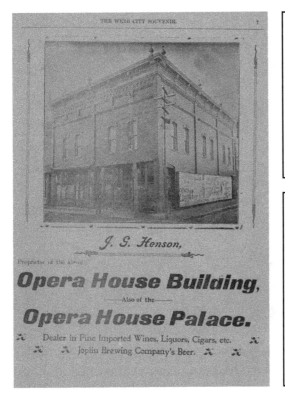

A page from the 1900 *Webb City Souvenir* shows the opera house at One South Allen (Main) Street when it was facing Broadway (at that time known as Main Street), prior to the remodel that made it a three-story building and facing Allen (Main Street).

The remodel of the Middlewest Building in progress. The building entrance was changed from Broadway Street, then known as East Main (north side of building to the west side of the building, facing Allen Street [now Main Street]). Plus the building was changed from a two-story brick building to a three-story building.

Remodel of the Middlewest Building. Photo by Eileen Nichols.>>

The impressive Middlewest Building after the remodel that changed the building to three stories and changed the building to be facing Allen (Main) Street. Photo by Eileen Nichols.

The Review

A 1906 report on the Growth of Webb City.

This is a report from a 1906 copy of *The Review*, which was the high school newspaper but more like a small annual. In this old school newspaper was a wonderful article titled "Webb City's Solid Growth" by Joseph E. Cobb. I would like to share this article with you. Other than the mining improvements, this article could be referring to today instead of 1906. Let's take a look at Webb City in 1906 through the eyes of development.

> Few towns are making more satisfactory progress on a firmer basis of prosperity than Webb City. This is due in part to the greatest improvement of late years in the character of mining in the immediate vicinity of the city. The opening of the vast area of what is known as the sheet-ore ground has changed speculation into safe investment—a characteristic of lead and zinc mining until recently never dreamed of, and nowhere realized except in the territory within a few miles radius of Webb City.
>
> Today Webb City is becoming known all over the world as the center of a distinctive mining district, which has not only the exceptional advantage of assured permanence, but also of being the greatest producer of mineral wealth of any similar area where lead and zinc have been discovered.
>
> It is worthwhile to remember, and to emphasize, that during the year 1905, the yield of this territory, stretching from Duenweg to Neck City and Alba, a dis-

tance of about six miles to the north and south, the lead and zinc mined and sold reached a value of six and one-half million dollars, equaling the value of the product of all the rest of Southwest Missouri, Southeast Kansas, Northern Arkansas, and the Indian Territory, in lead and zinc.

To be the center of such a marvelously rich district, which as yet had but started towards its full development, is surely a distinction of which Webb City may well be proud.

This city has also the very great advantage of being the natural center, for financial and business purposes, of a group of towns and cities all of whom are pushing forward with rapid strides in all that counts for solid progress and substantial prosperity. Nearly thirty-five thousand people are brought by the electric railways centering here in closer touch with Webb City than with any other commercial center. From Duenweg, Prosperity, Oronogo, Purcell, Alba and Neck City, as well as from the rich farming districts intervening, seventy-five percent of the people come here to do their trading and to get supplies for farm, mine and household needs.

These and other reasons which cannot be enumerated without going too much into detail have caused a great awakening among the leaders of public sentiment in this city during the past year or two. Starting with the street paving movement inaugurated by Mayor Moore, and carried through with enthusiasm by the heaviest property owners in the city, the spirit of civic pride has grown daily. Projects have been set on foot and are now being carried to completion such as would not have been seriously thought of two or three years ago. At the close of 1905, it was found by a census, that more than a quarter of a million dollars had been spent that year for new buildings, many thousands of dollars of public money has been put into sidewalks, sewers, and other public improvements; the erection of a $75,000 viaduct by the Southwest Electric Railway company has been commenced, and is now nearly complete; and besides all this, a score of business buildings, better than any hitherto in existence are nearly completed or in course of completion.

With so good a start as has been made, it is scarcely possible for any untoward event to stop the continued growth of Webb City. There is at the present time such an abiding faith on the part of every citizen that investments are being freely made by home capital. More new houses are at the present time in progress of erection than had been built in any five years prior to 1905. There are houses, too, such as any city might be proud of. The sentiment is growing also that all the streets of the city must be a prevailing characteristic and that every means possible must be used to beautify and render attractive the homes of miners and mechanics as well as those of well-to-do citizens

The Webb City that is to come will be made pleasant as well as prosperous. And it is gratifying to note that a healthy public sentiment now stands ready to endorse whatever measures may be found necessary to remedy and remove the wrong, and to establish and strengthen all that pertains to the betterment of the entire community; as well as the personal happiness of each individual citizen.

May we take the same attitude today and stand behind our community as it takes steps to improve and grow.

A few advertisements from the 1906 *Review*

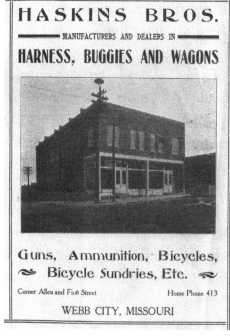

The City in 1909

Changes occur at all times. Webb City has been through many major changes throughout the years. Well, you can just imagine how many changes have taken place since 1876. Let's take a little journey back to 1909 and see what was going on in Webb City at that time, when the city was thirty-four years old.

The gas company bragged that you could do your cooking and laundry during the seven months of summer (that one got me) for 50–75¢ per month. Sugar was 4¢ a pound, coffee was 15¢ a pound, and eggs were 14¢ a dozen. Most women of the era washed their hair with egg yolks for shampoo and rinsed their hair in rainwater.

The average wage in 1909 in the United States was 22¢ per hour, with the average worker earning $200–$400 per year. Although certain trained positions made more money. A competent accountant could expect to earn $2,000 per year, a dentist $2,500 per year, a veterinarian between $1,500 and $4,000 per year, and a mechanical engineer about $5,000 per year. It wasn't anything near that in Webb City; our miners were making between $1 and $2 a day in the mines.

Ninety percent of all doctors did not have a college education, but many did attend a medical school that the government felt was substandard. Two out of every ten adults could not read or write. Only 6 percent of Americans graduated from high school.

Webb City only had one hospital in 1909, the Salvation Army Hospital, which was established in 1905 and located at 200 East Main (Broadway) Street. Jane Chinn Hospital would not be built until 1910. And the Tuberculosis Hospital was not built until 1916. Therefore, the majority of births were in the home. The five leading causes of death were pneumonia (influenza), tuberculosis, diarrhea, heart disease, and stroke. The average man lived to the age of forty-seven.

Another business that Webb City abounded in was photographers. Which is great, as that is one way that history has been preserved. One hundred years ago, we had the John Buck Photography, located at 307 West Daugherty; Spracklin's was one of the longest lasting photographers in Webb City history, located at 205 West Daugherty; O. C. Kerr was at 115 South Allen (Main) Street; Waldo P. Johnson was located in the Coyne Building at 110 West Main (Broadway) Street. Eman's Photo Studio was located at 110 North Allen.

Webb City was noted for the beautiful homes. Many had just been built between 1900 and 1910, as those who had accumulated wealth from the mining industry wanted a home to reflect that wealth. Only 14 percent of the homes in the United States had a bathtub or indoor plumbing and only 8 percent had a telephone. In 1909, Webb City had two telephone companies: The American Bell Telephone Company and the Home Telephone Company. The two companies merged in 1913. The phone company building, at 209 West Broadway, was built in 1907 (now part of the Webb City Police Department). The phone calls were handled by telephone operators who would connect you with the person you were calling. When you lifted the receiver, you would hear the operator say, "Number, please." Those telephone numbers were two or three digits. Some businesses would have two phones as their customers would be associated with the two different phone companies, and you didn't want to lose a customer because they couldn't reach you by phone. Some businesses were fortunate enough to get the same number with each company, so they would advertise like the Webb City Drug Store, "Both numbers 195."

In 1909, the Minerva Candy Company had three locations. The one we are all familiar with at 12 South Main in Webb City, and then 634 Main and 1038 Main in Joplin. Their phone numbers were 450 in Webb City and 955 and 926 in Joplin, all with the Home Telephone Company.

Webb City was such an active place in 1909 with lots of barbershops, saloons, grocery stores, restaurants, and confectionaries. The population in the 1900 census lists it at 9201, so I am sure it had increased in the nine years till 1909.

Statistics in 1909

Population: 15,000

Paved streets, 1905, natural gas, fine homes, beautiful parks, fine business district, four banks, five well-equipped school buildings, eighteen churches of different denominations, fire department, complete water and sewer system. Electric light and power system, a flouring mill foundry and machine shops, a plant manufacturing brick from cement and mine chats, an overall factory, opera house, three stone plants, ice plant, many neighborhood grocery stores, farm products, dairy farms, garden products.

A rare photo of the ice plant found in the 1954 thesis of Rosemary Burk Merker, "The First 25 Yearsof Webb City, Missouri."

Statistics in 1947

Population: Approximately 8,000; the 1940 census is 7,033.

Four-mile square area

.1000 above sea level

Average rainfall per year: Forty-two inches

Two parks, total of twenty acres

Two banks: Webb City Bank and Merchant Miners Bank.

Phones in service: 1,100

Eighteen churches with sixteen denominations

One newspaper

One hotel with twenty-six rooms

US Highways 66 and 71

Airport with three airlines

Automobiles registered: 1,100

Auditorium in the city seats 750.

Three movie theaters, seating 1,400 people.

Golf course, high school stadium, city swimming pool

One hospital with twenty-six beds

Library has ten thousand volumes.

Forty miles of city streets with twenty miles paved.

Fire department has one station and six firemen.

Police department has one station with four men employed.

After WWII, lead and zinc mining was making a comeback.

Factories: Elder's Mfg. Co. Big Smith Mfg. Co., Rex Metallic Casket Co., Webb Corp, dairy, mill, and grain, mill wholesale grocer

Transportation in Webb City includes air, train, bus, highway.

Close by are three large powder plants located nearby.

Prominent stores in town: The Hub, Huey's Department Store

City Departments

The Encyclopedia of the History of Missouri states that in 1901, the city offices were situated in the city hall, a two-story brick building, which also contains the jail, horse carriage room, and business offices. The building was built in 1891.

Mayors through the Years

Webb City incorporated as a city, December 11, 1976

Chairman of the board, trustee-led:

J. E. McNair	December 11, 1876–January 13, 1877 (became postmaster)
James Smith	January 13, 1877–January 1878
George H. Smith	January 1878 (first election of chairman of the board)

Mayors of Webb City incorporated as fourth-class city, mayor-led:

Ben C. Webb	April 1878–April 1880 (two one-year terms)
T. J. Harrington	April 1880–April 1882 (two one-year terms)
James Gammon	April 1882–July 1882 (resigned in July)
T. J. Harrington	July 1882–April 1883 (finished Gammon's term)
T. J. Harrington	April 1883–April 1886 (three one-year terms)
William Hilburn	April 1886–April 1888 (two one-year terms)
Peter McEntee	April 1888–April 1890 (two one-year terms)

Webb City changed from fourth-class city to third-class city, 1889

T. J. Harrington (ninth term)	April 1890–April 1892 (one two-year term)*
C. S. Manker	April 1892–April 1894 (one two-year term)
J. J. Funk	April 1894–April 1896 (one two-year term)
F. M. King	April 1896–April 1897 (served only one year)
J. W. Frey	April 1897–April 1898 (finished King's term)
E. E. Spracklen	April 1898–April 1900 (one two-year term)
S. T. Clark	April 1900–April 1902 (one two-year term)
D. F. Wertz	April 1902–April 1904 (one two-year term)
G. W. Moore	April 1904–April 1908 (two two-year terms)
Patrick McEntee	April 1908–April 1910 (one two-year term)
W. V. K. Spencer	April 1910–April 1914 (two two-year terms)
J. E. Locke	April 1914–April 1916 (one two-year term)
W. F. Gill	April 1916–April 1922 (three two-year terms)
A. G. Young	April 1922–April 1924 (one two-year term)
W. F. Gill (fourth term)	April 1924–April 1926 (one two-year term)
C. C. Harris	April 1926–April 1928 (one two-year term)
W. H. Tholborn	April 1928–April 1930 (one two-year term)
Walter Ragland	April 1930–April 1934 (two two-year terms)
Frank C. Nelson	April 1934–April 1936 (one two-year term)

Lee A. Daugherty	April 1936–April 1938 (one two-year term)
Dr. M. S. Slaughter	April 1938–April 1942 (two two-year terms)

Mayor changed to four-year term:

Don O. Adamson	April 1942–April 1946 (one four-year term)
Fred Nelson	April 1946–April 1950 (one four-year term)
Robert J. Cummings	April 1950–November 1951 (nineteen months of term)
C. S. FLY	November 1951–April 1954 (finished Cummings' term)
Ed W. Murray	April 1954–April 1958 (one four-year term)
Dr. Earl Baker	April 1958–November 1958 (seven months of four-year term)
Paul Hight	November 1958–April 1959 (five months of four-year term)
Don O. Adamson	April 1959–April 1962 (finished Hight's four-year term)
Don O. Adamson	April 1962–April 1966 (one four-year term)
Robert J. Baker	April 1966–October 1969 (thirty-one months/two years of four-year term)
Donald Scott	November 1969–April 1970 (finished Baker's term)
Robert Patrick	April 1970–April 1974 (one four-year term)
Sterling Gant	April 1974–1976 (two years of four-year term)
P. D. Crockett	1976–April 1978 (completed Gant's term)
P. D. Crockett	April 1978–April 1982 (one four-year term)
P. D. Crockett (health issues)	April 1982–October 1984 (two and a half years of four-year term)
Carolyn McGowan	October 1984–April 1985 (served six months of term)
Kathryn Patten	April 1985–April 1986 (served last year of term)
Bill Lundstrum	April 1986–April 1990 (one four-year term)
Phil Richardson	April 1990–1992 (two years of four-year term)
Sterling Gant	1992–April 1994 (finished two of four-year terms)
Sterling Gant	April 1994–April 2002 (two four-year terms)
Glenn Dolence	April 2002–April 2006 (one four-year term)
John Biggs	April 2006–April 2014 (two four-year terms)
John Biggs	April 2014–November 2015 (one and one half of third four-year term)
Lynn Ragsdale	November 2023

Webb City Police Department

The Encyclopedia of the History of Missouri states that in 1901, the police force consisted of a marshal, an assistant marshal, and three men, whose annual cost of maintenance was $2,800.

There's not much info on the history of the police force of Webb City. We do have a few stories that have been shared concerning citizens and the police force.

Died in action—On March 17, 1918, over one hundred years ago, Webb City lost a great chief of police; George D. Hooper died in the line of duty. I was informed, at the time of writing this article in 1990, that Hooper was the only Webb City police officer to die in action. I think that says a lot for our community and our police force.

Things weren't very calm in 1918. What started out as a quiet evening ended up tragic. George Hooper, chief of police, and George Rogers, deputy sheriff, had just ended their shifts at midnight and were headed home together since they were neighbors. They stopped by the Frisco Train Station in the west end to visit with the night patrolman, Oliver Rusk. After some political comments and good-humored retorts, they headed on toward home in Roger's car. Just as they crossed the Frisco train tracks, they were stopped by Joe Noland. Noland had heard some shooting in the direction of Charlie Kinney's home, a close friend of Hooper's.

Alarmed that his friend was in danger, Hooper and Roger headed north to Madison Street. In the distance, they observed a woman running and a man following her. Rogers drove his vehicle to the intersection of Central and Madison Streets and asked the lady what was going on. The lady said, "He's following me."

The pursuer made a swift turn onto Central Avenue, running or walking briskly, diagonally across the street. Both officers called for the man to stop as they took chase. In answer to the command, the man turned and fired. The bullet went into Hooper's right side, penetrating the lung and lodging in or near the spinal column.

Even though the bullet did mortal damage, Hooper stayed upright, managed to walk and to keep firing his gun toward the assailant. Hooper was between the assailant and Rogers, preventing Rogers from being able to fire at the assailant. As Hooper emptied his gun, and he began to collapse, the assailant stepped to the side, and Rogers was able to get aim and opened fire. Three shots from Rogers' gun found their target, and the assailant fell to the ground.

Rogers went to the rescue of Hooper. Hooper was able to speak a little. He said, "'You stayed by me, buddy. Stay by me now. I am done for. Don't let my head down on the ground."

But at that very moment, movement caught Rogers' eye, and he saw the assailant reaching for his gun. Rogers had to let Hooper lay back as he sprang for the assailant's wrist and secure the gun. As he commanded the assailant to lie quiet, the response was, "I'm done for."

As Rogers supported Hooper's head, he ordered the lady (Myrtle Page) to call for an ambulance. In her excitement, the lady called for a patrol car instead of an ambulance. Rogers had her hold Hooper's head while he summoned an ambulance because he knew Hooper was in bad shape, and every minute counted.

All efforts were in vain as George Hooper died at 5:40 a.m., at Jane Chinn Hospital. His assailant, Mortimer St. Clair Holmes, also known as Mont Holmes, died a little after 7:00 a.m.

Hooper was born January 13, 1879, in Ashgrove, Missouri. He was thirty-nine years old. He was married to Myrtle Bell Scott, and they had two small daughters: Vinita, age eight, and Ruth, age five. He had four half-brothers: Jim Woody, Grover Woody, John Woody, and Jesse Woody, all from Oklahoma.

Hooper's reputation was that of a faithful public servant. He never betrayed a friend, trust, or a principle. He fought fair, open, and above board. His speech was plainspoken, never with words to conceal thought, and always truthful.

George Rogers was the grandfather of Fred Rogers, who dedicated so much of his time and energy to the streetcar 60 that is located at King Jack Park. Fred provided the above information about his grandfather and police chief.

Her one true love—As a child, Kevin Costly would spend a lot of time at his beloved great-aunt Emma's house. Memories did stand strong of Emma's house at 709 North Prospect. Emma had a photographic memory and delighted in telling the many stories of her life and loves.

Emma McReynolds was born January 8, 1897, to John Wesley and Hettie Jane McReynolds. She was the second youngest of seven children born to the McReynolds' union. Their modest house, now torn down, was located on the eight hundred block of North Oak Street.

By nature, Emma was a rebellious child. She took pride in admitting this trait/flaw to family, friends, and enemies. Her rebellious personality did not blend well with her father's stern disposition. In those days, the man ruled over the household, and the concept did not sit well with Emma. She was an early feminist, born before her time.

At the young age of fifteen, Emma ran away from home to marry her boyfriend, Roy Springer. She always said that she "used their marriage as a ticket to get out of the house and away from Papa." According to Emma, Roy was a sweet boy, and she was a lousy wife. So she did the decent thing— she divorced him and "mercifully set him free!"

Not long after her divorce, Emma met Burney Newton. Burney was on the Webb City police force for several years. Emma was in love. They married and settled down to live happily ever after. The only problem was, they fought like cats and dogs.

Emma not only fought with Burney, she fought with Burney's mother, Amanda Newton. Emma and Amanda disliked each other mutually.

It was the custom with some women, each evening, after supper and dishes were washed, Mother Newton would sit on her rocking chair and dip snuff. Emma, not to be outdone, tried her hand at snuff dipping. She decided to give up the bad habit after only one attempt, claiming "it just about killed me!"

The marriage of Emma and Burney ended rather abruptly. They loved each other too much to live with each other. Burney went on to serve our nation during World War I. After coming back home from duty overseas, Burney came back to this area to work as a lead and jack miner. Working the mines, Burney contracted tuberculosis and spent his final days at the TB Hospital on Carl Junction Road (now Stadium Drive). Burney passed away in 1926 and took a part of Emma with him.

Not long after their divorce, Emma met and married a chef and pastry baker named Fred Garris. They both worked for the prestigious Fred Harvey chain restaurants. Linen and silver were used to accommodate the powerful and influential upper-crust guests. They later traveled all over the vast west to many fancy restaurants working as a chef-and-hostess team.

Emma said it was a great life. But eventually, Fred wanted to stay in California to strike it big in the business. The independent Emma stubbornly refused to stay in California and moved back to her hometown of Webb City. She found a good job as the administrator for the TB hospital and continued for thirty-five years.

Fred and Emma kept in contact over the years. They wrote back and forth, and in one of those friendly letters, Emma told Fred that she was going to give him a nice "birthday present"—a divorce! Then one day, the letters stopped, and she never again heard from Fred Garris. She assumed that Fred was dead. He was one of her best friends, and she later admitted her regret for ending their fun marriage. Emma Garris had several loves in her life. And each one carried a hilarious tale to go along with it. She even fell in love at the ripe age of seventy-five.

But all those loves paled in comparison to the greatest love of all—her policeman, Burney Newton. She never loved anyone as much as Burney. She often said that she would go to her grave loving that man, and she did. Up until she could go no longer, Emma visited Burney's grave. Fresh flowers adorned his grave. Each Memorial Day, she graced his grave with the American flag.

The picture shows a very serious police force on the steps of the post office. Emma had this photo on her living room wall for many years. She would often ask Kevin to point out the best-looking man in the picture. Kevin felt that the best-looking man was second from the left on the front row, but he knew better than to try to outguess his Aunt Emma. It turned out that the love of her life, Mr. Newton, was third from the left on the back row. Emma loved "big men."

Emma McRynolds Springer, Newton Garris, died on February 26, 1984, at the age of eighty-seven. On a snowy day, she was laid to rest only seven graves away from her love, Barney Newton's, forgotten grave.

Kevin's memory will never dim of the somewhat-unusual yet memorable love shared by Emma and Burney.

The Webb City Police Department standing on the steps of the post office.
1913 Webb City Police Department in front of city hall.

Webb City Police Department 1980

Webb City Fire Department 1913

Webb City Fire Department

During the early days, the greatest threat to the area was the threat of fire. A single blaze could wipe out an entire area in just a short time. Bucket brigades were formed to fight the fires, but usually to no avail. The town would lose up to a whole city block before the fire could be contained. Many buildings were being built with brick and blocks to try and outsmart the villain known as fire.

In 1883, there was a big fire, which took the Pacific Hotel and Parker's Saloon, along with four other buildings. The bucket brigade was able to put out small fires as they began, but the major fire itself just had to burn out with the brigade, trying to keep it from spreading.

Then in 1889, under the leadership of Colonel Henry Wonner and T. C. (Tom) Hayden, the official Webb City Volunteer Fire Department was organized.

One of the most active members of the organization was Charles W. Evans. Evans recalled being active with the bucket brigade when he was just a youth. During the big fire on the corner of Main (now Broadway) and Allen (now Main), at the Barnes Restaurant, Evans acted in what was referred to as an act of heroism, but in his later years Evans recalled it as just "youthful" heroism.

It was the custom for grocery stores to carry small quantities of dynamite, and the firm of Gammon and Henderson, in the same block of the fire, kept an open box of gunpowder on the premises. Evans rushed into the burning building to try to prevent—if possible—an explosion.

"If I had thought about it a moment," said Evans, "I expect I never would have taken the risk. The fire was burning furiously all around me when I went into the grocery store. I found the open box of explosives standing there in the rear end, just where I had often seen it when I bought a dollar's worth at a time. Picking it up, I carried it through a shower of sparks and bits of burning timber as thick as hail. I ran across Allen (Main) and west on Main (Broadway), I tell you nobody was better pleased than I, when I dropped it in front of the old Webb place, (John C. Webb's place later known as the Burgner place), and I found I had gotten free of the tricky stuff without an accident having happened!"

In 1899, under E. E. Spracklen as mayor, Webb City got its first organized paid fire department with an auto fire wagon, which cost $5,000. E. E. Spracklen gave a speech at Webb City's fifty-fifth birthday, in which he shared the story of the first paid fire department. He recalled that the city was in a paid fire department, and the city council was not too agreeable about the subject. Spracklen spoke with Colonel James O'Neill, who had just started the new waterworks for the city. O'Neill told Spracklen to go ahead and order the new horse-and-wagon fire truck and said that he (O'Neill) would pay for it. With the new wagon built and the horses bought, Jesse Kern took over as the first fire chief. The city council gave in and took control of the new city fire department.

Evans was born in West Hackney, County of Middlesex, England, on April 29, 1860, to Samuel and Elizabeth Evans. At the age of twelve, Evan stowed away on a ship to come to the United States. He reached Webb City in 1877, age seventeen, and began working the mines.

Along with every other miner, Evans dreamed of mining his own mine. This dream was accomplished. Evans was appointed as city assessor in 1921, a position he held until his death, September 15, 1929.

Evans married Sarah Elizabeth Yadon. They had seven children, including Harry E. Evans, Nellie May Evans, Kohnke Evans, Minnie Evans Shultz, Ina Frances Evans, and William Oscar Evans. All of the children were born at the old home place at Twenty-One South Ball.

Once again, Webb City is able to boast of a brave forefather who helped make our community the great place it is today.

In 1911, Charles W. Evans was appointed fire chief.

The Encyclopedia of the History of Missouri stated that in 1901, the fire department consisted of three men, with hose and hook-and-ladder equipment, is maintained at an annual cost of $1,800.

The first fire wagon—Colonel E. E. Spracklen said it was a hard fight to get the council to agree to purchase a fire wagon and team and keep men constantly on duty at headquarters. Spracklen was the mayor at the time. He said a majority was against the proposition. When the council had decided they were against a paid fire department, Colonel James O' Neill stepped forward and told Spracklen, "Go ahead, buy the wagon and horses. And if the council won't vote the money, draw on me, and I will pay the bill. But Spracklen said the council thought better of the plan. The money was paid without taking advantage of Colonel O'Neill's generous offer.

Photographer: Bill Bisher>>

Webb City and Carterville Waterworks

The latter part of the nineteenth century was a time of growth and improvements to Webb City, which had been incorporated in 1876. James O'Neill, who was heavily involved in the activities of the city, began to see a need for a water system. It was going to be an expensive project, and not too many local businessmen were willing to get involved. Colonel O'Neill was of the nature that when he got an idea, he usually carried it through, even if his friends thought he was making a financial mistake. They tried to warn him that it would be a costly investment with no guaranteed return on his money.

In research, there were several different dates mentioned concerning the building of the water-works. *The History of Jasper County*, by Joel Livingston said, "*In 1888 the Webb City—Carterville water works was built and on its completion the Carterville Fire Department was organized.*"

The *Biographical Record of Jasper County* stated, "*In 1890, Mr. O'Neill began the erection of the Webb City Water Works.*"

The 1937 *A History and Economic Survey of Webb City, Missouri,* compiled by school teacher Ms. Henrietta Crotty, stated, "*The Missouri Utility Company in Webb City was founded by James O'Neill 1888–1890.*" The name Webb City and Carterville Waterworks was changed to The Missouri Utility Company in 1937.

The *Encyclopedia of the History of Missouri (1901)* states that in May 1890, James O'Neill, the owner of the waterworks, established the waterworks for $120,000. By 1901, it was operated by the Webb City and Carterville Waterworks Company, with the water coming from Center Creek, and the pumping station is located on Center Creek, two and one-half miles north of Webb City.

Finally, the *1899 Webb City Gazette* gave this version, "*In the year 1889, James O'Neill with his never failing foresight, secured a franchise for putting in a system of water works in the city of Webb City and Carterville. The system was very complete in every detail, with ample capacity for all future consumption,' was completed and accepted by the cities May, 1890."*

The Webb City and Carterville Waterworks Company was incorporated on September 26, 1889, with James O'Neill as president and treasurer, Henry O'Neill as vice president, and George H. Bruen (James's son-in-law) as secretary and general manager. Mr. O'Neill, being the shrewd businessman that he was, kept a controlling number of the company stocks, nineteen-twentieths to be exact.

The dates may have varied, but each publication did agree—*the water was good!* The *1899 Webb City Gazette* went on to say, *"As pure and wholesome water as can be found in the entire west."* That was a mighty strong statement. Ms. Crotty, in her book, stated, *"No chemicals are needed either to purify or soften the water."*

In the beginning, the company had twenty-four miles of water mains in use (the black smoke stack water tower in Webb City was completed in 1890. One source says it was 145 feet tall and 12 feet in diameter. Another source says it was 14 feet in diameter). By 1907, the company had thirty miles of water pipe mains in Webb City and Carterville, plus 150 fire hydrants. In that year, it was reported that the company was *"unrivaled in the state for purity and safety and was recommended by the Missouri Board of Health, as safe and wholesome water for domestic and boiler use."*

By 1937, the Missouri Utility Company was supplying 350,000 gallons of water a day through thirty-six miles of water mains with 170 fire hydrants. By this time, there were five wells at the Center Creek plant and two wells within the city of Webb City. The pumping station was taken out in 1962.

There was a house built by Center Creek to allow the maintenance worker to live nearby in case of an emergency. Many families lived in the house during the years and have commented that the view was beautiful, but the house could get a little damp during the flood season.

Water Towers

Water towers tend to stand out as you enter a town. They loom over the area, and some are a bit intimidating. Some greet visitors with an announcement of the name of the town. Some towns have unusual-shaped water towers to represent a major industry that has made a name for the town, such as ketchup bottles, pineapples, etc. Webb City's main water tower shows the name of the city, our respect for the flag, and represents our city's nickname of the City of Flags. But we have had other water towers in our city that are long gone, and once again, we are reminded of the old saying, "Out of sight, out of mind," so let us just refresh our memories of days gone by.

The original black stack water tower was quite a landmark in Webb City. It was located where today's water now stands. It was the highest point in Webb City at the time, that black stack tower on Hall Street.

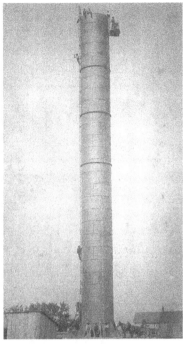

The present-day water tower. A second water tower, the original black smoke
pipe water tower, was added on South Hall Street in 1997.

Water Tower, Mount Hope Cemetery, Webb City, Mo.

This water tower originally stood in Mount Hope Cemetery, which was established
in 1905. The water tower served the three-story lodge, the office, and the watering
of the flowers and shrubs, which decorated the grounds of the cemetery.

Water tower at Brenneman Florist, Broadway Street Water Tower at Meinhart Nursery, Roane Street
to Oronogo. Broadway street to Second Street Liberty Street (from Fourth to Fifth Street).

Life at the Webb City waterworks—Here is a memory of one who lived at the waterworks. William Clyde Wood worked at the waterworks from 1895–1912. He brought his new bride, Gertrude Richardson Wood, to his home at the waterworks in 1903. Gertrude is the one relating the following experience in her own words.

"The first nine years of my married life, I lived at the waterworks pumping station in the country, two and one-half miles northeast of Webb City on Center Creek, where my husband was the engineer in charge of the pumping station. Our house was about fifty feet from the station. It had three rooms and a porch, which was enclosed and ceiled for a kitchen, and over one window, a piece of the ceiling had come off.

"On July 30, 1907, after spending about an hour at the station visiting my husband, I went over to the house, about five o'clock, to prepare the evening meal. I started the meal, then struck a match to light the gas stove. As I turned on the gas, I heard a hissing noise, like a gas leak, and immediately leaned over to examine the gas pipe. To my horror, I saw a huge snake coiled under the stove. I jumped back just as the snake struck. I ran through the house and out the front door, jumped over the fence, and ran to the station to get Mr. Wood.

"I was hysterical by the time I got there and was crying, but between sobs, I related what had happened. He came at once with me to the house, bringing the potato fork, which was standing by the gate. He laughingly said, 'Probably a garter snake.' But when he cautiously peeped in the door, one look was sufficient, for there lay the monster reptile, still in an angry mood, and evidently ready to fight.

"Mr. Wood recognized that he had a real job on his hands. He stepped into the room bravely and began his conquest with the snake. His attempts to crush the life out of the reptile were unsuccessful, for he would no sooner stick a prong of the potato fork in the snake than it would fight and tear a hole in its flesh where the prong was and get loose. Meanwhile, I had picked up a long poker, which we used when we burned coal, and put it in the gas flame, which I had lit earlier when I first came into the house.

"Mr. Wood had fought with the snake for thirty minutes, and besides being excited, hot, and almost exhausted, there was blood all over from the snake, and it had eluded him and gotten under a small cupboard where it was coiling itself. I hurriedly handed him the real hot poker, telling him to hold it toward the snake, as it was striking at everything in reach. He did, and immediately, the snake struck at the poker with its mouth open. My husband pinned it down to the floor, and as the odor of burning flesh spread through the house, the snake began to quiver and relax, but not without a fight. It would lash its tail against the floor, like it wanted to crush everything within its reach, each time growing weaker, until it finally lay dead. I was almost prostrate from my fright.

"The snake proved to be a coachwhip. It measured five feet and four inches long and was eight inches in circumference. We always thought that it got in the house where the piece of ceiling was missing over the kitchen window, and needless to say, the hole was repaired before anyone slept that night. No snake of its kind was ever seen there before or since, so the supposition was that it had come down the creek during the high water, which we had had only about a week before."

The Webb City Carterville Waterworks (as of 1937 became the Missouri Utilities Company) shut down in 1962. Each family that resided at the waterworks home on Center Creek experienced lots of flooding, but the view was beautiful!

I think the amazing part of the story was that she continued to live there for another five years before her husband moved her to town and started his own plumbing business out of his garage at 602 West Broadway.

Gertrude had handwritten this story for her family on December 10, 1932. Her daughter, Dorothea (Wood) Elliott, of Clearwater, Florida, brought in a photocopy to share with us in April of 1996.

The home that was supplied at the Webb City and Carterville Waterworks.

An interior view of the pump house located at the Water Works plant on Center Creek in 1907. The water works plant supplied water to Webb City and Carterville

Webb City Gas Company

The gas company was established by James O'Neill when he brought gas in from Kansas fields.

Electric company—According to *Jasper County*, by Marvin Van Gildner, the first gaslights in this area in the 1880s was produced by plants in Carthage and Joplin, in the case of public illumination, including streetlights and commercial buildings. The first brilliant white light produced by electric-powered bulbs were first seen in Carthage and Joplin in 1882 in a special exhibit presented by the traveling Cole Circus. The first streetlights were generated by G. W. Sergeant, generated from a generating plant located at 414 Joplin Street. Sergeant installed the first exhibition lamp at Fourth and Main Street, then obtained a contract to illuminate all the business streets of downtown. Homes in Webb City built during the 1890s were constructed with both gas and electric systems as the changes were coming. Electrical power was established for the streetcars. Public entertainment was equipped with electricity at Schifferdecker Electrical Park and Lakeside Park. Electrical power was used to move streetcars and then locomotives.

Telephone Companies

In 1908, you might have heard this conversation on your phone, "Operator, would you please ring me 450?" Or "Please connect me to the Minerva Candy Company." There is a strong possibility that you would be heard by at least four other people, as all lines were party to each other, meaning you could listen in on any conversation, which many did. It was more informative than the local newspaper.

Our telephone system has come a long way. There is a lot more privacy now. The operator is no longer the most-informed person in town.

Alexander Graham Bell invented the marvelous contraption called a telephone in 1876, the same year Webb City was incorporated. But our town did not get to enjoy this new modern convenience for another five years, in 1881. That was when Charles W. McDaniel installed the first telephone exchange, The American Bell Telephone Company. Mr. McDaniel's iron wires were strung on trees, fence posts, porches, or anything that would hold the wire. In fact, Mr. McDaniel had installed telephone exchanges in all the neighboring towns that same year. When the subscriber would crank up the phone, it rang a bell at the switchboard; the operator would then make the connection to the requested number. It took a while for this new convenience to make itself worthy to many, especially those who lived on the farm. Our telephone company was located in the Webb City Hall, a two-story-frame building located on the northwest corner of Allen (Main) and Main (Broadway).

Just a few more years later, a more sophisticated phone system was established in 1896, by G. M. Manker and W. C. Stewart, called the Home Telephone Company.

Charles McDaniel established the first telephone line in Webb City, The American Bell Telephone Company, in 1881. G. M. Manker and William S. Stewart organized and established the Webb City Electric Telephone Company. Two telephone lines in one town. But one line did not connect to the other line. The subscriber had to choose which telephone line they wanted. And you could not call anyone on the other line.

So the busy businessman had to subscribe to both telephone lines, as he couldn't afford to lose a customer because they had a different telephone line. Most businessmen had two phones sitting on their desk waiting for the customer to call. It soon became evident that if two different people called each line, the businessman could hold the mouthpiece of one phone against the earpiece of the other, and if he held it just right, the two clients could converse with each other. Modern technology is really a wonder.

In 1907, the unusual-looking building with the unique architecture at 209 West Broadway was built to house the telephone company. By 1913, both telephone companies had consolidated.

Southwestern Bell Telephone Company bought out the local phone company in 1925. It was in 1939 that the big change came, and you no longer had to crank the phone to get the operator. Webb Citians were treated to the newfangled battery-type telephone. It took several months for the telephone crewmen to install the new telephones in the homes and businesses of over eight hundred subscribers. It cost the telephone company $15,000.

Then in December of 1939, it was determined that a Saturday would be "the day," and it only took one minute to switch everyone over to the new system. Each subscriber only had to lift the receiver, and it would connect them to the operator. A light on the switchboard at the telephone office informed the operator that a subscriber wished to make a telephone call. This new service called for a slight increase in the monthly bill, but citizens were in favor of the switch.

The next big change came in July 1959, when the first dial telephones were installed. A new telephone building was built at Liberty and Broadway (the building is still there). That building held all the new equipment needed for the dial conversion program, which cost $630,000. The local office was in the same building.

You can't help but wonder what it was like to be a telephone operator. I was fortunate enough to get some telephone operator information from an actual telephone operator, Frankie Peek Pyle.

Frankie shares her memories of being a telephone operator and sitting at the switchboard day after day.

Frankie began working for the Southwestern Bell Telephone Company in June of 1948. Her chief operator was Marie Poole Leniton. Frankie said Marie stayed with the company until the dial-up phones in 1959. Most of the operators working when Frankie began had been there for many years. There were Juanita Billings, Mildred Watson, Maggie Parker, Gladys Shaner, and Josie Elliott. Little later, more operators were added: Ada Tabor, Mary Aylor, Betty Thomas, Crystal Hargis, Erline Cromer, Mary Neihart, Margorie Mayes, Patsy David, Lucy Storm, Barbara Studyvan, Barbara Alumbaugh, along with Frankie. Frankie is sure she probably forgot a few, and she is sorry. The operators were like a big happy family, and most of them stayed with the company for twenty to thirty years, usually until retirement.

Frankie recalls two times that the company went on strike, and one lasted for six weeks. The operators worked various shifts like 7 a.m.–4 p.m., 6 a.m.–3 p.m., 8 a.m.–5 p.m., 9 a.m.–6 p.m., 12 noon–9 p.m., 1 p.m.–10 p.m., 2 p.m.–10:30 p.m., and 3 p.m.–11 p.m. Frankie worked nights 10–6 for many years, while her husband was away in the service during the early '50s. Hours and vacation time were determined by the length of service with the company.

Frankie said, "We had breaks and a lunch hour. We liked to eat at Kallas' Drive-In right behind the telephone office. Also ate at the small café across from the post office. Mabel Covert had the best homemade pies in town. Safeway was right next-door for our convenience.

"The 'number please' job was one of the best I ever had. It was pleasant, fun, and educational. I made friends for life.

"When we converted to dial in July 1959, many of the operators retired, some transferred to Carthage and Joplin. Some just decided it was time to stay home. I transferred to Joplin, and it was so different from our small telephone family in Webb City. I worked until May 1961, and my son, Kevin, was born June 8, 1961. I was ready to stay home.

"I enjoy my family, friends, and my dogs. I have been truly blessed living in Webb City. I have lived here all my life. I was born in 1929, and Webb City is my favorite city."

Thank you, Frankie Peek Pyle, for sharing your telephone operator memories with us.

Corine Keys   Mildred Watson   Marie Poole   Josie Elliott

Classes to learn to use the dial phone—In 1959, as Webb City continued to grow and take on new technology, Ney Dean Cunningham, along with the business and professional women, decided to help out the housewife who did not venture out of the house and offer some classes. One class that Ney Dean taught and the BPW Club presented was a class about how to use a dial telephone. Some of those local ladies had only had an operator-assisted phone and had no idea how to go about using that new dial phone sitting on the end table. And some were hesitant to get the new phone until after they attended Ney Dean's class.

The 1953 telephone book—Oh, what fun! Looking at a 1953 telephone book of the Joplin-Webb City–Carl Junction–Carterville–Oronogo area. This over-sixty-year phone book has been entertaining. Such joy going through the Yellow Pages, with the wonderful advertisements of businesses gone by the wayside and some that are still in existence. The year 1953 was before we had the exchange numbers like MAyfair 3, MAyfair 4, for Joplin, ORchard 3 for Webb City, Carterville, and Oronogo, MIssion 9 for Carl Junction. The phone numbers of 1953 are two, three, and four-digit phone numbers. Those followed by a capital letter like J usually indicated a party line. My in-laws, Alvin and Mabel Newby, had the phone number 1429J. Their first dial phone was Orchard 3-2583. I dialed that number a lot when calling their son!

There were many unique types of businesses, such as: Joplin Weavers Company at 221 West Third Street (upstairs), phone 2399. This business advertised "Let us reweave your damaged garments—Moth holes, Burns, Tears." And down the block, at 521 West Third Street, was their competition, Magic Weavers, phone 286. Webb City's weavers were the West End Weavers, located at 926 West Daugherty, phone 1980; they even reknitted sweaters.

In an era when the local "five and dime" was one of the most popular places to shop, S. H. Kress in Webb City was at Four South Main, and their phone number was 88. I found it interesting that three of Joplin's four dime stores were located in the same block. S. S. Kresge & Co. 5 and 10 store was at 506 Main, phone 1991; S.S. Kresge & Co. Dollar Store (not really a 5 and 10, I guess) was at 514 Main Street, phone 3506, and directly across the street, at 517 Main Street, was the F. W. Woolworth Co., phone 2523. Ben Franklin was down the street at 1508 Main, phone 1006.

In this day and age, we see many computer stores around the area. I thought it was interesting that the Joplin-Webb City area had nine typewriter stores where typewriters could be purchased, rented, repaired, and bought used. That is a definite change in times.

There were fifteen moving companies listed in 1953, and the one that struck a memory for me was the Rex's Transfer & Storage Company, which was Webb City's own moving company. The main office was at 324 South Main (which was their home), and their phone was 1290. In later years, they moved to the one hundred block of East Daugherty.

Motels in the area were plentiful. Webb City had the Madison Motel, 1500 South Madison, phone 32; the Ozark Motel, 416 South Madison, phone 1234; and the Webb City Cabins, 1114 West Broadway, phone 9651. At the time, Webb City had several rooming houses, but they were not listed in the phone book. Visitors just drove down the main traffic streets looking for the sign that stated "Room for Rent" or "Rooms to Let."

Mining was still an active item in the Yellow Pages. Many mines had phone numbers to contact them. A few that caught my eye were: Sucker Flat Mill, Ninth and Pennsylvania, phone 11; Snapp Mine, North of Oronogo, phone 61; American Zinc Lead & Smelting Co., 1217 South Arch, Carterville, phone 93.

Webb City had a business named Monogifts Inc., 115 East Daugherty, phone 25, and they were listed all through the phone book, advertising their many services, like advertising promotional, sales aids, and advice on how to market your products.

Lumber companies were plentiful in Joplin and Webb City and area towns. Carterville Lumber was at 209 West Main, Carterville, phone 594; Carl Junction Lumber Co. was at 112 South Cowgill, Carl Junction, phone 7276; Home Lumber & Hardware Co. at 212 North Madison, Webb City, phone 34; Burgner-Bowman-Matthews Lumber Co. at 401 East Broadway, Webb City, phone 24. Some of Joplin's lumber companies are still open, such as Herrman Lumber Co., 301 West Second (different address) phone 83; C-Meek Lumber Co. at the stockyards, phone 6055.

The most called number was the Time of the Day, at the First National Bank, Fourth and Main in downtown Joplin, and the number then was 8000. Bob Baker's office was at 927 West Daugherty, and the phone number was 185. Nearby was the Myers Insurance Agency, 917 West Daugherty, phone 490, with Helen Myers as notary. Western Auto was located at 20 South Main, Webb City, phone 968; Oklahoma Tire & Supply, 106 North Main, Webb City, phone 69. Minerva Candy Company, same address as today but phone was 9666. Huey's Family Store, 16 South Main, Webb City, phone 98, their Joplin store was 1504 Main and phone 1702. The Hub was 1 South Main, Webb City, and their phone number was 708. Ray Holland's Service Station was at 401 South Jefferson, Webb City, and his phone number was 9630, and across the street, the Dairy Queen was at 404 South Jefferson with the phone number of 169. The Civic Theater at 217 West Daugherty had the phone number 133. The Bradbury Paint Store at 203 North Main, phone 288 was next-door to the Bradbury Bishop Drug Store, 201 North Main, phone 288.

We did notice that the stores that had four digits were able to adjust to the new exchange numbers by just adding the number onto the front. Allen Electric in Joplin had the phone number 3121, and later their number was 624-3121.

The listing of the Animal Shelter, out on Shoal Creek Drive, brought back memories as well as the Joplin Pet Shop at 115 East Sixth, on the alley where we always went to pet the puppies.

Found lots of memories from childhood except one. As a child in 1956, I wanted to take dancing lessons, and Mom just couldn't afford it, but that did not stop me from constantly turning the Yellow Pages to the page that had a drawing of a beautiful ballerina and just leaving it open next to the phone—power of suggestion. But it didn't work. Memories!

Thanks for traveling down memory lane of 1953, where we let our fingers do the walking!

Streets of Webb City

It seems only appropriate that the city of Webb City would have a street named in honor of the founder, John C. Webb. *Webb Street* runs from Fourth and Webb North. At the time it was platted, the street ran in front of the Webb home at 110 North Webb Street. Just to the north of Webb's home was *John Street*, also named on his behalf, but later (1922), John was renamed *Austin Street*.

Other streets throughout the city have been named in honor of certain people of distinction. *Tom Street* was named to recognize Webb's uncle Thomas C. Webb. Webb's oldest daughter, Martha, married William E. Hall, and *Hall Street* is in his honor.

Daugherty Street was named for William A. Daugherty, who was Webb's business partner in his first mining attempts. Daugherty also had another street named after him, and that was the one that ran in front of his home on the west side of Webb City (now the Dilworth Home), and it was called *Daugherty Lane*, but most of you know it as *Colonial Road*. In between being known by either of those names, it was called the *Hospital Road*, as it led to the Tuberculosis Hospital.

Colonel James O'Neill became a very important asset for Webb City as he established the waterworks, the gas company, the ice company, and the Newland Hotel. He was also busy in the mining industry and in purchasing land. He doesn't have a street named after him, but his home on the southwest corner of Broadway Street and Pennsylvania Avenue sits in tribute to him. The *Pennsylvania Avenue* in front of his home is the only street in Webb City named after a state, and it just so happens that is the state that the colonel hailed from. While living in Pennsylvania, the colonel invested in land that was rich with petroleum, and he worked the oil wells and made his fortune. So Pennsylvania was an important part of his history.

Aylor Street was named in honor of Joseph Aylor, who arrived in Jasper County after the Civil War and purchased land on what became known as Aylor Hill (located on the northeast corner of what is now Madison Street and Cardinal Drive, just east of Mount Hope Cemetery, and the hill no longer exists, torn down in 1979). Aylor invested well with Andrew McCorkle in purchasing land rich in minerals, amassing over two thousand acres in his name.

George W. Ball had the honor of *Ball Street* being named after him. He also had Ball Addition, which was easily recognized as each home had concrete balls on each side of the entrance from the main sidewalk. Some are still visible today but becoming scarce.

There isn't anything to document about *Washington Street, Jefferson Street,* or *Madison Street,* but we are assuming those three streets that run parallel to each other are named after the first, third, and fourth presidents of the United States.

College Street was named to guide you to the college at the west end of John Street (later Austin Street). The college faced to the east.

Oronogo, Galena, and Joplin were the towns located close to Webb City, and they were honored with streets bearing their names, but *Joplin Street* became Broadway in 1922. *Oronogo Street* has held its identity through the years. Carl Junction is to the west, and the Carl Junction Road started at Madison Street going west, and it used to go all the way to Highway 43 but was cut short with expansions to the airport. That street has been changed to *Stadium Drive* when the new stadium was completed (2011). On the south side of the airport that we have often referred to as Airport Drive was called *Webb City Road*.

Kos Elliott, who was the surveyor who surveyed Webb's First Addition, has *Elliott Street. Walker Street* was named in honor of a gentleman involved in the mining business.

A sign that stood for many years is now gone from Main Street across from the old Independent Gravel Company, and that is *Surface Avenue*, named in honor of Hubert Surface (and his wife, Hazel) who were instrumental in establishing the Independent Ball Fields and kept them maintained.

Broadway Road, a spur off Broadway Street, was named *Powell Drive* in honor of Sergeant Robert A. Powell, who was the first Webb City serviceman killed in Vietnam. He died June 10, 1966.

As many new building subdivisions are being established in Webb City, it is nearly impossible to note how the new streets have obtained their identity. But we have had some new names added to local streets. The west side entrance into King Jack Park off Hall Street bears the name of *Robert J. Baker Drive*, as Baker was one of the major enthusiasts that helped to establish King Jack Park. Along the Praying Hands, also in King Jack Park, we have *Dawson Drive*, in honor of the Dawson family whose talents and generosity have helped the city in many ways, which were done quietly and without a lot of fanfare.

Grant Wistrom Drive, just east of Madison and Crow, was named in honor of Grant Wistrom, who graduated from Webb City High School and made it as a professional football player in Nebraska.

Times change and names change, but it is nice to be able to honor some important folks with a simple street sign that bears their name and calls them to memory. And I can think of many very important and helpful folks who deserve a street sign in their name, but alas, there are not enough streets to offer that honor.

Street trivia:

Did you know, in 1891, Broadway Street (then known as Main Street) was the only road into Carterville from Webb City? Daugherty Street ended at Elliott Street.

Broadway had the nickname of "Red Hot Street." Some say that Broadway (which was Main Street until 1922) was called the Red Hot Street because of the Temperance Program which banned liquor in Carterville, and that was the street taken by the many miners as they came to Webb City to buy their liquor.

Original platting of Webb City Street—The city began with eight streets, seven alleys, and seventy-two lots.

Main Street (changed to Broadway Street on October 18, 1920) is eighty feet wide and bounded on the north by lots 31 and 40, and on the south by lots 21 and 30.

Church Street is fifty feet wide and bounded on the north by lots 11 and 20, and on the south by lots 1 and 10.

Joplin Street (changed to Broadway Street on October 18, 1920) is sixty-six feet wide, bounded on the north by lot 71, and on the south by lot 72.

Daugherty Street is fifty feet wide, bounded on the north by lots 51 and 60, on the south by lots 41 and 50.

John Street (changed to Austin Street on October 18, 1920) is twenty-five feet wide, bounded on the south by lots 61 and 70.

Webb Street is fifty feet wide, bounded on the east by lots 1, 20, 21, 40, 47, 60, and 61, and on the west by lots 71 and 72.

Allen Street (changed to Main Street on October 18, 1920) is eighty feet wide and bounded on the west by lots 4, 17, 24, 37, 44, 57, and 64; on the east by lots 5, 16, 25, 36, 45, 56, and 65. The alleys are sixteen feet wide, except on the extreme eastern and southern boundaries, which are eight feet wide

Malang, John M. Sr.—First Concrete Road

"Father of the Good Roads Movement"—When you hear stories about the good ole days, one thing that wasn't considered great was the road system. Those old cars with the narrow wheels would make some pretty deep ruts, and on muddy days, many a vehicle got stuck in the mud up to the rim of the tires. Something had to be done, and they chose the right man to do it—John M. Malang Sr.

John Malang was born September 29, 1866, in Nashville, Tennessee. Coming to this area in 1878 with his parents, they settled in Tanyard Hollow. John didn't get a lot of education. He started working the mines as a young lad and later became a mine operator.

John left the mining business to become partners in the Joplin Transfer Company.

At the age of twenty, in 1886, John married Anna, and they had a farm out on West Seventh Street, outside of the Joplin city limits. During several election campaigns, John, being a staunch Republican, would get into some strong debates with some of the attorneys, which was good practice for him, as he ran for the state senate in 1908 and won.

After leaving the senate, John became the superintendent of the Joplin Special Road District in 1914. His first project was the eighteen-foot-wide concrete highway from Webb City to the Kansas Stateline. This was the first concrete road in the entire state.

In 1919, the McCullough-Morgan Law went into effect (of which John was the author), and it provided for the appointment of a state superintendent of highways. You know the old saying "don't make a suggestion unless you are willing to do it!" Well, John was appointed and was also ex-officio secretary of the highway board.

He quickly went to work on developing the first Missouri road plan, which he entitled "Lift Missouri Out of the Mud." In 1921, his new campaign was called Farm to Market, and he worked on linking rural counties with the arterial highway system.

John Malang not only designed the main network of roads in the state, he also supervised the construction. He constructed a scenic route from Joplin to Neosho, a shortcut from Joplin to Seneca and a cutoff between Highways 16 and 38 for Pierce City, Sarcoxie, and Wentworth.

He was working on another bond issue for the highway improvement when he passed away of heart complications in a hotel in Kansas City. His funeral was attended by more than one thousand people. They ranged from miners, highway workers, to politicians, lawyers, friends, and relatives. The ceremony was held in the Elks Club at Fourth and Pearl Streets. The funeral procession went down the first highway made of concrete for which John was responsible for obtaining. He is buried in Mount Hope Cemetery, where his tombstone looks out over that very same highway (although throughout the years, it has been widened).

A special commemorative plaque was installed at the capitol building in Jefferson City, in remembrance of John M. Malang, "Father of the Good Road Movement." The plaque was dedicated on January 11, 1930, just a few hours before John's loving wife passed away to join him.

Powell Drive

A memorial to Robert Powell, Webb City's first Vietnam casualty.

Powell Drive was dedicated in honor of Rose's brother Robert A. Powell, who was the first Webb City citizen killed in action in Vietnam. Sergeant Robert A. Powell had been stationed in Germany two years before requesting a transfer to Vietnam. He was a dedicated soldier, a member of the First Calvary Division, Fourteenth Artillery, and he had been in Vietnam for three months when he was killed by a mine on June 10, 1966. He only had 228 days left on his tour of duty.

Powell was the son of Mr. and Mrs. William F. Powell and came from a large family of six brothers and two sisters. He had only been married five months at the time of his death. After the ceremony here in Webb City, Robert A. Powell received the honor of being buried in Arlington National Cemetery.

Rose said that since her mother was unable to travel to Washington, DC, she decorated the grave of the Unknown Soldier in the Webb City Cemetery. It's become a family tradition that Rose and her sister, Connie, have continued to honor.

Thank you, Rose, for sharing the information about your brother with all of us. Rose has donated Robert's hat, military dog tags, and telegrams received by their mother to the Webb City Historical Society.

Before being dedicated as Powell Drive, the street was known as *Broadway Road*, a spur off from *Broadway Street*.

Names of Webb City Streets

Colonial Drive was formerly known as Hospital Road, since it was the road that led to the Tuberculosis Hospital. But long before that, it was known as Daugherty Lane, since that was the road on which the W. A. Daugherty home was located. It is the oldest house in Webb City.

Question have been asked about the streets that were named after presidents and found it odd that we have a street named after the first president, George Washington; the third president, Thomas Jefferson; and the fourth president, John Madison. But for some reason, the second president, John Adams, was left out. I wonder why?

Did you know that the road that runs by the airport used to be referred to as the Webb City Road because that was the road that got you to Webb City from Joplin and Carl Junction? Joplin's North Main Road was the connection between Webb City and Joplin. At the time, Range Line Road was just a gravel road, not traveled much. Mostly used as a streetcar track.

Rumor has it that Ellis Street was named after the real estate agent who had the area surveyed and platted, John Ellis. The section of Sixth Street going west from Ellis Street to Zigler Street was called McClelland Street. Fifth Street from Ellis Street to Zigler Street used to be called Zoller Street. At Third Street and Madison Street, where the trailer park is located, was a street that was two blocks to the west and named Edna Street. Edna Street led back into a section of town that was secluded.

South of Edna Street was Forrest Avenue. Most people don't even realize that there is a Preston Street, Shenandoah Street, and Forrest Street in that part of town. The only way to get into the area is going west from Madison on Fourth Street, which used to be called Dermott. At the end of Dermott, you could turn left on Frisco Street, which was located just on the west side of the Frisco Railroad tracks, and Frisco went south to the city limits, which was only as far as Seventh Street at the time.

Before the mining of Sucker Flat, where King Jack Park is now located, there were roads that are no longer there. Liberty Street went south beyond Sixth Street, as did Webb Street. Between Liberty Street and the five hundred block of Main Street was Tracy Street, and between Liberty Street and the six hundred block of South Main Street was a street called Home Avenue. The hill that the Praying Hands statue is sitting on was not there when these streets were in existence.

Pennsylvania Street went to about Tenth Street, and there was a streetcar track that crossed over (and above) Pennsylvania Avenue. Many changes have taken place in Webb City over the years, with streets changing names and some even disappearing. Many houses were torn down to make way for progress, as when the new Highway 71 went through town. It's hard to imagine that there were normal city blocks where the highway winds its way through town.

There were mostly houses on Madison Street to Thirteenth Street. It was a wide street to make way for the streetcar tracks, but it wasn't the thoroughfare it is today. On past Thirteenth Street, you were out in the country with the cemeteries framing up the edge of the city limits. Across Madison Street, from Mount Hope Cemetery, was Aylor Hill where Mr. Aylor lived before building his mansion in town at Webb Street and Daugherty Street.

Stewart Street and West Street were located off Aylor, where Mark Twain School is now located. West Street ran north from Dermott (Fourth Street) past Aylor Street.

Starting at Broadway Street, west of Madison Street, were streets named First Street, Edna Avenue, Preston Avenue, Dermott Avenue, Zeller Avenue, McClelland Street, Seventh Street, Harrison Street, West Eleventh Street. Zoller Street went from five hundred block of Ellis, west to Zigler Street

Continental Avenue went from six hundred East Wood Street north to East Aylor Street. Also Continental Avenue went south from 600 East Fourth for two blocks.

Going south on Main Street, just past Tracy Street to the 600 block of South Main Street, was Home Street, which went from Main Street west to Liberty Street. Evidently taken out when Sucker Flat was created.

We adjust to changes so easily that it's hard to remember what things used to look like.

Jefferson Highway

The year is 1915, and the residents of Webb City are so excited about the completion of the new transcontinental international Jefferson Highway going through Webb City. The Jefferson Highway was a north to south highway extending 2,300 miles from Winnipeg, Canada, to New Orleans, Louisiana. The symbols were a pine tree and a palm tree, referring to the trees along the route. Many called the highway "the vacation route of America," and it came right through our town of Webb City. Originally it came into Webb City from Carterville on Daugherty Street to Devon Street, left one block to Broadway Street, which, at that time, was named East Main Street to Allen Street, now Main Street. Jefferson Highway then turned south to Fourth Street. Turning right (west) on Fourth Street, the highway went to Madison Street. Madison Street, at that time, was being worked on to transition it from streetcars to automobiles and trucks. The highway then continued south on Madison to Joplin. That route was short-lived, and a new route was determined that allowed travelers to see more of the city.

So the new route for the Jefferson Highway came into the city from Carterville on Daugherty Street, turning south (left) onto Main Street (Allen Street). This allowed the tourist to see the Merchants & Miners Bank, The Webb City Bank, and the Middlewest Opera House. Then the highway turned right (west) on Broadway (at that time known as West Main), past the Coney Island. Then there was that little jog on Webb Street immediately turning right onto Broadway (at that time called Joplin Street). The traveler was able to enjoy the beautiful sights of E. T. Webb's mansion, the Methodist Church, the O'Neill home, the Presbyterian Church, and the Baptist Church before turning left (south) on Oronogo Street, traveling four blocks to Fourth Street before turning right at the beautiful Eugene Field School at Fourth and Oronogo. Fourth Street carried the traveler to Madison Street. Heading south on Madison Street brought the traveler to the new concrete road, which started at Thirteenth and Madison, extending to Zora Street through Royal Heights to Broadway in Joplin.

The signs markings the route along the Jefferson Highway were always attached to poles, and they were square with a blue band across the top and bottom and a twelve-inch white band in the center, which held the initials JH attached to each other. Most of those signs were scrapped during the war. Some signs were painted directly on the poles, trying to have two at the intersection where the highway turned. One showing where you turned, and one showing you made the correct turn. According to a newspaper article, the Missouri Highway gang was in Webb City putting up directional signs to help tourists follow the Jefferson Highway through town. The highway had been in town for six years, so they must have been updating the signs.

The Jefferson Highway was in existence until 1929 when the highways bearing numbers began taking over. The North–South Jefferson Highway was replaced by the new Route 66, which changed the direction of the highway in a few spots.

The Jefferson Highway celebrated its one hundredth anniversary in 2015. It would be great to have the Jefferson Highway signs marking the route. Carthage, Carterville, Webb City, and Joplin all had the distinction of having the North–South Jefferson Highway and the East–West Route 66 both passing through their town and their history. Other Missouri towns, like Kansas City, Nevada, Jasper, Lamar, and Neosho, had the Jefferson Highway passing through their towns, but they did not have Route 66, which makes our area in Jasper County unique.

Completion of the Jefferson Highway brought travelers into town. The highway entered Webb City on East Daugherty to Devon, across to Broadway, west to Main Street, south on Main to Fourth street, west on Fourth to Madison, south to what would be the new concrete road, which began at

Thirteenth and Madison. The concrete highway extended through Royal Heights to Broadway in Joplin. The concrete road was built by the WPA.

Route 66

Let's take a nostalgic trip down Route 66 in Webb City. Many changes have taken place over the years, so let's look at the trip as it would have been many years ago.

As we leave Carterville, heading west toward Webb City, on the left is the very spot that John C. Webb uncovered that chunk of lead that started the town of Webbville, soon-to-become Webb City. Just a little more to the left brings us to the location of the Missouri Pacific Railroad Depot. Now we come to the *Y* in the road. Route 66 takes the left side of the *Y* on Broadway Street. There is a small gas station that is known as the *Y*, which is appropriately named. Heading west on Broadway, we notice Webb Corp on our left, one of the oldest businesses in continuous operation in Webb City's history. On the right, we have the lumberyard, which changed names throughout the years, but most of us today remember it as the Webb City Lumber Yard. When we arrive at the intersection of Broadway and Main Street, we notice Kress Dime Store sitting next to the Coney Island on the southwest corner. The northwest corner is the home of the Webb City Bank, established in 1879. The Middlewest Building on the southeast corner is home to The Hub (later Ben Franklin Dime Store). Continue west on Broadway, and we are heading straight for the Civic Drive-In Café which was quite a hot spot for dinner before going to your choice of theaters: The Civic, The Dickenson (Larsen), or the Junior.

The southeast corner of Broadway, as we turn left on Webb Street, is a service station, and we take a swing to the right as Broadway completes an *S*-curve. On the right is the Safeway Store, on the left is E. T. Webb's home (Liberty and Broadway), and on the right is Hedge-Nelson-Lewis Funeral Home.

Route 66 along Broadway takes you past the Methodist Church, The Presbyterian Church, and the First Baptist Church, all of which have been a major part of Webb City history for many years.

The southwest corner of Pennsylvania and Broadway is the home of Colonel James O'Neill, one of the most important forefathers who brought us water, gas, a fancy hotel, an ice company, and many other spectacular commodities of convenience.

The next southwest corner at Ball and Broadway is the home of Thomas Coyne, owner of a lumberyard, but more important is his dealings with establishing the Jane Chinn Hospital. Behind the Coyne home is the well-known Broadway Market, which made its impact on Webb City for many years. As you arrive at Washington and Broadway, you can't help but notice the impressive Webb City High School, built in 1912. What a fine building to represent the great school district of Webb City.

Whoa, don't go too fast, you have to make a left turn at Jefferson and Broadway. What a busy intersection as three of the four corners have service stations (two of those buildings are still standing today). Now you take a leisurely drive down a residential section of town as you head south on Jefferson Street for about four blocks, and then you are at yet another service station on the southeast corner of Jefferson and Fourth. On the northwest corner is a barbershop and Greyhound bus station. Across the street, on the southwest corner, is the ever-popular Dairy Queen, a great place to get an ice cream treat.

Route 66 heads south across MacArthur Boulevard, but we are unable to make that journey today because of a median in the road. But using your imagination and with a few twists and turns, you can get back onto Jefferson Street, heading south. We are in a residential area until you get to Twelfth Street where we find yet another service station on the southwest corner. At Thirteenth Street and Jefferson, the road kind of curves right toward Madison Street. Today you would find yourself between the Webb City Bank and Taco Gringo, but in those days, you were south of the Madison Café. Across from the Madison Café, as you turn left, is the Madison Inn. Just past the Madison Café on the left is Cobble's Service Station and Jerry's Café and then the Mobile Service Station. Across the street, at Sixteenth and Madison, on the west side of Madison, is Karbe's Grocery Store. Once you go past the Mount Hope Cemetery, you are basically heading out of town until you get to Zora Street, and Route 66 takes a right to Florida Street. You have left Webb City behind, but what an interesting trip the ribbon of Route 66 makes as it winds its way through the historic city of Webb City.

There is quite a bit of controversy about the famous Route 66 in the small local towns that were fortunate enough to be a part of the most popular road of today. Webb City has a wonderful rich history of mining, and Route 66 adds yet another flavor to Webb City's historical background. Take a walk, a bike ride, or a car ride and see what you might remember along Route 66 in Webb City.

Let's take a nostalgic trip down Route 66 in Webb City. Many changes have taken place over the years, so let's look at the trip as it would have been many years ago. Route 66 was officially finished from St. Louis to Joplin in 1930.

As we leave Carterville, heading west toward Webb City, on the left is the very spot that John C. Webb uncovered that chunk of lead that started the town of Webb Ville (1873), soon-to-become Webb City (1876). Just a little more to the left brings us to the location of the Missouri Pacific Railroad Depot. Now we come to the *Y* in the road. Route 66 takes the left side of the *Y* on Broadway Street. There is a small gas station that is known as the *Y*, which is appropriately named. On your immediate left is Swapper's Salvage, where lots of Webb City history spent its last days. The old plane (Joplin Jalopy) was moved from the airport to its final resting place at Swapper's. The original "Webb City, City of Zinc" sign that spanned Daugherty Street in the west end of town came to rest in an upright position at Swapper's, where folks coming into town by Route 66 knew they had just entered Webb City. Swapper's was not a beautiful sight, but to the inquiring minds, it was loaded with history. Heading west on Broadway, we notice Webb Corp on our left, one of the oldest businesses in continuous operation in Webb City's history (est. 1895). On the right, we have the lumberyard, which changed names throughout the years, but most of us today remember it as the Webb City Lumber Yard. The three hundred block of East Broadway was a popular spot to many teenagers as they worked on their hot rods. Johnson's Auto Salvage had the parts they needed, S. W. Rigg's & Sons could do the welding, Hamilton's Auto Supply could get the newer parts, and there was Mill's Auto Repair Shop behind the welding shop, in case the boys didn't know for sure what they were doing. They could also fill up on gas at the Clark's Oil Company filling station. Or they could continue one block west and find auto repair at Cardwell's or Sam Kelly's Auto Repair.

When we arrive at the intersection of Broadway and Main Street, we notice Kress Dime Store sitting next to the Coney Island on the southwest corner. The Coney Island was a wonderful little business established in 1923, when Sam Kallas introduced a special treat that he had tasted in Kansas City. He ordered his wieners from Chicago, the buns were made by the local Etter's Bakery, and he used his own recipe for the chili. You could buy a Coney Island Coney for 5¢ or six for 25¢. A new fad had begun. Sam leased the southwest corner of Main and Broadway from Kress Five and Dime and built the little café that stood there for many years. Later (1945) Sam and his son, Paul, moved their business to the Civic Drive-In Café at 110 South Webb Street. Paul told me in a 1992 interview that his dad sold those 5¢ Coney dogs and made $500 per day on the weekdays and $1,000 on Saturdays. That was a lot of 5¢ Coney dogs!

The northwest corner is the home of the Webb City Bank, established in 1879. The Middlewest Building (originally Webb City's finest opera house, established 1883) is on the southeast corner, at one time home to The Hub (later Ben Franklin Dime Store 1967). The Webb City Bank installed a drive-in bank (1962) on the northeast corner, which was quite a new concept for our small town. To the east of the drive-in bank was the Home Beverage Company with a drive-through window which allowed folks to purchase their alcoholic beverages, cigarettes, ice, or soda pop without getting out of the car.

Continue west on Broadway, and we are heading straight for the Civic Drive-In Café which was quite a hot spot for dinner before going to your choice of theaters: The Civic, The Dickinson (Larsen), or the Junior. Later this same address, 110 North Webb, was also home to The Myers Insurance Agency, Bill Myer's Law Firm, and Bob Baker's CPA offices. To the south, we have Dr. Ferguson's office at 105 North Webb and the Elks Club on the northwest corner of Webb and Broadway. The third floor of the Elks Club was where many teenagers enjoyed a Saturday night dance, with the windows open for fresh air and also to allow that great music to drift outside and lure more to join in on the fun.

Just before we turn left on Webb Street, we must look to the right and observe the Oldham Service station which was also home to the Western Union office and the bus companies, Greyhound and Crown. As we continue left, on the left is yet another service station (now known as the Route 66 Visitor Center and Chamber of Commerce office in the refurbished service station). And now, we take a swing to the right as Broadway completes an S-curve. On the right is the phone company where Bill Patten recalls, "As a child I used to go upstairs and watch the operators connect the calls by putting the wires in the right holes. Webb City may have been the last city in Missouri to see the advent of rotary phones." The next building on the right is the Safeway store, on the left is E. T. Webb's home (Liberty and Broadway), and on the right is Hedge-Nelson-Lewis Funeral Home. Sitting on the alley is a cute little block building which was home to Jelly's Market, one of many small neighborhood grocery stores.

Route 66 along Broadway takes you past the Methodist Church, The Presbyterian Church, and the First Baptist Church, all of which have been a major part of Webb City history for many years.

The southwest corner of Pennsylvania and Broadway is the home of Colonel James O'Neill, one of the most important forefathers who brought us water, gas, a fancy hotel, an ice company, and many other spectacular commodities of convenience. On the northwest corner of the same intersection is the illusive Masonic Lodge.

The next southwest corner, at Ball and Broadway, is the home of Thomas Coyne, owner of a lumberyard, but more important is his dealings with establishing the Jane Chinn Hospital. Behind the Coyne home is the well-known Broadway Market, which made its impact on Webb City for many years. Everyone remembers the outside watermelon tank which kept those watermelons ice-cold. As you arrive at Washington and Broadway, you can't help but notice the impressive Webb City High School, built in 1912. What a fine building to represent the great school district of Webb City. Across the street, on the northeast corner of Washington and Broadway, is a little café that fed many a student at lunchtime. Couraw's was well known for their chili dogs. Mr. Couraw would cut the wiener into fourths, long ways, and put that one-fourth of a hot dog on a bun, douse it with chili, and charge the kids a dime. Couraw's also made hard cinnamon candies which were a popular sweet treat.

Whoa, don't go too fast, you have to make a left turn at Jefferson and Broadway. What a busy intersection as three of the four corners have service stations (two of those buildings are still standing today). Now you take a leisurely drive down a residential section of town as you head south on Jefferson Street for about four blocks, and then you are at yet another service station on the southeast corner of Jefferson and Fourth. On the northwest corner is a barbershop, which also shared with the Greyhound bus station in later years. Across the street, on the southwest corner, is the ever-popular Dairy Queen (est. 1952), a great place to get an ice cream treat.

Route 66 heads south across MacArthur Boulevard, but we are unable to make that journey today because of a median in the road. But using your imagination and with a few twists and turns, you can get back onto Jefferson Street, heading south. We are in a residential area until you get to Twelfth Street where we find yet another service station on the southwest corner. At Thirteenth Street and Jefferson, the road kind of curves right toward Madison Street. Today you would find yourself between the Webb City Bank and Taco Gringo, but in those days, you were south of the Madison Café (a few blocks to the north was the Webb City Drive-In theater, established 1953). Across from the Madison Café, as you turn left, is the Madison Inn. Just past the Madison Café on the left is Cobble's Service Station and Jerry's Café and then the Mobile Service Station. Across the street, at Sixteenth and Madison, on the west side of Madison, is Karbe's Grocery Store. Once you go past the Mount Hope Cemetery, you are basically heading out of town until you get to Zora Street, and Route 66 takes a right to Florida Street. You have left Webb City behind, but what an interesting trip the ribbon of Route 66 makes as it winds its way through the historic city of Webb City.

There is quite a bit of controversy about the famous Route 66 in the small local towns that were fortunate enough to be a part of the most popular road of today. Webb City has a wonderful rich history of mining, and Route 66 adds yet another flavor to Webb City's historical background. Take a walk, a bike ride, or a car ride and see what you might remember along Route 66 in Webb City.

CHAPTER 3

Southwest Missouri Railway Association

A. H. Rogers, 1858–1946

A. H. Rogers, Founder

A. H. (Alfred Harrison) Rogers was born February 2, 1858, in Le Claire, Iowa, to Robert H. and Mary Jane (Caldwell) Rogers. The father was a state legislator for Iowa back when the state capital was Iowa City. Having a little bit of notoriety, Robert Rogers was also the cofounder of Le Claire, Iowa. He had a large interest in lumber, and he built the first steam sawmill west of the Mississippi River. The family relocated to Kansas City, Kansas, where Alfred H. Rogers graduated from high school at the age of sixteen. And the elder Rogers passed away.

A. H. Rogers taught himself Greek during his high school years by studying at night and, within eight months, had mastered the language (normally a three-year course) and entered Harvard at the unusually young age of sixteen. Within four years, Roger graduated from Harvard, in 1878. His first intentions were to study law, but his brother had established a lumber, grain, and milling business in Spring Hill, Kansas, following in his father's footsteps. He worked with his brother and continued his studies in law. He was admitted to the bar in Olathe, Kansas, within two years, in 1880. But he never practiced law.

His career kept changing when he left his brother's business and went to Wyandotte. He established the Bank of Wyandotte, which he managed for five years before selling the business. He contemplated what he would do in his life while working as a clerk at the Citizen's National Bank in Kansas City, Missouri. Liking the banking business, he worked for two years at the Bank of Springfield, Missouri. In 1888, he organized the Springfield Savings Bank. He kept that business but made the journey to Webb City to check out the needs of transportation for the local miners. That was when he established the two-mile mule-drawn trolley line from Webb City to Carterville

Some people have a natural ability to look at a situation and determine a need. Then they carry that talent a step further and "feed the need" with a solution. Such was the case for A. H. Rogers. He wandered into Webb City and Carterville in 1889 from the big city of Springfield. He saw the need of transportation for the miners. Rogers started out his plan to feed the need by building a two-mile mule car line between Webb City and Carterville, creating an interurban system. He obtained the city franchise under the name of the Twin Cities Street Railway.

In those days, Webb City and Carterville were often referred to as the twin cities, as they grew and developed at pretty much the same speed. Some folks refused to call it the twin cities and referred to it as the Webb City–Carterville Electric Line. Rogers worked as the head of his newfound business. But all the while, Rogers was looking into the future and making plans that would change the world of transportation for Jasper County. The work began with installing the rails between Webb City and Carterville in 1889. The mule-line streetcar business began September 1, 1890, and continued to March 1, 1893, when the new modern electric-powered streetcar was established in the area.

In the fall of 1892, Rogers discarded his mule-car system and took on a new approach, with the help of capitalists from the east. He used the right-of-way from the mule-car system and started an electric line, naming his new venture Southwest Missouri Electric Railway. He came up against a hard rock when local businessmen spoke up against an electric line between Webb City and Joplin, as they felt the customers would ride to Joplin and spend their money.

Mayor Charles Manker suggested to A. H. Rogers that the businessmen might be more agreeable if he would make Webb City the headquarters for the railway. Rogers determined that this was feasible, and he established the power plant, carbarn/repair shops, and offices in the west end of town, just a few blocks from where he had originally kept his mules and cars at Washington and Daugherty Streets. This was quite a financial boom for Webb City as the company employed almost 175 people. Webb City was only seven years behind Kansas City in providing electric transportation.

July 4, 1893, was the day of the first run of the Southwest Missouri Electric Railway Company between Joplin and Webb City. Three of the mule car drivers had been trained to operate the new electric system, and they were William Palmer, William Hamilton, and George Herron. Two of the electric cars were made in Joplin and were affectionately known as Henrietta and Julianna. Juanetta and Oriana were manufactured by Laclede Car Company in St. Louis, Missouri. The new cars traveled over railway tracks made with steel from Illinois Steel Company. The railway ties were made of oak from around Jasper County. The electrical power came from Webb City.

This new Webb City company was a pioneer company as the electric line system had only been in use nationally for eight years with the first system opening in Baltimore, Maryland, on August 10, 1885, by Leo Draft. Kansas City opened an experimental line that consisted of half a mile but operated its first successful electric line in the Armourdale District in 1889. In 1888, Richmond, Virginia, used an electric motor to operate their first streetcar. In 1886, the Dan Patch electric line declared that there was only eight miles of electric lines in the United States. By 1889, in three years, that number increased to 805 miles of electric streetcar tracks handling 2,800 streetcars.

Rogers added to his streetcar miles in 1896 by purchasing the Jasper County Electric Railway that ran from Carthage to Carterville. This purchase included the land of Lakeside Park, plus some land on Center Creek. This will be discussed a little later as that is where the magic of the era was born.

Rogers then purchased the Joplin Electric Railway and the Galena Electric Railway, making the Southwest Missouri Railway an excellent interurban service and adding even more miles with the addition of Joplin's Smelter Hill and Chitwood in 1903. With the growth of the company, a change was made in 1906 when the Southwest Missouri Railroad Company was organized and took over the Southwest Missouri Electric Railway and the Webb City Northern Electric Railway Company, which connected Oronogo, Neck City, Purcell, and Alba. It was all one company now. In Webb City, 1903, the new powerhouse and car shops were built on the northwest and northeast corners of Madison Street and Joplin (Broadway) Streets. Each year brought more tracks being built, and there was more activity in the constantly growing electric streetcar business.

Once again, Rogers showed his ingenuity by looking ahead and purchasing the right-of-way into small towns in Jasper County. In 1896, he purchased the Jasper County Electric Railway (the White Line) that ran from Carthage to Carterville, which included Lakeside Park. That same year, he purchased the Joplin Electric and the Galena Electric Railways. Rogers continued to add lines to extended areas like Chitwood and Smelter Hill, northwest of Joplin. By 1897, the electric railway was classified as the longest continuous electric railway in the world!

The old mule carbarn at Daugherty and Washington was replaced by the modern carbarn at Madison and Joplin (Broadway) Streets. The new powerhouse of brick and stone was built across from the carbarn on the northwest corner in 1903 and the building for the association. More information to follow.

This is not Rogers' only claim to fame as he ran the most accomplished electric streetcar line, which continued to grow each day. He fought the competition of J. J. Helm, a multimillionaire from Kansas City, who was determined to outdo Rogers. Rogers tangled with Gilbert Barbee and the Joplin Globe, so Rogers bought up enough shares to take over as president of the Joplin Globe. Rogers was king of the mountain until his death in 1920, at the age of sixty-two.

Year 1903 showed the company was doing well, as they built the new powerhouse at Broadway and Madison and added the clubhouse in 1910.

In 1906, the business regained purpose again with the newly organized Southwest Missouri Railroad Company absorbing the Southwest Electric Railway and the new Webb City Northern, which took the railway north to Oronogo, Neck City, Alba, and Purcell, which had been added in 1903. A freight line was added in 1906, with the purchase of three freight cars.

Thirteen new steel passenger streetcars purchased by the new company were heated by electricity, and the old potbelly coal stoves became obsolete in the streetcars.

Rogers was a shrewd businessman, and as he encountered problems along the way, his theory was if you can't lick 'em, join 'em. And that was what he did. In November of 1906, J. J. Heim, a millionaire from Kansas City, announced plans to build an electric line from Joplin to Galena to

Baxter Springs, and another from Joplin to Duenweg. Not being of the shy type, Heim stated his intentions to gridiron the entire mining camp with electric roads. The tug-of-war had begun.

Heim managed to gain twelve miles of streetcar line within the city limits of Joplin. Rogers already had ten miles of track, but when Rogers' attorney approached the city to ask for a few more blocks, they were denied. And Heim managed to get an electric line from Joplin to Pittsburg before Rogers.

Not to be outdone, A. H. Rogers began to buy shares of common stock of the Joplin–Pittsburg Railway Company, owned by J. J. Heim. Rogers managed to become a controlling stockholder and was present at each meeting when the company made plans to extend their line into Joplin, which he used his stock to vote against. This limited Heim to five miles of track in Joplin, and Rogers had obtained fifteen miles.

In 1908, the Spring River Power Company purchased Old Kate, which was a generator used at the world's fair in St. Louis in 1904. Two thousand kilowatts, this power was used for the Joplin and Pittsburg Railway Companies and the Southwest Missouri Railroad Company, later to be referred to as the Empire District Electric Company.

Another similar business transaction was handled by Rogers with his if-you-can't-lick-'em-join-'em attitude. It seemed that Rogers and Gilbert Barbee, president and stockholder of the Joplin Globe, were having a problem, and Rogers did not like the stories being printed about his company. In January 1910, Barbee sold his stock to some prominent men in the area, including A. H. Rogers, who took over as president and held that position until his death in 1920. At his death, his son, Harrison C. Rogers, became president of the publishing firm until his death in 1946. At that time, the executive position went to Clay Cowgill Blair and then to Blair's son-in-law, Frederick G. Hughes, and Harrison C. Rogers' son became the publisher. They held these positions until the paper was sold in 1970 to a newspaper company.

A. H. Rogers was a man who knew how to feed a need, how to handle a situation, and how to succeed. Thank you, Mr. Rogers, for helping us get around the neighborhood. We take this moment to recognize that the electric streetcar has been serving Webb City and the surrounding area for 114 years and to celebrate the one-hundredth birthday of the organization of the Southwest Missouri Railroad Company.

One other little tidbit about A. H. Rogers was that he went to visit Alexander Graham Bell in February 1877, just nine months after Bell had patented the telephone, and he had the opportunity of speaking into Bell's new invention. He always claimed to have "probably" been the first person from Southwest Missouri to speak into a telephone.

Southwest Missouri Electric Railway

A 1901 description of the railway found in the *Encyclopedia of the History of Missouri*:

This line of railway connects the principal cities in the Missouri-Kansas mineral region with its terminal at Carthage, Missouri, and Galena, Kansas, passing through the cities of Carterville, Webb City, and Joplin, with a branch from Carterville to Prosperity. It also affords local service in Carthage and Joplin. January 1, 1900, the total number of miles operated was thirty five. This was increased May 1, 1900, by an extension from Galena southwest to Riceville, a distance of three miles and by second tracks for a distance of ten miles at intervals between Carthage and Galena, increasing the trackage to a total of forty-eight miles. The rolling stock comprises ten single-truck cars, twenty double-truck closed cars, eleven double-truck open cars and three trail cars. The cars are provided with electric and hot waterheaters, and the interurban cars have powerful electric headlights. Eight of the cars, put on the road in 1899, are forty-four feet long, contain smoking compartment, and are modern in every detail. Double cedar poles and span-wire construction is used throughout, and the feed wire amount tonearly 300,000 pounds of copper. There are two power houses; one at Webb City and one at Lakeside Park, on Center creek is a combination station and carhouse. Besides the Lakeside Park carhouse, there is one in Webb City and another in East Joplin.

Two parks are owned by the company, Midway Park, near Joplin and Lakeside Park, seven and one-half miles from Carthage.

The splendid South West Missouri Electric Railway is an evolution from a muleroad, which was built in 1890 by A.H. Rogers, now president of the present operating company. It was known as the Twin Cities Street Railway and extended from the west end of Webb City to the east end of Carterville, two and one-half miles. It was operated with mules from September 1, 1890 until March 1, 1893, when it was purchased by the present company, and was extended six miles to Joplin and two miles to Prosperity. In 1890-1891 and electric railway was built from East Joplin to Blendville, a distance of five miles. The present company purchased this road in 1895 and the following year extended it from Blendville to Galena, Kansas, a distance of seven miles. In 1895 the Jasper County Electric Railway was built with Carthage capital, and extended from Carthage to Carterville, a distance of twelve miles. This property was purchased in 1896 by the South West Missouri Electric Railway Company, and this acquisition brought the system to its present comprehensive dimensions.

Streetcars

The streetcars brought magic to the area. There was a special feeling just riding the rails all over the area while sitting inside the streetcar. The excitement for a young child as they travel from Lakeside, downtown Webb City, busy streets of Joplin, past the mines where their daddy worked, or just out in the country between the small towns that they wouldn't normally get to travel was enlightening. Women used the streetcar to do their shopping and visiting. Men had a way to get to work. Students used the streetcar to get to school, library, etc. Sports teams traveled from city to city for competitions.

The early streetcars had seats that ran the length of the car. Later streetcars had the coach seats. Early seats faced the front of the streetcar, and as the streetcar arrived at the end of the line, the engineer would move to the rear of the streetcar as passengers stood to move the back of their seat forward to change seating directions. The streetcar could head back down the line with the conductor facing the front again, as well as the passengers. The early streetcars were heated with potbellied coal stoves, and the newer cars were heated with electricity, which seemed cleaner and safer.

The streetcar did not have the convenience of a restroom or drinking fountain. There were no snacks to be purchased, unless you purchased them at one of the depots, which were located quite a distance apart. The color scheme of the streetcars associated with the Southwest Missouri Railroad Association was pea green with a yellow number and yellow trim. Certain numbers attained some recognition such as 91 was the first streetcar built by the Webb City crew and 32 being the first car to run the Webb City northern route.

The old wooden streetcars of the early 1900s became the work cars for the maintenance men, eventually being switched out to the steel cars. Maintenance workers were of importance for the association as the entire scheduling system could be out of line with one streetcar down.

The charm of seeing a streetcar traveling over the streets in some of the old pictures of main streets in area towns is nostalgic. The opportunity to see old car 60 pulling out of the carbarn at King Jack Park adds its own charm to the city. The smiles on the faces of the young children as they ride Old 60 is contagious to all who watch the blending of new generations with memories of the old generations.

Each time the streetcar journeys out of the carbarn, we say a silent thank you to the wonderful men who donated their time and energy of rebuilding a wonderful piece of history that makes Webb City so unique.

Joplin 1902,   number 32 SWMo streetcar

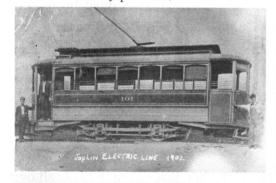

Joplin 1902,   number 32 SWMo streetcar

The main powerhouse—located on the northwest corner of Madison and Joplin (Broadway) Streets across from the Webb City carbarn.

Powerhouse after it was added onto.

The powerhouse located at Madison and Broadway; water tower to the right.

When the building was no longer needed as a powerhouse, it became the home of the Webb City wholesale grocery company. Through the years, the building has been a bowling alley, boat construction company, and skating rink.

The powerhouse and inn at Lakeside.

The Carbarn and Shops, a.k.a. Car House

The principal car house, located on the northeast corner of Madison and Joplin (Broadway) Street. A brick building, 143×200 divided into two longitudinal compartments. The northern compartment, 95×200, is the car house proper and contains six tracks, each two hundred feet long. The south compartment contains a suite of clubrooms for the employees, furnished with pool table, a reading room, which is supplied with periodicals and newspapers, card tables, etc. Back of this is the company storeroom. The supplies therein contained are catalogued and comprise a list of about three thousand articles. The stock of supplies has been charged to expense accounts.

Back of the storeroom is the armature room. The rest of the space in the building is occupied by the repair and paint shop, which contains two tracks, each two hundred feet long. The shop is well equipped with lathes, tools, etc. Complete new car bodies have been built in this shop, and all kinds of repair work is done there except wheel pressing.

By the end of the streetcar era, Webb City carbarn will have made thirty-three streetcars in this carbarn.

The other carbarns are located at: Galena, a frame building with two 120-foot tracks; *Lakeside* car house is located within the Lakeside powerhouse, made of brick, located on the north part of the building. There is an additional carbarn in Webb City on the southwest corner of Daugherty and Jefferson Street. Originally used as the mule carbarn, it became a storage barn, 60×190 feet.

The carbarn located northeast corner of Madison and Broadway

Layout of streetcar buildings

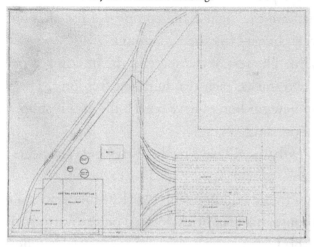

Carbarn

Offices

A two-story frame building located adjacent to the powerhouse. The lower floor is divided into four offices and a fireproof vault. The upper floors are the dispatcher's room, drafting room, a filing room, and room for lost articles. The building is electrically lighted, heated, and cooled.

Offices

January 1, 1922, photographer Frank Brooks offices

Clubhouse—Built in 1910

A. H. Rogers arranged for the building of a three-story clubhouse for his employees. It was erected on company property on the east side of Madison, just north of the carbarn. Employees with talent stepped forward and built this beautiful building. The building was used by the employees to relax between shifts. They could shower, change clothes, play checkers, sleep, or eat. The clubhouse was also used for banquets, meetings, or any special occasion. The clubhouse cleared up some space in the carbarn to allow more tracks to be installed and more room to work on streetcars.

The clubhouse was built in 1910. Employees with carpentry skills were put to good use on the clubhouse. Later years, the building became the Jasper County Health Department. It was the home of the Webb City Historical Society. They turned ownership over to the city in 2020.

Monument for Southwest Missouri Railroad Association in King Jack Park

Having been in the salvage business, Fred (Fritz) Rogers was knowledgeable about the procedures in procuring needed materials. This was the knowledge Rogers used when he went to the Conner Hotel as it was being prepared for demolition and talked to the necessary individuals about some of the beautiful art panels that were being removed from the grand old hotel. One evening, about 5:00 p.m., Rogers went down into the basement of the Conner Hotel to talk with the contractor. The French Renaissance design art panels had already been removed and were being placed in crates to be stored for future use. Arrangements were made for the Southwest Missouri Railway organization to buy two of the panels at $250 each. The contractor told Rogers that the panels would be on the north side of the building whenever he was able to make arrangements to haul them (the next morning, at 6:00 a.m., the Conner Hotel collapsed prematurely).

When Rogers went to pick up the panels, he was told that he could have them as a donation instead of paying the $250. The panels were stored at the airport until the site could be prepared for them.

Rogers knew he needed money to finish this project he had started, so he advertised that names of those donating $100 would be put on the plaque of the monument. He earned $7,000 to complete his project.

The Missouri Army National Guard moved the panels for Rogers, and a company in Carthage supplied necessary equipment for lifting the panels. Support of the citizens is what helped Rogers complete his task.

Arrangements had been made for Rogers to remove the actual Southwest Missouri Railway sign from the north side of the powerhouse. Being an actual part of the building, Rogers was to pay $250, plus replace the bricks where the sign had been. As Rogers thought about this task, he wasn't feeling too good about it. Jack Dawson suggested to Rogers that they could make a sign that would look just like the original. So that project began. They made a cement form, constructed letters out of Styrofoam, and glued them into the form. Cement was poured into the form with the Styrofoam staying intact. After the cement dried, they burned the Styrofoam, which caused it to melt right out of the concrete block. Many people have thought that sign really did come from the powerhouse. They did an awesome job of reproducing it without damaging a historical building.

As the monument came together, more structural support was needed for the upright concrete and marble. Ironically Rogers used three old streetcar bumpers for the props.

As mentioned earlier, Rogers restored streetcar 60 and put in many hours installing the streetcar tracks that go around King Jack Park. Before the arduous work began on installing the tracks, a fifty-year agreement was drawn up with the city. This agreement allowed the streetcar association to place the tracks in the park and gave it a twenty-foot easement on both sides of the tracks. Rogers said that agreement has an option for renewal after the first fifty years.

Fred Rogers has journals that record every movement made in building of the streetcar monument—the laying of the tracks, the restoring of the streetcar, the building of the depot, and even helping Jack Dawson with the Kneeling Miner Statue. It's recorded that Rogers helped Nancy Dawson keep mud mixed as Jack Dawson's magic fingers formed the Kneeling Miner. Rogers also built the base for the statue.

The Depots of the Streetcar Association

The streetcar transportation became quite a convenience in travel. Mostly the miners used the streetcar to get to work and back home. Many used the streetcar to travel to other areas to check on job availability. The housewife used the streetcar to do shopping for necessities. Students traveled to school and back home by streetcar. Schedules were posted so everyone could make their connections.

Not only schedules but location of the different depots became an important piece of information to make connections. Many connections consisted of only a stop beside the road to be picked up or dropped off. Some busy places were set up with actual depots to allow conveniences for the traveler. Some depots were given thoughts on planning in building, and many of the depots have lasted through the years; others not so lucky.

Streetcars made stops at every corner along the way. If you were traveling from Carterville to Webb City-Oronogo Depot, a waiting station where folks could sit and wait for the next streetcar. For a while, there was a small café in the back of the depot. When the depot no longer served the streetcar association, there were a few years it served as a community mining museum. The building still stands today in memory of the many miners and citizens who made daily trips on the streetcars.

Roy Ferguson (Oronogo) shared his memory, a few years ago, of the last streetcar ride of the Alba Line that he said was the spring of 1926. He recalled his teenage years when he remembers seeing three streetcars at one time with passengers hanging on at the Oronogo Depot. He said streetcars left every fifteen minutes going south and every thirty minutes going north. He recalled that the ticket from Oronogo to Webb City was 10¢ for adults and 5¢ for those twelve and younger. He did not think the counter at the depot was big enough to be called a café so much as a snack bar. Ferguson rode the streetcar. Back in the day, when they reached the end of the line, the passengers would reverse the back seat to go in the opposite direction, and the engineer would change to the rear of the streetcar as it became the front of the streetcar.

Subpower station—Power station and depot, located one and one-half miles north of Oronogo on the way to Alba. A Webb City resident, Laura Willard, once told me about her ride to Alba on the streetcar as a little girl and waiting at the subpower station for the connecting streetcar.

Prosperity Junction Depot, East Side of Carterville

For the longest time, the only way in and out of Prosperity Duenweg was by hack line. With the addition on the Prosperity–Duenweg streetcar line, activity and population grew.

The Prosperity Depot (made with mining timbers) was taken down in parts. The rock walls were left in place, and the roof, windows, and doors were moved to Webb City King Jack Park. They built a new rock building and added the roof, doors, and windows to remake the original depot. The building has been used as a depot for Old 60 streetcar which resides at King Jack Park, the office for the Webb City Area Chamber of Commerce and then home to the offices of the Webb City Parks and Recreation Department.

PROSPERITY, MO.   JUNCTION

Lakeside Waiting Station—the Waiting Station at times could be too small, but
during the summer months, especially on Sundays, there would be hundreds of
people waiting in line for the next available streetcar to take them home.
Once you were on board the streetcar, you traveled and stopped at each stop along the line.>>

After all these years, since the streetcar association began in 1889, 130 years ago, we still have wonderful buildings, a streetcar, cement pillars, and personal memories to keep this special piece of history alive in our hearts and minds.

Streetcar Association Picnic

Webb City is unique as it has a working streetcar. Many people refer to the streetcar as a trolley. Historically speaking, they were referred to by both titles; take your pick.

We have had several articles on the Southwest Missouri Railway Association, but I wanted to take a moment and talk about the employees. There were many dedicated men who worked long hours as conductors, motormen, maintenance, men at the power station and carbarn. It wasn't uncommon for several generations, brothers, uncles, etc. to have worked together on the streetcar line.

Each year, the Southwest Missouri Railroad would have a picnic at Lakeside Park. The employees (those who weren't working) would join in the festivities and good food. In 1912, it was noted that the Southwest Missouri Railroad Company employed 250 employees with half being from Webb City. And why not? Webb City was home to the main office, powerhouse, carbarn, and clubhouse.

Changes came with the change in the mining industry, and business on the streetcar began to decline. By 1931, the new president of the Southwest Missouri Railroad Company moved the main office to the Keystone Hotel in Joplin, which he happened to own. June 3, 1939, was the official end of the streetcar era as the buses, which had been running for a few years, were the new mode of transportation.

The dedicated employees of the Southwest Missouri Railroad Company were die hard, and they continued to meet every September for their annual picnic. Of course, they couldn't meet at Lakeside anymore, but they met at members' homes.

It is great that there are still dedicated men who give of their time and energy to work on the streetcar 60 in Webb City. And we are anxiously awaiting the repair of the tracks so we can see our glorious streetcar in operation again!

Streetcar going over bridge over Center Creek

Southwest Missouri Railway Time Line

1889—A. H. Rogers, *owner* of Springfield Savings Bank, arrived in Webb City from Springfield, Missouri.

1889—Saw the need and built a two-mile mule car line between Webb City and Carterville, creating an interurban system; obtained the city franchise under the name Twin Cities Street Railway. Some hated being referred to as the twin cities and referred to it as the Webb City–Carterville Electric Line.

1892—Rogers discarded the mule line and, with help from investors, started an electric line using the right-of-way of the mule line. Capitalists from the East Coast (Pennsylvania) helped with the financing.

1892—Rogers made Webb City his base for the new Southwest Missouri Railway Association. He established the powerhouse plant, carbarn, repair shops, and offices in the west end of town. SWMR employed 175 people. Rogers was only seven years behind Kansas City in providing electric transportation. He began purchasing the right-of-way into small Jasper County towns. The first four electric streetcars were manufactured in St. Louis. They were affectionately named Henrietta, Juliana, Oriana, and Juaneeta.

1893—To add to his run of tracks from Webb City to Carterville, Rogers bought the right-of-way from Carterville to Prosperity, on to Duenweg, Duquesne, and on to Joplin.

1893—July 4, the first run of the electric streetcars between Joplin and Webb City.

1896—Rogers purchased the Jasper County Electric Railway (a.k.a. White Line) that ran from Carthage to Carterville. This purchase included the land for Lakeside Park.

1896—Purchased the Joplin Electric and the Galena Electric Railways; continued to add extended areas like Chitwood and Smelter Hill, northwest of Joplin.

1897—The Southwest Missouri Electric Railway was classified as the longest continuous electric railway in the world.

1903—Built a new brick powerhouse at Broadway and Madison Streets, northwest corner, and the new car shops on the northeast corner. The company also added seven miles of track to the Webb City northern system.

1903—It was stated that there were as many as 150 streetcars a day between the Webb City carbarn and Lakeside Park per day. There were special tracks for loading and unloading at Lakeside, and it was estimated there were between forty thousand and fifty thousand people in Lakeside Park on the Fourth of July.

1906—Rogers reorganized the business, and it became the newly organized Southwest Missouri Railroad Company, absorbing the Southwest Missouri Electric Railway and the new Webb City Northern which had been built north to Oronogo, Neck City, Alba, and Purcell. Changing the name to the Southwest Missouri Railroad gave the railway authority of the railroads that it didn't have before. The capital of the railway was $150,000, but the Southwest Railroad had a capital of $5 million.

1906—A freight line was added with the purchase of three freight cars.

1906—Thirteen new steel passenger streetcars were purchased that were heated by electricity, making the old potbelly coal stoves obsolete in the streetcars.

1906—November, millionaire J. J. Heim, from Kansas City, announced plans to build an electric line from Joplin to Galena to Baxter Springs. With plans to build another line from Joplin to Duenweg, Heim announced his plans to gridiron the entire mining area with electric roads. Rogers already had ten miles of track, but when his attorney approached Joplin about purchasing more blocks, they were denied. Heim managed to get an electric line from Joplin to Pittsburg before Rogers.

1907—Rogers began to quietly buy shares of the Joplin and Pittsburg Railway Company until he became the controlling stockholder. He was present at every meeting when the company made plans to extend their line into Joplin, which he used his stockholding power to vote against. This limited Heim to five miles of track in Joplin, and Rogers had obtained an additional fifteen miles.

1908—Southwest Missouri System extended tracks four miles east of Joplin to Duenweg. This extension made a complete belt around the rich zinc and lead mines of the area.

1909—Rogers was having problems with Gilbert Barbee, president of the Joplin Globe. Rogers did not like stories being printed about the streetcar company.

1910—Barbee sold his Joplin Globe stock to some prominent men in the area, and Rogers managed to buy enough to have control and took over as president of the Joplin Globe and held that position until his death in 1920.

1910—The new clubhouse was built using employees with carpentry skills.

1916—Purchased twelve new streetcars, forty to forty-five feet in length, made of steel, with air brakes, double trucks, three step-up entrances. A new federal law stated all interstate trolleys must be steel cars, or at least have steel frames.

1917—March, work has begun on building the longest company-owned interurban bridge in Kansas. The all-steel bridge is being built across Spring River, entered Baxter Springs on Sixth Street.

1918—Service between Joplin and Baxter Springs began. The line between Baxter and Picher was completed. First streetcar went in to Picher on June 10, 1918. The fare from Fourth and Main in Joplin to Picher was 55¢, plus 4 pennies for war tax. The ride took one hour and ten minutes. A trip from Carthage to Picher could be made without changing streetcars.

1918—Prices went up. Carthage to Carterville was 20¢; Carthage to Webb City went from 15¢–25¢; Carthage to Joplin went from 25¢–35¢; Carthage to Galena was 55¢; Carthage to Baxter Springs was 75¢; Carthage to Picher was 90¢.

1918—Southwest Missouri Railroad Company reached its peak in revenue when the gross revenue reached $1 million, and the line became a first-class railroad.

1920—A. H. Rogers passed away. His son Harrison Rogers took his place in the business. Rogers was buried in the Rogers' mausoleum in Mount Hope Cemetery in Webb City. An elm tree was planted in memory of Rogers with a plaque. The elm tree is no longer there.

1920—The Southwest Missouri Railroad Company stopped producing its own power at the Webb City power plant and went under contract with Empire District Electric to buy its power.

1924—Business began to slow down and schedule changes were made.

1924—April 14, announcement made by E. J. Pratt, general manager of the Southwest Missouri Railroad Company, that Lakeside Park will be closed. The buildings will be razed and only grass and trees will be left.

1924—May 4, although the announcement was made that the Lakeside Park will be closing, insistent demands from hundreds of former patrons of Lakeside Park, including lodges, associations, societies, and chambers of commerce in every town and city along the Southwest Missouri railroad resulted in arrangement by the railroad company for the reopening of the park on May 15, for the season of 1924.

1925—Passenger business began to slow down so much that lines to Alba and the lines from Prosperity to Duquesne were abandoned.

1928—The tracks, power lines, and poles from Prosperity to Duquesne were taken down to keep from paying county taxes. The tracks were used to upgrade existing tracks.

1935—July 21, the last electric streetcar made the forty-mile trip from Carthage to Picher.

1935—July 22, the motor buses began their route, taking the place of the streetcars between Carthage and Joplin. The passenger streetcars continued to carry passengers on some lines.

1937—General Manager F. C. Wallower moved the offices of the Southwest Missouri Railroad to Joplin in the Keystone Hotel (owned by Wallower).

1938—Two streetcars in operation carrying passengers. The expense became too much.

1939—June, the Southwest Missouri Railroad Company from Carthage to Joplin was sold to Joplin Public Service Company for $2,000. The company failed to exist in the passenger business. Liquidating of property began.

Southwest Missouri Railway—The Men Who Worked with the Streetcars

The streetcar was described as the backbone of transportation for years for the miners, businessmen, schoolchildren, housewives, and farmers. Thousands of people have ridden the streetcar to work, school, shopping, and entertainment. The main source of entertainment was the wonderful Lakeside Park, the recreation spot of the district. More on this attraction later in this section.

When the original mule streetcar line was put in, the three drivers were William Hamilton, George Herron, and William Palmer. The railroad ties for the original tracks were hewn from native oak grown in Jasper County. The heavy steel rails were purchased from the Illinois Steel Company. When the streetcars went electric, instead of mule drive, the Webb City powerhouse generated direct current electricity for the streetcar at 650 volts.

At the time of the electric streetcar's introduction to Jasper County, it was still in its early phases. Just eight years earlier, 1885, Baltimore, Maryland, had just opened an electric street railway. Then Kansas City opened an experimental electric line only one-half mile long. In 1888, Richmond, Virginia, opened their first streetcar line. Kansas City opened an official electric trolley in 1889. So for A. H. Rogers to embark on this monumental crusade in Jasper County in 1892 was ahead of its time.

Gretz, Fred—Fred Gretz was born in Germany in 1855, at a time in German history when the country seemed to be constantly at battle. There were many uprisings. At a young age, Fred made the journey to the New World—the United States of America—where hopes and dreams were meant to come true. Everyone knew you could find happiness if you could just get to America.

Landing in New York, Fred found that it was such a busy place; a new immigrant could easily get lost in the shuffle. Surprisingly most immigrants that were eager to leave their own countries always seemed to gather together and make small communities of their own nationalities. It was just such a community that Fred met a lovely young German named Laura who had come to America with her parents.

After Fred and Laura had been married awhile, Fred heard about money being made in a small community in Missouri. So the small family loaded up and made the long journey by wagon to Webb City, Missouri, in 1884. Laura's mother and father were saddened to see their daughter leave, knowing they would probably never see her again. She was heading into the unknown, just as they had done by heading to America.

The young Gretz family joined the many others who were waiting in line for a chance at employment in the mines. The city of Webb City was growing at such a fast pace that there was a shortage of housing. Many families were housed in tents at the edge of town. Food was not always available, but Fred was one of those determined young men who always managed to find the right path to follow.

After a short mining career, Fred found himself in a new line of work, which seemed to suit him fine. Fred became an employee of the Southwest Missouri Railroad Company, which was a wonderful job for such a talented young man. Fred was superintendent of the undermining. He was in charge of keeping the right-of-way clear and unthreatened. Fred held this job with the Southwest Railroad Company for twenty-five years before retiring.

The Gretz home was located at 333 South Ball, and the Gretzes had six beautiful children. Family was an important commodity in this land. There was Charles Gretz, who worked the mines. He worked the sludge table. Charles was married to Gertrude, and they had three sons, Carl, Paul, and Walter, and two daughters, Lora Rose and Ruth Oldham. Carl's sweet wife, who is eighty-four, said the Gretz family was just good common folk who worked hard for their money.

There were two other sons in the Fred Gretz family, Harry and Fred Jr. Fred Jr. worked in the mines until he was forty-seven, and health reasons forced him to leave. He had Bright's disease.

Now there were three girls born to Fred and Laura. Minnie May Gretz married Albert Michie (more on that family in the future). Albert was postmaster in Webb City for a while. Lena Gretz became Lena Sanderson, and Mary gave up bookkeeping to become Mrs. Mary Fehrenberg.

The Gretz family was part of the backbone that made Webb City the community it is. Too often, we focus on mining tycoons who had the money to back the mines, but those mines wouldn't have made any money without the miners who gave more than their time in the mines. Many gave their health and lives.

Hess family—W. R. Hess and Margaret De Priest Hess made the move from the southern charm of Alabama to Shannon County in the middle of the state of Missouri. A son was born to this couple by the name of Isaac C. Hess. I have written a previous article about Isaac, as he was a very prominent man in Webb City. He was a member of the city council for several terms, beginning in 1898. He was involved in the Knights and Ladies of Security, the Odd Fellows, and he was an engineer with the Center Creek Mining Company. His reputation was spotless, and he was noted as one who was always willing to put his shoulder to the wheel for a cause that promised improvements for the citizens of Webb City.

Now let's move on to another member of the family, and that Isaac's brother, John A. Hess. Isaac hired John on as his second engineer, and they worked side by side every day. Each one was a credit to his career.

Before joining Isaac with the Center Creek Mining Company, John A. Hess had made a name for himself serving as an engineer with the Iron Mountain Railway Company. Below is a photo of John A. Hess standing to the rear of the train engine at a logging camp in the 1890s.

The next generation of the Hess family included another engineer/conductor, Homer Hess. Homer was employed by the Southwest Missouri Railway Association and seemed to carry the same trait as his father and uncle as he was always willing to put his shoulder to the wheel and work. His life was dedicated to the streetcar association.

His place of residence was 1302 West Daugherty, just a couple of blocks from his place of employment. He always had a smile on his face, as if life couldn't be better. The Hess family seemed to be drawn to the big transportation toys and enjoyed careers that let them play with those toys all day!

This is a special tribute to the Hess engineers of Webb City!

A photo of John A. Hess standing to the rear of the train engine at a logging camp in the 1890s.

Hood, Harry C., Sr.—A native of Southwest Missouri, Harry was born December 28, 1905, in Johnstown, just south of Carterville. He often said that he grew up within fifty yards of the Southwest Missouri railroad tracks, and his house was situated on mining ground. This area was in his blood.

As did most people born in the same era of Harry, he rode the streetcars to work and back. He rode out to Lakeside, and to get to any town in the area, he rode a streetcar. Harry said he didn't mind paying the fare to get where he was going, but occasionally, late at night, the conductor did not bother to collect his money from him. And many a time, Harry would just jump on the front steps and hang on till he got where he was going.

Harry did not grow up in a fancy house, it was just a home. The rent for his home sitting on mining ground was one dollar per year. His barrel of water was delivered twice a week by the tank wagon. He used his water for drinking and cooking. He lit his house with coal oil lamps, and he says his house was never painted.

Harry was not alone in his description of his life. He worked in the mines of Missouri, Kansas, and Oklahoma. For a change of pace, he even worked at the Carthage Marble Quarry in Carthage for a short while.

Harry is listed in this book because Harry was just an ordinary man, living an ordinary life in an ordinary little mining town. But the one thing Harry did was write down his memories for future generations to share. In 1976, as Webb City was celebrating her centennial, along with the United States bicentennial, Harry wrote *The Southwest Missouri Railroad*, a book about the streetcar association that was a major part of his life. He dedicated the book to Lawrence McMecham, who had been an employee of the Southwest Missouri Railroad Company and who assisted Harry in accumulating the information. He also gives mention to the employees and the officers of the Southwest Missouri Railroad, as well as all the people who spent their nickels, dimes, and quarters for the car fare on the streetcars.

And we thank you, Harry, for preserving a wonderful piece of history.

Long, Henry—"Henry Long had a 'long' streetcar career." In 1888, just twelve years after Webb City was established, a young man named Henry Long left his home in Hamilton, Ohio, and came to this prosperous mining community in Southwest Missouri. Twenty-year-old Henry had many dreams and plans for his future. He settled in Joplin on November 10, 1888, and immediately went to work for the Joplin streetcar line, working on the horse-drawn streetcars.

On September 1, 1891, Henry went to work for the Southwest Missouri Electric Railway Company. In 1896, Henry was a motorman for the first streetcar out of Carthage on the new and just-completed White Line between Carthage and Carterville. In those days, an extra motorman was needed to watch the trolley. On this memorable trip, his brother, Louis Long, accompanied Henry. It was not uncommon for families to work together on the streetcars—brothers, fathers, and uncles.

Railway work was not easy work. Employees worked hard and long hours. There were employees on call to take care of problems like breakdowns, derailments, and accidents. Many men worked seven long days a week without vacations.

These two brothers, Henry and Louis, not only worked together, they only lived two blocks away from each other. Henry lived at 928 West First Street, and Louis lived at 917 West Third Street.

When Henry passed away on March 25, 1920, at the age of fifty-two, he had the distinction of being the oldest motorman in point of service on the line after twenty-eight years (that was twenty-eight years with the Southwest Missouri Railway Company, but he had been in the railway business for thirty-two years). Upon his death, his brother, Louis, acquired that honor for twenty-six years.

Besides being well known from working on the streetcar line, Henry was also a member of the Modern Woodsmen of America and the Royal Neighbors Fraternal Lodge.

Henry G. Long and his wife, Emma, had one son, Roy L. Long, and one daughter, Viola Long. Here is a well-known young man who came to this area from Ohio and became a permanent resident of Webb City. Thanks to Fred Rogers for sharing this information about one of Webb City's special citizens of the past.

A note from George Rainey:

> *I read with interest the story on Henry Long. I didn't know of him. My stepfather Elmer Long was Louis' son. He lived at 917 West Third with my mom until he died. The corner of 3rd and Madison was known as "Long's Corner". 917 was the only house on the block at that time. My mom was secretary of the SW Mo. Railway Association for many years. She had the yearly meeting at her home. When she died I gave all the pictures and minutes to the streetcar at King Jack Park. Roy Long and Elmer were good friends and cousins. Elmer had retired from the U.S. Navy. Roy was the projectionist at the Fox Theatre. Jeanne, keep up the good work. George Rainey.*

Pratt, E. J.—E. J. Pratt was the efficient superintendent of the motor power and chief engineer at Webb City, Missouri, of the Southwest Missouri Street Railway Company. He was born in Allegany County, New York, March 4, 1862; a son of Garrison and Elizabeth (Tibbitts) Pratt.

The education of Mr. Pratt was secured in the schools of Franklinville, New York, and later he enjoyed a short period of study in Geneseo, where he had an opportunity to gain instruction in mechanical engineering, but he laid aside his books at the age of nineteen. His first important work was with the Erie Railroad Company as bridge carpenter, and he remained in that line for four years, being considered one of the most capable and reliable men in the employ of that great road.

In 1889, Pratt moved to Joplin, Missouri, and engaged in mining, being fairly successful, but he was not willing to resign the trade in which he had put so much study; therefore, when he was offered a position with the Joplin Street Railway as engineer, he accepted it. In 1892, he was given the position of foreman of the engineering force that built the roadbed between Joplin and Carthage.

In 1892, however, Pratt was given the position of mechanical engineer on the Southwest Missouri Railway. Much of the success of the Southwest Missouri Railway was due to his efficiency.

The marriage of Pratt was in 1888 to Ms. Kate Cameron, who was born in Ontario, Canada, and was a daughter of Dr. Charles Cameron. They had one son, Fred Cameron Pratt. Socially E. J. Pratt was a member of Joplin Lodge 335, AF and AM, Joplin Commandery. and also attained the thirty-second degree of the Scottish Rite. He also had membership with the Modern Woodmen of the World.

Rogers, Fred (Fritz)—Well, as we discuss people of the past in our area, a reader has submitted the name of Fred (Fritz) Rogers. Now here is a man who has so many different "hats" that he wore during his lifetime that I don't think it can be condensed down to just one paragraph. But I do believe his call to fame must center around the restored Old 60 streetcar that runs around the tracks in King Jack

Park. The timing is right as Old 60 has been idle for a space of time while parts were being repaired. During the inoperable time, Old 60 sat on display at the entrance to King Jack Park, right in front of the Southwest Missouri Railway Association monument (which was another of Fritz Rogers' projects). While the streetcar was on display, many tourists stopped by to check it out. Many questions were asked, and she seemed to have more attention while resting. She did look impressive sitting out for viewing.

Well, now she is up and running again, and I do enjoy seeing her as she goes by my house loaded with folks who want to take that trip down memory lane in style! What an impressive nostalgic piece of history that few towns can boast of having, but thanks to Fred Rogers and his associates, Webb City is on the streetcar map.

As Della Roger (his wife) once said about Fred, "He is the chairman of the board of nine members of the Southwest Railroad Association in Webb City. His heart, soul, and mind has been the restoring the streetcar 60."

Fred traveled all over the country finding parts for the streetcar, all the way to Kennebank Port, Maine, to San Francisco, California. He would be going through railroad yards, searching to find what he needed to complete the streetcar. He kept a diary for over ten years that detailed each step of the restoration of Old 60 and the men who helped. The money for getting the streetcar up and running was from donations for the nonprofit organization. Not to be outdone, Della often made sure everyone knew she was right there beside her man, Fred, as he searched for those streetcar parts.

Mentioning the Southwest Missouri Railway Association Monument, it was Fred's quick thinking that allowed us to have those beautiful art panels from the old Conner Hotel. As the Conner was being prepped for demolition, Fred went down into the basement to talk with the contractor. The art panels (French Renaissance design) had already been removed from the building, and they were being crated and stored for future use. Fred talked them into selling him two of the art panels for $250 each. The panels were stored on the north side of the building, waiting for Fred to find a way to transport them to Webb City. The very next morning, at 6:00 a.m., the Conner Hotel prematurely collapsed. Fred hurried over to get the panels, and he was told that he could have them as a donation instead of the agreed price. Fred got permission to store the panels at the airport until the site was prepared for the monument. Quick action and quick thinking on the part of Fred Rogers put those beautiful art panels in Webb City.

The laying of the railroad tracks in the park, the building of the monument, restoring the depot, and helping Jack Dawson with the Kneeling Miner information is recorded in that ten-year diary that Fred kept on the restoration of the streetcar. It is a treasure book of historical information. For twenty-eight years, after retiring in 1973, Fred did his volunteer work at King Jack Park. He said he couldn't have accomplished what he did without his faithful comrades from the streetcar association and the many donations from the citizens of Webb City. He took pride in the fact that he rarely spent much money on any of the projects, thanks to the generosity of those who wanted the best for Webb City.

Streetcar Old 60, established 1980—During this holiday season, I think we could safely say that the streetcar Ole 60 holds the spotlight of being the popular highlight of the area. Hearing the streetcar running constantly every Thursday, Friday, and Saturday (and during the farmer's market hours) around King Jack Park is so wonderful. And each time the streetcar goes around the park, it is full of excited children, loving parents, and history seekers. The park is decorated with dancing lights of the season that makes the children smile and point out the lights to their parents. What a wonderful addition to the Webb City's personality.

Our hearts go out to Fred and Della Rogers for the many years of volunteer work that went into the restoration of the streetcar 60. Fred (Fritz) Rogers, now here is a man who has so many different "hats" that he wore during his lifetime, I don't think it can be condensed down to just one hat. But I do believe his call to fame must center around the restored Old 60 streetcar that runs along the tracks in King Jack Park. There have been many times that the Old 60 has been idle while parts were being repaired. During the inoperable time, Old 60 often sat on display at the entrance to King Jack Park, right in front of the Southwest Missouri Railway Association monument (which was another of Fritz Rogers' projects). While the streetcar was on display, many tourists stopped by to check it out. Many questions were asked, and she seemed to have as much attention while resting as she did on the move. She did look impressive sitting out for viewing.

Well, now she is up and running during the holiday season, an impressive nostalgic piece of history that few towns can boast of having. Thanks to Fred Rogers and his associates, Webb City is on the streetcar map. As Della Rogers (Fred's wife) once said about Fred, "He is the chairman of the board of nine members of the Southwest Railroad Association in Webb City. His heart, soul, and mind has been centered on the restoring of the streetcar 60."

Fred traveled all over the country finding parts for the streetcar, all the way to Kennebank Port, Maine, to San Francisco, California. He would be going through railroad yards, searching to find what he needed to complete the streetcar. He kept a diary for over ten years that detailed each step of the restoration of Old 60 and the men who helped. The money for getting the streetcar up and running was from donations for the nonprofit organization. Not to be outdone, Della often made sure everyone knew she was right there beside her man, Fred, as he searched for those streetcar parts.

The many projects of Fred and friends, besides the restoring of Old 60, include: laying of the railroad tracks in the park, the building of the monument, restoring the depot, and helping Jack Dawson with the Kneeling Miner, information that is recorded in that ten-year diary that Fred kept on the restoration of the streetcar. It is a treasure book of historical information. For twenty-eight years, after retiring in 1973, Fred did his volunteer work at King Jack Park. He said he couldn't have accomplished what he did without his faithful comrades from the streetcar association and the many donations from the citizens of Webb City. He took pride in the fact that he rarely spent much money on any of the projects, thanks to the generosity of those who wanted the best for Webb City.

Fred Rogers definitely was a special person from the past that we don't want to forget. Webb City is one of the few cities to have a Streetcar still in operation. Old 60 was rescued, refurbished by the group of volunteers from the Southwest Missouri Railroad Association. They are now in partnership with the Webb City Parks Department, and that has allowed the streetcar to be able to operate during farmer's market, Polar Express, many different school groups, family reunions, high school reunions, and many festivities. Her popularity continues to shine.

Santa Clause and Mrs. Clause add to the holiday excitement at King Jack Park during Polar Express, but they have to share the limelight with another star attraction, and that is that beautiful green streetcar 60 that allows her passengers to step back in time and take a journey that will leave a special memory in the minds of all those aboard.

And let's take a moment to remember the master mind of this relic, Fred Rogers (and his associates), who had a mission that took years of hard work, lots of donations, and many hours of searching for parts to accomplish this dream that we all get to enjoy.

A special thanks to the Parks Department, the streetcar association, and the city of Webb City for sharing this special treasure with us and the many visitors from all over the area.

Webb City, the place to be during the Christmas season, the streetcar 60, the wonderful shops, the lights in the park, friendly people, beautiful homes, school activities, and so much more.

Webb City is one of the few cities to have a streetcar still in operation. Old 60 was rescued, refurbished, and is operated by a group of volunteers from the Southwest Missouri Railroad Association. The streetcar is on track in King Jack Park and is brought out for operation during city and park events, school field trips, family reunions, school reunions, farmer's market, etc.

Old 60 is authentic and a historical asset to Webb City.

CHAPTER 4

Southwest Missouri Railway Entertainment Lakeside

Back in the heyday of the Jasper County history, Lakeside Park was the main attraction of the area. Advertisement of the park over time is a bit confusing for folks, as it often lists the location in Carterville, Webb City, Carthage, and Joplin. The actual location was on the east side of Carterville, owned by the Southwest Missouri Electric Railroad Company, which was based in Webb City. Many employees were involved in the daily operations of the Lakeside Park, and the number of visitors of the park was amazing. The only way into or out of the park was by streetcar, so you were always warned to not spend your last nickel as you would need that coin to leave the park.

Lakeside Park was where people went by the hundreds to swim, boat, watch a ballgame, dance, watch a movie, or just to get out in the sunshine. Many a miner worked six days a week. They went to work before the sun came up and got off work after the sun went down. Time spent at Lakeside was their only time to enjoy the sunlight. They could sit in the sun, eat a piece of watermelon, and talk with their families.

I am sure the children of today would not enjoy Lakeside Park as much as the children of yesteryear, as it was a relaxing and romantic type of fairy-tale setting. Not the wild exciting setups like Silver Dollar City of today.

Lakeside first came into being in 1895. With the popularity of the area, a renovation took place in 1909. That was when the steel suspension bridge was put across the lake east of the boathouse to give access to an additional tract of land, north of the creek, that was opened up. A portion of Center Creek was dug deeper to allow for swimming. Large crowds made regular visits to Lakeside Park.

The sad part of this situation was that many of the motormen and conductors of the railway company were required to live at the park to start and finish their daily runs. They did not have proper living quarters for these men, and they slept in tents, in old streetcars, or any dry spot they could find. With the men being away from their families so often, divorce was becoming a problem. The Jasper County Railway Company decided to correct the situation by building a hotel, and then in 1895, they decided to build six cottages near the hotel to allow families to stay with the motormen and conductors. The cottages varied between three rooms and five rooms.

It was noted that Lakeside Park was one of the most popular entertainment areas in the county. During the Fourth of July, it was said that between forty thousand and fifty thousand people were in the park. The twelve streetcars ran every ten minutes from 5:00 a.m.–11:00 p.m. In 1902, for the Fourth of July, the last streetcar left Lakeside Park at 3:00 a.m.

A dear friend, Ken Kneeland, several years ago, wrote of his memories of Lakeside Park. I would like to share them with you.

The history of this area would not be complete without including Lakeside Park. It was operated by the streetcar company, located about ¼ mile upstream from the Center Creek Bridge (Highway 66 & 71), where they built a dam. There was a pier and bathhouses. The pier extended from the north side of the river with a diving board on the end. There was a waterslide about 20 to 30 feet high. Two tennis courts and a baseball diamond were on the north side of the river. The only way to get to the north side was by the swinging bridge just east of the swimming hole. The south side of the river had a rope swing and canoe rentals and lots of food booths and wares. Up the hill to the south was a dance pavilion. It was the most popular recreation spot in the Tri-State area.

In 1920, the well-loved theater caught fire and burned along with the café next to it. The Carterville firemen could not get there in time to save the theater but did an excellent job protecting the rest of the buildings.

In April 1925, it was printed that Lakeside would be closing permanently, but the public was not about to let that happen. The decision was rescinded and then in 1931 Lakeside went under another renovation with improvements to the bathhouses and arrangements made for new concessions.

Then, in October 1935, the decision became final and Lakeside Park became only a memory. Memories of a midway, roller coaster, shooting gallery, Japanese bowling place, merry-go-rounds, balloon ascensions and not to be forgotten, the Trolley Baseball League.

Some even wonder if, on a warm summer night, you can hear the laughter of happy children, the squeals of splashing bathers, or the floating music of an orchestra as couples dance the night away.

As Ken mentioned in his memories, with the streetcar association closing down, the announcement was made on April 14, 1924, that the Lakeside Park would be closing for good. The buildings (the ones that were left) would be razed, and all that would be left would be grass and trees, as well as many fond memories. The announcement was made by E. J. Pratt, the general manager of the Southwest Missouri Railroad Company. He said the park had not been a paying business for several years, and the expense of thousands of dollars would be prohibitive, as all the buildings, the swinging bridge, and roads would need major repairs before the opening season.

But then on May 4, 1924, the announcement was sent out that:

Although it had been announced a few weeks ago that Lakeside Park would be closed permanently because of expense of continuing operations, popular demand resulted in a change of plans. Insistent demands from hundreds of former patrons of Lakeside Park including lodges, associations, societies, and Chambers of Commerce in every town and city along the Southwest Missouri Railroad resulted in an arrangement by the railroad company for the reopening of the park on May 15 for the season of 1924.

The facility would be under the management of Ralph Putnam, who had, for years, had a keen interest in Lakeside Park. The equipment was inspected, and necessary repairs were made. In making this announcement, E. J. Pratt of the railroad company said the decision was the direct result of the many requests for the reopening of the park.

Though Lakeside is gone, its memory will remain in the hearts of those who were fortunate to be around when the atmosphere was ignited with the perfume of happiness and the fragrance of romance.

Karen Oheim made a discovery of a mention of Lakeside Park in 1896, when it was mentioned that the White Line Railway had its biggest day's business ever—an estimated ten thousand people, and the "woods along the park were black with teams, wagons, and buggies." *That must have been before the time it was fixed that you could only get into Lakeside Park by streetcar.* July 4, 1897 was mentioned that there would be a celebration at Lakeside Park.

Entertainment included all kind of food. Strolling around the park, you could munch on hot dogs, corn on the cob, watermelon, ice cream, and many other good summer treats. Men could take their ladies out for a romantic drifting along the river in a boat or take his lady dancing. He could show off his talents by tossing some horseshoes or hold her close as she got scared on the roller coaster.

Famous guests such as *John Phillip Sousa* appeared at Lakeside Park. A song, music written by *James Scott* and the words by *Ida B. Miller*, tells of the wonderful atmosphere at Lakeside Park. The words are:

Take me out to Lakeside that beautiful place, Where your life seems complete.
Orchestras playing and everyone swaying gives you such a treat.
Dancing and glancing with smiles so entrancing is all you can see,
The Waltz Hesitation is all the sensation, Oh come and dance with me.

Take me out to Lakeside Sunday afternoon,
Where the band is playing, Flowers are all in bloom,
Boys and girls together Happy as a lark,
Take me out to Lakeside Beautiful Lakeside Park.

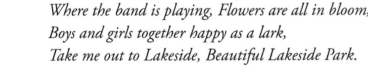

When twilight draws near and the whole world seems drear, And you've no place to go,
You may sit guessing but no thoughts expressing, the pleasures you love so,
You think of your only while you feel so lonely it all seems a dream,
So while you are pining there comes a reminding, A glorious thought it seems.

Take me out to Lakeside Sunday afternoon,
Where the band is playing, Flowers are all in bloom,
Boys and girls together happy as a lark,
Take me out to Lakeside, Beautiful Lakeside Park.

Another famous guest at Lakeside was in 1902 when the *Three Keetons* performed. Little *Buster Keeton*, age six, was an added attraction. *The Sentinel* said the Keetons were staying with Joseph Keeton's aunt, Barbara Smith, on North Roane Street.

One of the big events that drew a crowd was when they had the hot-air balloon ascensions. Many times the balloons were set up to allow people to be raised in the air and set back down, but occasionally, there would be balloon races which brought a large crowd.

Charles Douglass recalls the summer of 1949, when he was given a job with the Highway Department. He was assigned to a survey party that was monitoring the construction of a new highway between Webb City and Carthage. The project included three bridges, one of which was over Center Creek, about halfway between Carterville and Carthage. One day, as they were working on the bridge over Center Creek, the contractor was going to open up a dam a little ways down the river so as to lower the water level where the bridge was being constructed. The word was that the dam was part of an old amusement park called Lakeside.

The *tracks were removed* in January 1936, and all hopes of reviving Lakeside Park were gone. The best known resort in Southwest Missouri had become only a memory and definitely a legend. Charles went to see the contractor open the dam. Near the dam were the concrete piers where the bathhouse had been. He said he could see all kinds of things that had been dropped or thrown in the river. The thing that caught Charles's eye was an odd Coca-Cola bottle that was quite a different shape from the Coca-Cola bottles of World War II. Charles went home and asked his parents about Lakeside, and they told him it had been quite a place in its time. They told him of open-air streetcars that carried people to Lakeside on summer afternoons to swim and go canoeing. They said there were balloon ascensions, dances, movies, food stands, and just a lot of things to do. They said the demise was because of the loss of the streetcars.

The End

Major changes began to take place in Southwest Missouri. In 1918, the greatest ore strike in the tri-state district was discovered in Oklahoma. The beginning of the end for Webb City's mines. Quite a blow to the economy in Webb City, as miners hopped on the streetcar and headed to Miami where the mines were active, and there was no devil water to fight as there was in Jasper County. Not only did the mines begin to shut down, but many of the new motor cars were appearing everywhere. No need for the streetcars to travel from one place to another. The new concrete highway from Thirteenth and Madison Street through Royal Heights to Broadway Street in Joplin made it easier to travel between the cities. The end of the war brought many changes. The chamber of commerce went on a major campaign to find industries to move to Webb City to keep the city from dying due to the lack of mining.

An influenza hit the area (1919), closing down schools and businesses as folks were encouraged to stay home to stop the spread of the deadly disease. The streetcar association continued to expand as they extended their streetcar lines into Kansas, reaching an all-time high in revenues during 1918. The Southwest Missouri Railroad Company reached its peak in revenue when the gross revenue reached $1 million, and the line became a first-class railroad company. In 1920, the Southwest Missouri Railroad Company stopped producing their own electrical power at the Webb City Power Plant and started purchasing the power from Empire District Electric Company.

By 1924, business began to change for the streetcar company; schedules began to change. As individual streetcar lines began to shut down, such as the Alba line and the Prosperity line and the Duquesne lines shut down, and abandoned, and many rails were taken out to save the company from paying taxes on the abandoned lines.

On April 14, 1924, just prior to the opening of the 1924 season, E. J. Pratt, general manager, announced that the Lakeside Park would be closing with plans to tear down all the buildings. On

May 4, after the insistence of hundreds of patrons of Lakeside, along with many lodges, associations, societies, and area chamber of commerce in Jasper County, it was announced that the 1924 season would begin on May 15. In 1931, Lakeside was treated to an overhaul to improve the boating and bathing areas and new concession stands. But darks days were ahead as in 1935, it was determined that the beautiful Lakeside Park would cease to exist. The streetcars would no longer be running, and even though two highway entrances had been provided, the popularity of the resort was linked to the streetcar lines, and the last electric streetcar made the forty-mile trip from Carthage to Picher on July 21, 1935. The bus system started on July 22, 1935. A few short lines continued streetcar passage until 1935, when there were only two streetcars running. In June 1939, the Southwest Missouri Railroad Company sold to Joplin Public Service Company (bus lines) for $2,000. Thus the end of the Southwest Missouri Railroad Company, 1895–1939. The end of an era that had lasted forty-four years. Lakeside was the jewel of Southwest Missouri from 1896–1935 and an entertainment era of thirty-nine years.

The *Joplin Globe* asked:

> How many families can recall pleasant reunions at Lakeside? Reunions featured by sumptuous picnic dinners spread upon the grass, augmented by the laughter of happy children, shouts of splashing bathers, music of bands or orchestra floating down from the hilltop pavilion, the soft summer evening air? How many courtships began at Lakeside or marriage proposals were enjoyed. So though they tear down the buildings, close the entrance gates to the public, they will not destroy memories of joyous hours spent at Lakeside.

Lakeside Hotel

Picture

Lakeside Roller Coaster

A figure-eight roller coaster made of wood.

Lakeside Dance Pavilion

Burned in 1920 while workmen were burning leaves, as well as the café.

Dance Pavilion, 1899

Lakeside Ball Park—Home of Trolley League

They played area teams, and occasionally a well-known team would come to play. Admission was free, unless you wanted to sit in the bleachers, and then you had to pay 10¢.

The old Trolley League consisted of local talent who played baseball for the fun of it. The players were from Webb City, Joplin, Carterville, Galena, Carthage, and Alba. The league lasted about ten years. The games were free, unless you wanted to sit in the grandstand, then you paid 25¢. That money went toward team expenses like baseballs and transportation for away games.

Baseball, America's favorite pastime! Either you love baseball, or you don't! The baseball fields at King Jack Park seem to have quite of few loyal baseball fans who turn out every evening to cheer on a favorite son, daughter, grandchild, or maybe cheer on a favorite team. The joyous sounds coming from the ball fields seem to be a part of summer. Well, years ago, when Lakeside was in its heyday, baseball was in the limelight also. Many folks could hardly wait for ball season to begin.

Here is a memory shred by Walter Hilburn, 1945, as he recalls the first memories of baseball in Webb City. "In the early days, they were not known as a baseball club but as a baseball nine. There were only nine members of the team. When the pitcher stepped into the box at the start of the game, everyone knew he would pitch until the end of the game, no relief. If by any chance, a player was injured, someone from the crowd would be called in to take the player's place. The substitute would play in civilian clothes as there would be no extra uniform to wear.

"The first baseball club was called the Webb City Stars. They played all over southwestern part of the state and defeated almost every nine they played. The catcher was the only player to use a glove. It was a half-mitt with the fingers cut off." Baseball was such a hit at Lakeside, the Trolley League (started in May of 1909) consisted of many teams who played visiting teams and one another with gusto. So much of the history of the Trolley League is no longer available, it is hard to get actual names of teams or players. Players that included men from Joplin, Webb City, Carterville, Carthage. The games were free, unless you wanted to sit down in the new 60-foot grandstand of 1909 (later extended to 180 feet), then the ticket would cost 25¢. This added admission fee helped support the Trolley League in baseballs and transportation.

One name that was mentioned was Elmer Meredith, who played in the Trolley League in 1913 after he dropped out of professional baseball. Most players were just everyday miners who enjoyed the sport on their one day off.

There was so much going on at Lakeside Park in competition with the baseball game. Not long after the game would begin that there would be daylight fireworks, band concerts, balloon ascensions. But then again, there were over twenty thousand people at the park, and they couldn't all watch the baseball game, so there were many activities to entertain the crowd.

One advertisement for the Fourth of July 1926 tells of the fun at Lakeside. An old-fashioned Fourth of July featuring a new modern event of a Bathing Beauty Revue. The main event was listed as a display of fireworks on the Sunday, the fourth, and Monday, the fifth, with a small display on Saturday, the second. Balloon ascensions and parachute leaps, dances on Saturday and Monday nights. Bands would play music all day long to add to the atmosphere. Water events, greased pole climbs, movies at the theater, and more events than could be attended all in one day!

Ball grounds. Lake Side Park, Webb City.

Lakeside Swinging Bridge

LAKE SIDE PARK, CARTHAGE, MO.

Lakeside Tennis Courts

Lakeside Memories

Myrtle Allen said that her dear husband, Jimmy Allen, when he was a young man, sported a red wool sweater, trimmed in white, that proclaimed Jimmy to be the "Lakeside Skating Champion." This got my attention because I had recalled there being a skating rink at Lakeside, but evidently there was. Myrtle said roller-skating was quite a popular activity.

Myrtle remembered Lakeside Park's swinging bridge and picnics, which were big events in her childhood.

Harry Hood Sr. described Lakeside Park as the "park that boasted of entertainment of every description in those days, and this included a boathouse, dance pavilion, theater, roller coaster, picnic grounds, baseball park, and even a boat on which, for a small charge, you could be taken on a short trip up Center Creek to see the beauties of the woodlands on either side. For those who wished to spend the night or several days at the park, there was the Lakeside Hotel nearby."

Hood told of an advertisement that boasted:

> Attractions tomorrow are of the unusual high standard, including two free band concerts by Jolley and his band, the championship ball game between Joplin and Alba teams of the Trolley League and a grand display of fireworks at night. The movie shows in the park are free to everybody. Next Tuesday night a grand ball will be given free in Lakeside Pavillion, the music to be furnished by Putman's Orchestra. Everybody is invited to dance. No gate admission, the only cost being car fare to Lakeside.

Boat at Lakeside!

Lakeside Falls

VIEW OF BOAT HOUSE—LAKESIDE PARK—S. W. MO. ELECTRIC RY.

Lakeside boathouse

Lakeside Balloon Rides

Lakeside celebrations and events:

June 22, 1920—Masonic St. John's Day was celebrated by all the Masonic lodges in Jasper County with a picnic at Lakeside Park.

Walter Harrigan, on April 1, 1897 secured the privilege from the Lessees of Lakeside Park to sell cigars, newspapers, etc. at the park this summer. He will have two stands, one at the station and another at the restaurant building on the hillside. Both will be complete in every way and he will carry a full line of cigars, tobacco, fruit, soda pop, confectionary, newspapers, and periodicals. Mr. Harrigan will open his place of business sometime next week.

Special firework display—Free attraction; display of Japanese daylight fireworks at 3:30 p.m. Entirely new feature. Definitely worth seeing.

Streetcars provided transportation to many events.

Grade school and high school students rode the streetcar to and from school. Athletic teams and fans rode to and from various contests in neighboring towns. Many lawyers rode the streetcar to attend court trials at both Joplin an Carthage Courthouses.

Circuses in Joplin, at Twentieth Street and Maiden Lane, carried many people to the event. Carthage held an annual Chautauqua, Webb City had an annual harvest show, Joplin had their annual Spanish street fiesta, Galena had old settlers' picnic and celebration, and Baxter Springs had a street fair.

CHAPTER 5

Transportation

Webb City has always had a good mode of transportation with a stagecoach company carrying folks into the new city as soon as word of the discovery of lead reached outlying areas. The Missouri and Northwestern Railway (the Frisco) Depot was built in the west end of town in 1879. Two years later, the Missouri Pacific Railroad Depot was built on the east side of town. A. H. Rogers started the first mule-drawn streetcar between Webb City and Carterville in 1889 but quickly grasped the invention of the electric streetcars and established the Southwest Missouri Railway Association in 1893, with the headquarters being established in Webb City. A miner could reach any local mining town by hopping on a streetcar.

Horse and wagon between Webb City and Joplin

Horse and Carriage, Buggy, or Wagon

Let's think back, if you will, to the days before automobiles. Webb City had dirt roads; the fire wagon was pulled by horses. The streetcars (trolleys) were pulled by mules. Farmer's wagons were pulled by horses and mules. And most families got around in a buggy-pulled horses. Even the hearse was pulled by beautifully matched horses. Some men traveled the area on horseback, and travel took a bit longer to get from one place to another. Men would ride their horses into town, stop by the saloon, and tie their horses to the hitching post outside of the business they were visiting. Sometimes the men would stay too long at one saloon, and the horses would stand outside all day long. The city was dismayed at the pile of droppings that would accumulate as the horse would stand there. City workers were kept busy with shovel and bucket as they cleaned up the droppings that made for an unpleasant smell and difficulty wading through the mud.

Many homes were not set up for the care of a horse and buggy. They relied on local businesses to care for their equipment and animals. The livery stables in town did the best they could to keep their customers happy. They housed the horses and kept them in great condition, including doctoring their hooves. The owner of Burris Livery Company, located at 109 and 111 East Main Street (Broadway), was known to give the public his utmost attention. He also rented out any type of transportation a person might need, from buggies to wagons.

Another well-known livery was located at Tom and Daugherty Streets and named the J. V. Wyatt Livery, Feed, and Sale Stable. Mr. Wyatt had a reputation of being friendly and helpful, which accounted for his long business history

On Webb Street, between First and Second Street (where Elder Shirt Factory was later located), was F. M. Hancock, a general blacksmithing and scientific horseshoer. He kept the horses disease-free and the carriages in tip-top shape.

Life in Webb City improved with the invention of the automobile and with Mayor George Moore paving the streets with brick in 1905.

Carriage Houses

When Webb City was first incorporated as a city in 1876, the most common mode of transportation was wagons pulled by horses or horse-drawn carriages. Men often rode by horseback, and many miners traveled by mule, as they were cheaper to come by.

As homes were built, it was necessary to build barns, sheds, or carriage houses to keep the horses or mules. Most homes of modest income just had a small shed out back, with a stall for the horse and a cover for the carriage. Wagons were a cheaper mode of transportation, and carriages were a sign of distinction. Surreys allowed more family members to ride together.

The streets of Webb City were a constant concern to the city, as the horses would leave droppings along the way. A street department being led by the street commissioner was in charge of keeping the main streets clean. It was frustrating to the city employees, as some men would leave their horses or mules tied up outside of the bars most of the day, and it was impossible for the men to keep the droppings picked up. There was talk of limiting the men to the amount of time they were allowed to tie their horses to the same post (they needed parking meters even back then!). When the streets were paved with brick, it made cleanup a little easier than the dirt roads.

Meanwhile, back at home, the horses were kept in the carriage house located not too far behind the main house. Several of the large homes in Webb City had such a carriage house. The E. T. Webb home at Liberty and Broadway had a large and rather impressive carriage house just west of the main home. It was torn down at a later date to allow room to build the Methodist Church. Many years later, when they were resurfacing the parking lot, many items were uncovered that were probably from the old carriage house.

The Andrew McCorkle home at 106 South Webb Street had a carriage house directly west of the house, in approximately the same location as the new kitchen that has been built on the back of the original house. The carriage house extended to the south. Many carriage houses were torn down as the automobile came into use. It didn't take as much room to house the automobile as it did to house the carriage and horses. Many homes built garages in the early 1900s as the automobiles became more popular. And those residents who have some of those old garages can tell you that the new SUVs and large trucks can't begin to fit into those rather small garages.

The Hatten home on Ball Street has an unusually large garage built to the southwest of the house. Mr. Hatten did have horses on his farm (as he liked to refer to his home). But Mr. Hatten also was the first citizen of Webb City to obtain a red automobile, and he had a great place to keep his car out of the weather.

The home on the southwest corner of Ball and Daugherty has a unique carriage house that opens on both ends to allow the driver to drive through.

The addition of automobiles to the local streets started out rather slow at first, but by 1919, the streets were bustling with cars lining both sides of Allen (Main) Street. This was the reason Mr. Hatten special-ordered the first red car so he could find that car when he was parked among other cars at city functions. There are drawbacks to that idea, as everyone can also recognize you as the car that may have pulled out in front of them or cut them off too soon. Laura Willard has recalled many childhood memories of Mr. Hatten's driving ability!

Some of the homes had outside kitchens, so the main home would not be heated up during the cooking of dinner. Some kitchens were located in the basement of the home. This kept the heat away from the dining area and also kept the clutter out of sight. It would be a lot cooler to cook in the basement, since those were the days before air-conditioning.

The problem with carriage houses, outside kitchens, and sheds was that citizens were taxed for the outbuildings. And as the indoor plumbing was added, they were also taxed for each of their water closets.

Carriage houses and outdoor kitchens are mostly memories of the past. Those who are fortunate enough to still have the existing carriage houses have a wealth of history. An era gone by as cars replaced the carriages, and now the new cars are so big, they are requiring the old garages to be replaced.

Webb City Railroads

Webb City has always had a good mode of transportation with a stagecoach company carrying folks into the new city as soon as word of the discovery of lead reached outlying areas. The Missouri and Northwestern Railway (The Frisco) Depot was built in the west end of town in 1879. Two years later, the Missouri Pacific Railroad Depot was built on the east side of town. A. H. Rogers started the first mule-drawn streetcar between Webb City and Carterville in 1889 but quickly grasped the invention of the electric streetcars and established the Southwest Missouri Railway Association in 1893, with the headquarters being established in Webb City. A miner could reach any local mining town by hopping on a streetcar.

Newcomers, railroad depots—During the early history of Jasper County, the only railroad was located in Oronogo, and people coming to this area had to ride a stagecoach into the bustling town of Webb City. That stagecoach ride was not pleasant as the road consisted of mud—and lots of it. The stagecoach trip from Oronogo to Webb City took close to an hour. The condition of the roads slowed them down. But as the town continued to prosper, the railroad companies thought it a wise move to locate to Webb City.

The Frisco Depot, later noted as the finest depot in the state of Missouri, was built in 1870. It was a modern brick structure with commodious waiting rooms.

The Missouri-Pacific Depot was built in 1881. Between the two depots, Webb City was the railroad center and metropolis for Carterville, Oronogo, Prosperity, Alba, Duenweg, and many other small towns nearby.

Throughout the history of Webb City, many people have entered the city limits, some for a lifetime, some for only as long as the mines held up. If the walls of those depots could talk, they would probably have some interesting stories to share. The Frisco Depot is one of the oldest buildings in Webb City.

During the wartime, the soldiers left from the Frisco Depot, then many returned from war to the Frisco Depot among the cheering and crying of family and friends.

Train robbery—It started out just like one of those old Western movies, with a group of men sitting in the back of a dark saloon in Empire City, a small town just north of Galena. The men were plotting a train robbery, and they were discussing the plans in detail.

Off to the side was a young lad whose job it was to sweep the floor. He lingered a bit as he heard the plot to rob the Frisco train, then hightailed it to the police station to report what he had heard.

The robbery was planned for that night as the westbound Frisco mail train would leave Joplin at 12:40 a.m. and arrive in Empire City at 1:16 a.m. Empire City didn't have a station; there was just a green box in which the conductor had to get off the train to register his time of arrival at that location.

It was a perfect setup for a robbery. While the conductor was busy, the robbers could force the engineer and fireman to uncouple the mail and baggage car and send them down the line. The passengers would not be aware that anything had happened.

The Frisco Secret Service sent word to the Joplin Police Department, Empire City, and Galena police asking for volunteers In the meantime, another witness stepped forward to report the planned plot. He had been approached to join the gang in the robbery. But he did not have confidence that the scheme would work, and besides, two of the gang members had been mean to him, so he refused the offer. He then told the Galena constable of the plans.

So a posse was formed, which included Frisco train detectives, a couple of Joplin policemen, and about forty armed and determined men, organized by Marshal McManamy. More officers wanted to join in on the event, but fear that it was a plot to empty the towns of police officers for other destruction convinced each city to keep ample protection on hand. Even a local newspaper reporter joined in with the posse. Not one posse member had any doubt that the robbers would be taken. Dead or alive.

It was decided that Constable Hardwick and two other officers would ride with the engineer for protection during the holdup. So at 12:40 a.m., the Frisco train left Joplin with the posse of forty armed men, along with Joplin officers Rhubart, Robinson, and Collier, and headed to Galena. A few officers, the Constable Hardwich, and the Empire City marshal boarded the train in Galena. There were plenty of men to apprehend the five men who were expected to try to hold up the train.

None of the passengers were aware of the number of lawmen aboard the train until Conductor Guinney ordered the lights on the train to be extinguished, and the passengers began to question what was happening. As soon as the porters began turning down the lights, the armed forces aboard the train began to pull their Colts out of their clothes; before that, they were just like normal passengers and kept their guns concealed as they discussed fishing, politics, and a recent Europe assassination. The newspaper reporter hid under the seat occupied by a blind gentleman, who began to have medical problems of paralysis during the commotion.

As the train neared its destination at Empire City, unknown to the posse, Conductor Guinney took matters into his own hands and ordered the engineer to pull the throttle wide open. Instead of slowing down as they entered Empire City, the train took on speed, and when the train passed the junction where the robbery was to have taken place, the train had reached the speed of forty-eight miles per hour. It was by far the fastest run between Galena and Baxter Springs.

The engineer had been only too happy to follow the conductor's orders, as his promised bodyguards had failed to show. Needless to say, with the train passing by Empire City at such speed, the robbery did not take place. With a description in hand of what the robbers looked like, the officers noted that none of them were seen around Galena or Empire City.

The headlines the next day read "Large Force on the Train to Capture Brigands, but the Conductor refused to Stop so That Holdup Could be attempted… The plot to hold up the Frisco fast mail train at Empire junction as outlined in yesterday's paper was not carried out."

Well, maybe the robbers read in the paper that armed guards would be on the train, prepared to fight to the death if need be? Nothing like an advanced warning.

It is hard to imagine our area having the marshal, constable, police, and posse out in pursuit of train robbers. Almost a Keystone cop situation, though when you think about those train robbers hiding and waiting for the train to stop and to see it go flying by without slowing down a bit. Or were they even there after reading the paper?

A piece of history that would have been forgotten if someone had not taken a moment to write it down, even if part of it was the day before the robbery.

Thanks to a special reader for sharing this unique story.

Automobiles

The streets of Webb City have seen many different types of automobiles through the years. Streetcar and automobiles shared the streets with each other.

Bev's Super Market at Sixteen South Main Street has several old cars that weren't old at the time this photo was taken.

Cars parked along the one hundred block of West Daugherty Street.

More automobiles parked on the 100 block of West Broadway. In the background you see John Webb's house and Hiron Insurance Company

Automobile garages—The addition of automobiles to the local streets started out rather slow at first, but by 1919, the streets were bustling with cars lining both sides of Allen (Main) Street. This was the reason Mr. Hatten special ordered the first red car, so he could find that car when he was parked among other cars at city functions. There are draw backs to that idea, as everyone can also recognize you as the car that may have pulled out in front of them or cut them off too soon. Laura Willard has recalled many childhood memories of Mr. Hatten's driving ability!

Cooley, George T., mills and automobiles—It is time to take a trip into the past and learn about one of our forefathers, George Cooley. You have heard about men who seem to turn everything they touch into gold; well, George Cooley had that talent.

George T. Cooley was born in 1848 on his grandfather's land, in Casey County, Kentucky. The land had been awarded to George's grandfather John Cooley for his loyal service during the Revolutionary War. The three thousand acres of land included the land that Daniel Boone had built his log cabin. It did not bother Boone, as he felt Kentucky was becoming overpopulated, so he loaded up and moved to Missouri, which had plenty of woods to hunt and plenty of solitude.

George's parents, Thomas and Letitia Cooley, moved from Kentucky to Springfield, Illinois, but George did not mind as he was adventurous, and most of all, he loved change in his life. After graduating from the State Normal School, George enrolled at the Wesleyan University. After completing three years, George felt the need for change, and he dropped out to start a new profession. He served as an apprentice in the joiner's trade, later becoming a journeyman in the joiner's trade.

George saw a need for a mechanical-stair-building business and, along with his friend Dan Harkness, started this new business with no competition. They were very successful, but after five years, Dan passed away. George once again felt the need for change, so he sold his business and became a millwright at the Union Iron Works in Decatur, Illinois. Having owned his own company, George realized he needed to be his own boss again. He started building grain elevators. He did such a great job that his reputation spread all over the country. One of his most famous mills was the Schellenbacher Mill in Wichita, Kansas.

At the age of thirty, 1878, George once again felt the need for change, so he moved his wife of two years to Twin Grove Township in Jasper County. He obtained some land but leased it out as farming was not his style.

In 1883, a terrible cyclone hit the town of Oronogo, which brought change to George's life, as he took charge of the men who had been hired to rebuild the town. When that project was completed, George needed another change, so he erected a zinc site mill of the concentration type for Stolz & Illsing. Trying something different, George used 2×4 studs instead of the usual boards. The experiment proved a success, and George patented the idea. As he became a specialist in building concentrators, once again, he was sought after all over the United States. In Jasper County alone, he built over three hundred concentrating mills.

In 1900, George invented a coal washing jig. He invented a sludge table which played a major role in the mining industry. George incorporated the American Concentrator Company, which held fifteen of his patented mining inventions. The need for change encouraged George to sell that company in 1908. In 1909, at the age of sixty-one, George started the Cooley Manufacturing Company, which manufactured concentrator tables and did general machine work for mines.

The year 1912 brought a new change to George's life as he saw a future in automobiles. George built a building at 410–412 South Pennsylvania Street in Joplin. This building held one of the finest garages in the area. Many years later, it became the R&S Motor Sales Company.

George had many sons to assist him in his business, and a successful business it was. They built another garage in Webb City operated by son Julian Cooley. Back in Joplin, George added onto his Pennsylvania building with a building that faced East Fourth Street. At the top of the building at 214 East Fourth, you can read "Cooley…R&S… Wilson."

The large Cooley family consisted of sons and one daughter: Archie Frances Cooley, Jessie L. Cooley, George Elmore Cooley, Julian Arthur Cooley, Charles Thomas Cooley, Sidney Earl Cooley, Dixon (Dick) Cooley, John Norman Cooley, and Broadwich Cooley Fly.

The biggest change in George's life occurred in 1920, when he retired at the age of seventy-two. He lived until the age of eighty-three. What a great inventor, builder, and businessman was George T. Cooley. What an impact he made in Jasper County with the mining business. Cars brought to the area by George were all over the Jasper County area. The family lived in Joplin, Webb City, and Oronogo. He was known all over the United States.

Even though the mills built by George have long since disappeared, the inventions have become obsolete, and the automobiles have been replaced with modern forms of transportation, it is nice to know that the name Cooley still shows at the top of a building in Joplin. Not much to show for his brilliant talents, but a piece of history all the same.

Automobiles and Hot Rods

Transportation is a constantly changing chapter in our lives. What did you drive when you were a teenager? Driving by the high school, it is so amazing to see the number of cars on the school parking lot. Of course, I realize they have a lot more students than the high school days of the '50s and '60s. The high school parking lot was rather small, and a few of the students parked on the street, but there seemed to be only a few fortunate kids that had a car of their own. I myself was offered the family's 1956 Ford station wagon, and when I snarled my nose at the thought, Dad said, "Fine, you can walk." And I did! My younger sister learned from my mistake, and when she was offered the old 1959 international truck, she took Dad up on the offer and learned to love that old truck as much as Dad did!

In looking at old annuals, I noticed that during the '50s, there was only one school bus at the high school, and it was driven by Clarence Hare. The 1958 annual said that Mr. Clarence Hare made two trips each morning and evening to transport students from outside the city limits to and from school. But we had twelve crossing guards, as most students walked to school. By 1961, Clarence had help as the school hired Bob Carey to be a second bus driver and bought a second bus. That has changed over the years also!

Not too many of my friends had a car, so for entertainment, we rode the city bus to Joplin and felt the bus fare of 25¢ was well spent as we went shopping, watched a movie, ate lunch, and visited the Joplin Humane Society to see all the cute animals (do you remember the humane society being downtown in Joplin, just a half-block east of Main?).

Note: when the Joplin Public Service Company was established in 1939, the cost of a bus ride in the city of Joplin was 5¢, and you had to pay 10¢ to go to Webb City.

It was usually the guys who were driving cars of their own. They would work to earn the money to pay for their cars. You had to mow quite a few lawns to save enough cash to buy a car. They would pay $50–$75 for a car and spend lots of hours getting it in good running condition. Many a girl learned to sit patiently and wait for the love of her life to finish tinkering with the car before he would show her some attention. It became a challenge to become a distraction to pull them away from the car!

Wouldn't it have been neat to know the future and to have held onto that used '57 Chevy, '64 Chevy, '65 Ford Mustang, etc. that you bought for a fairly low price, knowing that it would be worth $20,000 down the road! And there is always something special about the first car you owned. As the men get older, they have a tendency to buy a piece of that memory. Some buy them already restored, and others enjoy the labor of restoring it themselves.

Another thing I remember about the good ole days was that a guy was happy to have a car—any car—and he wasn't embarrassed about mismatched doors or fenders. He was still cool to have his own wheels. You could watch weekly improvements to the car as money was earned, and time was spent lovingly fixing up the hot rod!

Nowadays, you can see those souped up hot rods at the local cruise nights on Main street. Those cars do look sharp. There is a lot more money being put into those cars today than there was in the past. And wasn't it fun, way back when, to go to the junkyards to get the parts for the old cars being fixed up? And the used parts were quite a bit cheaper back then.

Cars in the past were shown off at the drive-in theaters, at the local hamburger stands, and at the bowling alley. But the most fun had to be driving the circle around the swimming pool at Hatten Park. Guys were openly eyeing the girls in their swim suits, and girls were secretly eyeing the guys in their wheels. And before you knew it, that guy would be driving the circle to show off the gal he had sitting next to him in his sharp wheels.

Here in Southwest Missouri, we didn't have too many races for pink slips, like they did in the movies. There might have been a few races to show off the motor under the hood and what it could do. But it was even more fun to go to the demolition derbies. That is why those old cars of yesteryear are worth so much money today. Only a few survived the final destruction of the demolition derbies. The crazy things we did for fun in those days!

Living in Southwest Missouri did have its advantages—the chats! What better place to have a little car racing fun without worrying about hitting anything of importance. Of course, there was the danger of mine holes and the legend of the Hatchet Man, but that is a story for another day!

Airplanes and Airports

The first area airports—When I first became interested in the history of Webb City, I talked with many old-timers, and I heard many tales that had been passed on to them or that they had remembered from their childhood. One of those stories that I have often shared turns out to be one of those uh-ohs that wasn't quite right.

I had been told that the Joplin Airport, located on Webb City Road (now MacArthur Drive), was originally called the Webb City Airport, and that Webb City sold it to Joplin many years ago. Well, many years later, when I finally got around to doing some research on the airport, I found the rest of the story, and I will share it and hope to make the matter right.

The story starts way back in the spring of 1919, when a new company was established in Joplin at Third and Kentucky Streets, and it was known as the Hiland-O'Brien Airplane Company. The goal of this new company was to manufacture aircraft of the Curtiss type. They were also planning to head up an aviation school with the chief pilot being Thomas Webber, who had recently returned from overseas service.

By the fall of 1919, this prosperous company, now listed as the Hiland Airplane Company, had completed its seventh airplane in just a few short months. It was suggested that Joplin should become a port of call for cross-country fliers by establishing a municipal landing field with hangars.

As the Hiland Airplane Company would complete each plane, they would be launched from Schifferdecker Park. Many pilots would come to this area to have their planes repaired, and they also used the park for landing and taking off. Many stated that they would be willing to use the services of Hiland Airplane Service, except for the lack of suitable landing fields. The nearest airplane repair service and factory other than Joplin was in Chicago.

It wasn't until October 1927, eight years later, that those plans were to become a reality. Plans were made to acquire 100 acres close to the intersection of Seventh and Schifferdecker Streets. The land purchased was just west of the Empire District Substation. The main advantage to this location was that the Schifferdecker Golf Links were located to the north, and the Oak Hill Golf Links were located to the south, providing emergency landing fields if needed. The Joplin Municipal Airport was dedicated on November 11, 1927, and it included 160 acres between Seventh Street and Thirteenth street.

By the following January, 1928, it was announced that a company known as the Ozark Association had received the contract to provide school, transport, and concession rights at the municipal airport. Ozark built a new hangar and started out with four aircrafts.

To get the public better acquainted with the sensation of flying, Ozark offered scenic tours of the region. The trip included a flight over Galena, Riverton, and Shoal Creek Valley at a cost of $5 for each passenger. The flights went out at two, four, and six o'clock each afternoon. For $12.50, a person could see the sights of Galena, Lowell, and Baxter Springs, Commerce, Miami, Seneca, and Neosho. The most elite flight, for $25, would show the beauty of the Ozarks by flying over Monett, Aurora, Crane, Galena, Branson, Hollister, Lake Tanneycomo, Ozark Dam, Forsythe, and Springfield.

Ozark Association received a bit of competition when Southwestern Air Fast Express joined the airport in March 1929, and they offered flights from Joplin to Tulsa for $13, and from Joplin to St. Louis for $33.

By 1932, Joplin had become a popular stopping point for many aircrafts, and the need for a new airport was in demand, not to mention the danger of the high-tension lines of the Empire District Electric Company, which cut across the corner of the airport on Seventh Street.

Joplin was looking at a four-hundred-acre tract of land just north of Stone's Corner and just north of the Joplin-Webb City Road. As the land was being cleared in preparation for the new airport, the uprooted trees were cut into stovewood by unemployed forces and were furnished to needy families through the Health and Welfare Association.

The Junge Municipal Airport was one of the best airports in the area. To make it known to the world and any planes flying overhead, gravel-filled trenches which spelled out Joplin, Mo., were completed in February 1934. The letters were forty feet across; they looked enormous from the ground, but from the air, they were merely large enough to distinctly outline the words. Perfectly proportioned and spaced, the gravel-filled trenches were dug by the CWA workmen, who were helping to build the new airport.

History was made in April, 1936, when a twin-engined plane landed at the Joplin Municipal Airport, marking it the largest craft to land at the new airport. Mr. Pomeroy was the pilot, and he was accompanied by W. Alton Jones, formerly of Webb City who had moved to New York with the Cities Gas Service Company.

The 750-pound revolving aeronautical beacon was installed at the airport in the summer of 1936. In April of 1937, Joplin Municipal Airport was approved as a daytime landing field for mail planes and commercial planes hauling passengers.

The hangar was completed in December of 1937, with the offices on the north side of the building being highly modern with gas for heating and water from the airport's deep well. The first night flight, which required the turning on of the runway lights, was recorded in July of 1945.

So even though Webb City has shared the airport with Joplin all these years, it truly was originally the Junge Municipal (Joplin Municipal) Airport. Many houses located on the north side of the Joplin-Webb City Road (MacArthur Drive) were moved to different areas, but most were moved to Stone's Corner, including the home of Ma Barker and her boys.

The Flying Professor
By Bob Chancellor (2011)

Bonham Chancellor moved his family to Webb City in the summer of 1943, to take up the position as principal of the junior-senior high school. We moved from Shelbina, MO., where there was no airport; and he had grown up around Boonville, MO., where there was no airport, so the move to Webb City was certainly his first exposure to airports and flying. But his interest and enthusiasm for flying took effect quickly and strongly.

His first flight, a 30-minute demonstration, was logged October 9, 1943 with pilot/instructor Tim Merritt. He next flew in February of 1944, and had been in the air 21 times by the end of June. These were all dual hours, with instructor N.A. (Gus) Skoglund, a former Navy pilot. Simultaneously with flying, he was taking the required ground training courses, and in May, 1944, he applied for a student pilot license.

At least 60 hours of flying time, both dual accompanied by an instructor, and solo, were required before the student pilot could attain a private flying license. The instructed hours included lots of take-offs and landing: circle the field, land and take-off again; emergency landing, plot and follow a course to Pittsburg, KS, or Neosho. With 10 hours 40 minutes under his belt, Bonham Chancellor made his first solo flight June 23, 1944. That was followed by a few more instructed hours and lots of solo time, reaching for the goal of 60: take-off, turns, stalls, landing, and "playing around."

Flying activity in those days was centered at a large hangar, right by the highway between Webb City and Stone's Corner (now West McArthur Dr.) There were two or three trailers that functioned as offices for the various flying services—there was no Joplin air terminal or commercial air service at that time. The airplanes were single-engine, high-wing aircraft: Cessna 120 or 140, Luscombe or Aeronica.

Bonham Chancellor's big day came more than a year after his first solo flight. With 63 hours of solo time and 85 hours total air time, he was tested and awarded his Private Pilot's License October 14, 1945. Now, he could take up passengers. That was a beginning of a chapter in which many people in Webb City, young and old, would take their first airplane ride.

His first passenger was my younger brother, Sam, who was five years old. The next ride was mine, I was nine. And then my mother. It appears that he hoped Mother would get the flying bug, and perhaps take instruction for her own license—during the first year she was his most frequent passenger and he even purchased her own log book.

There was a notation in his log book that his license had cost $571: $184 for instructed time and $387 for solo time plane rental. That sounds incredibly cheap for these times, when earning a private license can cost 8 to 10 thousand dollars. But those were the days of 20 cent gasoline, and as principal of the high school he earned $6000 per year, so learning to fly was a substantial investment.

But the flying professor found a way to finance his expensive hobby. During the summer vacation periods, he worked for the flying service, maintaining and cleaning planes, pumping gas and pushing aircraft into and out of the hangar. He also worked on the apron, spinning and starting propellers in those days when small planes did not have electric starters. For pay, he took one hour of flying time for each hour of ground work. He did this for several summers and amassed a large balance of free flying time.

He loved to fly. I think it was because of the precision and preparation it took. And he loved to share his enthusiasm of flying. He always was looking for someone to fly with him. After receiving his license, he made 513 flights; 390 of those times he took a passenger. In fact, the first 63 flights after he was licensed, he had a passenger with him.

I flew with him 32 times, amassing 18 plus hours in the air—pretty heady stuff for a pre-teen. My mother surpassed me, with 19 hours in 26 flights and even younger brother Sam, barely able to see over the dashboard, made 20 flights and logged nearly 11 hours.

But here's where it gets fun—the number and names of other people he took aloft. Sometimes it is difficult to determine the names or partial names, or initials entered into his flight log books, but in approximate order over the years, they include: 1945–46: science teacher G.C. (Willie) Williams was his first (and frequent) non-family passenger, followed by Mrs. Williams, John K (?), Jack Lowe, Jack Cogbill, Geltz Zentner (a trainer), (?)Hood, Alec Parson, John K., D.D.G. and Mrs. D.D.G., Dick Burdick, Tommy Byrd (a next door neighbor), Jim Finley (flying company owner), Carole Byrd, Mel Snead, Nelda Snead, (?) Bachler, Miss Winter, Harry Howel, Wilma McDonald, Glen McDonald, Earl Webb, an un-named sailor, Madge James, Al Fahrman, Miss Coleman, Alice Gaor, Rosemary Parish, Mr. Foley, Bob Laster, Kate and Clayton, (?)Preston, Mrs. Brixey, Ed Kluba, Charles Brown, Mr. Cannon, (?)O'Neil, Jr. Elliott, Archie Smith, Jack(?), (?)Essex, (?)Bachler, Joe Stanley, Dick Lewis, Vernon Babbitt, Mr. Ward, Ray Shonk, relatives of Jim Finley, my aunt Phoebe Kennedy, my grandmother Louise Tearle, (?)Cooley, (?)Watkins, Bachelor's son, Archie (?), Mr. Housman, (?)Locke, (?)Bruff, (?)Wheeler, (?)Fahrman, (?)Shaner, (?)Choate, (?) Inman, an unnamed school boy, Jack Hill, (?) Lowe, (?) Rodarme, (?)Danhart, Ed Murray, Mutt Hughes, (?)Hatcher, Terry James, (?)Bair, Joan Smith, Mary Lee Stewart, Woody Oldham, Bennie Welcher, and Jerry Watson.

That was just the first full summer. High school students, friends, fellow teachers, Lions Club members, or if you were just hanging around the airport when it was time to go flying, you were invited. In mid-1946, he had passed the examination for his Commercial Pilots license, which meant he could be paid for flying, and many of the logged flights logged appear to be familiarization flights for prospective students. He was not licensed as an instructor, however. And many flights were not paid flights—he took people aloft for the sheer joy of flying.

1947: (?)Locke, Bud Schoekels, Joy(?), B. Tomlinson, (?)Collier, Bob Morris, Bob Lassiter, Mr. Crawford and son, Shirley Ferrell, Beverly Smith, Pat Greene,

Eugenia Craig, Frances Hopper, Jack Cogbill, Dorothy Dennis, Shirley Bradbury, Jay Stever, (?)Hulen, (?)Gardner, Eugene Long, Charley Brown, (?)Lacey, Bob Finley's friend, John Owen, Ted Parrish, Oliver (?), Jack Carmack, (?)Greninger, (?)Glover, Joe Babbitt, Bob James, Boyd(?), Glen McDonald, and Mrs. Byrd.

Ed Kluba, Ed Murray, Ken Davis, Donald Davis, Bill Mace, Old John, Bob's friend, my uncle Marsh Kennedy and Phoebe, Carl Gerlich, Rusty Martin, Carole Byrd, Elmo Webb, Ralph Rusk, Jack Carmack, Gene Crocker, Robert Woods, Mary James, Mrs. Williams, Charles Tudor, Fred Nelson, Mott sisters, Henry Hulett (probably where a lot of aerial photos of Webb City came from), and Karl Lee.

1948: Bart Hancock, Henry Norman, Maley Ray, Miss Stinnett, Mutt Hughes, Elmo Webb, Jim Harsh, Joe Sullens, Jim Owen, Jim Harsh, Herb Munsen, Galen Longnecker, Clayton Johnson, Phillips family, (?)Woods, Tommy Byrd, (?)Newton, Gerald Roberts, Bob Bradbury, Hortense Hackbarth, Clint Cooper, Junior Harper, Bob Richardson (6 times), Ed Kagin, Lee Dew, Anna Kluba, Tommy Kluba, Clark (probably Robert, the superintendent of schools), Gary Cooper, Fred Nelson, Peggy Walters, Shirley Roland, Elmo Webb and family, an auditor for Eagle Pitcher, my uncle Skipper Johns, Richard Armstrong, Carl Brooks. trainer Gretz, John Peck, Joe Babbitt, Frank Doll, Carol Knost, Miss Hubard, Richard Cruse, Bob Nieswanger, Jim Finley, and Ed Kagin.

By 1949, the pace and the enthusiasm had slowed down, in part because he had used up most of the accumulated flying hours from his summers of work, and the costs of a family of three boys forced him to seek remunerative summer employment elsewhere. He had attained a Ground Instructors license, and taught aeronautics for the Civil Air Patrol in which he was an officer and for Finley's Flying Service… He also taught aeronautics in 1948 at Webb City High School; one of the few public high schools in the country to offer such a course. And of course, he and his class painted the famous sign on the high school roof, which photographer Henry Hulett captured.

Passengers in 1949–51: Bernie Leonard, Ed Kagin, Dale Gilliam, Jim Coffee, Bob Farris, John Campbell, the Hughes kids, Glen McDonald, Ed Kluba, Bob Stults, Dick Rowlette, Henry Hulett, Mel Kennedy, Bob Richardson, Jack Boyd, Kenny Johnson, Jerry Drachenberg and Dick Rowlette.

There was a year and a half gap from September, 1951 until February, 1953 when he made five solo flights. Bonham Chancellor's last logged flight was a 35 minute jaunt on March 28, 1953, at which point he had logged 355 hours flying time. Ironically, he was never again in an airplane until 1972 when he boarded an airliner to Washington, D.C. for the wedding of his first passenger, Sam Chancellor.

Joplin Jalopy—In August 1946, the Joplin Airport was alive with enthusiasm as city officials, media, and area citizens gathered to welcome the arrival of the famed Joplin Jalopy. War history describes the fame of the Joplin Jalopy as a B-24 Liberator bomber that completed sixty-three combat battles over Germany.

Most people would not have been impressed with the war-worn silver aircraft that "limped" into the Joplin Airport, but to the citizens who helped raised the funds to purchase the bomber in the first place, it was a thing of beauty, a trophy of sacrifice, dedication, and patriotism.

The bomber was set aside at the east edge of Joplin Airport. It became a fascination to young boys who climbed on the plane and dreamed of being pilots of fame as they flew their imaginary missions of war.

With the plane being located so close to the Webb City side of the airport, it was mostly the Webb City youth that have fond memories of the Joplin Jalopy. Many a youth from the late '40s can relate tales of playing around the bomber and winning many imaginary battles.

It was an indignant end to a glorious life, as the Joplin Jalopy was eventually sold for scrap metal. It may have been removed from the airport, but it can never be removed from the minds and hearts of the young men who spent many hours flying the skies on the east edge of the Joplin Airport.

Merle Lortz recalls playing on the Joplin Jalopy as a youth and is the proud owner of one of the few photos of such a magnificent memory.

Jim Bunch says that about 1949 or 1950, he loved to go over to the salvage yard located at the Y, where East Broadway curves to join in with Daugherty Street before heading on to Carterville. The Swappers Salvage Company, 517 East Broadway, was owned and operated by S. W. Firth, and he had two sons, Dick and Jack. The salvage yard was just east of the Webb Corp and was an interesting place for young boys to rummage and play. One day, a plane arrived at the salvage yard, the Joplin Jalopy had a new home, and a new group of boys found the thrill of playing on the old plane.

Jim recalls that the plane didn't have to do a thing. Just sitting there allowed them to travel over Berlin, have many air battles, and kept their active imaginations going full force. Every movie they had seen came to life as they flew that plane over Europe and back home to safety.

Daugherty trees—Webb City wouldn't be here if it wasn't for the great pioneer families such as the Webbs, Daughertys, Ashcrafts, Corls, Stewarts, Hardys, McCorkles, Huletts, Chinns, Pattens, Coynes, Aylors, Hattens, Mankers, O'Neills, and many more, too numerous to mention.

I recently read a 1942 newspaper article from the *News Herald* which brought me even closer to the Daugherty family. As you may recall, the Daugherty family was one of the early pioneers to the area, living just east of what is now the Joplin Airport. W. A. Daugherty moved to Jasper County in 1870 (Webb City was established in 1876) and purchased 260 acres on the west side of what would eventually become Webb City. His original home was west of Colonial Road on what is now the airport. The newspaper article I read refers to the old homestead.

Judge Lee A. Daugherty, grandson of W. A. Daugherty was having some difficulty adjusting to changes being made on the old homestead. In 1941, the judge had sold some of the family land to Joplin to allow them to expand the airport, making it suitable for use by military airplanes. But he kept the land just south of the airport, an area that once held the family homestead.

Along the yard of the old homestead stood seven maple trees, which had stood like soldiers guarding the Daugherty homestead for the seventy-five years that the Daughertys had owned the land. But closer examination showed the trees to be nearing the century mark. Daugherty thought that by keeping that piece of land, he would be able to protect the family trees.

But the Civil Aeronautics Authority came to look over the airport, and they determined that the trees, even though they set back a ways from the airport, created a hazard to heavy aircraft and were a definite obstruction. They noted that the trees stood in line with the south end of the long runway, and heavy airplanes taking off or landing might not be able to clear them. They said the trees had to come down.

The article was quoted as saying:

> Eighty-years ago those trees may have offered shade and rest for weary civil war Calvary men who ranged this country. Today, they are sentenced to death because, in modern warfare, they are "just in the way." And because "only God can make a tree" and man loves them, Presiding Judge Lee A. Daugherty of the county court was just a little saddened today, he admitted, by that death sentence.
>
> The old Daugherty farm home has long since been moved, and the field in which they stand is planted to grain, but the Daugherty family, for sentimental reasons, has kept the trees as landmarks of the old home place.

The newspaper article mentioned that the span between Civil War and World War II seems long in the life of man, but just a little while to a small grove of trees.

The Daugherty farm had moved to the east, and the new homestead was located at Three Colonial Road, still a part of the original 260 acres (he eventually owned over 4,000 acres). This house is still in the Daugherty family and is owned by W. A. Daugherty's descendent Cathy Dilworth and her husband, Larry. Quite an honor to have land that has been in the same family since 1870.

When you turn north onto Colonial Road (once known as Hospital Road), a cement block fence went down both sides of the road. The Daugherty family built the fence in the late 1870s, and it still stands today.

CHAPTER 6

The Men and Women Who Built Webb City

Webb City's history is loaded with travelers. A new town seems to attract a variety of folks. There were some who left a legacy, and some who quietly enjoyed life without much fanfare. Those who made the biggest impact in Webb City history have buildings, streets, and businesses named after them. That allows them to live on in time. Then there are those who made an impact on the development of Webb City, but it may have been from the sidelines. Listed below are a few of those people who were there for the beginning days of Webb City through the years.

The People Who Built This City

Webb City has a wonderful history, with a glorious past revolving around the mining industry. As we look at the beautiful buildings downtown, many display names of past businessmen who helped Webb City grow. Streets carry names of those who went above and beyond the call of duty to establish a city that has endured. These men and women from the past still linger in our minds as we recall their generosity and ingenuity.

Name-Dropping

Let's mention a few names from Webb City history.

Of course, we can't drop names without mentioning John C. Webb, the founder of (Webbville) Webb City. Webb moved here from Tennessee in 1856, uncovered a chunk of lead in 1873, and established the town of Webb City in 1876. Webb built the first brick house, the first brick business building, the first hotel. John and his son, E. T. Webb, started the first bank of Webb City in 1882.

W. A. Daugherty lived just southwest of John C. Webb on what is now Colonial Road. He stepped in to get a piece of the mining action when Webb and a friend, Murrell, got discouraged with trying to mine the first mine shaft in what would soon become Webb City. Daugherty also became the founder of Carterville. He built the first building in Carterville other than the Carter farmhouse, which was located way out on the backside (northeast) of what would soon become Carterville.

Granville P. Ashcraft was known as the "man of first" in Webb City. He was in partnership with W. A. Daugherty, and they were first to uncover a large chunk of lead in what would become Webb City, bringing up fifteen thousand pounds the first week. He was the first to market the lead and first to ship it out. His daughter, Bernice, was the first child born in the new incorporated town of Webb City. He built the first frame house in Webb City (located where the senior citizen building is located today) as John C. Webb and Daugherty were living in log cabins at the time. Ashcraft also purchased the first automobile in Webb City.

James O'Neill came to Webb City in 1879 at the age of forty-three. He had become quite wealthy in the Pennsylvania oil fields by investing in land rich in petroleum. He began investing in land in Jasper County and Kansas and, once again, struck it lucky. He decided to take on a new business, against all of his friends' advice. He started the Webb City Waterworks. Once again, his investment paid off. He also built the Newland Hotel.

Elijah Lloyd came to this area from Kentucky in 1867. He was a civil engineer, worked for the railroad, and did surveying. Assisted in laying out the town of Joplin in 1871, then he was employed by John C. Webb in 1874 to survey and plot a town, which would be called Webbville. He leased a mine in 1874, struck payload in 1882.

James E. McNair had the distinction of being the first executive officer (mayor) of Webb City. A position he held for one month and two days before being honored with the position of the first postmaster. Before moving to Webb City in 1875, McNair had served on the legislature of Tennessee, elected as a delegate to the Southern Loyalists Convention and worked for the St. Louis–San Francisco Railway as a bridge carpenter. He built Mr. Webb a home at what are now Tom and Daugherty Streets.

George W. Ball came to town without a penny to his name or shoes on his feet but with a dream to strike it rich. It didn't take him long to realize that only the mine owners got rich, not the miners. He was offered a mine that kept flooding. He corrected the leak and struck it rich. He built a beautiful home on the southwest corner of Daugherty and Washington.

A. H. Rogers established a horse-drawn streetcar line from Carterville to Webb City, and then in 1893, he consolidated with the Joplin Electric Railway and the Jasper County Electric and established the Southwest Missouri Railway, which took miners as far away as Oklahoma.

Jane Chinn was well known for her donation to the city that allowed the construction and furnishing of the Jane Chinn Hospital. But Elizabeth Jane Webb Stewart Chinn was a strong independent lady who had a sharp business mind. She owned several mines and invested in many more.

Thomas F. Coyne came to Webb City in 1876 with his parents. He attended the Sedalia Business College and began working at the W. C. Bank. He soon realized that to become wealthy meant owning a prosperous mine. Coyne began investing and soon became one of Webb City's wealthy people. He opened the Coyne Lumber Company which was located at 308 Main (Broadway) and one in Miami, Oklahoma. His success in business is attributed to the fact that he was a fair man. His home was located on the southwest corner of Ball and Broadway.

James A. Daugherty was the son of W. A. Daugherty, and he was helping his father farm the land, which is now Carterville, when they discovered that the farmland was loaded with ores and minerals. Although his father owned the mines, it was James's brains behind the successful mines. James donated generously to the W. C. College. He became a business partner with W. S. Gunning in the mining and mill business. Several well-known family names united with James A. Daugherty's children. His daughter Nancy married W. A. Corl; his daughter Myrtle married C. R. Chinn Jr.

If you hear the name of E. T. Webb, you think of that little alien in the movie *E.T.*, or you think of John Webb's son. And when you think of John's son, you can't help but think of that beautiful house behind the Central Methodist Church at Liberty and Broadway Streets. E. T. also was in the banking business with his father. E. T. gained national fame with his collection of valuable paintings.

But I also want to do a little name-dropping of a different type. If you heard the name George W. Waring, would you know that he was a Webb City citizen who became nationally known as a chemist? Keeping up with the Joneses might be a little tough if you are competing with Elmer T. Jones, a one-time Webb City citizen who became the president of the Wells Fargo Company.

Judge Ray Watson and Captain Fred Nesbitt were distinguished in World War service. Mrs. Rosine Morris Bachrach hailed from Webb City, but most folks didn't know it as they listened to her play for the Minneapolis Symphony Orchestra.

Webb City's very own Zoe Thralls wrote several geography books, some even used for the schools (I wonder how you go about writing a geography book? Do you travel, or do you go by old maps?) Either way, she helped put Webb City on the map.

Robert Landrum was a tenor soloist on the national broadcasting system of New York City. I know that we have many young people who have gone on to become great singers and entertainers or great newspaper reporters, television correspondents, and many other careers that seem rather glamorous. But we know that many long and hard hours go into making those careers.

A great botanist, Ernest Jesse Palmer, who was a professor at Harvard, became well known when he wrote a couple of books. One was called "catalogue of plants in Jasper County," and he cowrote *A Catalogue of All Known Plants of Missouri.*

Additional information on Ernest Jesse Palmer—he once maintained an herbarium in Webb City that contained twenty thousand species. He published a book of poetry in 1958 when he was eighty-three years of age.

We've had a few inventors from Webb City and some wonderful artists who still reside in Webb City. There are musicians, actors, singers, and businessmen who have made a name for themselves and still call Webb City their hometown.

There are many names that I could drop such as: A. D. Hatten, Colonel James O'Neill, George Ball, J. C. Stewart, J. P. Stewart, W. S. Chinn, Joseph Aylor, C. E. Matthews, Andrew McCorkle, Colonel A. A. Hulett, S. L. Manker, C. M. Manker, W. A. Ashcraft, Grant Ashcraft, W. S. Gunning, George Bruen, J. M. Burgner, H. C. Humphreys, E. E. Spracklen, W. A. Corl, G. F. Corl, W. E. Patten, L. J. Stevison, S. H. Veatch, James Roney, and many more. More information to follow on the prominent men and women of Webb City history.

Variety of Pioneers

In the 1850s–1880s, many families were tearing up roots and making journeys into the unknown west. The government was offering land for free in some areas, at a very low price in others, and some were tempted by the promise of getting rich in the mining business. As the folks headed west, some went on out to Colorado, California, New Mexico, and other untamed areas.

Some folks began settling around Southwest Missouri in Sarcoxie, Granby, and Joplin. Some of those early pioneers purchased land and lived out in the woods, all by themselves, enjoying the beauty of Jasper County.

Many times, we have mentioned some of our well-known early pioneers of Webb City who came to town and left their mark. Well, I'd like to take a moment to mention some of the more common folk who came to town to make a living and did just that. They aren't mentioned very often in history books because they were just trying to get by, but without them, some of our history might be changed. These folks were very important to the development of Webb City, even if it was from the sidelines.

Josiah Van Buskirk left his home state of Indiana in 1870, stopping in Kansas for a while. He moved to Joplin in 1871, trying his hand at mining and smelting. When Webb City was incorporated in 1876, Josiah decided he would head to where the action was. He and his wife, Lauretta, moved into town, and he continued his line of work in smelting. But in 1879, Josiah and Lauretta decided there was a need for a small grocery store, so they changed their destiny and took a gamble. The grocery store was a success, and business continued to grow, as did the Van Buskirk family. They had four children: Martha, Theodore, Jeannetta, and Ira. Although Josiah isn't remembered as some fantastic businessman who was listed among the famous pioneers, his business made a difference. He had many friends, was a member of the AOUW, and was remembered as being socially pleasant!

Samuel S. Barclay, at the age of seventeen, in 1862, entered the Eighth Missouri State Militia and served in the Civil War under Colonel McClurg. Samuel and his wife, Martha, settled in Granby, and Samuel served as the Granby marshal in 1875. When Webb City was established as a town, Samuel and Martha moved to be in on the excitement of watching a new town get settled. Having had experience in law enforcement, it didn't take long for young Samuel Barclay to leave his mark. He was elected as the marshal of Webb City in April of 1882.

Note: One of the reasons Webb City became incorporated as a town in 1876 was due to the fact that they were having such a bad experience with lawbreakers, they needed to be incorporated to establish law and order.

John Anderson was born in Germany. In 1865, at the age of twenty-four, he came to America. His first stop was Indiana, and in 1866, he made it to Kansas City before stopping in Parsons, Kansas. He opened a mercantile store in Parsons and established quite a good business until 1877, when he heard about the great commotion in Webb City. He sold his business and made the move to the hustle and bustle of the new mining town. He opened his mercantile store and never regretted his decision. In 1881, he married Ms. Anna Cook and established his permanent roots in Southwest Missouri.

Dr. W. M. Whiteley hailed from the state of Wisconsin, graduated in 1874, and settled in Joplin in 1875. He married Ms. Evadney Myers of Joplin, and they were content with their lives, until 1879 when Mr. Whiteley saw a need for doctors in the fairly new town of Webb City. He moved his wife and family to Webb City and set up practice. His three children were Albert, Daisy, and Nora. Once again, the call to come to Webb City seemed to echo through the air.

Dr. Whiteley's father-in-law, Edward Myers, had a busy life. Edward was born in England and made the trip to New York City in 1847 at the age of twenty-three. He acquired employment in a clothing store on Chatham Street as a salesman. He moved westward and worked as a clothing salesman in St. Louis. Still having that desire to move west, Edward headed on to California to follow his dream. He stayed in Sacramento for thirteen years, working in the hotel business and clothing business until he tried his luck in the theater in San Francisco as Professor Myers, the "American Magician." This new profession took him all over the west as he performed his exhibitions. He retired from show business and settled in Middle America, in Joplin. He opened an auction house with several branch stores. The business failed, and he moved to Webb City in 1882 and engaged in a clothing store and a saloon. His new adventures seemed to finally slow down the ever-busy Edward. But during his leisure time, his active mind just wouldn't slow down, so he began inventing gadgets. He invented a safety attachment for railroad cars that kept them from leaving the track, and a safety switch. Both inventions were deemed very valuable. Having traveled so much in his lifetime and being so diversified in his careers, Edward Myers was a very interesting person to talk to, and he had an inexhaustible amount of stories to share.

John W. Spencer and his wife, Mary, came to Missouri from Illinois in 1882, where his five brothers and their father all enjoyed the same career of carpentry. The newness of the mining town was gone of Webb City, and life seemed to be more settled. John used his carpentry as a means to earn money and began to establish himself in the mining business. He had a level head and commonsense which made him a popular candidate as supervisor for a few of the mines. Several of his mining enterprises flourished, and he eventually put up a mill on Center Creek, which created quite a profit when he sold it. John and Mary had four daughters: Narcissia Shawgo, Mary Olive

McCann, Sarah Schiers, and Hazel A. The six sons in the family were Clyde, John Jr., Clarence, Earl, Harry, and Stephen. Not only did John add to the history of Webb City by establishing the mill, but also he added tremendously to the population!

John G. Lofton and his wife, Sarah, moved from Illinois to Barton County in 1871. They made their move to Webb City in 1877, as the city was in its hectic early development. Seeing a need, John began a livery business, which prospered. Being an honest man who showed pride in his work, John was recognized as one of the leading businessmen of the city.

Arthur Myers left his home in New York City at the age of thirteen, with dreams of making it big on his own. He stopped for a while in St. Louis, then traveled on to Denver. Arthur served throughout the Civil War under General Hancock, being engaged in many famous battles and serving in Washington, DC, in the pension office after the war. He acquired a bookkeeping job in Chicago until the great fire in that city. He traveled in the south for a couple of years and settled in Joplin in 1877. In 1882, as Webb City continued to flourish, Arthur made the move to town and opened a clothing business. He was classified as a gentleman of culture and rare social qualities. He was said to have an inexhaustible fund of wit and humor.

These folks were just common everyday folks that left a piece of history in Webb City. They don't have any monuments in their honor, but if they hadn't moved to Webb City, there would have been a void in the development of our fair city.

Abbott, Freddie

In going through some notes, I ran across a story about a young lad that I want to share with you.

The year was 1880, and spring was in the air. The date was March 25. All the tiny flowers were beginning to bloom, and the birds were singing. As the teacher rang her brass bell, the students ran out of the building, whoopin' and hollerin'. They had had to sit quietly at their desks all day, and that pent-up energy was busting loose.

One little nine-year-old, named Freddie Abbott, was running with his friends, and he couldn't seem to get enough of the fresh air. The boys started playing leapfrog, and Freddie was the littlest one of all, and as the boys pushed down on his back, he felt their weight, but he didn't complain because he wanted to fit in with the crowd—he wanted the boys to like him. This was the first year that they hadn't called him the runt, and he just knew they were starting to like him!

It's about a mile to Freddie's house. His father had a doctor's office in the house. So when Freddie gets home, he has to do the chores and keep quiet so as not to disturb the patients who are waiting to see the doctor.

As Freddie was running and playing, the thought of the chores crept into his mind, but he quickly pushed those thoughts away and continued to play games with his friends. The boys decided to play tag, and as they were running, someone bumped into Freddie, and he fell against a jagged stone. The pain that shot up Freddie's leg was almost unbearable, but he couldn't let the other boys see him cry, so he had to be brave.

One of the boys ran over to have a look. His face turned pale as he saw the bone sticking out of the gash on Freddie's leg. Freddie reached his hand up for the lad to help him get up, but his hand was waving in thin air as the boy had run off. He ran to the group, and he's telling them something, and now they were all running off.

"Please, help me. Don't leave me. Hey, you guys, come back." But Freddie's pleas were not heard as the boys scattered in several directions.

Try as he might, Freddie just couldn't get up. The pain was getting more and more unbearable, and the tears were beginning to trickle down his cheek as he still tried to be brave, just in case one of the boys might come back to help him.

Then Freddie saw some older boys—young men—walking down the street. As they came into view, Freddie pleaded with them, "Please tell my papa to come get me, I think my leg is broken." But the young men walked right on by, as if Freddie is invisible. The anguish overcame Freddie, and he laid his head in his arms and sobs. He didn't care who saw him crying, and he didn't care who thought he was weak. He wanted his dad, and he didn't see any way of getting home.

Finally a young man by the name of Alex McClaron happened to be walking down the other side of the street when he heard Freddie's sobs. He crossed over and examined Freddie's leg, and he knew the boy was in a lot of pain. He gently picked up the young lad and carried him to the Abbott home.

Dr. Abbott was able to mend little Freddie's leg and relieve some of the pain. It's nice to know that someone like Alex McClaron will come along when you need a friend. It's a shame that the boy had to lay there and suffer, as there were plenty to give him assistance, but they had no compassion. But I can't imagine being able to walk right by someone in need of help and not doing something about it.

They say that we have reached a time that we are reluctant to help someone in need for fear of being put in a compromising situation. But I would hope that society has not forgotten the parable of the Good Samaritan.

It doesn't hurt anyone to hold the door open for a senior citizen, or to reach something high on a shelf for someone in a store. Or maybe let a young mother, loaded down with small children, ahead of you in a line. Don't let this hard cruel world take away the pleasure of assisting someone in need.

Adams, F. E.

F. E. Adams was born in Greene County, Pennsylvania, on February 17, 1856. His parents were the Reverend Jesse and Jane (Gallagher) Adams. Reverend Jesse Adams was a clergyman with the Cumberland Presbyterian Church and a farmer. Jane Gallagher Adams was the daughter of John Gallagher, also a farmer, located in Fayette County, Pennsylvania, in the vicinity of Uniontown.

F. E. was raised on a farm but attended public schools and attended college at Waynesburg College, from which he graduated in 1882. He started his career in newspaper work on the editorial staff of the *National Stockman*. His father passed away in 1885. Adams married M. Louise Carpenter (1885) of Brandon, Vermont, whom he had met in college. In 1886, he moved to West Plains, Kansas, and began to study law. He was admitted to the Kansas Bar in 1887 in Springfield and started his law practice.

Along with law, he also became associated with the Bank of Seward County. In 1890, F. E. moved to Ava, Missouri, and he was in partnership with J. M. Adams in the starting of the Bank of Ava, and he served as the cashier for three and one-half years.

Adams moved to Mansfield, Missouri, in 1895 and once again opened a law practice. While in Mansfield, Adams dabbled again in his journalistic work.

An opportunity presented itself, and Adams moved to Webb City, Missouri, in 1899 and purchased the Webb City *Daily Sentinel,* which was in financial difficulties. It did not take Adams long to use his skills to bring the *Sentinel* into a solid newspaper with a reputation of being not only the best newspaper in Webb City but in Jasper County (according to the *Biographical Record of Jasper County*). The *Sentinel* was an eight-page newspaper with eight columns on each page. Adams had twenty-three employees.

Allen, Charles C.—Colonel, State Senator

Charles C. Allen, a special person of interest in the history of the area was in the political campaign of 1876 (the same year Webb City was founded), which will live in history as one of the most exciting and momentous elections on record. Allen, being the candidate on the Republican ticket for the second highest office in the state of Missouri, running for the office of lieutenant governor, made his mark in local history.

Mr. Allen was born in Orleans County, in the state of New York, August 1832. One branch of the family from which he is descended was connected with the old Dutch families of New York. His father, Benjamin Allen, was a lawyer of the town of Sandy Creek, Orleans County, New York, and died when the son was but three years of age. Two years later, his mother removed to the west and settled in Stephenson County, in Northern Illinois. There Charles C. Allen spent his early childhood. That part of Illinois was, at that time, very thinly settled, and Mr. Allen was a pupil in the first schoolhouse ever erected in Freeport. He had, however, no superior educational advantages. He was at school in all about three years, eighteen months of which were spent at an academy in Mt. Morris, Illinois, where he went in the year 1850, at the age of eighteen.

He had learned the printing business at Freeport, and while yet underage, he established a newspaper at Savannah, Illinois, called the *Savannah Register,* of which he remained in charge about a year. He left Savannah to take control of the *Dixon Transcript,* in Dixon, Illinois. In 1857, having succeeded in disposing of this paper, he removed to Iowa and went to farming at Waverly, in which pursuit he was occupied till the breaking out of the war of the rebellion.

In 1861, he enlisted in the Third Missouri Regiment Infantry, was connected with other regiments, and finally commissioned as captain of the Thirty-Fifth Missouri. He was major in the

Missouri State Militia. He served in Missouri and Arkansas, was employed on staff and bureau duty, and most of the time acted as provost marshal in St. Louis. In the year 1864, C. C. Allen was discharged from the army by reason of disability.

Establishing himself in the hardware business at Waverly, after his return from the army, he remained there till 1866, when he removed to Booneville, Missouri, and again commenced farming, however, a business which he was not particularly successful.

In the year 1869, he became a resident of Carthage and undertook the lumber business. While living in Jasper County, he has been closely identified with its interests and became one of its foremost enterprising and progressive businessmen. He was the originator of the Carthage Foundry, which owed its success mainly to his enterprise and energy. His establishment, of which he was president, was the first of the kind started in Southwest Missouri, west of Springfield, and contributed to the growth and prosperity of Carthage.

Previous to the war, Mr. Allen voted with the Democratic party. After the war, he became a Republican and acted with that organization. In the year 1870, he was elected to the state senate from the sixteenth senatorial district. In the senate, he assumed a position as one of the leading spirits and representative men of that body. He was known as an effective orator, was always at his post, attentive to local and state interests, and watched with a careful eye and keen perceptive faculties with every movement on the political chessboard. He was chairman of the Penitentiary Committee and served his district and the state with honor. The service record he set in the legislature made him widely known throughout the state, and on the assembling of the Republican State Convention in the summer of 1876, his name was vigorously urged as a candidate for lieutenant governor as the strongest that could be placed on the ticket. He was nominated on the first ballot, and almost without opposition. His election was not expected. To overcome the heavy Democratic majority was more than could be hoped for, but with Mr. Finkelburg, the candidate for governor, he made a flattering canvass of the state. He has been a member of the city council of Carthage in whose welfare and prosperity he has taken a deep interest.

He was married in 1854, in Asbury, Illinois, to Harriet E. Bates. He was a member of the Masons, headed the exploration party for the Carthage cave, prepared legislative papers for incorporation of Carthage, March 7, 1873, and was a mining landowner in Carterville.

In 1882, Colonel C. C. Allen of Carthage offered a handsome gold medal to be contested for by the young men of Southwest Missouri. The first contest was, from a literary standpoint, a complete success, as it brought to Carthage a number of young men who were the best debaters of their respective towns. A. L. Sherman, a law student in the office of L. P. Cunningham in Joplin, won the medal at the first contest. In 1884, the medal was again contested, but in 1885, on account of the lack of interest, the offer was withdrawn.

In 1884, Carterville's company of military cadets, organized by Reverend R. J. Downing, began to be recognized for their ability at precision drill, and they were enrolled in the Company F, Fifth Missouri State Guard Infantry, under the command of Colonel C. C. Allen of Carthage.

The question has often been asked about the naming a busy street, Allen Street in Webb City. There have been a few citizens in the history of Webb City who would have fit the definition of being honorable enough to have a street named in their honor. But after quite a bit of research, Charles C. Allen seemed to step ahead of the others, as he kept himself involved in the happenings and the history-making of Webb City. Friends with John C. Webb and interested in the mining of the area alongside Webb, Allen placed himself in line for the honor of having a street name Allen Street. Alas in the year 1921, Webb City officials made the decision to change the name of Allen Street to Main Street. Webb City's Main Street became Broadway Street. Allen Street was no longer in existence, and the fame of C. C. Allen went by the wayside in Webb City.

Allen, Edward David

Ed Allen was born in 1873. He was a real estate dealer for forty-three years and a resident of Webb City for sixty years before he passed away in January of 1951. His office was located at 113 East Daugherty, and he lived upstairs.

Ed had four sons: Cleo Allen, N. R. Allen, Paul I. Allen, and Fred Allen, and one daughter, Mrs. Paul Russell. He had three sisters: Mrs. Terris Sloan, Mrs. Cordelia Marchall, and Mrs. C. A. Armstrong, and two brothers, Robert Allen and Amos Allen.

Ed Allen was a colorful character in Webb City's hall of history.

His grandson Dave Allen shared some of Ed's activities. He claimed that his grandfather Ed "almost tipped over the family tree." Ed had been blessed with six wives and was engaged at the time of his death at seventy-eight years of age. He had twenty-six children and ten stepchildren.

Ed's father was David Crockett Allen, a Scotch Irish immigrant who worked the Illinois coal mines before moving to Webb City and continuing his mining career in the lead mines. David Crockett Allen had eleven children, with six of them listed above.

Ed's grandson Dave Allen claims that Allen Street (now Main Street) was named in honor of David Crockett Allen. This is a controversial subject, as it is not stated in any Webb City history for whom Allen Street was named.

Back to Ed Allen; he worked in the lead mines also but soon discovered that it was much easier, not to mention more profitable, to own land and let others work the mines. Being naturally frugal and having a discerning eye, Ed went into the real estate business full-time.

Ed served the city well as a long-time Realtor and justice of the peace. Being cautious in spending money but always ready for a good investment kept Ed with a cash flow. During the Great Depression, Ed was one of the enviable few who had cash on hand. Folks would come to his office when they were at risk of losing their homes. They would put their house on the market, and within an hour, Ed would have purchased the home and then offered the seller a chance to rent the house they had just sold. Of course, Ed was a shrewd businessman, and he purchased those houses at 50–75 percent of their value. But the seller had money in his pocket and a place to live at a discount rate with head held high to make it through some pretty rough times. Some folks were thankful, but others were resentful, but Ed felt he had helped. Many who refused to go to Ed for help usually lost their home to tax sales and then would search out Ed to rent a house. Most renters were given the option to apply a portion of their rent toward the purchase of the property with interest. Ed was seeking a profit, but he was not out for blood, according to his grandson Dave Allen.

Ed eventually owned so much property that he put some unfortunates to work. He started a work crew of about twenty or thirty men to maintain his rental property. He continued to be frugal in his expenses, so repairs were often made with stucco, hence his nickname, the Stucco King.

One of the odd things about Ed was his distrust in banks due to the crash of '29. Dave said that when Ed died in 1951, they found cloth sacks full of silver dollars hidden in the walls, behind the bed, in the office, and in the warehouse, some hanging from ropes. It took several wheelbarrows and a couple of hours to cart the bags of money to the Merchants and Miners Bank to be counted and deposited. The money was placed in escrow until the estate was settled. Along with the bags of silver, the family also discovered worthless mining stocks for mining explorations in the tristate area: New Mexico, Colorado, Arizona, and Utah.

What looked like quite a valuable inheritance was diminished tremendously after the settlement with eight ex-wives and twenty-six children

Anderson, A. G. and Lillian—Centenarian

It's a beautiful Sunday morning in the early 1960s. The sun was shining, and the birds were singing as the morning dew shone upon the grass. Down the road was a familiar sight of "Gus" Anderson strolling along on his way to church at the Pleasant Hill United Methodist Church. The two-mile trek was made more enjoyable as he was joined along the way by several children who had waited for Uncle Gus to walk with him.

This seemed like such an ordinary feat, except the most important factor was that Gus was almost one hundred years old. Born in Atorp, Sweden, on November 24, 1863, A. G. "Gus" Anderson came alone to the United States in 1879 at the age of sixteen. After living in Brooklyn a very short time, Gus came to Jasper County, Missouri.

As usual, in that time period, Gus worked in the lead and zinc mines. Determined not to work the mines for the rest of his life, Gus saved every penny he could. Finally, in a dream come true, Gus was able to purchase four hundred acres of land in the Twin Grove Community, in Jasper County.

In 1888, Gus married Lillian Olson. They built a two-story-frame residence on the four hundred acres and raised their two children, Floyd and Lillian. Lillian came to America with her parents in 1869. Her father was a section hand and followed the Frisco Railroad as it extended its line from St. Louis to Seneca, Missouri. He left the Frisco Railroad Company at Seneca and settled on a farm in Twin Grove's established Swedish community.

Gus was a successful businessman and served as the director of the Citizens Bank of Carl Junction. And Gus was very active in his church, serving as lay leader, superintendent, teacher, and trustee.

One of Gus's many accomplishments was his natural ability to preach. On the spur of the moment, Gus could be relied upon to offer a speech. Many times, he would offer the prayer in his native Swedish tongue.

On the twenty-fourth of November 1963, Gus celebrated his one hundredth birthday with his many friends. He was awarded a certificate—Together Magazine Century Club—by the Methodist Church.

Gus died the following year on June 10, 1964. Gone but not forgotten. Many a child will remember walking to church with Uncle Gus, and many will remember that his long life was attributed to leading a Christian life, his kindness, and his understanding, according to his daughter-in-law Marie.

Anderson, John

John Anderson was one of the first mercantile merchants in Webb City, building his business in 1877. John was born in Schalveg, Germany, on October 3, 1841, to C. and E. Anderson. Coming to America in 1865, at the age of twenty-four, made Indiana his first location, and he learned the art of shoemaking. One year later, he moved to Kansas City and two years later moved to Parson, Kansas, where he continued to make shoes for eleven years. He heard of the building of the new town of Webb City and decided to get in early on the development, so he moved and started a mercantile business. On December 18, 1881, he married Ms. Anna Cook. Mr. Anderson was a member of the IOOF (Oddfellows Lodge), the Good Templars, and a member of the Congregational Church.

Ashcraft, Granville "Grant" P.

A pioneer is someone who goes before, preparing the way for others. Pioneer is also defined as being one of the firsts of its kind. Well, both of those definitions fit the description of Granville P. Ashcraft. His pattern in life seemed to be that he was always the first to do something.

Granville, or Grant as he became known, was born December 13, 1842, in Cass County, Missouri, to Eli and Abigail (Plummer) Ashcraft of Kentucky. They were pioneers of a portion of Bates County, which later became Cass County, Missouri, as of 1836. They had moved to an area still inhabited by the Indians and wild animals.

Living in the wilderness as they did, Grant didn't receive a formal education. He began work at an early age at a sawmill. He drove the horses, which furnished the power to the mill. He earned only $10 a month, and he saw no chance for advancement, so after four months, he quit. With the money he made, he bought a suit of clothes from a store in a neighboring town. His was the first suit of ready-made clothing worn in that part of Missouri. This gave Grant a prominence in the neighborhood that was pleasing to him. Thus it became his desire to be first at many accomplishments throughout his life. His mother had died when he was two years old, and his father died when Grant was fourteen. His education consisted of attending a small country school during the winter months for a few years.

At the tender age of seventeen, Grant made a trip to California over the Santa Fe Trail. The journey took over five months, meeting danger and hardship along the way. While in Stockton, California, Grant hardly gave himself but a few hours rest before he went to work as a painter. But an adventurer such as Grant could not live that close to the California Gold Fever without catching it himself. He went to work for Mr. Fair and Mr. Mackey and became one of the four men who dug the first shaft on the famous Comstock Lode, which made millionaires of the men for whom he was working.

Five years later, Grant headed back to Missouri after a visit from his brother Sam. He got sidetracked along the way in Denver, Colorado, and did a little successful mining. But the longing for home overpowered the need to continue his mining. He had stayed in Colorado for eight years (quite a detour) on his trip back home. It was 1872 when Grant arrived in Joplin, which, at the time, was a small developing community of only a few houses and businesses.

Almost immediately upon arriving in the area, Grant got the mining fever again. He originally bought into what was later known as the Oronogo Circle Mines for $1,500 but got mad about a deal he was involved in, sold the investment for $50, and left Oronogo for what was later named Webb City. He remained here until his death in 1911. Ashcraft bought many mines and, at his death, was one of the largest property owners of the area.

Grant leased some of the mining land belonging to John C. Webb and was the first to bring in lead from the Webb City mines. The first week alone, he took out fifteen thousand pounds. He was also the first to ship ore out of the area. In 1874, Grant married Theressa Belle Baker, a native of Springfield, Illinois. They were the parents of three children: Bernice Ashcraft (who married Earl Bunch); another daughter, Mae Ashcraft (1877–1946), who married Allen Hardy Jr.; and a son, Eli Ashcraft. Bernice was the first child born in the new town of Webb City. Theressa Belle Ashcraft died January 18, 1929, at the age of seventy-two. She moved to Culver City, Colorado, to be with her daughter after Grant's death.

Upon arriving in the area of the Webb mines, the only thing in sight was John C. Webb's log cabin. Ashcraft bought some land from Webb and built the first frame house on a city block area that was surrounded by Pennsylvania Street, Daugherty Street, Ball Street, and John Street (later known as Austin Street). His house faced Pennsylvania. Later he built additional houses on the land. Land was important to Ashcraft, and he kept adding land to his assets. He purchased 260 acres west of Webb City. When the mines paid off, Ashcraft purchased more land and eventually owned more than 4,000 acres of mining land and agricultural land in Jasper County.

Grant may have been first in a lot of his achievements, but he was definitely first in the eyes of the citizens of Webb City. His death on July 24, 1911, was deeply mourned. The statement was made that it was the death of "*one of the most prominent and highly honored of the citizens of Webb City and Southern Missouri.*" Theressa Ashcraft died in 1929, at the age of seventy-two.

Granville was named after a childhood neighbor, Granville Swift, who later gave Grant a place to live in California on the Swift Ranch where Granville Ashcraft learned about horses, which became a major hobby throughout his lifetime. Sam Ashcraft once said, "Grant knew a good horse as well as any man in Jasper County, perhaps, and no end of stories could be told of his venturesome and daredevil exploits. One day, in the early days of the old 'red plan,' a Frisco train was passing when he was on his way to Webb City. He made a bet with the man who was riding with him that he could beat the train to town. No doubt, he did his best to win the bet, as was shown by the fact that in his mad race, he killed a cow on the roadway and had to pay the owner for the loss of the animal, besides getting unmercifully joshed by his friends for years afterward."

Samuel Ashcraft, Grant's brother, made the comment that Grant always backed his own judgment, rarely told anyone what he intended to do in business matters, and never asked advice of anybody. He was a hard man to persuade into anything, but once he gave his word, everyone knew he could be relied upon to do just what he said.

While in California, Ashcraft developed a love of horses and acquired quite a bit of knowledge on the subject. That became Grant's favorite hobby throughout his life. Many came to Grant for advice about horses.

Ashcraft's daughter Bernice was the first child born in the new town of Webb City. And Ashcraft purchased the first automobile in Webb City. His list of firsts continued throughout his life, but when he passed away on July 24, 1911, it was obvious that Grant Ashcraft held the position of being first in the eyes of the citizens of Webb City. As was the custom, Grant's funeral was in his home on Pennsylvania Street.

Granville "Grant" Ashcraft wandered into the area that would eventually be named Webb City and made it his home. He became a legend in the history of Webb City. He was definitely a Webb City forefather worth remembering.

Grant's wife, Theressa Belle Ashcraft, went out to Culver City, Colorado, to live with her daughter after Grant's death. She died of a heart attack on January 18, 1929, at the age of seventy-two.

G. P. Ashcraft's home on the northwest corner of Pennsylvania and Daugherty Streets.

Ashcraft, Leander Leon "Lon"

Lon Ashcraft came to this area from Iowa with his parents in 1875 at the age of three. He was born in 1867. Lon was a loyal member of the community, and he kept involved. He married Carrie L., and they did not have any children, but he was devoted to his five nephews and one niece. Lon and Carrie lived in a beautiful home at 222 South Pennsylvania. Lon served two terms as county clerk, from 1902–1910. He was Carthage postmaster from 1922–1926. He served six years as deputy sheriff under L. M. Thomas. He was vice president of the Jasper County Title Company at the time of his death in 1936, from a liver disorder. Lon and Carrie were members of the Webb City Presbyterian Church, and Lon was a member of the York Rite and Scottish Rite Masonic Bodies.

Attended Drury College studying law. Elected county clerk for two terms, 1902–1910. Served as Republican Party chairman. Served as Carthage postmaster, 1922–1927. Married Carrie Overstreet in 1897. Lived in Carthage while in politics. Moved to Webb City after that and lived at 222 South Pennsylvania. In charge of and vice president of the Jasper County Title Co., Mason, Shriner, Scottish Rites, First Presbyterian Church. Lon and Carrie lived at 123 North Ball when first married.

Lon passed away in May 1936, in his home at 222 South Pennsylvania, and his funeral service was at home also.

In his will, Lon left everything to his wife, Carrie, except his fishing tackle, which he left to his best friend, A. E. Spencer Jr., and $1,000 to a friend, Mrs. Cecil Marr.

**Lon L. Ashcraft, in a speech given on April 2, 1931, recalled his memories as a small lad in the early days of Webb City. He said his family arrived here in 1875 when Lon was just a boy. His father was one of the original town trustees. He recalled them burning the entire prairie in the fall of 1875 as they prepared to lay out the town of Webbville. Ashcraft recalled in later years, a Carterville gang raided Webb City as a way of seeking revenge for one of the gang members being confined in jail the night before. A merchant was killed during the raid. The city jail was burned, and Ashcraft added that one man's mustache was shot from his face.

Ashcraft, Samuel P., Sr. (1837–1933)

Sam Ashcraft was devoted to his brother, Granville "Grant" Ashcraft, in whom he dedicated his life to watch over and protect. He lived at 216 North Ball with his wife, Mary Margaret Worsham Ashcraft, just a block west of Grant. Mary was born in Kentucky in 1857, and her father was Judge Worsham of Lexington, Kentucky. Sam and Mary had three children and their son Samuel Ashcraft Jr. was a Joplin city engineer. Mary died March 15, 1928, and her services were at the home, and she was buried in Mount Hope Cemetery, alongside Sam. She was a member of the United Daughters of the Confederacy.

Ashcraft, W. A.—On the First Board of Trustees of Webb City, 1876

W. A. was a cousin to Granville Ashcraft. W. A. was married to Emily, and they had four children: Norris, William, Mary, and Leon (Lon [information on Leon listed above]). The family moved to

Jasper County. W. A.'s grandson Edward M. Flournoy served as marshal in 1884. Mary Ashcraft graduated in 1894 from Webb City High School.

W. A.'s wife, Emily Ashcraft, was tending to a calf on September 9, 1886, when she fell and broke her hip. The doctor calmed her down as best he could and left, but Emily was still agitated and couldn't rest. Sadly she died three days later, on September 12, 1886. W. A. would live for another twenty-two years, passing away in September 1908.

Aul, William Henry

William Henry Aul was born in Pennsylvania, July 7, 1864. At the age of eighteen, young Aul made the journey from Pennsylvania to the booming tristate mining fields in Southwest Missouri to make his fortune. He helped to develop the Webb City-Carterville-Oronogo Fields. He eventually opened his own company, the W. H. Mining Company.

In 1888, W. H. married Ms. Martha Francis Vaughn in Webb City. They purchased a home at 325 South Oronogo, just across the street east from the two-story Eugene Field Schoolhouse, which was located on the northwest corner of Oronogo and Fourth Street.

The Auls had two daughters, Lula (May) and Murl E. The town of Webb City didn't hold fond memories for the Aul family. In 1908, their sixteen-year-old May Aul committed suicide across the street, in the Eugene Field School outhouse, by shooting herself in the chest and running home to fall at her mother's feet on their front porch.

At her sister's dying request, Murl Aul went on to marry her sweetheart, Loraine E. Johnson. The invitations had been sent out two weeks previously. After lingering for fifty-six hours, May passed away during the wedding ceremony, but Murl was not told of her sister's demise until after the wedding.

The Auls eventually bought a home in Joplin, at 101 South Conner, and both lived to be in their late seventies.

Aylor, Joseph W.

Joseph Wheeler Aylor left quite an impression in Webb City with his unusual home on the southwest corner of Webb and Daugherty Streets. Born in Rappahannock County, Virginia, September 29, 1839, to Stanton Aylor and Malinda Quaintance Aylor, Joseph was one of fourteen children.

Having been to school for only two months and nineteen days in his entire lifetime, Joseph became smart in business through actual experience and keeping a cool head about him. His word was as good as a bond.

In 1859, at the age of twenty, young Joseph ventured west to the new territory of Missouri. By 1861, Joseph found himself to be a member of the army with Pindall's battalion of sharpshooters. Under the command of General Parson, who was attached to General Price, Joseph was actively engaged at the battles of Lexington, Pea Ridge, Prairie Grove, Jenkins' Ferry, Arkansas, Pleasant Hill, Louisiana, and numerous other places, serving under the Confederate flag.

In 1865, Joseph Aylor was mustered out with his command in Shreveport, Louisiana. He soon found himself in Texas with only $5 to his name. He invested the $5 in a horse. He groomed, trained, and took good care of the horse as he waited until he could sell the horse for more money. In the meantime, he proposed to and married Ms. C. M. E. Webb on January 21, 1866. Ms. Webb hailed from the state of Texas. With the extra money he made from the sale of the horse, Aylor and his new bride made the trip to Jasper County, Missouri.

Joseph invested the rest of his horse money in purchasing some farmland in Jasper County, and the land was rich in minerals. Aylor built his home on Aylor Hill, as it was called, located east of what is now Mount Hope Cemetery. Going into partnership with Andrew McCorkle, the two men bought as much land as they could and mined a good portion of the land. Both became quite wealthy, as they began mining as early as 1869 in neighboring towns.

Joseph Aylor, being wealthy, was a very paranoid person. He built a grand three-story brick home on the southwest corner of Webb Street and Daugherty Street, adding precautions for protection. He was concerned that someone would kidnap him for his money. When he built his new home, he put a beautiful etched glass window on the second floor that allowed him to view who was at the door when the maid answered. He felt confident that if it were someone up to no good, he could make a hasty retreat before they were even in the door.

In the basement of his home, Joseph Aylor had a tunnel that went south to the John C. Webb home, which was right next-door. It's been said that the tunnel was often used for the young ladies as they traveled from one house to next without worry of messing up their clothes or hair. It also served as a hasty retreat for Aylor if he felt threatened in any way. He could go down the back stairway of his home to the basement and through the tunnel to Webb's house. Aylor also kept a safe under the stairway of his home to keep his personal papers and spend cash safely out of harm's way.

As Aylor's wealth continued to grow, he invested in more land and built a beautiful home in Carthage and a million-dollar estate in Kansas City. He let his daughter and her husband, S. Nilson, live in the Aylor home on Webb Street, and he lived mostly in the Carthage home, which he loved. His son, Ben, had a tendency to live in the Kansas City mansion.

One day, in 1912, as Aylor was taking care of his garden in Carthage, he had a seizure and landed in the fire he was tending. He wasn't badly burned, but he had inhaled smoke and flames to the extent that his health was greatly impaired. He died in Kansas City in 1917, leaving his wife, Blanche, and two adult children to mourn his death.

At the time of his death, he owned the Webb City home, the Carthage home, the Kansas City estate home, two thousand acres of land in Jasper County, and twenty-nine sections of land in Texas. His net worth at the time of his death was estimated to be over $2.5 million. Just imagine, he started out with $5 after the Civil War.

The Aylor home, southwest corner of Webb and Daugherty
Streets. The second brick home in Webb City.

Aylor, Ben

Son of Joseph Aylor, was born in the year 1870. Ben was on the board of directors for the Merchant
& Miners Bank (1905). Ben died January 31, 1941, at the Aylor estate in Kansas City. Ben had two
daughters, Margaret Aylor and Mrs. Ivan Chadwell.

Ben had a good life and a rough life. He was a credited citizen of Webb City and dealt in banking (former director of the Merchant & Miners Bank) and real estate. He lived in the family home
at 128 North Webb and the family mansion in Kansas City.

In 1932, when Ben was sixty-two years old, he was mixed up in some bad business in Kansas
City. He had purchased, in 1923, the Rochambeau Hotel at 3736 Broadway in Kansas City for
$185,000. By 1932, the hotel was empty and not bringing in any money. Aylor had insured the
empty building for $90,000.

Hugh E. Thompson, a real estate salesman, had approached Aylor about burning down the
hotel. Aylor said he didn't want anything to do with such a scheme. Well, Thompson did it anyway.
He hired Charles P. Mueller to torch the building with the understanding that he would not get
paid till the insurance paid the claim. Then Thompson threatened Aylor, and he paid Thompson
$12,000 of the $79,000 he had settled with the insurance company.

Thompson got greedy and decided to blackmail Aylor. When Aylor wouldn't pay up, Thompson
threatened to kidnap Aylor's daughter. Aylor went to a friend for advice, and the friend told the

police. So on April 14, 1934, two years after the fire, Ben Aylor and Hugh E. Thompson were both arrested. Charles Mueller was able to evade the police. He was also being sought for the robbery of the First National Bank of Leavenworth, Kansas, in April 1932.

Ben C. Aylor passed away on January 31, 1941, at the age of seventy.

Bacon, David E.

David Bacon was born in Dayton, Ohio, February 22, 1848, to Thomas and Nellie McCarty Bacon. Thomas was from Pennsylvania, and Nellie hailed from Ohio. They were married in Ohio but moved to Sangamon, Illinois, in 1852 where David was raised.

The family moved to Missouri in 1867, settling in Polk County, making their final move to Joplin in 1879. David tried his hand at mining for several years and was quite successful. But in 1882, he made the decision to open a grocery store in Webb City and found his niche in life. David became one of the important businessmen of Webb City that kept the town going.

David died in Wichita. He had three children: two daughters, Mrs. George Magruder, Mrs. Carl Cushman; and one son, Charles D. Bacon, who died in 1936.

Ball, George Washington

During Webb City's mining era, many men lost what little money they had saved and wound up with only sore hands and aching backs. But there were some that struck it rich. Many times, the deciding factor in making it or breaking it was simple common sense. One such story of common sense was about a young man named George W. Ball.

The beautiful Ball home, at 804 West Daugherty, has a wonderful history, as it reflects the amazing rags-to-riches story of George W. Ball. At the tender age of sixteen, George W. Ball came to Webb City in search of a job. He was barefoot, penniless, and full of dreams. It didn't take long for this young man to find employment. They put him to work in one of the large mines north of Webb City. George was a strong husky boy, and he did a good job each day as he earned his $2. Occasionally the mines would fill in with "devil water," and work would be cut back as they tried to pump out the water and get the mine back in working order. The miners were out of work during this time, and it put quite a strain on the mine owners. If it happened too often, the mine owners would just shut the mine down, sell it, or just close it up as a loss.

That is exactly what happened to the mine where George was working. The mine owners had been keeping their eye on George because he showed a lot of promise and seemed to be long on horse sense. So they made him a proposition. They offered him the mine on a royalty basis; he would be an owner instead of a worker. This did interest George, but that horse sense he was noted for jumped in and told them he should think it over before jumping in headfirst. In the meantime, George went down into the mine and searched to find where that devil water was getting in.

George found a large crevice in the rock bed of Muddy Creek. He ordered loads of baled hay and stuffed them into the crevice. He then poured a thick layer of concrete over the hay. He then leased the mine from the owners. The next time that Muddy Creek filled to the edge, George's mine stayed dry, money came in, and George became quite wealthy.

George went into partnership with A. D. Hatten, which was another smart move on his part, as everything Hatten touched seemed to turn to gold!

George married Martha in 1879. They had seven children: Walter Claude (wife Ethel), Jack W., George Bryon, Charles J., Grace (Morton), Ethel (Chenoweth), and Mary (Quigg, Bradley), Fant (wife Katherine Sutton).

George died March 19, 1928. The entire town was shut down in honor of George during his funeral.

Ball, Walter Claude

Walter, born February 16, 1880, followed in his father's footsteps (George W. Ball) and went into the mining business. Not to monopolize his money or time, Walter ventured into other fields. One of his major businesses in Webb City was when he went into partnership with W. S. Gunning and the Boyd & Gunning Mill on Madison became the Ball & Gunning Milling Company.

Not to be too far from his family, Walter and his wife, Ethel (Peggy) Deane Ball, built a beautiful home on the southwest corner of First and Washington. It was noted as the first and only home in Webb City to have an elevator.

Walter died August 1940, at the age of sixty. He was a member of the Presbyterian Church, serving on the board of trustees. He was a member of the Webb City Rotary Club, Charter Member of the Elks Lodge 861, and also served on the school board and the board of trustee for the Jane Chinn Hospital.

Walter and his dad were both active in the community. It was noted that when George passed away in 1928, the entire town shut down during the funeral.

Home of Walter Ball, 804 West First Street. First home in Webb City with an elevator.

Barbee, Frederick H.

Hailing from the state of Illinois, Frederick was born in Gifford, Champaign County, Illinois, on March 25, 1877. His father, Ira Alvah Barbee, was born in Kentucky, being of French descent. Frederick's mother was Rhoda Matilda Knight, coming from the New England area, was proud of her early heritage in the Land of Stars and Stripes. Alvah and Rhoda were married in 1868 and had three sons and five daughters. Three of their children died in infancy. After residing in Illinois for a number of years, they moved to Kansas in the 1880s before moving to Webb City, Missouri. Alvah passed away April 21, 1898, and Rhoda lived until July 17, 1910.

Frederick attended his first years of education in the rural schools of Cherokee County, Kansas. Moving to Webb City put Frederick in the public school system, graduating from the Webb City High School. Claiming teaching as his career, Frederick started his teaching in the blackberry district of Jasper County, 1895. He left his rural school position for a teaching job at a grade school in Galena, Kansas, 1898. Fred advanced into high school teaching and moving on to becoming principal of the Galena High School.

His experience as principal brought him back to Webb City to serve as the principal of the high school in 1904. Nevada, Missouri, lured Frederick in their direction as principal until 1910, when Joplin offered Professor Frederick Barbee the head position of their high school.

Frederick was united in marriage on November 27, 1901, in Webb City, to Clara Narcissus Long, daughter of W. J. Long, a prominent citizen of Webb City, living at 314 Ball. Clara was a teacher for

153

Webb City. Her brother G. A. Long was active in business and involved in the Independent Order of Odd Fellows. Frederick and Clara had one son, Frederick Herbert Barbee.

Frederick came from a family of musicians. He hailed as a Republican for national elections but locally gave his support to the man he felt superior in measures. He was a member of the Odd Fellows, Knights of Pythias, Niangua Club of Joplin, and the Commercial Club. He was a member of the First Christian Church, of which he served as an elder and superintendent of the Sunday school.

Barclay, Samuel S.

Barclay was a born Missourian, having been born February 2, 1845, in Dallas County, Missouri, to Daniel and Jane E. Barclay. Daniel Barclay hailed from Alabama and was one of the early settlers of Polk County, Missouri.

At the age of seventeen (1862), young Samuel entered the Eighth Missouri State Militia, under Colonel McClurg, and served throughout the Civil War, mostly in Missouri.

Following the war, Samuel married Ms. Martha S. Michael of Newton County, Missouri. He served as the marshal of Granby, Missouri, from 1875–1876. Moving to Webb City, Missouri, Samuel Barclay was elected marshal of Webb City in April 1882. Samuel and Martha had three children: Charles W., William W., and F. D. Barclay.

Barnes, Henry

Henry Barnes moved to Webb City in February 1876, becoming one of the first wonderful merchants and businessmen of Webb City when he purchased the City Restaurant with his wife, Mary Wheeler Barnes, a native of North Carolina. They were married in August of 1871.

Hailing from DeWitt County, Illinois, Barnes was born June 26, 1836, to George and Rebecca Barnes. His parents had settled in Illinois after moving from Ohio, where they were one of the early settlers.

In 1869, at the age of thirty-three, Henry moved to Burton County, Missouri, where he practiced his trade of carpentry and farming. In February 1876, he journeyed to the newly incorporated Webb City, where he purchased the City Restaurant and was one of the major contributors to the success of the new town.

Barnes, James

Young James Barnes worked in the Sunflower mine, north of Carterville. On a Thursday in 1911, twenty-three-year-old James had a rough night when he dreamed a boulder fell down a shaft and hit him in the head. The dream was so vivid that James mentioned it to his wife and a friend at work the next morning.

Later on that day, James, who normally worked as a shoveler, was told to work the tub hooker's place. A little while later, a bucket fell down the shaft, just missing James. He laughingly remarked, "Well, that's the end of my dream!" At 2:55 p.m., a boulder fell from the tub that James was working with and struck him on the head, ending his life, just as he had dreamed the night before.

Barnes, Jesse M., Dr. (Ophthalmology) 1871–1955

Dr. Jesse M. Barnes was a man of distinction in our area. At the time of his death in 1955, Dr. Barnes had the oldest license of ophthalmology in operation. He had opened his first office in Carthage in 1902.

Jesse M. Barnes was born December 26, 1871, in Poplar Bluff, Missouri, to Mr. and Mrs. John Barnes. They were a fairly normal family; one son, Jesse, and one daughter, Laura.

Jesse graduated from Zock College of Ophthalmology, Topeka, Kansas, in 1898 at the age of twenty-seven. It is a wonder of how Jesse chose this college, or did the college choose him? It was quite a ways from his hometown. Then after graduation, he settled in Carthage, and after a bit of working for someone else, he opened his first office in 1902. His business in Carthage was in existence from 1902–1926.

Dr. Barnes, seeking a new adventure, in 1926, at the age of fifty-five, opened two offices: one in Webb City and the other in Joplin. He worked out of those two offices from 1926–1941. He lived out by the Jasper County TB Hospital (now Webb City Rehabilitation). Taking a more leisurely look at his career, at the age of seventy-one, Dr. Barnes closed both of his offices and began practicing from his home. The change did not seem to discourage his patients as his business continued to flourish.

At the close of World War II, at the age of seventy-three, Dr. Barnes purchased a landmark in Webb City. He bought the E. T. Webb home at Four South Liberty. He and his wife, M. Viney, proceeded to take up residence in the Webb house, and he established his office in the home as well. This office was in operation from 1945–1953, when Dr. Barnes retired at the age of eighty-one. But he kept his license active, so when he passed away in 1955, he had the oldest active ophthalmology license.

Dr. Jesse Barnes had another secret passion in his life besides working—he loved to write. He centered on writing religious books.

Dr. Barnes and his wife had one daughter, Mary.

E. T. Webb home. Dr. Barnes had his office in this home from 1945–1953.

Bates, Judge Sardius

To be able to claim patriotic ancestry is quite an honor. One such gentleman in our local history not only claimed that honor but also added to it.

During the Revolutionary War, Andrew Bates, who had come from England, fought for independence.

His son, Adam, married Elizabeth Metcalf of Irish descent, and they settled in Sandusky, Ohio, where their son, William H. Bates, was born. William fought in the Civil War, serving with the Seventy-Second Ohio Volunteer Infantry. He served under General Sherman and Colonel Bucklan in such famous battles as Shiloh, Vicksburg, and Corinth. William settled in Rising Sun, Wood County, Ohio, and married Mary Inman, whose ancestry was also of revolutionary stock. Her family had served in the Revolutionary War and the War of 1812. Her mother's brother, Captain William Jennings, served under General W. T. Scott in the Mexican War.

A son, Sardius W. Bates, was born to Mary and William. The only boy in a family of three girls—Zela, Estella, and Leila—Sardius was born in 1876 and proved to be an avid learner. After finishing school, Sardius spent two years as a teacher. Deciding to continue his education, he attended Heidelberg University in Tiffin, Ohio.

The Spanish-American War interrupted his plans, as Sardius enlisted in the Second Ohio Volunteer Infantry. He was stationed in Chickamauga, Georgia; Knoxville, Tennessee; and Macon, Georgia.

In 1905, at the age of twenty-nine, Sardius took a collegiate course and received a degree at Otterbein University in Westerville, Ohio. In the fall of 1905, Sardius made the decision of a lifetime as he started studying law at the Ohio State University, moving to the University of Missouri in Columbia, and graduating with his law degree in 1907.

In 1908, at the age of thirty-two, Sardius located in Webb City and began his practice with L. E. Bates (unable to determine if L. E. was related or not). Later Sardius went into business with Mr. Robertson and then with R. T. Abernathy.

The lovebug hit in 1909, and Sardius married Georgie A. Jones Collier. He also settled down with a law partnership with Judge Robertson. Life took on quite a hectic but rewarding pace.

In 1910, Sardius Bates became the city attorney. In 1912, at the age of thirty-five, he was elected as prosecuting attorney under the Democratic ticket, getting re-elected in 1914. Then in 1916, he received the honor of being selected to serve a one-year term in the Missouri Senate to replace the late Colonel C. H. Phelps.

World War I interrupted any of Sardius's plans as every able body enlisted. Having served in the Spanish-American War, Sardius was sent to Officer Training School in Fort Riley, Kansas, and commissioned a captain in the depot brigade. He later advanced to the rank of major with the Tenth Division and went overseas.

Returning home to his law practice, Sardius still had the desire to serve politically and ran for judge of Circuit Court Division 1 in 1922. He won the election and served as judge until 1929.

In 1932, at the age of fifty-five, Sardius ran for a position on the Missouri Supreme Court, but he was defeated.

Under his belt of accomplishments, Sardius served as chairman of the State Bar Committee of the Twenty-Fifth Judicial Circuit. He was also credited with having been largely instrumental in the success of organizing the central drainage district of Webb City. With the help of the government, mining fields in Webb City, Carterville, and Oronogo were drained to resume mining. Sardius spent almost five months in Washington, DC, working on this project.

In 1936, while Georgie was out of town, Sardius became ill. He left his office and went home to rest. Dr. George W. Sanz stayed with Sardius throughout the night, and by morning, he seemed greatly improved, so the doctor left to attend to other business.

An hour later, Judge Bates called his best friend, C. W. Oldham Jr., and requested that he go see him. When Oldham arrived, the judge seemed to be resting comfortably, and they conversed a few minutes. Suddenly the judge had a severe heart attack and went unconscious. At the age of fifty-nine, with a long list of accomplishments, Judge Sardius W. Bates passed away, another face etched into our monument of Webb City history.

Beckman, Martin

Owner of Beckman Grocery on West Daugherty Street. Lived at 816 West Second Street. He and his wife were married in 1895.

Bowman, J. A.

Jacob Andrew Bowman was in the lumber business. He moved to this area from Centralia, Kansas, where he was the manager of a lumberyard. After arriving in Webb City, Bowman started the Burgner-Bowman Lumber Company in 1903, with J. M. Burgner, the son-in-law of founder J. C. Webb.

In a fast-growing town like Webb City, there were many lumberyards. And many of the lumberyards changed hands through the years. The location of the Burgner-Bowman Lumber Yard was 401–408 East Broadway. That was an active lumberyard, as it changed names starting with the Stewart Lumber Yard in 1877, which was owned by brothers Joseph Stewart and W. C. Stewart, organized when Webb City was only one year old.

The Burgner-Bowman Lumber Company moved their general office to Kansas City, so the lumber company had two locations. Eventually the Bowman family moved to Kansas City where J. A. Bowman died in December 12, 1951.

Brenneman, Samuel S.

Samuel S. Brenneman was born December 2, 1846 in Rockingham County, Virginia. When he was twenty-one, he moved to Jasper County with his parents in the fall of 1867. In June of 1879, Samuel married the lovely Ms. Kate Haycroft.

Some people have a green thumb when it comes to raising fruits and vegetables, and I guess this couple must have had green hands. Everything they attempted to grow would blossom beyond compare. Samuel and Kate had a 120-acre farm, considered to be located in the country, and located between Fourth and Fifth Streets, including and north of what is now MacArthur Boulevard. They grew fruit and vegetables to sell in town. According to the *1883 History of Jasper County*, he sold as many as two thousand quarts of blackberries in one year. He had melons, peaches, and apples. He would net about five hundred bushels of apples and one hundred bushels of peaches from his orchards.

Along with fruits and vegetables, the farm also consisted of a dairy of twelve cows. Now this area was Kate's expertise. She handled the dairy farm. She would yield about forty pounds of butter each week, which she molded and sold for the highest market price. Kate enjoyed the care and feeding of the dairy cattle.

With Samuel doing so well with the agriculture, and Kate doing so well with the dairy, it was only common business sense that allowed them to pay off the farm. Samuel decided to set up a florist and greenhouse in town. Located at 604 Joplin (Broadway), southwest corner of Roane and Broadway, it was one of the largest in Jasper County. Both locations had their own water tower. Brenneman's Florist went from Broadway and Roane to Broadway and Oronogo Streets and back to First Street. The farm was more wholesale, and the city location was more retail.

Brenneman Florist consisted of seven greenhouses, fifty thousand feet of glass. Along with the florist business here in Webb City, there was also a retail florist business at 408 Main, in Joplin. S. S. Brenneman and his lovely wife, Kate, had a hand for farming and a head for business. After thirty years of hard work and labor of love, they sold the business in 1910 to Julius E. Meinhart. He changed the name from Brenneman's Florist to the Webb City Greenhouse. Although he did put the name Meinhart on the water tower at the farm, replacing the name of Brenneman. Julius and his family lived at 416 South Pennsylvania on the farm area (where the present Park Department barn is located today). Meinhart ran the business for almost twenty years before he passed away in April of 1929, at the age of fifty-eight.

When the new MacArthur Drive came through Webb City, it went right through the greenhouses on the farm, and they were removed. That was the end of the nursery.

Bill Perry II grew up on Fourth Street, just north of the greenhouses, and he recalled that he and some of his friends would gather lead chunks from Sucker Flat, which was just east of Meinhart's greenhouses. They would stand back, about a half-block, and use their slingshots to shoot those chunks of lead into the air, aiming for the greenhouses. He said they loved to hear the glass shatter! As soon as they heard the sound of the glass shattering, he said there wasn't a boy to be found close by; they scattered. He recalled that the highway is where the greenhouses were located off Pennsylvania Street. He also remembered that the greenhouses were not the only targets for these young boys, they also enjoyed shooting out the streetlights that were suspended over the city streets. His quote was, "Several streetlights were brought down without the presence of a single boy."

Burch, Edward M.

A dedicated doctor and one of the founders of the Rotary Club. He served as president at the beginning, from 1917–1919. Burch graduated from Washington University Medical School in St. Louis. He was giving a speech on August 4, 1933, to the Rotary Club, and as soon as he finished his speech, he passed out. His son-in-law, Dr. Emery J. McIntire, tried to revive him, but he passed away. He died doing something that pleased him so much—addressing the Rotary Club.

Burch, William C.

One of the early pioneers to our area was Edward M. Burch. He came here from Virginia and was proud to say he heralded from stanch English stock. Being active in mining, it's no wonder that Edward should come in contact with one of the most eligible young ladies in the district, Ms. Louise J. Daugherty, daughter of W. A. Daugherty. Daugherty was the smart businessman who went into partnership with John C. Webb when the first chunk of lead was unearthed on Webb's land. Then they added Grant Ashcraft to that great venture in mining.

Edward and Louise settled in Carterville, the town that Louise's father had founded. Edward continued his interest in mining and showed an expertise in farming. To this union, four children were born, but I only have information on three: W. C. Burch, Earl A. Burch, and Annie L. Burch Gass.

Annie L. Burch married Frank L. Gass, and they lived a very comfortable life. Frank came to this area from Indiana in 1900, at the age of twenty-eight, but he was only here for a short stay. He left to continue his education, receiving his law degree at the University of Indiana. He must have liked what he saw while visiting here because he returned in 1910 and set up his law office in Carterville. He became Carterville's city attorney, from 1916–1924, and became probate judge in 1922 and continued in that capacity until his death, twelve years later, in 1934, at the age of sixty-one.

Frank and Annie lived at 329 East Main in Carterville. Annie continued to live there after Frank's death, and later, her brother Earl came to live with her.

Earl A. Burch was born in 1873. He was a mine operator, as his father had been, and he also married into a strong mining family. In 1898, at the age of twenty-five, Earl married Bernice Ashcraft, daughter of Grant Ashcraft. Earl dealt in insurance and real estate, but his heart was in mining. Along with his father-in-law, he was an associate with Ashcraft and Burch, in association with Standard Lead & Zinc in Prosperity.

Earl's wife, Bernice, seemed to have been a very strong-willed lady. She was a bookkeeper at the First National Bank of Carterville and known as a lady of knowledge and quite a social leader.

I don't know if the marriage was a success or not because Earl moved in with his sister, Annie, and passed away at Annie's house in 1931, at the age of fifty-one.

Now the oldest son of Edward Burch was William C. Burch. He seemed to have been the child with the head on his shoulders. Born in 1872, in Carterville, William was only nine years old when his father passed away. Leaning on his grandfather for support, William became a bookkeeper in the mining industry for about two years, when he decided to work for his grandfather's bank instead. Starting out as a clerk in the First National Bank of Carterville, William worked his way up to assistant cashier and eventually moved on to become vice president of the Webb City Bank, and on up to be president. That's quite a climb up the ladder. He also started a real estate and insurance office, located at 124 North Webb.

William married in 1907, at the age of thirty-five, to Ms. Jessie Ethel Litteral. Jessie's father was Jacob Litteral, a farmer and miner. He made sure that his daughter was well educated. She had attended Central College in Lexington, Kentucky, and Forest Park University in St. Louis.

William and Jessie settled in a beautiful house in Carterville, located at 410 East Main (the home is still standing and has been well preserved. It was recently the home of Steve Gannaway, but they sold it last month). The Burches did a lot of entertaining in their home, and it was the location of their daughter's wedding. Halycon Anne Burch was married in 1932, to Henry Hook Harris, and the newspaper account of the wedding suggests this was the wedding of the century, with four bridesmaids, four groomsmen, and the works. The yard and home were overflowing with the 150 guests who attended.

Jessie and William also had two other children, Mary Louise Burch, who married William Wilson Waggoner, and W. C. Burch Jr., who married Mary Margaret Davis.

In the *History of Jasper County*, it states that "William C. Burch was one of the best known and enterprising citizens of Carterville. Mr. Burch's individuality and energy have left a permanent impression for welfare and upbuilding of the town."

Some may say that having a well-known grandfather like W. A. Daugherty, the founder of the town you grew up in, might have influenced the progress one makes in life, but I think William succeeded on his own because personality makes a major impact in life also. Just because you are related to someone rich or famous doesn't mean people have to like you, but the people of Carterville respected William. And William did the Burch name proud.

Carney, Fred S.—Doctor

Fred Carney was born February 29, 1892, in Gilman, Iowa. He was a professional singer and a dentist. He moved to Webb City in 1941. He was choir director of the Presbyterian Church. A member of the Webb City Rotary Club, a member of the Southwest Missouri Dental Society. During World War II, he promoted the sale of war bonds. He was married to a professional piano player, Marguerite Carney. Dr. Carney went to Kansas City to court the lovely Marguerite and brought her back to Webb City. She taught piano lessons to many of the youth in town. They are buried in Mount Hope Cemetery.

The original George Hardy home became the home of Dr. and Mrs. Fred Carney in 1941.

Carpenter, John "Seth"

John Carpenter was born July 17, 1842, in Montrose, Iowa. John served in the Civil War. He and his wife, Mahala, moved to Webb City in 1899 and lived at 127 North Roane. They had four sons: Clarence Lonton "Puss" Carpenter, Walter G. Carpenter, Stephen Herbert "Bert" Carpenter, and Jesse A. Carpenter, and one daughter, Maude Irene Carpenter.

John was active in the OP Morton Post 14, GAR, and served as commander at one time. This organization helped promote the observance of Memorial Day and Flag Day. At one time, this organization entertained the famous General Sherman in 1883.

John also belonged to the Last Man's Club (Civil War vet organization). John lived to be eighty-eight years old, passing away in 1930, and his wife, Mahala, lived to be eighty-one, passing the same year as John in 1930. Many Civil War veterans moved to this area after having served in the war and seeing the beauty of the country.

The children lived in the Webb City area, except for Walter who moved to Sheridan, Missouri; St. Joseph, Missouri; and Washington, Missouri. The rest of the children shared a common address of 303 South Ball. Clarence (Puss) was a painter for the Southwest Railroad Company, and before that, he was an interior decorator working in defense plants. He had one daughter Ruth. He died in 1944, at the age of sixty-five. Stephen was a painter, just like Clarence. He had two children, Robert and Mary. Jesse was a driller.

Chenoweth, Lincoln Curtis—Doctor

Born March 20, 1862 in McDonald County, Lincoln, Chenoweth continued a family legacy and became the fourth generation of his family to practice medicine. He graduated from the Missouri State Medical College (later known as the Washington University) in 1887 and started his practice in Pineville, Missouri. One year later, 1888, Dr. Chenoweth and his wife, America Levina (McNatt) Chenoweth moved to Webb City.

His wife, Levina, was born in 1868, in one of the first houses built in Aurora, Missouri, before her family moved to McDonald County where her father built and operated McNatt's Mill and founded the town of McNatt. Levina attended a seminary for girls in Pea Ridge, Arkansas. She married Dr. Lincoln Chenowith on July 10, 1887, just after he graduated from medical school.

In 1905, Dr. Chenoweth established the first hospital in Webb City in the residence of Captain S. O. Hemenway on the northwest corner of First and Webb Streets. A pioneering physician of the boom era of the Webb City mining field, the doctor had a colorful career in administering to miners injured in accidents and explosions.

Later Dr. Chenoweth established a hospital at the Salvation Army building on East Main (Broadway).

The Chinn Family

Chinn, Charles R.—Charles R. Chinn was born August 17, 1833, in Henry County, Kentucky, to W. S. Chinn, whose family had come from Norfolk, Virginia. His grandfather Thomas Chinn was also from Virginia. W. S. traveled west with his family, settling in Missouri where he helped to establish the county of Shelby, which was named in memory of his Kentucky home of Shelbyville. W. S. Chinn became one of the first judges of the county court.

C. R. Chinn was the youngest of ten children. He married August 3, 1853, to Ms. Milissa Sodowski of Kentucky. They were married in Jasmine County, Kentucky. He engaged in the mercantile business in Kirksville, Missouri, in 1855 at the age of twenty-two. In 1860, he was elected treasurer of Adair County. In the spring of 1862, he took a journey out west to live among the mountains but never found a place he liked as much as Missouri, so he headed home. He stayed in Clarence, Shelby County, for seven years and engaged in the mercantile business. He then went back to Kirksville, Missouri, for another three years. In 1877, seeing a favorable market in the newly incorporated town of Webb City, Missouri, C. R. opened the largest dry goods store in the city. He and Millissa had one son, W. S. Chinn, born January 16, 1855. He was in the mercantile business with his father at Parker, Chinn & Co.

After the death of his wife, Milissa, Charles married Elizabeth Jane Webb Stewart in 1897 (a.k.a. Jane Chinn) and moved into her home on the southwest corner of Third and Pennsylvania. C. R. was a Master Mason, a member of the Webb City Lodge (he was a charter member), and a member of the IOOF (Oddfellows). He was a Democrat in politics. He was described as an active progressive man, taking an interest in all that tends to advance the community in which he resides.

C. R. and his wife, Jane Chinn, donated enough funds to build and equip the Jane Chinn Hospital.

This was the home of Jane Webb Stewart Chinn. The cousin of John C. Webb, her second husband, was Stewart, who died, and she married Charles R. Chinn. While married to Stewart, he and Jane built this beautiful home on the southwest corner of Third and Pennsylvania. When she married C. R. Chinn in 1897, they moved into this home of Jane Stewart Chinn. Jane never lived in one of the Chinn homes, but C. R. Chinn moved into Jane Stewart's home.

Chinn, W. S.—W.S. Chinn was the son of Charles R. Chinn Sr. and Millissa Sodowski Chinn. W. S. was born January 16, 1855. He was a partner in the clothing firm of Parker, Chinn & Company of Webb City. His wife was Minnie Manker, daughter of S. L. Manker, a pioneer hardware merchant of Webb City. W. S. became an employee of the Webb City Bank. He died in 1909.

Chinn, Charles R., Jr.—Charles Chinn Jr. was the son of W. S. and Minnie Chinn, and grandson of Charles R. Chinn Sr. He was born December 29, 1882, in Webb City, Missouri. After graduating from Webb City High School, Charles went to Kemper Military School at Boonville, where he graduated in 1901. He then attended the University of Missouri. He returned to Webb City and entered employment with the Webb City Bank as a clerk. At the death of his father, W. S., in 1909, Charles was promoted to succeed his father as cashier. He eventually made it to be president of the Webb City Bank from 1915 until he retired in 1929. He also served as the city treasurer.

Charles married Myrtle Daugherty on June 10, 1908. Myrtle was the daughter of James Daugherty and granddaughter of W. A. Daugherty. Myrtle was born on the Daugherty farm on the west edge of Webb City, which is now part of the airport property.

Charles and Myrtle had two children: a daughter, Mary Elizabeth, who married Thomas McCrosky Jr.; and a son, William R. Chinn. Charles passed away in 1940 and Myrtle in 1950. They made their home at 204 South Webb Street.

Home of Charles R. Chinn and his wife, Myrtle, 204 South Webb Street. Their son was W. R. Chinn.

Chinn, Elizabeth Jane Webb, Stewart—Jane Chinn, "A name that remembered fondly in the city she cared so much about."

Elizabeth Jane Webb was born June 27, 1829, in the state of Tennessee. Elizabeth Jane Webb, daughter of James C. Webb (uncle to John C. Webb, founder of Webb City), from the state of Tennessee, moved as a family to Jasper County in the 1850s. With not too many families living in the area at that time, Jane, at age nineteen, married her cousin, Ben C. Webb. They had a happy home in Jasper County until the Civil War began, and they went to Texas to be close to family during the conflict. After the war was over, they settled in what would later become Webb City.

Ben was the brother of John C. Webb, founder of Webb City. He served as mayor of Webb City and as justice of the peace. The branch that runs between Webb City and Carterville is named Ben's Branch, after Ben Webb.

Ben passed away a few years after they moved back to Jasper County. He was buried in the Harmony Grove Cemetery in Duenweg. The widow Jane Webb proceeded to invest her money in the mining industry. She bought mines as they became available, and she invested in others. A smart move; as the mining industry continued to grow, so did Jane's bank account.

After about five years of widowhood, Elizabeth Jane married Daniel Stewart. They built a beautiful home on the southwest corner of Third and Pennsylvania Streets, 302 South Pennsylvania. The filigree design made the home quite a showplace, surrounded by a wrought iron fence. Jane continued with her mining investments and her involvement in the community and the Methodist South Church. As her business became more involved and continued to develop, Jane became known as the wealthiest woman in the county.

Not having any children of their own, Jane and Dan became foster parents to a young lady named Pearl Stewart, who married Roy Gale. Jane was also closely involved in the lives of her many nieces and nephews on the Webb family side, such as Ada Aylor Nilson, Ben C. Aylor, Eliza Webb, Lee Webb, Sam Taggert, Victoria Bushear, Clara Gage, Eli Glasscock.

Daniel passed away in 1895 and was also buried in the Harmony Grove Cemetery in Duenweg. Jane, being the independent woman that she was, continued in her business endeavors and continued to succeed. Then in 1897 (age sixty-eight), Elizabeth Jane Webb Stewart, after being a widow for a couple of years, married Charles R. Chinn Sr., and that's the name she is most remembered by—Jane Chinn.

Jane married Charles R. Chinn Sr., another pioneer in Webb City's history. Chinn, the youngest of ten children, moved with his parents to Missouri where his father, W. S. Chinn, helped to establish Shelby County, Missouri. In 1877, Charles and his wife of twenty-four years, Milissa, moved to the new town of Webb City and opened the largest dry goods store in town, Chinn's Dry Goods.

The widower Charles Chinn Sr. married at the age of sixty-four, to the widow Jane Stewart, age sixty-eight, in 1897. They moved into Jane's home on Pennsylvania and lived a very peaceful and happy life. Thirteen years later, at the age of eighty-one, Jane and Charles Chinn decided that the growing city was in need of a hospital. So in 1910, they donated $60,000 to build and supply the hospital. They also made necessary arrangements to keep the hospital financially stable. They had the miners donate 50¢ a month, and the mine operators paid $5 a month, which was enough to keep the hospital operating. In honor of the generous donation, it was deemed that the hospital would be named Jane Chinn, and if for some unforeseen reason, the hospital should no longer exist, the building would be left to the heirs of Jane and Charles Chinn (Jane's and Charles's pictures hung in the entryway of the hospital).

Jane Chinn was a remarkable woman, a strong independent lady who had a sharp business mind. She was involved in mining in the area. She owned several mines and invested in others.

One can't help but wonder if the hospital had not been named Jane Chinn, would we have forgotten this strong women born before her time? Would we have remembered her for her business ability? Most women in that time era weren't allowed to use their brains for business matters. It was considered unladylike to think of anything but charity events, household problems, and raising children.

Jane Chinn passed away December 31, 1913, just three years after the building of the Jane Chinn Hospital. Jane had two brothers, Thomas Columbus Webb and John Webb of Texas (not John C. Webb, founder of Webb City).

With the opening of the apartments in the old Jane Chinn Hospital (2008), it renewed an interest in the Lady of Webb City known as Jane Chinn. Many of the early pioneers of Webb City's history have their names on buildings, streets, businesses, etc. Most of those pioneers are men. Very few women left their mark in Webb City's past, except Jane Chinn, and that was because she had a hospital named in her honor.

The sad part is, the lady did so much more than just donate $60,000 to have a hospital built. She was a remarkable woman with a business mind that put many men to shame. She seemed to have complete control of her life, starting with her early marriage at the age of nineteen.

The Chinn family was connected to many other Webb City pioneers. Charles's son, W. S. Chinn, married Minnie Manker, daughter to S. L. Manker, a pioneer hardware merchant. His grandson, Charles Jr., married Myrtle Daugherty, daughter of James Daugherty and granddaughter of W. A. Daugherty, mining pioneers and founders of Carterville. Jane was related to C. M. E. Webb, who married Joseph Aylor. The Harmony Grove Cemetery, east of Joplin, near Kensor Road, is the Webb family cemetery.

Clark, Jerry

Jerry Clark came from a very large family. His father, Thomas Clark, and his mother, Nancy Combs, had twelve children, and at the time of their deaths, they had 140 grandchildren, plus great-grandchildren and great-great-grandchildren. And Jerry's maternal grandmother lived to the ripe age of 108 years.

Jerry managed to get a good education and even attended a private school in Arkansas for one year in 1868. After his graduation, Jerry taught school for one year, decided that wasn't what he was cut out to be, and tried his hand at farming, as his father had done before him.

In 1871, Jerry heard about the mining going on in Granby. He decided that might be the line of work he would like to try, eventually heading into Webb City as the mining excitement began. He proved to be very talented in the mining business. He became a third partner in the Maud B. mine and a second partner in the Mosley mine. The Maud B. turned out to be a wealthy investment, and Jerry became financially comfortable.

Jerry and his wife, Elizabeth Jones Clark, had a daughter, Roxie May, who was born in Webb City in 1876 and graduated from Webb City High School. Roxie married a druggist by the name of R. M. Jones, thus having the same name as her mother's maiden name.

The Clarks were well known in Webb City and thought of in the highest regard. Jerry continued his good success in the mining industry.

Clark, Joseph A.

Joseph Clark's father, Thomas A. Clark, was born in Penworth, Cumberland, England, and was apprenticed to the tailoring business. He married Tamar Vipond, and they headed to America to check out the opportunities, locating in Wolcott, New York, where they opened a tailoring business. Little Joseph A. Clark was born November 4, 1870, and the family had a strong desire to return to England. It may have been the desire of Tamar Clark, for as soon as she passed away in 1885, Joseph and his father, Thomas, returned to America, where Thomas's business had flourished better than in England.

The two Clark men settled in Springfield, Missouri, where Thomas opened his business and happily worked there until his death in 1907. Joseph, in 1887, went to Clinton, Missouri, where at the age of seventeen secured the position of assistant postmaster. He only kept that position for one year, as he felt the calling to be a tailor like his father. To perfect his career decision, Joseph apprenticed himself to N. J. Rumbeck for three years, from 1888–1891. After learning all that Rumbeck could teach him, Joseph traveled around the vicinity, working in various places. After about one and a half years, he decided to settle in Aurora, Missouri, and opened a tailoring business. Joseph married Adie L. Knocker, daughter of Andrew Knocker, on August 8, 1895. This union yielded three children, all boys: Percy R. Clark, born in Newton, Missouri, April 3, 1897; Trevor Clark, born in Aurora, Missouri, on September 17, 1899; and Harold Clark, born in Aurora, Missouri, on August 14, 1901.

In 1907, after his father's death, Joseph sold his interest in his shop and moved to Webb City, Missouri, after learning of the superior educational and business possibilities of this fair city. He opened his business at 107 West Daugherty Street. His fine workmanship put the business in good favor with the city.

Joseph Clark was listed as a Republican nationally, but in local elections, he was independent, giving his support to the one he considered to be the best fitted to fill the position. He belonged to the Aurora Blue Lodge, AF and AM, became a member of the Webb City chapter, holding the rank of sir knight; the BOE(Elks) in Webb City.

Conner, John

Jacob and Ida Conner raised ten children and spent their last years in their home at 511 West First, in Webb City, where they were able to visit with many of their descendants each day.

One of their most famous descendants is Bart Conner, 1984 Olympics double gold medal winner. He is now more famous for being the husband of Olympic perfect ten Nadia Comaneci. Each August, the Conner family reunion is held at the W. C. senior citizens' building. Usually sixty to ninety descendants of Jacob and Ida gather to renew contacts and to honor the remaining members of the Conner family.

The subject of this story is Jacob and Ida's son, John Conner. Born in Mayes County, Oklahoma, in 1901, John learned to farm, play guitar, and sing. Even in his later years, he would sing all the verses of "The Old Rugged Cross" while he worked. John and his wife, Beulah (DeMoss), raised four children: Johnnie May Conner Huey, Harold "Bud" Conner, Myrtle Lee Conner Babbit, and Dee Conner. The parents, like most Depression survivors, insisted that each child achieve significant goals in school and graduate from college. All four children had outstanding careers in teaching, accounting, engineering, and/or management. The grandchildren, great-grandchildren, and many great-great-grandchildren carry on the family tradition of achievement. Several of the descendants still live in Webb City.

John Conner left many monuments to his hard work and skill in Webb City. As a skilled mason, he completed over one hundred masonry projects with his distinctive style that can be seen in many buildings around Webb City and the area. Many customers wanted the mixed look of Carthage marble masonry, which was the signature of John Conner's work.

For over forty years, the Conners lived at 216 South Ball. This beautiful home is an example of the unique masonry construction that John Conner was known for.

Throughout the town, many homes were given that special touch, which changed an old deteriorated home into a showplace with the stone masonry that only John could seem to accomplish. Some customers would request sandstone or brick, but John knew his expertise was in Carthage marble, not brick.

It seems that John Conner has left another legacy in Webb City. According to his son, Harold, John requested the installation and paid for the construction of the elevator in the Central Methodist Church. Beulah Conner benefited from that elevator, as many others have, I'm sure.

A special thanks to Harold Conner for sharing information about his father. I've always admired that particular masonry as my husband's aunt and uncle, Grace and Walter Klein, lived in one of those houses on Ellis Street.

Several of the Conner family members helped John in his construction projects. Sons Bud and Dee worked on many of the houses and even completed several on their own. John's brother Basil, brother-in-law Jim DeMoss, nephews Lloyd Wingo, Donald Lee, and others worked on many of John's masonry projects.

I couldn't have said it any better than Harold did in his letter, "The legacy of visual monuments of John's artistic masonry" is always a pleasure whenever descendants return to Webb City. He is remembered not only for the benefits of hard work by a strong man but as a good person and good example for the whole Conner Family.

Thanks again, Harold, for sending us these wonderful memories of John Conner (1901–1983).

Craig, Charles Henry—Doctor

Charles Henry Craig and his wife, Lucy, moved to Webb City on August 19, 1890, from Jefferson City. In Jefferson City, Craig had been the assistant prison physician at the state penitentiary for three and a half years.

Born June 8, 1857, Dr. Craig came from a poor family, the oldest of ten children, so he had to work hard to earn money to make it through medical school. He graduated from the State

University of Missouri in Columbia and the Missouri Medical College of St. Louis. He became a medical doctor in 1887.

Dr. Craig was active in the community. He was a Master Mason, an Odd Fellow, and a Woodman of the World and a member of the Order of Knights and Ladies of Security. He was a Democrat and a Methodist.

He went on to continue his education by attending the College of Physicians and Surgeons in Chicago in 1907. Dr. Craig became known and recognized as one of the leading physicians and surgeons of Southwest Missouri. He was the railroad surgeon for the Kansas City, Fort Scott, and Memphis and the Frisco railroads.

Both of Dr. Craig's sons were born in Webb City. Charles Maurice was born September 23, 1895, and Joseph Franklin was born October 12, 1901.

Dr. Craig was of Scotch Irish descent. The first of his line to come to America was his great-great-grandfather, Reverend John Craig. He arrived in America on August 17, 1734. He established two churches in Virginia. Reverend Craig married Kitty Kennerly and had a son, George Russell Craig, Jr., who married Polly McMullen.

George Jr. was the Craig who made the move from Buffalo, Virginia (which is now West Virginia), then to Fulton, Missouri, in 1835. That's where most of the Craigs still reside. George and Kitty had a son named Joseph L. Craig, who married Mary E. Jones. These two are the parents of Dr. Charles Henry Craig.

*Additional information about the Craig family: In 1978, Helen and Dick Woodworth purchased the Craig home at 711 West Broadway where Dr. Craig also had his office. The house had been empty for many years, and when the Woodworths entered the home, the only thing left inside was a box full of photos of the Craig family. There was one newspaper clipping in the box, and it was of Dick Woodworth when he was a boxer. Spooky! Also in the box was Dr. Craig's medical certificate.

Dr. Craig married Lucy Wren of Fulton, Callaway County, Missouri, October 31, 1888. When the Craigs first moved to Webb City, they lived at 122 North Liberty, and his office was on North Allen, above Wright's Drug Store (Bruner's Drug).

Corl, George F. C.

Born in North Carolina in 1846, George Corl was twenty-nine when he came to Jasper County in 1875 and opened a general store in the area where Carterville would eventually be located. In March of 1890, he moved to Webb City to open a larger store.

When Webb City was incorporated in 1876, George Corl was right there as one of the leaders helping to organize the town. He became one of the six directors of the city with the other five being C. C. McBride, A. A. Hulett, W. E. Foster, George Robinson, H. C. Gaston, and J. P. Stewart as treasurer. George served as a justice of the peace. He was a brother of W. A. Corl.

George died in November of 1930.

Corl, William Alford

Born in Gold Hill, South Carolina, in 1863, W. A. Corl moved to the new town of Carterville in September of 1883 at the age of twenty. He went to work for his brother, G. F. C. Corl, in his frontier-type general store. Later he moved to Webb City and started his own mercantile business. He operated a bookstore at 10 1/2 Main Street for many years. He was the president of the Interstate Grocery Company, the Independent Gravel Company, and the General Steel Products at the time of his death in 1938. He had previously served on the board of directors and the secretary of the Merchant & Miners Bank of Webb City.

W. A. was married to Nancy E. (Daugherty) Corl, the daughter of James Daugherty and the granddaughter of W. A. Daugherty.

To the left, the 1894 photo of W. A. Corl's home. Below: the same home in 1990.

Coyne, Thomas F.

Thomas F. Coyne was born in the state of Wisconsin and, with his Irish parents, moved to Webb City in 1876. Thomas's father worked the mines, as most immigrants to the area did. The family built the Transient Hotel on East Broadway. Tom started working the mines at the age of twelve but still managed to keep up his schoolwork. Thomas graduated from Webb City schools and took a course at the Sedalia Business College in 1889. Next he went to work for the Webb City Bank. He worked as an assistant cashier for nine years. Finally Thomas decided the only way to make money was to get involved in the mining business, not as a miner but as an owner. Tom eventually made it to being vice president of the Webb City Bank.

Thomas Coyne found out the big money was in the buying and selling on mining property. He had interest in the Mosley Mine, which was sold at a very large profit. After erecting a mill at the Coyne Dermott Mine on Center Creek, this property brought a healthy profit to Thomas. He also opened a mine in the Center Valley, which he sold. Thomas was superintendent of the Ada Mining Company and the Stevenson Moore Mine, which was purchased for $33,000 and later sold for $60,000.

It seems that Thomas Coyne might have been one of those men that whatever he touched, it turned to gold. Later Coyne opened the Coyne Lumber Company, which was located at 308 East Main (Broadway) Street. He also had a lumberyard in Miami, Oklahoma. His success in business was contributed to the fact that Thomas F. Coyne was a fair man. He sold his goods strictly upon their merit, nothing could be said against the quality or the price of the merchandise at the Coyne Lumber Company.

Until the opening of the Jane Chinn Hospital, there was an organization that was known as the Webb City Hospital Association, and the president of this organization was Thomas F. Coyne. This association had $2,000, which they donated to Jane Chinn Hospital for the support of the institution.

Thomas Coyne married Louise Miller from Wisconsin, and they had two children, Roy Raymond Coyne and Mary Louise Coyne. This prominent family of Webb City lived on the southwest corner of Broadway and Ball Streets.

I'm sure if Thomas F. Coyne would have the opportunity to come back to this era for a visit, he might be surprised at Jane Chinn Hospital. The building has now been remodeled into lovely apartments.

Additional information on Thomas F. Coyne.

His parents were both native of the Green Isle of Erin (Ireland).

The Coyne building is located 110 West Broadway.

Thomas Coyne's sister, Sadie, married Amos D. Hatten in 1888.

The Coyne building at 110 West Main (Broadway)

4 South Ball—Thomas Coyne home

Cummings, Coach Charlie (1908–2003)

I received a wonderful letter from a 1925 WCHS graduate, Galen Campbell. Galen was prompted to write after learning of a reunion in Indiana. Now what does a reunion in Indiana have to do with our Webb City history? Well, a lot if a member of that reunion was a past WCHS graduate and a past athletic coach for Webb City students.

I'm referring to a young gentleman by the name of Charlie Cummings, known to most people as Coach Cummings. Charlie graduated in 1925 with Galen Campbell and with another buddy, Woodson Oldham. The three were able to get together for a visit before Judge Oldham passed away.

The reunion referred to was to celebrate the Indiana State Championship of 1946 which was won by the Anderson High School team under the talented coaching of Coach Cummings. The sport being celebrated was basketball, but Coach wasn't limited to just basketball—he also mastered football.

After graduating from high school and leaving behind quite a reputation as being adept at sports, Charlie went on to college from 1925–1929. Then he shared his talent in Carterville, coaching that first year out of college. Webb City took advantage of the opportunity to snatch up this up-and-coming young coach, and he began with the WC school system in 1931.

According to the 1933 annual, he was highly thought of. The annual states:

> This was Coach Cummings third and most successful year as coach of the Cardinals. During his time here he has produced the two best football teams W.C.H.S. had ever had. Perhaps this can be attributed to the loyal devotion he inspires in his players, and the high grade of football he teaches them. Webb City High School would be sorry to lose Coach Cummings, as the loss would be a hard blow to athletics.

Well, all good things must come to an end, and W. C. did lose their coach. Charlie went to Indiana and was well appreciated and stayed there until his retirement. He coached at Crawfordville, Indiana, before going to Anderson, Indiana. Later he became the athletic director of Anderson schools.

Upon retirement, Coach and his wife, Gladys (Kungle) Cummings (who retired from teaching also), moved to Arkansas. After Mrs. Cummings passed away, Coach went to live with his son, Michael, back in Anderson, Indiana, where he is among many friends and admirers.

Gladys (Kungle) Cummings family lived outside Carterville and owned the Kungle Orchards. Coach's father was John Cummings, and he worked for the Joplin Globe for many years.

Coach is now eighty-seven years young and seemed to really enjoy the reunion in Indiana with former team members. He had many fond memories of the state championship, but he also had one sad memory. The morning after the big win, Coach called his father to discuss the triumph, only to discover that after listening to the championship game on the radio, John Cummings passed away in his sleep. But I'm sure his last thoughts were happy ones as he recalled the success of his son.

I would like to give a special thanks to Galen Campbell for taking the time to share this information with us. He seemed to know Coach pretty well to supply all this wonderful information. He also recalled that one of Coach's team members that he coached was Kenneth Kneeland, whom Galen states was a star athlete, which is the same description Galen gave to Coach, so, Kenneth, I think that's quite a compliment!

Cunningham, Ney Dean

Do you remember going down Main Street and seeing the unmistakable sight of Ney Dean Cunningham walking down the sidewalk, holding her purse on her left arm and striding for city hall to take care of bookkeeping. Ney Dean worked her way into the hearts of all she met with her smile, eyes squinted with crinkles on the side as her smile lit up her face. She never met a stranger and usually found a common thread that connected you in some distant fashion.

Ney Dean Sequoiah Cunningham was born to L. F. and Rosa Cunningham in 1911. She grew up at 801 Wilson and became unofficially a true Ms. Webb City. Ney Dean could be found at such meetings as the chamber of commerce, Business and Professional Women, Mining Days, and many area organizations, usually serving as the treasurer or secretary as that was where her talent flourished. She went to Kansas City as a young lady to get her secretarial and financial training.

Ney Dean loved a good time, and that attitude helped her join in the steering committee in 1979 to plan out a city celebration to be held in King Jack Park. As usual, Ney Dean served as treasurer and assisted in organizing some of the fundraisers to raise money to start the new celebration. Ney Dean loved music, and she served on the entertainment committee, and she faithfully hired the Paul Jensen Band every year.

Ney Dean had a change of pace and served as the first president of the Webb City Business and Professional Women when the organization was formed in 1950, and she stayed with that group up until the day she passed away.

The Methodist Church was fortunate enough to have Ney Dean as a loyal member of their congregation, and Ney Dean walked with God on earth as she does now in heaven. What a dedicated promoter of the good deed of her Heavenly Father.

Probably the group that showed Ney Dean's exquisite and humorous personality had to be The Joy Belle Jubilaires, a kitchen band formed in 1970. Each instrument in the band was homemade except the piano, and each lady was not shy as she worked her unusual-sounding musical invention made from kitchen gadgets. And each member played a kazoo in this rare and unusual band. Ney Dean was spokesperson/band director, and she was so much fun as she proudly named each player and the unique-sounding names associated with the homemade instruments. The word spread quickly, and soon the calendar begin to fill, and the ladies were on the road to wonderful places like Branson, St. Louis, Kansas, Oklahoma, etc. Television spots were on the *Carol Parker Show*, and local nursing homes enjoyed the many costumes the ladies wore at each event. I'm sure that Ney Dean would be reminding me about this time that I had not mentioned the other members of band. The Joy Belles band consisted of Glenda Adams, Helen Brock, Nancy Carlson, Ney Dean Cunningham, Nadine Drachenberg, Ruby Gregory, Helen Hogan, Helen Jackson, Helen Johnston, Marie Mammen, Neva Oerhing, Bea Spille, and Mildred Toomey.

In 1959, as Webb City continued to grow and take on new technology, Ney Dean, along with the Business and Professional Women decided to help out the housewife who did not venture out of the house and offer some classes. One class that Ney Dean taught and the BPW Club presented was a class about how to use a dial telephone. Some of those local ladies had only had an operator-assisted phone and had no idea how to go about using that new dial phone sitting on the end table. And some were hesitant to get the new phone until after they attended Ney Dean's class.

Ney Dean passed away in 1994, and she is greatly missed but deserves a mention in the people-to-remember list. If she were here, she would be the secretary or treasurer of that list!

Dale, Frank—The Inventor

When you think of inventors, you automatically think of men like Thomas Edison, Eli Whitney, etc. Well, Webb City had a famous inventor. Born in the small community of Prosperity, Frank Dale proved to the world that even small-town people could be an asset to the world.

The small-town boy moved to the big city of New York to work for the Quaker State Oil Company. While employed as sales manager, Frank put together a mechanical man made out of oil drums and oilcans. He used this mechanical man at a meeting to promote Quaker State Oil. It created such a sensation that Frank Dale decided to experiment a little more. He eventually set up a workshop in the basement of his home in Pleasantville, New York.

In 1938, Frank Dale founded Mechanic Man, Inc. of New York City. Once his creative juices started flowing, there was no stopping this genius of invention. Business slowed down during wartime because of a lack of material to work with, but as soon as the war was over, full-scale production began again.

Frank's specialty was to promote trademarks to increase sales. Many brand names were advertised with the help of Frank's mechanical dolls. There was a child in pajamas carrying a candle advertising it was time to "Re-Tire with Fisk tires." A mechanical butler would smile and offer some Ballantine's Ale to passersby. A high-stepping majorette promoted Chesterfield cigarettes; a young girl would kick a spark plug (Autolite) into action. But the most famous of all was the lifelike baby lying in the basket with arms and legs waving. This baby was mostly used to advertise baby clothing, medical supplies, and diapers. Many merchants and production companies were seeking help from Frank Dale, the Mechanical Man, Inc.

Frank had an even better idea, and he contacted Mae West and signed a contract for worldwide use of her face, figure, and costumes for advertising. The cost of the first Mae West mechanical figure was $3,500. The doll looked just like Mae West, and the latex skin was remarkably lifelike. Although plans were to create many of the Mae West dolls, only two were actually produced. One is in Gabe's Doll museum in Tombstone, Arizona, and the other just recently sold at an auction in Scottsdale, Arizona.

Gabe's Doll Museum is home to many of Frank Dale's famous dolls. They stand as a memorial to the famous man who started a new enterprise that was a benefit to many advertising companies. Before Frank Dale, mechanical mannequins were so complex and expensive that most merchants couldn't afford them. Frank Dale not only was able to make them more affordable, he even worked out a leasing operation so that even the small businessman could have special displays to promote sales.

If we were to commemorate the famous inventor from our community, we would have to memorialize his birthplace in Prosperity; his home in Pleasantville, New York; his Webb City residence for many years, 510 North Webb Street; and the building on the northwest corner of Daugherty and Tom Streets where he had his office. There are probably more places that haven't been mentioned, but we should be proud to have such an important man associated with our history.

A special thanks to Bob Hunter for the information on Frank Dale and his many accomplishments. And if you are heading west on vacation, don't forget to stop by Gabe's Doll Museum and let them know—you are from Frank Dale's hometown.

Daugherty, William Armstrong

William Armstrong Daugherty was born August 19, 1829, in McMinn County, Tennessee, to Mathew (Ireland/Tennessee) and Nancy Cass Daugherty (North Carolina). Mathew Daugherty's father was Charles Daugherty, a soldier in the Revolutionary War and served as a major in the army during the War of 1812. In 1847, William married Nancy (Nina) Riggs, who was born in 1827 in McMinn County, Tennessee. W. A. was a farmer and a cattleman. Trying to take care of his wife and seven children convinced W. A. to move to greener pastures. They moved to Washington County, Missouri, in 1864 when W. A. was thirty-five years old. They then moved on to Austin, Texas, in early spring of 1867 where Nancy passed away in July of that year. With the hardship of raising a family alone, W. A. moved to Jasper County in October of 1867. He resumed his profession of farming and stock operations.

In 1870, W. A. purchased 260 acres of land just west of what would later become Webb City. He soon purchased 320 acres east of Webb City. His farm and mines began to pay off, and he eventually owned 4,000 acres of mining and agricultural land in Jasper County. The property east of Webb City became the city of Carterville (of which W. A. is one of the founders, along with his son James).

Life had been a difficult struggle for W. A. as he tried to raise his family. Even though he possessed some land, there was not always necessary funds to take care of the needs of the family. But perseverance paid off, and he began to reap the rewards of his years of hard labor.

The oldest of his children was a son named James Alexander Daugherty, born August 30, 1847, in McMinn County, Tennessee. James was a levelheaded young man with ideas and knowledge that helped his father to achieve the rewards he so greatly deserved.

In 1874, William A. Daugherty wandered over to his neighbor's farm, John C. Webb, and observed the mining endeavors of Webb and a partner, Murrell. Seeing Murrell's frustration over the mine filling with water continuously, Daugherty offered to buy Murrel out for the hefty sum of $25. Murrell jumped at the opportunity; after all a miner usually made only one dollar a day. John Webb Was getting as disillusioned as Murrell as the mine kept filling in with devil water, which was frustrating. Ashcraft came to town to visit Daugherty and made an offer to Webb, who leased the land to Daugherty and Grant Ashcraft, giving him royalties from what was the beginning of the Center Creek Mining Company.

W. A. Daugherty and his son James formed a partnership with C. C. Allen, W. M. McMillin, and T. N. Davey to form the company known as Carterville Mining and Smelting Company. This company opened the North and South Carterville Mines, which proved to be the richest in the Webb City and Carterville districts.

W. A. Daugherty

The story continues—William attended school no more than three months in all of his life. His education was self-acquired. He worked a farm during his boyhood.

William was married at age seventeen, on November 4, 1846, to Nancy Riggs. They borrowed $21 to furnish his log cabin and $200 to purchase hogs. They paid off both debts within the first year.

Served as a Confederate lieutenant in the Fifty-Ninth Tennessee Regiment, serving mostly in Knoxville. He saw service at Cumberland Gap and in the Atlanta campaign. He was captured by the Federalists at his own home but was quickly discharged without being asked to take the oath of loyalty.

In 1864, William moved to Washington County, Illinois, then in 1867, the family moved to Texas where his wife passed away in June of 1867. They had nine children: James, works with his father; Louisa Jane was the wife of E. L. Thornton an, engineer in Carterville; Benjamin A. was a farmer; Lucinda married B. F. Hatcher, mine owner; Martha Melissa became the wife of Thomas Burch, died and left two children, Alice Burch, who was married to G. W. Davis, and Nancy Caroline Burch, wife of Carterville postmaster L. C. Gray); Tennessee Daugherty died in Illinois at the age of eighteen months; and another infant child (unnamed) died in Texas (I am assuming Nancy died giving birth to this child).

After the death of his wife in 1867, William moved the children to Jasper County, Missouri, which he had passed through on his way to Texas. Jasper County was mostly unsettled, and those who did live there were spaced far apart. William rented a house and barn for his family about four miles southeast of the future Carterville.

In June of 1868, W. A. married Sarah B. Davis of Joplin, a native of Tennessee. No children were born to this union. W. A. had stated that he needed help in raising his family.

In 1874, William A. Daugherty wandered over to his neighbor's farm to the northeast, John C. Webb, and observed the mining endeavors of Webb and a partner, Murrell. Seeing Murrell's frustration over the mine filling with water continuously, Daugherty offered to buy Murrel out for the hefty sum of $25. Murrell jumped at the opportunity; after all, a miner usually made only one dollar a day. John Webb Was getting as disillusioned as Murrell as the mine kept filling in with devil water, which was frustrating. Ashcraft came to town to visit Daugherty and made an offer to Webb, who leased the land to Daugherty and Grant Ashcraft, giving him royalties from what was the beginning of the Center Creek Mining Company.

In 1876 Daugherty went into partnership with T. N. Davy, C. C. Allen, and W. M. McMullen. This partnership bought the Carter Lands eighty acres, laid the foundation for the Carterville mines. James A. Daugherty became the manager of the Carterville mines. One hundred twenty acres were added to the Carterville Mine Co. Daugherty also purchased one third of the Cornfield Tract. W. A. now owned about four thousand adjoining the new town of Carterville, which he founded. He built the first building in the new town.

W. A. purchased the First National bank of Webb City. His grandson Charles Whitworth Daugherty was cashier and the youngest man in the state to occupy so high a position.

In 1896, Charles died, and W. A. moved the bank to Carterville. W. A. was the president, and James was the director, Ashcraft was the vice president, W. B. Kane was the cashier.

W. A. was a Democrat, a Methodist, a Mason, and an Odd Fellow.

In 1900, W. A. Daugherty, at the age of seventy-one, claimed to be in robust health, still working in banking and mining interests which have made him extremely wealthy.

Time line of W. A. Daugherty:

1829—August 19, born in McMinn County, East Tennessee
1846—November 4, married Nancy Riggs
1847—August 30, son James A. Daugherty was born in McMinn County, Tennessee

1849–1861—Farming and stock raising

1861—Entered the Confederate Army as a lieutenant in the Fifty-Ninth Tennessee Regiment

1864—Moved his family to Washington County, Illinois

1867—Moved his family to Texas

1867—Wife died in Texas

1868—Moved his children to Jasper County, Missouri; rented a farm southeast of present Carterville.

1868—Married Sarah B. Davis

1872—J. C. Webb found ore on his land.

1873—Bought out Murrell, who was mining partner with Webb

1874—Partnership with Ashcraft

1876—Ashcraft retired, went into partnership with T. N. Davey, C. C. Allen, and W.M. McMullen.

1876—Business group purchased 80 acres of Carter property; added 120 acres.

1877—Total purchase of land was four thousand acres; organized Carterville Mining and Smelting Company.

1877—Founded Carterville. Built first building.

Daugherty, James Alexander—Judge

Some men are so highly endowed by nature with executive ability, financial genius, and capacity for large affairs that they can carry on gigantic enterprises without apparent effort, making everything work so smoothly that all events and circumstances seem to minister to their welfare, their very difficulties and obstacles being turned into wings for their progress or weapons for their defense. Their operations are imperial in range and sweep, and hold a princely rank among the industrial achievements of every age and race. One of the most impressive illustrations of this fact is furnished by the career and achievement of James Alexander Daugherty, of Webb City, Missouri, who has put in motion and conducted to emphatic success business enterprises of such a character and magnitude as to forcibly engage the attention and almost stagger belief in the West, where men have vision adapted to colossal proportions in everything. This glowing and impressive description of James Daugherty was noted by Joel Livingston in his book *History of Jasper County* in 1912. It would seem to be a hard description to live up to, but James Daugherty seemed to prove this description in his actions and deeds throughout his life.

James was born at Athens, McMinn County, Tennessee, on August 30, 1947, to William Armstrong and Nancy (Riggs) Daugherty. Raised on a farm, James learned much about farming and stock.

Receiving his scholastic training in public schools, when the family moved to Texas, James engaged in a career of cutting wood in the mountains for the government.

Young James Daugherty moved to the Jasper County area with his father in October of 1867. His father, William Daugherty, resumed his farming and stock operations in his new location, and James assisted him. James also spent one winter cutting and making rails in the lumber region.

James married Susanna Freeman of Ashley, Illinois, on December 30, 1867. They had eight children: (1) Nancy Elizabeth Daugherty, who married W. A. Corl with the W. C. Mercantile Company; (2) William Alva Daugherty, a mining superintendent; (3) Charles Whitworth Daugherty with the First National Bank of Webb City; (4) Dora May Daugherty; (5) Lee A. Daugherty; (6) J. Arthur Daugherty; (7) Myrtle Daugherty, who married C. R. Chinn Jr.; (8) Lula Alice Daugherty. Their mother, Susanna, died December 29, 1908, and James married Mrs. M. E. (Boone) Parker on April 20, 1910.

James was a gentleman of great ability. He could operate a business of great magnitude with such ease. James A. Daugherty was assisting his father, W. A. Daugherty, in cultivating the farmland east of Webb City, in an area that would become Carterville, Missouri, when they discovered the farmland was loaded with ores and minerals.

He became quite well known for his work with mining companies. The mines belonged to his father, but James was the reason the mines were successful. He followed in his father's footsteps to become the president of the National Bank of Carterville at the time of his father's death (1907). He served as vice president of the Interurban Ice Company; director of the City National Bank of Wagoner, Oklahoma, and the Citizens Trust Company of Wagoner, Oklahoma; president of the Henson Lumber Company, Carterville; and had valuable holdings in the First National Bank of Carterville. James Daugherty was also associated with James Gammon Grocery House, a pioneer grocery establishment in Webb City.

James proudly hailed to be an uncompromising Democrat in politics and served his party as well as possible. James served two terms as an associate judge for the western district of Jasper County and was a member of the legislature for one term.

Being an advocate of education, James was generous in his donations to the institution of learning, especially the Webb City College. He also served as director of his school district for over twenty years. November of 1910, James Daugherty was elected to the House of Representatives from the Fifteenth Congressional District.

James was active in the Masons, the Mystic Shrine, and the Scottish Rites. He faithfully attended the Methodist Episcopal Church, also serving as a trustee and a steward of the church.

William A. Daugherty was a man of eminent ability, and he passed this great attribute on to his son James. Under his instruction, James learned the mining industry, but James went one step further and soaked in all he could learn about the mining business from anyone willing to teach him. James became a universally respected and admired citizen. He was known for his honesty, great business ability, and high character.

W. A. and J. A. were two great forefathers to be proud of, and each one can be remembered as we see their name on the street signs in Webb City and Carterville. They deserve to be recognized for their many contributions of time and energy to the growth and development of our area.

Additional information about James A. Daugherty: He served as an associate judge of the western district of Jasper County for two terms, as a member of the legislature one term, and as school director of his school district for a period of twenty years or longer. In November 1910, he was elected to the national House of Representatives from the Fifteenth Congressional District.

Description of James A. Daugherty: A man of enterprise and excellent judgment; while energetic in the prosecution of a purpose, he was conservative in all that preceded action. Integrity was a marked feature of his character, and his acceptance of a trust was assurance of its thorough and conscientious discharge. A most commendable trait was his interest in educational affairs. His own school advantages were of the poorest, though his converse and conduct in business affairs would not betray it. Appreciating the value of a liberal education, he cheerfully served his school district as a director, aiding by his best effort in providing suitable instruction for the children of his neighbors. His own family had had every available educational advantage, and he had been a liberal donor to the establishment of the Webb City College.

The information on the time lines of W. A. Daugherty and James Alexander Daugherty have been acquired from the *Encyclopedia of the History of Missouri,* volume 2 (1901).

Time line of James Daugherty:

James Alexander Daugherty, son of William Armstrong Daugherty and Nancy Riggs Daugherty. Born August 30, 1847, in McMinn County, Tennessee.

1864—James and his family moved to Illinois.

1867—The family moved to Texas where his mother died in June of 1867.

1867—William A. Daugherty moved his children to Jasper County, Missouri.

1867—December 30, James Alexander Daugherty married Susanna Freeman of Mississippi. They had eight children: Dora May Daugherty died quite young; Charles Whitworth Daugherty, cashier at First National Bank of Webb City, died February 3, 1896; Nancy Elizabeth Daugherty, married W. A. Corl of the Webb City Mercantile and Mining Company; William Alva Daugherty, mining superintendent, died November 19, 1899; James Arthur Daugherty, a graduate of the Sedalia Business College, worked his father's farm west of Webb City where James lived; Lee Alexander Daugherty, graduated the Sedalia Business College; Myrtle Daugherty attended Webb City College; Lulu Alice Daugherty attended Webb City College.

James Alexander Daugherty became an associate with his father in the mining industry and financial transactions. Became the Superintendent of the eighty acres that his father was one-third owner, along with T. N. Davy, C. C. Allen, W. M. McMullen. The company was known as the North and South Carterville Mines.

James A. Daugherty became a partner in the James Gammon Grocery House.

1899—James became the president of the Spurgeon Wholesale Grocery Company of Webb City.

Large stockholder in the First National Bank of Carterville and a member of the board of directors of the bank.

A Democrat and a member of the Methodist Church South branch, a Mason, a member of the Joplin Commandery of Knights Templar, and with Ararat Temple of the Mystic Shrine at Kansas City.

1890—Was elected associate judge of the western district of Jasper County, re-elected in 1892.

1896—Elected a seat of the general assembly

1897—James was a two-year member of the district school board.

Daugherty, Benjamin A.

Benjamin Daugherty was a son to William A. and Nancy Daugherty, born January 17, 1852, in McMinn, Tennessee. He was the third of seven children. The family left Tennessee when Benjamin was eleven years old; they moved to Washington County, Illinois. Three years later, they moved to Austin, Texas, where his mother passed away on July 8, 1867. The family moved to Jasper County, Missouri. He met and married Ms. Missouria T. Caldwell, born January 4, 1851; they were married June 9, 1875.

Benjamin and his wife settled on a 120-acre farm, with all the land being cultivated, and they lived in a two-story framed house. He planted an orchard on the farm. They had four children: William F. Daugherty, Mary I. Daugherty, Louetta M. Daugherty, and Benjamin A Daugherty.

Davey, Thomas N.—A Manufacturer, Inventor, and Mine Operator

Davey was born in Cornwall, England, in 1835, and came with his parents to the United States in 1852, at age seventeen. The family settled in Philadelphia, Pennsylvania. Davey was apprenticed to a machinists' trade at Baldwin Locomotive Works. Desiring to work with mining machinery, Davey left Philadelphia and apprenticed himself with the mining machinery works in Pottsville, Pennsylvania. He extended his education to include the actual mining affairs to acquaint himself in all aspects of the industry. After his apprenticeship was completed, he traveled to over sixteen states to learn as much about mining as possible. Davey made friends everywhere he went.

In 1859, Davey found himself in Louisville, Kentucky. Davey married Ms. Anna Stealey in 1861 and established a foundry and a machine shop. In 1872, he sold his shops and moved his family to Carthage, Missouri. He became superintendent of the Carthage Machine Works. During his four years with this company, he built the first Cornish force pumps used in the lead mines of Jasper County. In an effort to help the Southwest Missouri Mineral District, he made many improvements in the way of mineral machinery. His inventions proved worthy to the district. He invented of an improved hoister for ores, including three different patents. He invented the Carthage pump clack and the Carthage pumps, hoisters, and clacks.

In 1874, Davey joined in with the mining operations of the Center Creek Mining Company with John C. Webb and W. A. Daugherty, as his invention helped to clear the water for them to continue mining with Grant Ashcraft.

Davey joined in with W. A. Daugherty in establishing the mines of Carterville. His business was always successful, and he knew how to get what he wanted. He felt that any sober, frugal, and diligent young man could have as good an opportunity for the acquisition of honors and wealth in Southwest Missouri where "nine-tenths of the natural resources and wealth are yet to be developed."

Thomas N. Davey was a Republican and a member of the Episcopal Church.

Time line of T. N. Davey:

1835—Born Cornwall, England

1852—Arrived in the United States, age seventeen, Philadelphia, Pennsylvania

1852—Apprenticed as a machinist at Baldwin Locomotive Works of Philadelphia

1859—Went to Louisville, Kentucky

1861—Married Anna Stealey in Louisville, Kentucky

1868—Established a foundry and machine shop in Kentucky; sold the business in 1872

1872—Arrived in Carthage, Missouri

1872—Superintendent of Carthage Machine Works

1872–1876—Inventor and builder of mining pumps and other mining appliances

1874—Engaged in mining operations with W. A. Daugherty and J. C. Webb. Purchased the Carterville land, several mines including the Cornfield.

David, Oscar and Wivi

It was a hot July in 1921, but two young people in love weren't concerned about the weather. All they were thinking about was getting married. They had grown up together in Stanberry, Missouri, where most of the teenagers hung out at the post office.

Oscar David and Wivi Fisher made the decision to elope. The first place they went couldn't marry them, but they found a preacher in Maryville who married them in his parlor.

As they were heading home to let the family know what they had done, they met Oscar's big brother coming to get them. Needless to say, both families were pretty uptight with the couple for rushing into this marriage. It must have been meant to be, though, because Oscar and Wivi will have been married for seventy years on July 18, 1991.

Wivi (pet name for Vivian) was seventeen, and Oscar turned nineteen the day after the marriage. Both looked young for their age.

Once they went to the Bethany County Fair with another couple. There weren't hotels as we have now days; instead you usually rented rooms from private individuals (boarding homes). Well, when they approached this lady about renting her rooms, she informed them that she didn't think they were old enough to be married, and she wouldn't rent to them. She finally agreed if the two young ladies would share a room and the two young men share a room. So for the first time in their young married life, the Davids had to spend the night in separate rooms.

Oscar and Wivi were blessed with two beautiful daughters who, in their eyes, couldn't have been more perfect. They were a strong family. After Oscar and Wivi were married, they took in Wivi's little sister, Zelma, and raised her as their own. So basically, they had three daughters: Zelma, Patsy, and Peggy. One day, several years later, according to family legend, friend Patty Green was invited over for dinner and never left, becoming a part of the family.

Peggy has a son, Patrick Platter, who is an attorney in Springfield and the apple of his grand-parents' eye.

After working for the Railway Express Company for forty-seven years, Oscar thought he would retire. One day, he went to help Kenton Fly with the inventory at the hardware store. He enjoyed himself, and Kenton must have known because he said, "Oscar, you're not doing anything, why don't you help me out?" Oscar helped him for fourteen years.

Some people have talents in many things, and Wivi had a natural talent when it came to sewing. Her father (Poppy) bought her a sewing machine for $5, and she trained herself to sew. Her daughter brags, "You could just show mother a picture, and she could make the item without a pattern." This talent resulted in Wivi becoming quite a quilt expert. She makes lots of quilts and gives them away to the church and different charities.

In this day and age, when one in two marriages are ending in a divorce, we asked Oscar and Wivi what advice would they give to young couples to help their marriage last longer. Oscar jokingly advises, "Don't get married!" But they both agree that the secret to their happy union has been giving 100 percent, not just 50 percent. Also you have to learn how to give and take. If you don't know how to give in a little, you'll only have contention. Don't try keeping up with the Joneses; live within your means.

Since the Davids weren't blessed with a honeymoon, when they first got hitched, their children took them to Niagara Falls on their fiftieth anniversary. It's been said that the family is so close, usually if you see one, you'll see another family member close by (that's another secret to the Davids' long happy union).

Congratulations to Oscar and Wivi for seventy years of a happy marriage in 1991. And thanks to them for sharing some of their memories with us.

Davids move to Webb City, Wells Fargo/American Railway Express—Oscar and Wivi David were transferred to the Webb City area in 1938. Oscar had been with the express company as it went through its many changes in names. He started out with Wells Fargo, which changed to American Railway Express, which became Railway Express and finally, the REA Express. He said he worked for four different companies, yet worked the same job for forty-seven years.

When the Davids came to Webb City by railroad, Wivi said that if there had been another train heading out of town, she would have been on it. Her first impression of Webb City consisted of views of chat piles. But they have changed their opinion of Webb City over the years and have come to love it as their home.

Oscar's office was located behind the Webb City Water Department (corner of Church Street and Webb Street), and for the first time in her life, Wivi (pet name for Vivian) was going to work outside of the home. She was going to be in charge of the books. The only problem was that Wivi didn't know how. Oscar told her to just watch her debits and credits, and she wouldn't have any problems. Wivi said she didn't know a debit and credit from a hole in the ground.

One day, when a company boss came to visit, Oscar made the mistake of saying to Wivi, "The only way you could be dumber is to be bigger!" This didn't sit too well with the petite Wivi, so she gathered up her belongings and slammed the door behind her. Oscar wasn't worried; he said, "She'll be back." Well, he was wrong—the office was closed for three days! When asked how he got Wivi to return, Oscar said he got down on his knees.

Their business with the express company was done totally on commission. So the amount of income varied each day. It was getting close to Christmas one year, and money was pretty tight. One day, they only made 46¢ in commission, and they were feeling a little depressed. The very next day, Oscar got a shipment with the Atlas Powder Company, and that day, they made $56, which was a lot of money in those days, and it saved Christmas for the Davids.

When we hear the name Wabash, most of us think of Johnny Cash's "Wabash Cannonball." Well, Oscar has different memories. He was to be the express agent (baggage agent) for the Wabash. He made the route from Moberly to Kansas City, Moberly to St. Louis, and Moberly to Des Moines, Iowa. Oscar has many wonderful stories he tells of his many years with the railroad and the different express companies that he has been affiliated with.

We want to thank Oscar and Wivi for sharing their memories.

Dermott, John

Webb City's history is full of stories of men going from rags to riches, men making it big in the mining industry and losing it all, and those who struck it rich just kept making more money. I enjoy the rags to riches stories the best. One such story begins in Ireland, concerning the Dermott brothers, James and John.

In Ireland, there were daily letters from the lucky Irishmen who had saved enough money to take their families to America. The letters might have been loaded with a bit of Irish blarney as they told of the streets of gold, plenty of money, and never a want for food. Those letters encouraged many to leave their motherland and make the long journey to America.

One young man had a dream to go to America, the land of opportunity, and his name was James Dermott. As he saved his money and dreamed his dream, he soon found that he was not making this journey alone. His parents had also read the letters, and they knew their youngest son would have a better chance in America and sent their young son, John, off to America with his older brother, James, in 1889.

Even at a young age, John had a determination to succeed. He became a mining operator and was involved in mining companies, such as Oronogo Circle, Pleasant Valley, and Margerium. Knowing how quickly a person could lose all their money with the failing of a mine, John Dermott invested in real estate and other businesses.

John built an impressive building at the Thirty-Four South Main (at that time known as Allen Street), the northwest corner. His name is featured on the front of the building. To add to his real estate ventures, John built a second building in Webb City. He built the Zinc Ore Building at Eight South Main, the present home of the *Webb City Sentinel*. Dermott replaced the original wood-frame building with a three-story brick building. Dermott used one of the upstairs rooms as his office.

Dermott platted out a section of land known as the Dermott Subdivision, 1907 (and he even had a street named after him, located west of Madison where West Fourth Street is now located).

John Dermott had one child, a daughter named Belle Dermott. Belle married Thomas J. Roney, who was elected to office as a state representative of the central district of Jasper County, and he also had an office in the Zinc Ore Building, rooms 1–4.

At the age of seventy-three, John Dermott passed. His name will live on in the Dermott Addition, the Dermott Building, and the Zinc Ore Building. Alas his street is no longer in existence but is known as West Fourth Street.

John's brother, James Dermott, settled in Lamar, and they remained close through the years.

The Dermott Building has had many occupants; many stayed for quite a while, such as F. M. King Grocery for many years. The Dermott Building has been home to Herrod Groceries and Meat, J. W. Herrod proprietor, and Marr Grocery. In our days, we can remember Downtown Pizza and, most recently, the Work Out Center. The upstairs has mostly been apartments.

The Zinc Ore Building showed up on the Sanborn map in 1906. Dermott leased out the bottom floor for retail, starting out with gentlemen's clothing, furnishings, and shoes. Most of the top floor was meant to be used for a lodge hall and, for the most part, remains unchanged. Bob Foos says there is still evidence that the Sisters of Pythias met there.

The home of John Dermott was 110 North Ball. That home seemed to stay in the family for quite a while. Representative Thomas J. Roney's father, James Roney, passed away in 1925, and he was listed as living at 110 North Ball Street. In the city directory of 1928, Thomas and Belle Roney were living at the home address at 110 North Ball. Chester Roney, son of Thomas and Belle, was listed as living at the home address. Chester later moved to 212 South Pennsylvania Street. And in 1947, the widow Belle Roney was still at the home address. The home at 110 North Ball Street held a few generations of the Roney family. James Dermott was the first generation. Still in the first generation was James Roney's father, State Representative Thomas J. Roney. The next generation was Thomas and Belle Roney, son of James Roney and daughter of James Dermott. The son of Thomas and Belle Roney was their son Chester who lived in that home until he married and moved to 212 South Pennsylvania. In the 8 South Allen Street (Main) Street, the Zinc Ore Building, James Dermott had an office, Thomas J. Roney had an office, and Chester had a store in the Zinc Ore Building.

The retail portion of the Zinc Ore Building shows the gentlemen's clothing continued at that location for quite a few years. In the 1919, city directory Sol. H. Baum Clothing was listed as the main concern with M. R. Lively in an office upstairs. By 1928, the city directory listed the Zinc Ore Building as home of the Webb City Bakery, with the lawyer offices of M. R. Lively and Ray E. Watson located upstairs. By this time, the Sisters of Pythias had moved to their new hall at 110 1/2 West Broadway (the Coyne Building).

The 1947 city directory for Eight South Main, the Zinc Ore Building has The Gambles Store, selling automotive and farm supplies and appliances. The upstairs offices were rented to a lawyer named Wayne Wheeling, Webb City & Joplin Ballast Company, and the Webb City & Joplin Sand & Gravel Company.

In later years, Chester Roney put in a little gift shop where he sold lots of miscellaneous, and he loved to put stickers on knickknacks that said they were a souvenir of Webb City and purchased at Roney's.

The upstairs offices were later occupied by Max Glover. Lettering on one of the office doors bore the name John Webb, who was a lawyer and state representative. A doctor's office was in the back.

A 1953 telephone directory listed Chester Roney's hardware store in the Zinc Ore Building, with Chester living at 212 South Pennsylvania and his mother, Belle Roney, still living at 110 North Ball Street. Max Glover's law office was still located upstairs. The Roney family was a close family.

Each of the buildings standing in Webb City represent lots of history and memories. Each building is well worth restoring to enable them to last into the future.

The street going west from Madison on Fourth Street used to be called Dermott Street.

Dickson, Josiah

In the early morning light, you could hear the sound of a milk truck moving along from house to house in Webb City. The jingle of glass bottles broke the morning silence. The stray cats in the neighborhood followed along, hoping to be close by in case some milk should spill.

As Josiah Dickson made his deliveries, his mind would wander back to the day he married his lovely bride, Elmira Louisa Obert Dickson. She had looked so beautiful in her lacey wedding dress, and he was proud to share his name with her. Together they had produced a family of nine children (including two sets of twins). Elmira was always ready to follow Josiah in his many whims, even when it took them all the way to New Mexico. That had been in 1913, and their fifth and sixth children (the first set of twins) had been born in the new territory they were visiting.

The trip back from New Mexico was rather tedious, with the small twins, a two-year old, and a four-year old. The two oldest boys, ages nine and eleven, helped with the covered wagon. That's the kind of trip that determined what pioneers were really made of.

Once back in good old Jasper County, Elmira and Josiah decided this was the place to stay. They had married in Carthage in 1901 and started their family in that beautiful city. The last of their three children were born in Carterville, and then they moved to Webb City. With such a large family, the perfect place to raise them just happened to be the old W. A. Daugherty home on what is now Colonial Road.

Raising a large family was a tough job, but it became even tougher for Elmira when Josiah passed away in 1924, at the age of forty-eight. The youngest girls (twins) were only three years old. Elmira continued to work the farm with the help of her oldest boys, twenty-two-year-old Bill and twenty-year-old Leo. Once again, she showed the stamina that was necessary for early pioneers.

The nine children of Josiah and Elmira were William, Frank Leo, Fern Elizabeth, Josiah Cecil, Marion Lee, Mabel May, Ray C, Helen Jeanette, and Hazel Annette. Each of these children grew up with great respect for their parents who suffered great hardships to raise their beautiful family.

Reverend William Dickson (1797–1884), Josiah's grandfather, had the family Bible, which he passed down to his son, who passed it along to his youngest daughter, and after she passed away, the Bible couldn't be located. Well, just recently, a young man in Oklahoma found the Bible in a bookstore in Oklahoma City, and he purchased it, thinking some family would be searching for it. He advertised it in a genealogy magazine, but his ad went unanswered. A year later, a member of the family was going through old issues of the magazine and found the ad. Taking a chance that he still had the Bible, a phone call was made, and the Bible was finally returned to the Dickson family. That prized possession won't get lost from the family again!

Donehoo, Thomas—Doctor

Thomas Donehoo was born May 1838, in Allegheny County, Pennsylvania, to John Donehoo (Ireland) and Belle McElhaney Donehoo (Virginia). Being on his own by the age of sixteen, he ventured to Platte County, Missouri, and studied medicine in Weston, Missouri.

In 1861, he graduated from St. Louis Medical College and relocated to Leavenworth County, Kansas, to practice his profession. He moved on to Medoc, Jasper County, Missouri, in May of 1867 to practice as a doctor and also to open a drugstore. He ventured to also purchase real estate and stock and sell dry goods and groceries. Not only being a good doctor, Donehoo showed his ability and integrity to be an astute businessman. He also purchased real estate in Webb City on Main Street. His son, John J. Donehoo, also became a doctor and practiced in Joplin, Missouri.

Donehoo building located at Church and Main. The building burned in 1888, and Donehoo rebuilt it, and the brick building burned in January 1989, one hundred years and one month later.

Dumbauld, D. F. and W. A. and B. A.—Doctors All in the Family

In the late 1800s, as the mining industry was booming, two brothers moved into the area from Michigan, and they were both doctors, Dr. D. F. Dumbauld and Dr. W. A. Dumbauld.

Dr. D. F. settled in the Sarcoxie area as he saw a need for a physician. In 1913, he built a new home in Carl Junction and moved from the Sarcoxie area. He passed away in 1915 at the age of fifty-four. He was survived by his widow

Dr. W. A., along with his wife, Elizabeth, and three children, B. A., Della, and Lida, moved to 203 West Main in Carterville.

Dr. W. A.'s son, B. A., started out his career as a hoisterman in the mines but decided he wanted to follow in the footsteps of his father and uncle and study medicine. He graduated from the University of Louisville, Kentucky, and joined his father's practice in 1905. Then he decided to set up his own practice in Webb City in 1906. His office was located at 114 North Webb Street. Dr. B. A. completed several post-graduate courses in New York and at the Mayo Clinic. He served during WWI as a physician and was commissioned a captain. He carried a good reputation all over the area as an outstanding physician.

Dr. B. A.'s nephew and grandson of Dr. W. A. Dumbauld, Richard Newkirk, also carried on the family tradition of joining the medical field.

When Dr. B. A. Dumbauld passed away, his list of pallbearers and honorary pallbearers were a list of distinguished citizens. Pallbearers were Dr. H. C. Vincent, Dr. E. R. Hornback, Dr. R. L. Neff, Dr. Jesse E. Douglass, Dr. R. M. Stormont, Dr. P. L. Pritchett. Honorary pallbearers were Fred Nesbitt, J. M. Hirons, John A. Skinner, Roy Teel, Robert Burress, F. C. Nelson, Woodson Oldham, Harry Easley, William Burch, Don Adamson, J. C. Veatch, Harvey E. Newell, Ben Reynolds, R. D. Toutz, O. B. Landrum, Willard Smith, Tom Goodwin, J. P. Niel, Clarence Walker, H. B. Sanders, Clarence R. Hunt, J. M. Jackson, Dr. H.B. Kerr.

Wife of B. A. Dumbauld was Blanche Dumbauld. His sister was Lida Newkirk, whose son was Dr. Richard Newkirk, and a son named Guy F. Newkirk employed at Empire District Electric Company.

Dunlap, John

John Dunlap was a wagonmaker and carpenter. He was born in Adams County, Ohio, May 8, 1830. His father, William Adams Dunlap, was a Virginian, and his mother, whose maiden name was Margaret Beedle, was a native of Kentucky. He was raised and educated in Ohio, where he attended the common schools and followed farming until nearly manhood when he learned his trade of wagonmaking and carpentry. After finishing his apprenticeship, he came to Scotland County, Missouri, where he resided until 1856, when he went to Andrew County and worked his trade for five years, spending a short time in Kansas. He returned to Scotland County, and from there, he went to Marion County, Iowa, where he remained ten years and then came to Jasper County, Missouri, in 1876 and has since worked his trade in the new town of Webb City. He was married to S. Callaway in Scotland County, Missouri, on October 5, 1851. They have six children: W. J., M. E., Margaret V., Paulina G., Anna B., and John H.

John Dunlap was a member of the Webb City Lodge 512, AF and AM, of which he held the office of SW.

Earles, John Wesley

John Wesley Earles was in partnership with Jerry Clark in the ownership of the Maude B. Mine. John was a schoolteacher in Ohio until he enlisted in the Civil War and served under General Sherman. He never missed a skirmish and quickly rose from private to captain. Even being wounded twice, Earles remained in service until his honorable discharge in 1864.

He returned home to Ohio and was elected sheriff for two years and, in 1867, was appointed United States Deputy Marshal, a position he also held for two years. He then headed to Kansas to try his hand at farming and finally came to Jasper County in 1875 and got involved in mining. He moved to Webb City in 1882. His investment in the Maud B. Mine was his best move. He served as the superintendent of the street from 1884–1886 and claimed to have built many of the main streets of Webb City.

When Earles voted for his first time, he voted for Abe Lincoln.

Etter, John Henry

It's the wee hours of the morning, and the smell of fresh bread filled the air in the west end of Webb City. The aroma was coming from the Etter's bakery, at 1005 West Daugherty Street. After the bread was baked, it's loaded into big wooden crates stacked outside the door. The wooden crates were then carried east across the street to the Frisco station to be loaded onto a train. The train delivered the fresh bread all over the area to small towns not fortunate enough to have a great bakery like Webb City.

John Henry Etter was an apprentice baker to Henry Worner in Centralia, Kansas, Etter's home-town. Worner later moved and opened a bakery in Webb City at the northwest corner of Allen (Main) Street and John (Austin) Street. Worner was open-minded and saw a need for more than one bakery in a booming mining town, so he contacted Etter, who was living in Neosho at the time, and suggested that he give Webb City a chance.

So in 1897, John Henry Etter and his new bride, Fannie Phelps, opened a bakery at the south-west corner of Second and Main Streets (where city hall now stands). After about five years, in 1902, Etter relocated his bakery to the west end of town, at 1005 West Daugherty Street. Etter's bakery was the first wholesale bakery in Webb City. By shipping his bread all over the district, Etter's bakery became well known. With such a great location so close to the railroad, Etter was able to ship his bread by train.

As business grew, so did the need for a larger building. In 1918, John built a modern two-story brick building around the older frame building, continuing baking operations throughout the time of construction.

There were twelve rooms upstairs above the bakery. Fannie was responsible for keeping them rented, and the money was hers to spend.

John built a home for his family just four doors down from the bakery, at 1023 West Daugherty Street. John and Fannie had three beautiful children: Marie (who later married Norval Matthews), Phelps (who married Catherine Hardy), and Maxine (who married Max Miller).

Each day, the children smelled the fresh bread as it came from the oven. They watched with amazement as the bread was loaded into the big wooden crates. Their childhood memories recall the big sacks of flour with the name Ball & Gunning printed on the sides (the Ball & Gunning Mill was located just a block to the north of Etter's Bakery).

Maude Nelson was the bakery bookkeeper, and she was more like family than employee. The Etters had a way of making everyone feel like family. Many wonderful stories have been shared with Marie and Maxine about their father and his kind ways.

A special thanks to Maxine Etter Miller for sharing her photos and information Our town has had so many talented people and so many colorful stories about the good ole days!

Etter's bakery, 1005 West Daugherty, 1902

Brick building of Etter's same location, 1918 later, Matthews Coffee

Fetters, Joseph—Justice of the Peace

Native of Ohio, Joseph Fetters was born in Carroll, Ohio, December 6, 1831. His father's name was Jacob Fetters, who was born in Germany in 1806 and came to this country as a child with his parents. Joseph's mother was Mary A. Shoemaker, a native of Pennsylvania, born in 1808. Jacob and Mary brought Joseph to Missouri in 1839 and settled in Scotland County where he remained until 1869 when he moved to Crawford County, Kansas, staying there for four years before moving to Jasper County, Missouri. In 1877, he settled in Webb City, Missouri, becoming engaged in mining and becoming very successful. He married Elizabeth Myers of Scotland County, Missouri, in 1856 and they have three children: Osmer Fetters, Joseph M. Fetters, and James T. Fetters.

Joseph Fetters was elected justice of the peace in 1878. Having a pleasant demeanor and social graces, the people of Webb City loved and respected him as justice of the peace. He was a Democrat with liberal religious views. He was as strong Union man and was opposed to secession.

Fitzpatrick, Robert C.

Born March 4, 1846, in New York, came to Missouri in 1869, settling in northern Jasper County in 1879. A miner by heart, he did serve one year as marshal of Webb City, Missouri, and one year as sheriff of Joplin Township.

Forlow, Frank L.

Frank Leslie Forlow is not a name that we are familiar with. There isn't a street named in his honor or a building with the Forlow name in the cement or many residents with the name of Forlow. But that name, in the late 1800s and the early 1900s, would have sparked a conversation of respect and admiration for Frank L. Forlow.

Frank was born in Hicksville Township, Defiance County, Ohio, on October 31, 1858. His parents were Amos and Eliza (Myers) Forlow. Amos was born in Ohio, and Eliza came from Pennsylvania. Frank L. Forlow's paternal ancestors came to America from Ireland prior to the Revolutionary War. He grew up on the family farm and attended school in Defiance. He went on to the Northwestern University and graduated in 1878. He started his career as a schoolteacher but only as a way of earning money to obtain his true desire which was to become an attorney.

After teaching for five years, in 1883, Frank gave up teaching and entered a law office in Defiance to complete his preparation for admission to the bar. He came to Joplin, for a short time after he received his law degree, in 1885, and met a fine young lady named Ms. Ida May Harmony, daughter of W. S. Harmony, on Jackson Avenue in Joplin. They were wed on September 16, 1885. It must have been a whirlwind romance. After the wedding, the couple moved back to Defiance for Frank to get established in his legal career.

In 1894, after nine years with the law firm Thompson, Forlow & Company, Ida and Frank moved to Webb City. Frank had an urge to be with a growing and developing territory, and Webb City definitely fit that description. He opened his legal office at 112 North Allen, and that was where his business remained until the day of his death on March 28, 1927. Allen Street was changed to Main Street in 1920, so Forlow did not change the location of his business, but the address did change.

Throughout the years, Frank developed a reputation as an honest upright citizen. He was involved in the community, and according to the resolution made at his death, "He performed well all of his duties to his community, state, and government." What a nice way to be remembered. It also stated, "He had a high regard for his profession and conducted himself in a way to gain respect."

His duties to the community included six years on the board of education, with which he was a voice and an active participant in raising the standard of the schools. He was on the school board during the time of the bond election to build a new school. He was a member of the Elks Lodge (first joining in Ohio). He was president of the National Bank, starting out as just a member of the board before becoming vice president and moving on to president. He was president at the time of the consolidation of the National Bank and Webb City Bank.

At the time of his death, Frank had served ten years as president of the county bar association and was a Democratic member of the state board. Frank had such a good reputation as a prominent attorney that there wasn't enough time to accept all the cases presented to him, but those that he did accept were treated with the utmost respect and courtesy.

Mining was such a strong force in the area that Frank couldn't help but become involved in that line of activity. His efforts were rewarded. Mostly his success was due to the fact that prudence and foresight governed his investments. Frank Forlow was always the master of the situation with all its powers and opportunities in his control.

So as you walk or drive past the building to the south of the old Merchants & Miners Bank building, remember that there used to be an upstairs with a legal office belonging to Frank L. Forlow for thirty-three years, from 1894–1927.

Freeman Brothers: Van, Ira, Henry

A native of New York, Van Freeman was born November 22, 1852, to Frank and Margaret Clem Freeman. Frank was a native of New York, and Margaret was from Ohio and was of German descent.

Van Freeman was raised on the family farm and received his education in a public school. In 1871, at the age of nineteen, Van went to Sedgwick County, Kansas, to begin a career of buying and selling stock. In the early part of 1882, Van decided to join his brothers Ira and Henry Freeman in their business, Freeman Brothers Butchers, in Webb City. Freeman Brothers did a most extensive business in Webb City and Carterville, opening their business in 1882.

Fredrickson, Charles

Charles Johan Fredrickson was not a stranger to the mining field. It was the talk of an ore strike in a small southern Missouri town that prompted Charles to leave his family in Motala, Sweden, in 1888, at the age of twenty-one.

Webb City was a booming mining, town and as the work spread, people came by horseback, wagons, train, and on foot. Jobs were scarce. Men were forced to sit around the shafts of the mines, waiting for someone to get killed so they could have his job.

A mining injury caused Charles to have a deformed spine that resulted in a hump on his back. But this did not dampen the spirits of this bright young man. Charles was able to feel at home in the midst of the Swedish community of Webb City. There were many picnics, footraces, and singing fests.

Because of his back injury, Charles was determined to never work below in the mines again. Being friends with Tom Coyne, a mine operator, they became partners in the drilling business. Charles eventually owned his own drilling rig.

In 1906, Charles Fredrickson married Emma Anderson. Emma was also from Sweden, a little town called Kristinebergs. She had come to Webb City to stay with an aunt who owned a boarding house for miners. Charles was thirty-nine, and Emma was sweet sixteen. As a wedding gift, Tom Coyne told them to pick out any furniture they wanted, and he would pay for it. Charles and Emma did not want to take advantage of their good friend, and they were very conservative in their selections.

The Fredricksons had a very beautiful family. The children were Hulda Evelyn Fredrickson, born in 1907; Carl Adolph Fredrickson, born in 1909; Thomas Fredrick Fredrickson, born in 1913; Emma Louise Fredrickson, born in 1916; Mary Frances Fredrickson, born in 1926; and then at the age of forty-five and sixty-eight, they had their last child, John Eric Fredrickson, born in 1935.

In 1913, Charles took time out from his drilling to go to California to acquire some mining leases on property in the Waco area. He was given an interest in the mines in exchange for obtaining the leases. Throughout the years, Charles had seen many men become millionaires, but he had also seen many men lose everything they owned. So being the conservative that he was, Charles sold out his interest in the mines for $8,000 (which was a lot of money in those days). But you can't help but wonder, would Charles have been one of those millionaires we read about if he hadn't sold his interest in the mines? But Charles had nothing to regret about his life. He had come to America to prove that he was *somebody*, and he had succeeded!

A special thanks to Evelyn (Fredrickson) Surgi for sharing the history of her father.

Fredrickson family lore keeps story of car alive for years.

Charles Fredrickson had traded his old 1913 Ford in for a new 1924 model. It was a beauty! His family was the envy of neighborhood, as the parents drove to the graduation ceremony for their daughter Evelyn, with their son Carl behind the wheel. Once they got there, Carl decided he didn't want to go to a silly program, so he wrote a note to his family, put the keys in the car, and left on foot. When the family came out after the ceremony, the car was not to be found. Charlie was mad at himself for allowing Carl to take the keys and especially mad at himself for not buying insurance.

After a thorough search, the police informed Charlie they couldn't find his new Ford. Charlie gave up hope of ever finding his car again.

But that wasn't the only thing ever stolen from Charlie and Emma. Two years after the disappearance of the car, Emma's chickens were stolen. Emma was a steady self-reliant woman, and those chickens represented her accomplishments, not to mention her spending money.

Emma kept her eye on the newspaper, and as soon as some men were arrested for stealing chickens, she went to check it out. Emma even went to the trial to see if she could figure out if they were the same men who had stolen her precious chickens. As the trial progressed, she heard it mentioned several times that the thieves were driving a 1924 Ford. Emma's mind was working—could it be the Ford that was stolen from them two years ago?

Straight to the garage where the car was being stored went the steady self-reliant Emma. She wanted to check that Ford. She wrote down the serial numbers off the car to check with the title when she got home.

Being a patient person, she waited until after supper that night before she asked Charlie to get out the title of the Ford to compare the numbers she had acquired that day. Sure enough, they matched. Those thieves had not only stolen all of Emma's chickens, but they had used her own vehicle for the getaway!

The next morning, Charlie and Emma went to the police to report what Emma had uncovered. After investigation, the police determined that the chicken thieves had bought the car from a member of a car theft ring out of Oklahoma.

Charlie got his car back, and he learned to keep those keys close at hand. He wasn't taking any chances anymore. As for Emma and her chickens, she gave them up. She said it wasn't worth it anymore if she had to spend all that time running down car thieves and chicken thieves.

A special thanks to Evelyn Surgi for sharing this interesting story about her parents.

Frising, Nic—The Cartoonist

In writing about people of the past, we cannot pass up a great artist that drew pictures for the *Webb City Sentinel* for about twenty-five years, and that is Nic Frising. I don't know about you, but I couldn't wait to see what event had caught Nic's eye for the week and what cartoon he would draw to highlight that event. He had such humor in his drawings and usually captured the special features of the selected character he would choose to grace his cartoon of the week. What talent Nic had, and we are so thankful he shared that talent with us.

Nic loved to draw caricatures and enjoyed teaching others to draw. You could find him at many city activities with Sharpie in hand and a long line of willing victims (I mean models). His work was published in many magazines and newspapers. You could catch some of his charming drawings in local cookbooks, church history books, and, of course, on many T-shirts. Nic and his wife, Nancy, had a T-shirt business with the appropriate name of Sparkle Graphics, which took Nic's drawings out to the public even more.

You could recognize Nic's distinctive work by his trademark sparkle that he would add to his drawings. A sparkle that brought a smile to your face before you even looked at the cartoon because you knew it was a Nic Frising original. He once said that the sparkle was his personal thank you to God for his talents and blessings. He was quick to help those in need and to give a smile to cheer up someone feeling down.

Nic had another passion besides his artwork—he loved bicycles. You could always catch his ad in the paper each week as he searched for old bicycles. He had a storefront on Main Street in Joplin where he could display some of his restored works of art on two wheels.

His passion for bicycles took him into the world of motorcycles and the Harley Davidson circuit. He was also a member of a local group of men known as the Macho Club, whom he would feature in many of his weekly cartoons.

We miss his smile, his sense of humor, and his weekly cartoon. Nic definitely fits into our list of people to remember.

Fullmer, Daniel

Around the late 1800s, many families migrated to this area. Daniel and Caroline Fullmer moved to the Prairie Hill district in Jasper County in about 1877.

A farmer and landowner, Daniel Fullmer had been noted as being a success in his business career and is respected for his honorable methods and reliability.

Born in St. Clair County, Illinois, on September 28, 1838, to Peter (Germany) and Eva Uninger (Germany) Fullmer, Peter came to America in 1834. Daniel is the sixth child and fourth son of eight children.

Daniel married Caroline Marker (Illinois)in 1873, in Washington County, Illinois. They had five children: Katie Jane Fuller, who married John Newby; George Fullmer, who married Ella Webb; Alpha Fullmer; John Leonard Fullmer; and Jerome Fullmer, died in infancy.

Daniel Fullmer voted for Abraham Lincoln. In 1865, he enlisted for service in the Civil War, becoming a member of Company B, 149th Illinois Volunteer Infantry, in which he served until the close of hostilities. Two of his brothers also participated in the struggle, one, John Fullmer, laid down his life on the altar of his country. William Fullmer was also a member of the 149th Illinois Volunteer Regiment. Daniel was a member of the GAR post in Carl Junction. His religion was Protestant Methodist. He was active in anything and everything pertaining to the welfare and advancement of Jasper County.

Gammon, James

Silas and Margaret McLyra Gammon had a son named James Gammon, born on November 15, 1837, in Orange County, Indiana. Silas was from Pittsylvania County, Virginia, and Margaret hailed from East Tennessee. Not long after they were married, they moved to Indiana when it was still a territory. In 1850, they made another change in their lives by moving the family to Clay County, Illinois, settling on a farm near Xenia.

James grew up learning about farm life and continued that line of work after moving to Missouri in 1863. He had married Ms. Elizabeth Flemming (a native of Ohio) on January 10, 1856, and he moved his family with him. When he moved to Jasper County, Missouri, in 1869, he added stock-raising to his farmwork.

Desiring a change in life, James Gammon started a mercantile business in Webb City in 1875, just as the city was being constructed, and the mining excitement was in full force. He invested in some mining companies, becoming partner in several large companies. Speaking of large companies, James and Elizabeth had nine children: Levy, Cora, George, John, Lemuel, Lillie C., Silas O., Addie, Lewis, and Alfred, who passed at a young age. A large family comes in handy to help with farmwork.

Geiger, George W.

John and Rachel Yergey Geiger worked hard every day on their little farm in Pottsville, Pennsylvania. John came from a farming family, having been born in Pennsylvania in 1814, and his lovely wife came from a farming family near Pennsylvania's Dutch colony.

Farming was not an easy profession, and even though it was passed down from generation to generation, there were some that just didn't "cotton to it." One of those was John and Rachel's son, George W. Geiger. George was born January 10, 1864, on the Geiger farm. He didn't take too well to school, and his parents needed his help on the farm, so he left school at an early age to assist the family.

His mother died in 1877, when George was only thirteen years old. Life on the farm changed after his mother was gone, but George was only looking for an excuse to leave a lifestyle in which he didn't feel comfortable. So at the age of sixteen, he headed out into the world to learn a trade. He didn't go far at first, apprenticing himself to C. O. Swinhart in Pottsville as a tinner. He was a good student and learned quickly. He finished his apprenticeship in Mahoney City, Pennsylvania, and continued to work there for one year, and then his journeys began.

George traveled from one place to another, landing in different towns only long enough to get a job, save a little money, and then venture on to the next chapter in his life. For sixteen years, George traveled from the Atlantic to the Pacific and from Canada to Mexico. He hit all four corners of the United States. Exciting as his life seemed, George began to have a desire to settle down and have a family. So in August of 1897, at the age of thirty-three, George arrived in Webb City, Missouri. He worked for Harrison and Lloyd, and within a year, he was married to Julia McCool. George was the father to two children, Anna and Lee.

George went to work for A. V. Allen in Joplin as a tinner, and when the tin line was slack, he took up employment in the mines, earning $1.25 a day. He worked hard to make extra money, which he saved up with a goal in mind. Finally in 1904, he had saved enough to fulfill his dream, and he purchased his own tin shop.

He soon discovered there wasn't enough business in tinware alone to do more than barely gain a living, so he added furniture and hardware to his stock. His hardware became one of the best in the area. His store was located at 109 South Main.

After the death of his wife, Julia, in 1912, George remarried, and he and his new wife, Mary, lived at 102 South Tom Street, just around the corner from the store. Because of his extensive traveling as a young man, George had many stories to share about his journeys. Some of his friends began to bore of his stories, so he learned to keep the stories short and sweet to keep his audience. He quoted an old wheelwright who said, "The longer the spoke, the bigger the tire."

Along with the hardware, new and used furniture, and tinwork, George also sold and repaired stoves. His motto was "You can find what you want at Geiger's."

Well, in 1926, George was hard at work transferring part of a furnace from Webster School to the old Eugene Field School at Fourth Street and Oronogo Street. He was riding down Fourth Street, on the back of a truck, holding the furnace in place. He lost his balance and fell, striking his head on the pavement. George Geiger died doing the work that he loved. After sixteen years of searching for his niche in life, he had spent twenty-two years in the hardware business and twenty-nine years in a little town called Webb City. His reputation of being an honest man with which to do business shows that he loved his work, and he loved the people of his town. At the age of sixty-two, George left his mark in the world.

Gentry, Colby Claborn—Doctor

Doctor Gentry passed away October 1913. He died of erysipelas. He contracted this deadly disease while taking care of his wife, who died one week earlier from the same disease. Mrs. Gentry, age sixty, was buried in Harwood, Missouri. Dr. Gentry was buried in Sturgeon, Missouri. They had one son, T. E. Gentry, who had moved to Chicago, Illinois. They had a foster son, Paul Gentry.

Glasscock, J. W.

J. W. Glasscock was born in Jasper County, Missouri, March 20, 1856, to Eli and Nancy Glasscock of Tennessee. The third of four children, J. W. was educated in Jasper County. In 1877, he married Margaret Vancil. They lived on the family farm and had two children, Nora and Zula. J. W. worked for the post office as well as farming.

Green, Leander—Judge

Josiah Green was of Virginia. His grandfather Jeremiah Green of North Carolina (a cousin to General Green of Revolution fame) was a Revolutionary soldier and served all seven years of the war.

Josiah's wife, Rebecca Long Green, was from Kentucky. Josiah and Rebecca lived in Kentucky until they moved to Sangamon County, Illinois, near Springfield in, 1830, making that their home and living there until their deaths in 1850 and 1854. They raised nine children.

Their fifth child, Leander Green, was born February 27, 1828. He married Ms. Mary E. Baker in Christian County, Illinois, in December of 1852, and they had two children, William and Harry.

Following in his family's footsteps, Leander Green served for years in the Forty-First Illinois Infantry, enlisting at Decatur, Illinois, August 5, 1861. In 1862, he was commissioned second lieutenant of Company I and, shortly after, advanced to first lieutenant. He was soon transferred to the quartermaster's department and stationed at Springfield, Illinois, where he served until the close of the war.

Leander Green, with the title of judge, moved to Medoc in Jasper County, Missouri, in April of 1868. He opened a general mercantile business which he worked for ten years, and he dabbled in farming for five years. In 1872, he was elected a member of the county court of Jasper County. He served one year.

In 1880, he moved his family to Webb City, Missouri, and opened a drugstore. Living in Webb City, Judge Green could not resist the temptation to have an interest in mining. Joining in with Captain J. G. Reid, they owned two paying mines, which they supplied with the latest improved mining machinery. They kept a working force of twenty men.

Judge Green was a Republican and had been nominated for the office of General Assembly of the state of Missouri. He and his wife were members of the Christian church of Webb City.

The judge's son William was a prominent attorney in Carthage with Thomas & Green.

Green, P. B.—Doctor

Green was born in DeKalb County, Alabama, June 28, 1852, and the son of Dr. A. B. and Ella Bruce Green, both natives of Tennessee.

Dr. P. B. Green received his medical education from Vanderbilt University in Nashville, Tennessee. He began his career practicing with his father in DeKalb County. He practiced in Waco, Texas, for one year. He also practiced in Pine Bluff, Arkansas, and Galena, Kansas, before locating to Webb City, Missouri, in 1881.

The Gretz Family

Fred Gretz was born in Germany in 1855 at a time in German history when the country seemed to be constantly at battle. There were many uprisings. At a young age, Fred made the journey to the New World, the United States of America, where hopes and dreams were meant to come true. Everyone knew you could find happiness if you could just get to America.

Landing in New York, Fred found that it was such a busy place, a new immigrant could easily get lost in the shuffle. Surprisingly most immigrants that were eager to leave their own countries always seemed to gather together and make small communities of their own nationalities. It was just such a community that Fred met a lovely young German named Laura, who had come to America with her parents.

After Fred and Laura had been married awhile, Fred heard about money being made in a small community in Missouri. So the small family loaded up and made the long journey by wagon to Webb City, Missouri, in 1884. Laura's mother and father were saddened to see their daughter leave, knowing they would probably never see her again. She was heading into the unknown, just as they had done by heading to America.

The young Gretz family joined the many others who were waiting in line for a chance at employment in the mines. The city of Webb City was growing at such a fast pace that there was a shortage of housing. Many families were housed in tents at the edge of town. Food was not always available, but Fred was one of those determined young men who always managed to find the right path to follow.

After a short mining career, Fred found himself in a new line of work, which seemed to suit him fine. Fred became an employee of the Southwest Missouri Railroad Company, which was a wonderful job for such a talented young man. Fred was superintendent of the undermining. He was in charge of keeping the right-of-way clear and unthreatened. Fred held this job with the Southwest Railroad Company for twenty-five years before retiring.

The Gretz home was located at 333 South Ball, and the Gretzes had six beautiful children. Family was an important commodity in this land. There was Charles Gretz who worked the mines. He worked the sludge table. Charles was married to Gertrude, and they had three sons: Carl, Paul, and Walter; and two daughters, Lora Rose and Ruth Oldham. Carl's sweet wife, who is eighty-four, said the Gretz family was just good common folk who worked hard for their money.

There were two other sons in the Fred Gretz family, Harry and Fred Jr. Fred Jr. worked in the mines until he was forty-seven, and health reasons forced him to leave. He had Bright's disease.

Now there were three girls born to Fred and Laura. Minnie May Gretz married Albert Michie (more on that family in the future). Albert was postmaster in Webb City for a while. Lena Gretz became Lena Sanderson, and Mary gave up bookkeeping to become Mrs. Mary Fehrenberg.

Of this hardworking family, the only ones left in this area are Mrs. Carl Gretz and her son, Melvin, and his family. But the Gretz family was part of the backbone that made Webb City the community it is. Too often, we focus on mining tycoons who had the money to back the mines, but those mines wouldn't have made any money without the miners who gave more than their time in the mines. Many gave their health and lives.

Gunning, William S.

William S. Gunning was born in Farmersville, Ohio, in the year 1867. By the age of two, his parents made the move to the uncharted area north of what is now Oronogo.

William grew up in a very industrious territory. He watched men get rich off the mines, and he observed those who lost everything they owned when their mines failed.

The first business adventure that William delved into was a livery stable in Oronogo. Business was good, and William was happy with his choice, but in the back of his mind, he yearned to try his hand in the mining business. Making some choice decisions, William went into mining with another industrious young man by the name of Walter Claude Ball.

You will recall from a previous story that George Ball came to town without a penny to his name and no shoes on his feet. By doing a good job and showing what a hard worker he was, he was given a chance to take over a mine that kept filling up with water and was of no use to the present owner. Using his skills to figure out the problem, Ball was able to get the water under control and became quite wealthy in the mining business. George's son was named Walter Claude Ball.

Ball and Gunning owned several mines together; one of the most famous was the Oronogo Circle. Others included the Little Mary, Dinger Mine, Bird Dog Mine, and the High Five Mine.

William and his wife, Sarah, moved to Webb City in 1900. William had the chance to enter into another business adventure. He and J. W. Boyd bought the S. H. Veatch Milling Company at Austin and Madison Streets. The business was going great when the name changed to Boyd & Gunning Milling Company. W. S. Gunning was the manager, and his goal was to continue the reputation that the milling company had with the Veatch family of "honesty in their products and fair dealings with their customers." Gunning did that and then some, as he gave his personal attention to the business.

Boyd eventually sold his share of the milling business to W. C. Ball, and the name changed to Ball & Gunning Milling Company. Gunning continued to manage the mill, and business continued to flourish.

William Gunning invested his money in several other mills in the area. There was the Monett Milling Company and a grain business in Fort Smith, Arkansas. He also invested in real estate in Webb City, as he knew that the land would always be worth money.

W. C. Ball and W. S. Gunning must have had a lot of mutual respect for each other, besides being good friends, because they continued as investment partners. They not only shared the milling company and several mines, they also shared interest in the Joplin Globe Publishing Company.

It's a shame that such a good business mind had to leave us at such a young age. By the age of fifty-eight, in 1925, William S. Gunning passed away from heart disease. His wife continued to live in Webb City for another twenty-five years. Their farmhouse was located right where McDonald's sits today. In talking with Eddie Vaughn, who is W. S. Gunning's grandson, I learned that the Gunning home was moved to Prairie Flower Road when the highway (MacArthur Drive) came through. Of course, after the Gunning home and before McDonald's at that location, there was the Ozark Motel and Restaurant.

William and Sarah had three daughters: Fern, who married Lawrence Vaughn; Lola, who married Earl Beale; and Treva.

Hall, William E.—John C. Webb's Son-In-Law

William E. Hall was born in Jasper County on March 14, 1845, and his father, Winston Hall, was born in North Carolina in 1818 and came to Jasper County in 1837, married Jane Roberson, also from North Carolina, and she came to Jasper County in 1840. They purchased 240 acres in Jasper County, built a log cabin.

William's parents, Winston (born 1818) and Jane Robertson Hall, were of Jasper County pioneer stock whose families moved here in 1838 and 1840 from North Carolina, with Winston and Jane being married not too long after the families were settled. Their son, William, was born March 14, 1845, on the 240-acre family farm. When Winston passed away in 1863, eighteen-year-old William took on the care and upkeep of the farm.

Not too long after taking on this challenge, William accepted the call of the Civil War and joined the Confederate Army, being one of the first soldiers sent to the front with the newly formed unit from Jasper County. William served under General Shelby, General Standwaite, and General Cooper.

With an honorable discharge at the end of the Civil War in 1865, William went to Texas to assist his mother, who had moved there for safety during the war. He made a quick trip back to Jasper County to marry Margaret Glasscox, and they returned to Texas.

In 1869, William's mother, Jane Hall, passed away, and sadly one year later, his wife, Margaret Hall, passed away, leaving William alone. He made the journey back home to familiar territory in Jasper County and soon worked up a career in the stock industry with transporting cattle from Texas to Missouri.

Starting a farm not far from the Webb farm in Mineral Township, William spent quite a bit of time visiting with John Webb. It was not a surprise when twenty-six-year-old William married Webb's eighteen-year-old daughter, Martha, on May 7, 1871. Since their farm was close by, William was there when John C. Webb established the town of Webb City in 1876. He even had a street named after him, Hall Street.

William worked as the Mineral Township assessor in 1874–1876 and, in 1878, became the county collector. The commute between the farm and the Carthage Courthouse was very tiring, especially with keeping up the farm, so the Hall family (William, Martha, Winston, Ed, C. Tom, and Ruth) moved to Carthage.

In 1883, William purchased an eight-hundred-acre farm just east of Webb City and west of Carthage and named it Hallwood. The farm became well known across the state as William raised some of the finest trotters and saddle horses. Once again, the family moved back to Carthage in 1889, but William still worked the farm.

In 1894, Jasper County formed the United Confederate Veterans Camp, and William Hall served as the treasurer since he was one of the first called to duty in Jasper County.

William and Martha had four children: John Winston, who died at age eighteen; Ruth, who became Mrs. Harry A. Vanderford of Nashville, Tennessee, and who passed away in 1897; Thomas, who married Mary H. Hendrix of Fayette, Missouri, and resided in Carthage; and Edward, who was engaged in the stock business on his father's farm.

William E. Hall died in 1907 at the age of sixty-two. He was described as a Democrat, he belonged to the Masons fraternity. He was a Methodist. He was a man of very strong convictions, and his integrity stood as an unquestioned fact in his career. The business policy he always followed was most commendable. His career was one which would bear the light of the closest investigation and scrutiny. He was faithful to duty with strict adherence to a fixed purpose in life, which will do more to advance a man's interest than wealth or advantaged circumstances. William Hall was accounted as one of the wealthy residents of Carthage.

Martha and her son Ed moved back to Hallwood. The exact location of Hallwood Farm was from Carthage, driving west out of town on State Highway 96, which is north of the old US Route 66, there is a sweeping curve in the road. At that curve, turn right to the north on County Road 180. Cross a small bridge, and just north of that bridge, there is a small road that turned back to the west that led to Hallwood Farm. The fifteen-room home was a wooden frame building with extremely nice furnishings that Martha had accumulated.

Tragedy struck the Hall family on Friday night, April 28, 1916, when a fire started in what might have been the rear of the house, maybe the kitchen area. Martha's son was awakened by the screams of his mother, and then he smelled the smoke. Ed could not find his mother or her maid, Alma Shaw, anywhere in the flames, so he went outside to see if she was there and headed back into the burning building. Ed received burns all over his body and finally had to be held back as he wanted to continue hunting for his mother.

The remains that were located in the house were impossible to identify which was Martha's and which was Alma Shaw's. Ed was taken to the hospital about midnight and passed away the next day from the burns and damage to his lungs.

The Hallwood mansion, since it was not in the city limits, was equipped with a waterworks system in the walls to prevent such a fire, but the walls collapsed quickly during the hot fire and disabled the water system. About midnight, according to the *Carthage Press*:

The Fire Chief S. T. Mathews and Fireman James Mealey, of the Carthage fire department, were taken out to the farm in a taxicab, arriving there about midnight. They took with them six of the small chemical fire extinguishers of which the department has a supply, but they could do nothing, as the walls had fallen in and lay in the basement, a mass of glowing coals.

There was a large turnout for the triple funeral. The remains that were found and unidentifiable between Martha and her maid, Alma Shaw, were put into a shared coffin. The coffins were placed in the mausoleum in Park Cemetery.

It was stated in the Carthage Press:

Mrs. Hall was noted for her philanthropy, although she made no great show of charity work that she did. Many young people, less fortunate financially than she, were indebted to her for their privileges of attending school. She was one of the most widely and favorable known women of the county.

She formerly was one of the most substantial members of the Methodist Episcopal church, South, of this city, having been active in the work of that church and many of the church organizations. She was the organizer of the missionary society of the church and took an active part in promoting other activities. She was a member of the Methodist Episcopal church, South, of Webb City at the time of her death. She formerly was active in the Eastern Star Lodge and other clubs and lodges. She was a member of the Rocking Chair Club, the Ianthe-Vincent C.L.S.C. and the Sixth Street. The funeral was characterized by the large number of lodges and society members who attended. At the Mausoleum the Eastern Star lodge had charge of the funeral rites over Mrs. Hall, and the Elks Lodge had charge of the services over Ed Hall.

At the time of her death, Martha was survived by her son, C. T. (Tom) Hall, and her brother, E. T. Webb. Quite a sad ending for a member of Webb City's first family.

More information on Hall listed with the Webb family.

Hancock, James C.

Hancock was a native of Wayne County, Kentucky, born October 12, 1834. His father was Benjamin Hancock, born 1779 in South Carolina. His mother was Elizabeth Vickery, German descent of Kentucky. His grandfather, father to Benjamin, was a Revolutionary soldier.

James graduated from Monticello Academy and attended Columbia College in Kentucky. His health began to fail, so he taught at Duval's Valley, Kentucky, for seventeen months. He began to travel, heading to northern Missouri in 1860. In 1864, he headed to Montana to engage in a mining and stock-raising business before returning to northern Missouri in 1867 to try his hand at farming. He married Elizabeth Owen Morris in Randolph County, Missouri. In 1873, he traveled around until he landed in Arkansas in 1874. His wife died while in Arkansas, June 12, 1876. He remarried again in Boone County, Arkansas, to Ms. Mary A. Lowe. On the move again, he came to Webb City, Missouri, in 1878. He started up a furniture business with a partner, Hancock & Lowe.

Hardy Family

Hardy, Joseph Allen, Sr.—The following information about a well-known forefather of Webb City was gathered by Harry Hood, Emily Hardy Kramer, and Leslie Myers. What a lifestyle and legacy left by this man's history. According to family legend, Main Street, which was once called Allen Street, may have been named in honor of this man, but alas, the street was changed to Main Street, and fame was set aside and forgotten.

Joseph Allen Hardy, an early-day mine operator in the Webb City district, was born August 15, 1840, in Ralls County, Missouri. He was the son of Joseph Arnold and Julia Anna (Gardner) Hardy, who both were born in Frankfort, Kentucky, the father in 1812–1879 and the mother in 1810–1890.

A little history of the father, Joseph Arnold Hardy, shows that just a short time before the Black Hawk War, Joseph Arnold went from Ralls County to Illinois and signed up for duty to battle with the Indians. He became acquainted with Abraham Lincoln, who also served in the Black Hawk War.

In 1846, Joseph Arnold moved to Shullsburg, Wisconsin, and became a mine owner. Joseph Allen spent the greater part of his boyhood in Shullsburg and, at the age of fifteen, began to work in the mines. He was trained in the mining business from youth. So it was that he became a great authority on mining and an expert in his judgment of mining properties and mining problems.

In 1873, Joseph Allen and Emily Edstrom Hardy, daughter of Paul Edstrom of Boston (married September 15, 1962), moved from Wisconsin to Oronogo, Missouri, and continued in the mining business, learning as he worked. In 1882, they moved to Webb City and opened the Hardy and Lillibridge Mine. The mine sold quite profitably in 1891. During the early 1880s, Joseph was instrumental in convincing the Bishop Lillis of Kansas City to establish the Sacred Heart Catholic Church in Webb City. Joseph was a liberal contributor of the parish. He was also on the board of directors for the purchase of land for the Mount Hope Cemetery, serving as president from 1905 till his death in 1917.

Joseph, in 1891, developed the Richland Tract, which was later sold to the Richland Mining Company. He also mined some property in Duenweg in 1895, which he sold to Louis and Otto Duenweg from Indiana, and the area was named Duenweg. He then moved on to another mining area known as the Porter Tract, which he sold to the Cordell Lead and Zinc Company of which he was president and manager.

Joseph Allen Hardy was identified with the Democratic Party. He never was one to seek a political position; however, he did serve as a member of the school board while living in Oronogo. He was also a member of the Order of United Workmen and director of the Mine Producer's Association.

Ten children were born to the union of Joseph Allen and Emily Edstrom Hardy, and they were: (1) Harriet Hardy, who married James McKenna, a foundry man of Joplin; (2) Mary Hardy, who married Dr. Tyree; (3) George Hardy, known as Georgie, was also involved in mining since the age of fifteen, married Margaret (Maggie) Cochran, built the beautiful house at 302 South Ball. He had five children, one of which was Helen Hardy Myers (honored with the title of Missouri Mother of the Year); (4) Alice Hardy, who became the wife of George Burgner of Joplin; (5) Catherine Hardy; (6) Anna Hardy, who was the wife of Benjamin C. Aylor of Webb City; (7) Joseph Allen Hardy Jr., married Granville Ashcraft's daughter Mae Ashcraft. Joseph Allen Jr. built a home on Madison Street where the north side of the Walmart parking lot is located. Leslie says that the Hardy house on Madison was known as the Hardy Craft for the former streetcar junction that ran near their house; (8) Thomas J. Hardy married Nellie M. Boyd; (9) Agnes Hardy attended school at a convent; and (10) Charles Herbert Hardy, known as Herbert, married Eunice Peebles. The Joseph Allen Hardy home was located at 122 North Ball.

A successful businessman, a public-spirited citizen, and gentleman of strict integrity, Hardy left to his children and grandchildren not only the fruits of his labors but the legacy of a well spent and useful life and an untarnished reputation.

So could the family legend be true that Allen Street was named after Joseph Allen Hardy, who went by the name of Allen? We have never been able to establish where the name of Allen Street originated, but having a family legend is one step closer!

Harry Hood and Emily Hardy Kramer have passed on, but Joseph Allen Hardy's great-great-granddaughter Leslie is digging the archives as she researches the family name. Thanks to all for this compilation of family history.

Webb City's Hardy Boys built some long-lasting homes.

In watching old movies, you can't help but run across an occasional *Hardy Boys* adventure. When I hear Hardy boys, I automatically think of the Webb City Hardy boys.

In 1873, Joseph Allen Hardy and his wife, Emily, whom he had been married to for eleven years, decided to move to Jasper County. Joseph was in the mining business. In 1882, they settled in Webb City. The J. A. Hardy home was located at 122 North Ball Street. They needed that big house, as they had ten children—six girls and four boys. Two of the boys also built large homes in Webb City (some of the other children may have built homes in Webb City also, but these are the only ones that I have information on at this time).

122 North Ball—home of Joseph Hardy

J. A. Hardy Jr. built a big two-story home on the west side of South Madison at a time when Madison Street was a rural area. Most people heading to Joplin went out Joplin's North Main Road. J. A. Hardy Jr.'s home has changed a little through the years, as the top floor was removed, and then a few years ago, Steve and Becky Walker added dormer windows.

The house was removed when Walmart built the supercenter

Another son, George Hardy, built a Victorian home at 302 South Ball Street. The house sat on over three acres and included a carriage house. George was born January 22, 1868, and died May 21, 1933. He married Margaret Ethel Cochran, and they had five children to fill his home. It has become better known as the Carney home for many years during the '60s up to 1997.

Joseph Hardy Sr. had many children and grandchildren and great-grandchildren that continued to live in Webb City and carry on the great Hardy tradition. I don't want to attempt to name them all, but I will mention a few: Helen Elizabeth Hardy Myers, Mary Hardy Bennett, Emily Hardy Kramer, and J. Philip Hardy. These are just a few that I have had the privilege of coming in contact with through the years. So now when you hear the Hardy boys mentioned, maybe you'll think of Webb City's very own Hardy boys!

Published March 22, 1991
Photo of the Hardy family
Joseph Allen Hardy (122 North Ball) and his grandchildren included **Granville Hardy, Helen Hardy Myers, Charley Hardy, Margarete Cummings, James Hardy, and Joseph Hardy. There was Josephine Cummings, Jamie Aylor, Bill Hardy, Agnes Hardy, Maria Aylor, Mary Lois Hardy, Catherine, Martin Tracy Walker, Emily Hardy, Agnes Cummings, Paul Hardy, and Allen Walker. The babies were J. Philip Hardy and Joseph Hardy.**

"Life was successful for the Hardys."

Joseph Allen Hardy was born near Hannibal, Ralls County, Missouri in August of 1840. Joseph's parents were Joseph and Julia Ann Gardner Hardy, and his grandfather was Casper Hardy. Joseph came from a family with integrity and prominence. At the early age of fourteen, Joseph was working in the lead and zinc mines alongside his father and older brothers in Shullsburg, Wisconsin.

In 1862, Joseph took Ms. Emily Edstrom as his bride. Together they had ten children—four sons and six daughters: Harriet Hardy McKanna, Mary Hardy Tyree, George Hardy, Alice Hardy Burgner, Catherine Hardy, Anna Hardy Aylor, Joseph Hardy Jr., Thomas Hardy, Agnes Hardy, and Herbert Hardy.

Joseph and Emily moved to Jasper County in 1873, and Joseph continued to mine and learn every detail of the business. Then in 1882, they moved to Webb City from Oronogo and opened the Hardy and Lillibridge Mine. The mine sold quite profitably in 1891.

During the early 1880s, Joseph was instrumental in convincing Bishop Lillis of Kansas City to establish the Sacred Heart Catholic Church in Webb City. Joseph was a liberal contributor of the parish. He was also on the board of directors for the purchase of land for Mount Hope Cemetery and served as the first president of the Cemetery Association until his death in 1917.

Joseph often remarked in his early mining days how he worked much of the time for little or nothing. He was highly pleased when he earned a dollar a day. His earnings were carefully saved, however, and in time, he became an investor. His thrift and sound judgment made him a man of means and influence.

In 1891, he developed the Richland Tract, which was later sold to the Richland Mining Company. He also mined some Duenweg property for about four years before selling that to move on another piece of land known as the Porter Tract, and selling it to the Cordell Lead and Zinc Company, of which he was president and manager.

This is one more fairy tale come true of a man-made success. It was more than being in the right place at the right time. It had a lot to do with knowing when to buy and well and when to hold on to the right investment.

A special thanks to Emily Hardy Kramer for sending the information about grandparents Joseph and Emily Hardy. Emily said she has a brother in Joplin, a sister, Mary Bennett, in Webb City, and nieces, nephews, and cousins in the area. So this is one forefather who still has many family members around to honor him.

Hare, L. D.

L. D. Hare was born in 1864. He came to Webb City and joined in the livery business with J. E. Pyle on East Daugherty Street. They built a two-story concrete building at Tom and Daugherty Streets. Hare had a wagon and carriage factory in that building.

L. D. Hare lived at 205 South Liberty.

Several years before moving to St. Louis in 1919, Hare decided to go into partnership with A. W. Hand (brother-in-law) in the grocery store business at Broadway and Webb Streets.

Hare passed away February 17, 1944, at the age of eighty. He was buried at Mount Hope Cemetery. He called Webb City his home!

Harrison, Ella

A modern woman in the late 1800's

In this modern world, we are getting used to the sight of women as doctors, lawyers, highway workers, electricians, and plumbers. But in the old days, women were expected to stay home, take care of the house, and have babies. If some misfortune found them without a husband but with children to support, they could take in boarders, do laundry, or cooking. Some women opened little shops downtown, such as millinery shops or cafés.

But in the late 1800s, there was a lady who stood out among ladies. Her name was Ella Harrison. Ella was born in Upper Sandusky, Ohio, in April of 1859. At the age of ten, she moved with her parents, Mr. and Mrs. D. A. Harrison, to Jasper County. They lived on a farm eighteen miles northeast of Carthage, later moving to Carthage.

Ella graduated from Carthage High School in 1881 and followed the natural routine for a young single woman. She started her career as a schoolteacher at Summit School, northeast of Carthage. Her mother had named the school.

The move to Carthage changed the Harrisons' lives tremendously. Ella's father, D. A., had given up farming and made a major decision. He went to law school and became a lawyer, later becoming a judge. Maybe it was this special spirit of her father's that Ella inherited because she wasn't satisfied with just a teaching career.

And what a career Ella developed. She went to the University of Iowa to study law. She also went to the Stanford University at Palo Alto, California. While there, she met Herbert Hoover, who was a member of the first freshman class of Stanford. She also met Herbert's future wife, Lou Henry, the only woman geology major attending Stanford. After finishing her studies at Stanford, Ella became a roving reporter in New York, Washington, DC, Seattle and other major cities.

Ella Harrison was a strong supporter of the women's suffrage cause from 1890–1900. She was president of the Missouri Women's Suffrage Association and traveled throughout the country organizing suffrage groups.

In 1911, Ella Harrison became the war correspondent for New York American in New Mexico. She was a reporter for the Arizona House of Representatives. She practiced law with her brother, Tom Harrison, in Carthage. She not only followed in her father's footsteps by becoming an attorney, she also became the justice of the peace for Jasper, the city that her father had platted.

Ella passed away in 1933, at the age of seventy-four. She had led a full and active life. She was far from the traditional lady that lived in Jasper County during that time. She met a lot of important people, visited a lot of wonderful places, and left her mark in history. If she were alive today, she would probably be holding office in Washington, DC. Perhaps she was a lady born before her time!

Harrison, J. C.

A man of distinction being related to President William Henry Harrison and President Benjamin Harrison, J. C. hails from the state of Virginia, born May 2, 1855, where both sides of his family were active in the Civil War and the ministry. J. C. left Virginia with his parent to resettle in Woodford County, Illinois, where they worked on their farm.

At the age of twenty, 1875, J. C. set out on his own to check out Iroquois County, Illinois, where he met and fell in love with a young lady, Clara Laird, whom he convinced to marry him. Four years later, he talked his young bride into moving to sunny Kansas where they settled in Iola, Kansas, and where they were miserable. Fighting starvation and a dismal outlook, it was 1893 before they were able to escape with the hope of finding a better life in Jasper County, Missouri, where they heard there was opportunity for wealth.

J. C. came to town with the hope of success. He started out with a butchering business. Nine months later, he was almost broke except for the small amount of dry goods stock he received in exchange for his Kansas property. He placed these items on the shelves and sat down to wait for customers. This was not something he felt comfortable with, so he hired a girl to watch the store, and he went to work in the mines to bring in some money. He watched the store in the evenings. This did not work as he barely sold enough goods to pay the rent. So he auctioned off his supplies and got a job at the *Webb City Daily Register* as a manager in the circulation department.

Getting more acquainted with the citizens of Webb City, after a few years at the *Webb City Register*, Harrison felt more confident, and he began to sell real estate and insurance. He really liked helping people get homes on the easy-payment plan. He finally felt he was at home in his business and his community. He helped secure many homes in Webb City. He was a member of the Commercial Club, serving as president many times. He, with help from others, organized the state municipal league.

J. C. and his wife, Clara's, children include Nora H. Harrison Covert, who had four children: Elmer, Theodore, Hazel, and Harry; Jessie H. Harrison Young, mother of three: Clarence, Byron, and Grace; W. Frank Harrison, proprietor of the Crescent Laundry with one child, Joseph Harrison; Edna Harrison Troxel, with two children, Fred and Jack; Willis Harrison; Viola Harrison; and Eugene Harrison.

J. C. Harrison was a man of enterprise and energy who never gave up. He knew there was a niche in life for him, and he kept persevering until he found it. He held a place of prominence and influence among the leading real estate business. His special aim was being able to help men with limited means to obtain homes for their families on the easy-payment plan.

308 South Main—J. Harrison

Haskin Brothers

"Haskin Brother's hardware diversified."

Nowadays businesses seem to come and go with much speed. For a business to say they have been established for more than ten years is quite an accomplishment. The economy makes it tough to keep a business going.

Although the economy has its dips and curves, many past businesses were able to scrape by and survive. One of those businesses that seemed to last forever in Webb City was Haskin Brothers' Hardware Store.

Frank E. and George Haskin set up their business in June 1900, when they purchased the building at the southeast corner of Main (Allen) and First Streets for $2,500. They bought it from Koonz Trading Company.

Frank E. was married to Judge Solomon Kerr's daughter, Elizabeth, who came to Jasper County in 1867, settling out by the old water plant. Frank and Elizabeth lived at 1124 South Jefferson Street.

George's first wife was named Pattie. After her death, he married a woman named Ida. They lived at 327 South Roane Street.

The Haskin brothers kept their business alive through the mine shutdowns and the Depression era. There was a lot of competition to face. Many hardware stores came and went.

As the new automobile was introduced, the Haskin boys began to handle auto supplies and tires. They had a good business going up until they retired and sold the building for $3,000 in 1946 to Fred Casada (C&W Furniture).

For forty-six years, the Haskin brothers did a business with the residents of Webb City. That building was sold to Edith Richards in 1971, who, in turn, sold it to the Sweets (Home Rug and Furniture) in 1973. We mostly remember it as the American Legion Hall until they built their new facility. Duke Mallos' family owns the building, and it became the home of the New Testament Church. In 2020, the building was remodeled by Paul Taylor and the home of a winery, restaurant, and bar A Taste of Life.

Note: The building that housed the Haskin Brothers' Hardware Store, 111 South Main, originally was the home of the very first hardware store in Webb City. Owned and operated by S. L. Manker, it was deemed the largest hardware house in Southwest Missouri. Manker's business began in 1877. It is noted that he had to rebuild his building in 1883 when damaged by high winds.

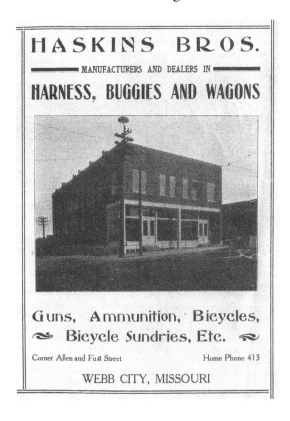

Hatcher, Benjamin Franklin

He was the man who helped pull the water out of the very first shaft from which mineral was hoisted, and thus assisted in the foundation work of the immense mining industry.

Benjamin recalled, "When Ashcraft first came over from Oronogo and undertook to sink the shaft on Center Creek, where there had been the first lead find in this district, I started with him to run the pump. My recollection is that it took a relay of seven horses, working each horse for two to three hours at a time, to keep the pump going, and all we had then was literally horse power. It wasn't much of a shaft, as we should think now. It was something less than thirty feet deep, and some lead had been taken out, that was in the dump, but none had been sold. It looked very doubtful about getting any more, as the water was so strong it came out of the top of the hole within a few hours whenever the pump stopped. We kept at it until he got enough out to make several sales of lead, but under great difficulty, and when there was high water, there was nothing doing.

"People didn't know much about pumps in those days, not around here anyway, and I remember that Thomas N. Davey, then and for a long time after in the foundry business at Carthage, devised a new kind of pump that he had hoped would prove adequate to the water proposition, as we should call it now, at Center Creek. But it didn't work, and for years, there was little else but discouragement as to continuous work, for when the pump shaft was down, none of the numerous prospectors were able to get in the ground. Among those interested in working this shaft in the early day were Ben Webb and John C. Webb, on whose land the discovery was made, Thomas N. Davey, W. A. Daugherty, S. R. Corn of Joplin, and a practical miner named Mike Jones, who came from Oronogo."

Pauline Jane and C. J. Hatcher were married in 1842 in Overton County, Tennessee. They had ten children of which two died in infancy, one at a later age, leaving three sons, Harris, Benjamin, and John. Four daughters were Mrs. Litteral, Mrs. Stith, Mrs. Thurman, and Mrs. Stellar.

The family moved to Jasper County in 1857. C. J. Hatcher was killed in the Civil War, and that left Paulina with the burden of raising her family alone. Pauline died in 1905.

Benjamin Franklin Hatcher was born April 7, 1847, in Tennessee to Charles Jabez Tall Hatcher and Paulina Jane Webb Hatcher (sister of John C. Webb). Charles was a teacher and a miner. He served as a Jasper County associate judge.

Benjamin Hatcher resided in Webb City and enjoyed the mining industry until 1888, when he purchased 140 acres in Carterville and built the family homestead on the hill of North Pine Street. The property included the home, barns, loafing sheds, and other outbuildings. The Hatcher Farm (homestead) was considered an exemplary model of the time. Ben also had two other 165-acre farms, one in Newton County and one in McDonald County, by Indian Creek. He held onto five mining plants in which he received royalties.

Benjamin married Dora Daugherty, daughter of W. A. and Nancy Daugherty. They had seven sons and four daughters: William, married to Effie Hurley; Frank, married to Myrtle Ball; Walter Janes; Nancy Pearl married Alexander Burkett Campbell; Benjamin; Daugherty; Grover C.; Eulalia; Ruth; Era P.; and Ada B (died at the age of twelve months).

Benjamin was a leading member of the Methodist Church in Webb City, a member of the Masons, IOOF, and served one year in the Confederate Army, Company A, Shelby's regiment.

The Hatcher homestead was purchased by Nancy Pearl and Alexander Campbell. The acres had decreased to 3.3 acres.

A thankyou to Julie Anna (Campbell) Riley for sharing this information on her family.

Hatcher, W. L.

W. L. Hatcher came from a fairly large family. He had four brothers: Anthony, Grover, Roland, and George. Two sisters in the midst of the five boys were Mollie and Dora. W. L. Hatcher and his wife, Mary, were living in Arkansas when they made a very important decision—they were ready to move and start a new life. They loaded up their family of two daughters and two sons and journeyed north to Missouri, settling in the pleasant community of Webb City. The year was 1918.

W. L. Hatcher was a carpenter by trade, and he found contentment in this small town that provided a warm environment for his family to flourish. Their home at 409 South Tom was the gathering place for the family, even as they headed out into the world to start their own families.

One of W. L.'s sons, George Hatcher, found employment with Hercules Powder Company. George and his wife, Mazie, had two children, Phyllis Hope Hatcher Trent and Jack Hatcher. George and Mazie lived in the family home at 409 South Tom after the death of George's father in 1928 and raised their own family. Three generations of the Hatcher family lived in the Hatcher home.

After the death of George and Maizie, Jack continued to live in the family home until he was put in a nursing home where he passed away. Jack was known all over town as he did not know a stranger. He would volunteer to help anyone he felt was in need of help. Jack was born with some health difficulties, but he never let that stop him. The citizens put a park bench on Main Street in Jack's honor.

Hatten, Amos, D. (Uncle Pete)

Another one of my favorite Webb City forefathers is A. D. Hatten. What a generous man who definitely loved Webb City. I thought I would just take a moment to mention the highlights of A. D. Hatten activities and generosity. Hatten kept a wonderful scrapbook of newspaper clippings of his family and of friends which included lots of history of Webb City. His granddaughter Sarah McKibbon shared a copy of that scrapbook with me, and I am deeply indebted to her.

D. Hatten's great-grandfather Samuel served in the Revolutionary War under George Washington. His grandfather William also served in the Revolutionary War. Both Samuel and William worked for George Washington following the war. Samuel and William were some of the first settlers in Wayne County, Virginia.

In 1883, A. D. Hatten arrived in Webb City and purchased the Center Creek Mine just east of the city between Webb City and Carterville. Hatten purchased the mine from Granville Ashcraft for $8,000, putting down $2,000 in cash, the rest in payments. He paid off Ashcraft in a few months and his investors in five years, in which they drew quite a bit of interest from their investment.

In 1887, he and Otto Raymond took some of their mining profits and built the second brick building in Webb City, on the northeast corner of Allen (Main) Street and Daugherty Street, for $21,000 (still standing).

D. Hatten was a stockholder of the Webb City Bank from 1890–1928 and served as president of Webb City Bank from 1928–1945. When the Mineral Bank in Carterville went under, Hatten deposited enough money in the Webb City Bank to cover all the depositors that had money in the Mineral Bank. He covered all the depositors and other monetary obligations. The total of the loan deposits were $67,000, not counting the other obligations. None of the Carterville Bank customers lost any money.

There were many mines in the area that were organized by Hatten. Also he started the Emma Gordon Mine in Oklahoma, which he named after the Indian maiden who originally owned the land. The town built by the mine was named Hattenville and kept that name until the Indian Territory joined the union and became Oklahoma, and the name of the town was changed to Commerce, Oklahoma. Hatten went to the Indian Territory after having a dream that showed him going to the Indian Territory and finding the zinc and lead. That turned out to be a very profitable dream.

January 13, 1930, A. D. Hatten deeded to the city a tract of land on Madison Street. Then he proceeded to have the Hatten Athletic Field built with WPA labor, Webb City's first official football field. Harrison Kash recalled that his father was working for the WPA at the time, and he was in charge of the job. He drew the plans out on a piece of paper that Harrison still has in his attic. He noted that the other WPA workers thought Mr. Kash was wasting his time drawing the design out on paper; they felt they should just start building and design it as they went!

May 1, 1933, Hatten deeded to the city a tract of land adjoining the Hatten Golf Course in the west part of town to be used as a city park. The land had previously been the grounds for the college. The basement was converted into the Webb City municipal swimming pool located in the Hatten Park. The rock walls and the cement picnic tables were built by the WPA.

Webb City was fortunate in having many WPA (Works Progress Administration) projects due to the fact that A. D. Hatten's son-in-law, Harry Easley, was the director of personnel of the Missouri Division of Works Progress Administration (WPA). Another major project was the cement road from Webb City to Joplin.

Hatten organized and operated the Home Land & Loan Company which allowed him to build many new homes in Webb City. As a landlord of rental property, Hatten was more than generous with those having hard times. Hatten also owned the most extensive collection of iris plants (flags) for miles around. He was generous, and each fall, as he divided the plants, he offered them to Webb City citizens at no charge.

Harry S. Truman was a dear friend to A. D. Hatten. When Judge Harry S. Truman came from Independence to visit Hatten in 1934, Truman stood on the back of a truck on Main Street for Hatten to introduce the judge to Webb City. Hatten then proceeded to prophesy to the citizens that if they voted Truman for senator, that he thought Truman had a great future ahead of him, and he could even become the president of the United States. Just ten years later, that prophecy came true when Truman served as vice president for just a few months before becoming president in April of 1945, at the death of FDR. He was re-elected in 1948.

In the *History of Jasper County*, the description of A. D. Hatten it states:

> *In all Mr. Hatten's dealings he is absolutely straightforward, and his word is as good as his bond. Shrewd business man though he is, he is not hard in his dealings. Many a man who is down on his luck has been given a boost by Mr. Hatten. He is genial and whole-souled, a man whom it is a delight to meet. His loyalty to Jasper County and above all to Webb City is unbounded. He never loses an opportunity to put in a good word for either one, nor does Webb City or Jasper County fail to reciprocate in kind. They are proud of him as he is of them and they have been mutually helpful.*

A fun story of A. D. Hatten is he lived in a time era when all the vehicles were black. He would get so frustrated when trying to locate his car, and they all looked alike. So he had his car painted red. It stood out, and he delighted in being able to locate his car no matter how many vehicles were around! He has the honor of owning the first red vehicle in Webb City.

This particular Webb City forefather was quite an asset to Webb City, and we admire this great man and his contribution to the history of Webb City. The Hatten home stands on Ball Street between Sixth and Seventh Streets and between Ball and Roane Streets. One city block that used to house an orchard and beautiful iris garden that Hatten nurtured with his own two hands.

The Hatten-Raymond building, second brick building

Hatten home

RESIDENCE OF A. D. HATTEN.

The house Hatten lived when
he first got married.

The home Hatten lived in (northeast corner of Pennsylvania
and Daugherty) while building his country home.

Hatten, A. D.

As you drive around town during the month of May, lovely irises are in full bloom with such a variety of colors. They seem to stand so tall and proud. I myself can't think of irises without thinking of A. D. Hatten.

Amos Davis Hatten built a lovely home out in the country, which is now known as the Hatten home, located on a square block bounded by Ball, Sixth, Roane, and Seventh streets. Being out in the country, Hatten had planted an orchard behind his home, but the most spectacular plantings were his irises on the north side (Sixth Street) of the house. Hatten was well known for his wonderful display of color in his irises. He was even known to spend as much as $30 for a start of an iris that he didn't have in his garden. I don't know if his garden was known worldwide, but he was known nationally. These beautiful flowers of varied colors were also referred to as "flags," which brings us to one of the old tales as to how Webb City became the "City of Flags."

Each year, when the irises (flags) were in full bloom, Hatten would have a public viewing, which allowed anyone in town the opportunity to walk through the Hatten flower garden. At the end of the season, Hatten would thin out his plants, and he would advertise in the paper that he was giving away Iris bulbs. There would be a truckload, and folks could come by and help themselves. What a generous man!

After doing this for several years, many homes around Webb City had the beautiful plants in the yard. During the blooming season, you could drive all over Webb City and see the most spectacular view as the iris flowers were blooming in almost every yard. Hence the name Webb City, City of Flags (now there is another version to how Webb City got the name; it is located elsewhere in the book).

A. D. Hatten was a well-thought-of gentleman, and he is known for more than just his irises, but during the springtime of the year, it is only right that we pay tribute to the man who spread his love of irises all over the area.

Hatten, A. D.—Our Hero

In the Wild West days, every town had its heroes. There were such figures as Wild Bill Hickock, Wyatt Earp, Bat Masterson, etc. Well, Webb City had its heroes also. And one of those heroes was Amos D. Hatten (or Uncle Pete, as he was affectionately called).

Amos D. Hatten was born September 7, 1859, in Wayne County, West Virginia, to Milo and Emmeline Newman Hatten. Both of Hatten's parents came from old West Virginia families. They were content to stay on the family farm. In fact, Milo was born, lived, and died on the same farm. Unlike his dad, Amos had the spirit of adventure.

When Hatten was nineteen years of age, he made his way to Nevada, Missouri. He found a job working on a farm, and when the summer was over, he made his way to the mining district around Webb City. No jobs were available, but that didn't stop Hatten from checking out the territory and learning everything he could about the district and the mining business. He went on to Colorado and, after three years, decided that Jasper County was where he wanted to establish his residency.

In partnership with his Uncle Alvin, Hatten began his career in the mining business. Throughout the years, he organized several mining companies, a real estate and loan company, insurance company, and many other businesses. If Amos D. Hatten was involved in a business proposition, you could be assured that it was an upright and honest business. He didn't make his fortune by taking advantage of the out-of-luck businessman or miner. Just the opposite. Hatten usually helped out those who were down on their luck. One such time was when the Mineral Belt Bank went defunct. Hatten made a large deposit in the Webb City Bank, and each and every depositor of the Mineral Belt Bank was able to obtain his or her money through the Webb City Bank. Hatten had deposited well over $67,000 just to cover the deposits. He also covered any outstanding debt the bank had.

On November 8, 1888, Amos D. Hatten married Sadie C. Coyne, daughter of Patrick Coyne and sister of Tom Coyne (one of Hatten's business partners). Amos and Sadie were both well thought of in the community. Never a sour word was said of either one.

Hatten's love for Webb City was obvious, especially with his donations to the city. Hatten donated the land where the old football field was located (where the high school is now). Mr. Hatten felt that if he cut up the land into building lots, the schoolchildren would be deprived of the area where they loved to play, so he donated it to be used for football and baseball, with the only stipulation that it be known as Hatten Athletic Field. That was January 13, 1930.

Mr. and Mrs. Hatten also deeded the city some land on the west side of the city to be used as a park. Mike Evans, a mine operator, owned the area, and he cooperated with Mr. Hatten to obtain a clear title for the city. The land was originally the campus and grounds of the Baptist College. Plans were immediately formed to use the basement of the college for the Webb City public swimming pool. There would also be four tennis courts, a croquet ground, playground, picnic area with camp stoves, and a bathhouse. The land was deeded on May 1, 1933, and the work on the park began May 2, 1933, to be completed by June 15, 1933. That was fast work (not like construction today!).

Almost everyone knows of the Hatten house that sits in the middle of a block between Ball and Roane Streets. When Hatten started building his home, he decided he wanted to live in the country, so he built the Hatten house. Needless to say, it is no longer considered the country. It cost $5,000 to build the mansion.**

Hatten was very fond of irises. Rumor has it that is how Webb City became known as the City of Flags. Hatten had so many irises that people came from miles around just to look at his yard when the irises were in bloom. Hatten was known to have spent as much as $30 for some of his iris starts. Whenever he thinned his plants out, it would be advertised in the paper, and truckloads of iris starts would be given away to the citizens. Soon the city was full of beautiful irises (or flags, as they were commonly called.)

This man did so much for Webb City that many more articles could be written about him. He left a legacy to Webb City that cannot be matched. The newspapers were always reporting little tidbits of information on this wonderful man who had the Midas touch. Not only did everything he touch turn to gold, but everything he touched brought happiness to those around him. Webb City was lucky that he chose this city to call his home.

A special thanks to the relatives of A. D. Hatten, who wrote to remind us of what a wonderful forefather we were letting slip from our memories. You have someone to be very proud of, and we are proud of him also.

Hatten, A. D.

Speaking of the name Hatten, in 1916, while breaking ground for A. D. Hatten's new home (he wanted to build out in the country to the south of Webb City) at Six Hundred South Ball Street, the construction workers uncovered two petrified ears of corn with kernels still intact. Mr. Hatten determined the artifacts to be several thousand years old, and the *Sentinel* headline of the discovery stated they were five thousand years old. Hatten laughingly dubbed Webb City as Noah's cornfield. They also uncovered fossils of starfish, shells, lizards, toads, and the age-old trail of a serpent that could plainly be followed in its windings round and round in and among the solid rock. Hatten kept the petrified corn in his Home Land & Loan office (108 North Main) for citizens to view his find. He later donated his corn and mineral collection to the Mineral Museum in Joplin.

Once again, A. D. Hatten was in the news when the city of Webb City dedicated their new stadium (donated by Hatten) on Madison Street just north of Crow Street on October 5, of 1930, as football fans watched a game between Pittsburg High School and Webb City High School. The event was celebrated with a parade down Main Street. The drum corps opened the ceremony of the field. The Webb City municipal band played the "Star-Spangled Banner," followed by a short

---

* A former neighbor of Amos Hatten came into the *Sentinel* to state that the reported construction price for the Amos D. Hatten house was wrong. He said it cost $25,000, not $5,000. Jeanne isn't one to argue but says she got the figure from a newspaper story in A. D. Hatten's personal scrapbook. Both Jeanne and the former neighbor say the cost figures they stand by were consistent with the cost of similar houses constructed in the same era.

concert. In his dedication speech, Ray E. Watson stated, *"This stadium should not be dedicated for victory, for victory does not always mean the highest scores. We shall dedicate this stadium and field to the good citizenship and the future citizens of Webb City, trained in our schools, and this is being done in the name of good sportsmanship."* The stadium was located west of what is now the Buck Miner Swimming Pool. The stadium had an eight-foot-high rock and concrete wall (built by the WPA) that went around the entire field and had a seating capacity of 2,500 (two hundred feet long, forty feet wide, and twenty feet high).

Laura Willard shared a bit of sage advice she received from Mr. Hatten. He often shared some of his memories with her when she worked for the family. He told her that he always put half of his earnings into savings and lived on the other half. Never touching the savings, sometimes were a bit lean, and other times, life was good. She also shared the fact that Mr. Hatten's huge heart showed when he would help the widows by paying their mortgages and letting them pay him back whenever they could afford it.

What a neat connection to the past. A. D. Hatten arrived in Webb City the year John C. Webb passed away, 1883, and purchased the very mine that Webb started (Laura recalls that Hatten told her he paid $2,000 down when they offered to sell him the Center Creek Mine for $10,000). And here is Laura Willard, sharing sage advice from this man who was a major part of Webb City's history. Thanks, Laura, for being our link to the past.

A few mines and businesses of Hatten:

> A. D. and his uncle Alvin purchased the Center Creek Mines in 1883. They put $2,000 down on the purchase of $8,000. They paid off Grant Ashcraft in a few months. The investors were paid off in five years at a great profit.
>
> Purchased another mine in the Center Creek mining area with his cousin-in-law, Otto Raymond. They made $26,000 in eight months. Took the earnings and built the second brick building in Webb City on the northeast corner of Allen (Main) and Daugherty Streets. That building became the home of Humphrey's Mercantile.
>
> 1904—A. D. Hatten, Tom Coyne of Webb City, S. R. Snook of New York organized the Osceola Lead and Zinc Mining Company. In 1907, the same three men organized the Rochester Land and Leasing Company.
>
> Organized the C. C. & H. Mining Company.
>
> Organized the Emma Goodwin Mining Company of Ottawa County, Oklahoma
>
> Organized the Ideal Mining Company near Joplin
>
> Organized the Home, Land & Loan Company
>
> Laid out the Hatten Subdivision, Villa Heights, Joplin

Hayden, Tom C.

The Hayden Dairy Farm was located on Fourth Street and Liberty Street to the highway. In his spare time, Tom fiddled around with cars, which he loved. When Tom built his section of the Century Building, Twenty-Seven South Allen (Main) Street, where he opened his auto business, he sold his farm, and he and his wife, Gladys, moved into the upstairs.

Thomas Cass Fletcher Hayden was born in 1865 and moved to the Webb City area in 1884, at age nineteen, to get involved in the mining business. Instead he became interested in dairy farming and opened a harness and buggy store which later became an automobile company.

During the Lakeside days, Hayden took an interest in the great pastime of baseball. He was a former president of Joplin Western League Club and active in the Old Trolley League. President and owner of the Parson's Franchise in the Kansas State League. The year 1905 placed the Webb City team in the Missouri Valley League. Owner of Pittsburg, Kansas, and Springfield, Missouri teams.

During his dairy farm days, Hayden did quite a livestock business. And in his later years he was a Jasper County stockman and a civic worker. Through the chamber of commerce, he was involved in the sales day Saturdays, on the agricultural committee, and the industrial committee.

In 1921, Hayden, as president of the Webb City Chamber of Commerce for several terms, had fostered a horseshoe pitching grounds on a vacant lot in the business district, saying it would attract farmers and tourists. Other merchants disagreed with Hayden and asked the mayor and marshal to stop Hayden. When Hayden learned of the move against him, he resigned as president of the chamber of commerce. As much as he had supported the city, the city wasn't willing to support him.

The Hayden Auto Company was listed in the city directory as late as 1928. Hayden died of double pneumonia in 1935. His wife continued to live in the building long after Hayden was gone.

The Century Building, 1900—Twenty-Seven South Allen (Main)

Hemenway, Silas O. Captain

Captain Silas O. Hemenway was described in the *1899 Webb City Gazette* as energetic, a progressive businessman, a miner, unselfish, untiring, and willing to sacrifice his own interests for the benefit of friends, employees, and neighbors. As if that isn't enough, the man was described as a writer, a fluent speaker, and an adviser for public and private interests.

The captain hailed from the state of New York, and his wife's name was Minerva. The editors of the *1899 Webb City Gazette* gave Hemenway praise for his kind acts in assisting with the publishing of the *Gazette*.

He built a house of distinction on the northwest corner of First and Webb Streets. It included the charming captain's walk on the third floor. Captain Hemenway decided to retire with his family to Webb City, where he spent his last years just as active as he had spent his entire lifetime. He was active anywhere he felt he was needed.

Captain Hemenway had an eventful life that ended October 8, 1905, as he was reading the newspaper about a friend passing from apoplexy and stating that is the way he would want to go. Almost immediately, his head dropped backward, and his wish was fulfilled. He was buried in St. Louis.

The next owner of the Hemenway home added more historical value to this unique house in 1905, as Dr. Lincoln Curtis Chenoweth opened the first hospital in the Webb City mining area in this very house. Dr. Chenoweth had graduated from Missouri State Medical College in St. Louis in 1887 and started his practice in Pineville, Missouri. Within the first year of his practice, Dr. Chenoweth decided he needed to move to Webb City where the miners were in need of medical attention. It took him seventeen years to get the hospital that was desperately needed.

Dr. Chenoweth originated from McDonald County, and he was a fourth-generation doctor. He was dedicated to his profession, which was evident in all that he did to assist Webb City in the medical field. He eventually moved the hospital from the Hemenway home to the second floor of the Salvation Army building on East Main (Broadway).

He was instrumental in the building of the Jasper County Tuberculosis Hospital and served on the board of directors. He convinced the state to take over the TB Hospital after the county completed construction in 1916. Dr. Chenoweth also assisted in the building and managing of the Jane Chinn Hospital in 1910. His brother, Charles B. Chenoweth, was a druggist, and his place of business was at Twenty South Allen (Main) in the Newland Building.

Dr. Chenoweth's son, John Albert Chenoweth (fifth-generation doctor), began his medical practice in Joplin (1915). Young Dr. Chenoweth went to war in 1918, and Dr. Chenoweth moved to Joplin to take care of his son's practice while he served our country. He continued to work with his son after the WWI and went to the office every day until he was seventy-seven years old, passing away at the age of seventy-eight.

The next owner of the Hemenway home was another doctor, Dr. Stormont. Dr. Stormont's contribution to the home was his love of gardening. He put in a fishpond, lots of flowers, trees, and a beautiful backyard garden. It looked like a park.

Captain Hemenway had the first frame schoolhouse of Webb City, located to the north of his home. Dr. Chenoweth had the central school building (brick) located to the north, but Dr. Stormont had the Smith Shirt Factory which had been built with the bricks from the old central school. Dr. Stormont noticed that the shirt factory ladies would gather outside as they nibbled on their lunches and enjoyed the beauties of nature. He also noticed that they seemed to admire his backyard garden, and it seemed to brighten their day. So Dr. Stormont fixed a special sitting area just for the shirt factory ladies. He took a small area of the shirt factory parking lot, southeast corner, and put in flowers, a small sitting bench, and a few shrubs. Now the ladies had a great place to sit and enjoy their lunch and nature.

Hess, Isaac

A man who loved Webb City—Most of the prominent citizens we focus on seem to have one thing in common: their love for the community. One such individual from our past was Isaac C. Hess.

Isaac was born in Shannon County, and his parents were from Alabama. Isaac married Ms. Rosa Wisby of Franklin County, and they had four children: Lee, Gertie, Earl, and Lester.

A well-known Democrat of the area, Isaac was elected a member of the city council of Webb City in 1898, 1900, and 1902. He was also active with the Odd Fellows and the Knights and Ladies of Security.

Isaac and Rosa lived in a beautiful home at 307 East Daugherty Street. Their pride in the community showed in their willingness to serve and to put their shoulders to the wheel to help start or maintain any movement that promised to advance the interests of any of the citizens of Webb City.

Isaac was the engineer of the Center Creek Mining Company and in charge of mining station 1. The second engineer who assisted him in his duties was his brother, John A. Hess (who was formerly an engineer for the Iron Mountain Railway Company).

Isaac felt a favorable impression in this community. He proved himself as a worthy elected official, and those who knew him believed he could handle any position given to him.

Hitner Family

Frank Hitner—Each depot began to look the same to Frank Ewing Hitner, as he made his way across the country. He would stop at each little community, check into a hotel, and show his line of silk and lace to merchants. He was a manufacturer representative for an import company out of New York.

Hitner had been born in Taylorsville, Kentucky, on December 5, 1874, to John K. Hitner and Phoebe Broderick Hitner (Phoebe's mother was married to the governor of Kentucky).

After graduating from Westminster College in Fulton, Hitner began his career with the import company. Even though the long dusty trips were monotonous, Frank still managed to have a good time occasionally. On one scheduled trip to Carthage, a department store owner, Mr. Rose, introduced Frank to a lovely young lady at a dance. There was no question in Frank's mind that he had found the woman of his dreams, Dorothy Moore.

After a short move to St. Louis, where they enjoyed the pleasures of the 1904 World's Fair and Exposition, Frank and his lovely wife moved to Carthage to be near family.

A couple of years later, the opportunity of a lifetime came into view. Frank Hitner and Frank Payne, as partners, bought the Humphrey's Mercantile of Webb City. Humphrey's was already established as a well-known department store. It employed approximately thirty-five to forty employees, and the building took up half a city block.

Business continued to be good for Hitner and Payne until the end of the mining era. This disaster prompted Frank Payne to tell Hitner he wanted out. Hitner bought out Payne and continued the business. Payne went on to California with JC Penney and ultimately died a millionaire.

Meanwhile, back at Humphrey's, Frank was striving to make it a success. Humphrey's had everything imaginable. A quote from the *Daily Sentinel* stated, "We will endeavor to make Humphrey's store such an institution that no one will need to go out of the city or send out of the city to buy a single article."

Frank Hitner was an asset to the community. He would go out of his way to promote Webb City. Whatever he did for the store, he did for Webb City. Frank was president of the chamber of commerce, director of the YMCA, an officer in the Jasper County Fruit Growers Association, and an elder in the First Presbyterian Church.

An active man, Frank still found time to spend with his family. Many an outing was made to Lakeside Park. Baseball was his favorite pastime. He was a lefthander and often would pitch for both teams and umpire at the same time. A valuable player!

At a time in Frank's life when he should have been resting for his health, his main concern was still for the welfare of Webb City and his department store. Frank passed away on January 29, 1933, of what was known as flu heart. Webb City lost a great citizen.

A resolution written by W. W. Wampler and J. D. Baldridge states, "The community has lost a valued citizen, one whose services were ever at call of any movement for the betterment of the community. To know him was to love him."

Frank's son, Robert, shared these special memories with us.

HATTEN & RAYMOND BUILDING.

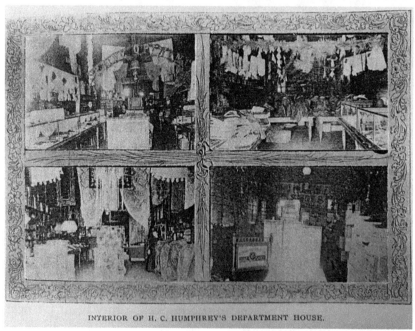

INTERIOR OF H. C. HUMPHREY'S DEPARTMENT HOUSE.

Frank Ewing Hitner
By Robert Hitner (November 5, 1991)

"Faith of our Fathers" was my Dad's favorite hymn so Mother had it sung at his Services when he passed away. His death was by far the most difficult experience of my life and at 12 years of age an impossible thing to understand. Why would God let it happen to the most perfect man on earth? Everyone who knew him said so. I cried myself to sleep many a night. It has not been a great deal easier as the years have gone by and my religious experience should have made me much more understanding.

I am going to relate as much about my Dad as I can remember so that you and as many other folks in subsequent generations as possible will know and appreciate more about him.

Frank Ewing Hitner was born in Taylorville, Kentucky on December 5, 1874 to John E. Hitner and Phoebe Broderick Hitner. I have written a brief biography of John K. Hitner. Phoebe Hitner was the daughter of the Governor of Kentucky.

I would like to know more about the childhood of my Father. He attended Westminster College at Fulton, Missouri which was a boys school of 300 students. By this time Grandfather was an iterant minister in Missouri. Quote from the Paris, Missouri Mercury of 1896, "Frank Hitner graduated at Westminster last week. He is a bright and promising young man—He has been an energetic and faithful student and has thoroughly equipped himself for the battle of life. The Mercury wishes him success in whatever field he may enter."

I would like to know more about Dad's life for the years after school, about 1900 when he was a Manufacturer's Representative for a silk and lace importer in New York. He would travel by train across the country stopping at cities and checking in at a hotel where he would show his line to the leading merchants of the community as his Belgian lace was displayed in his room. It was on one of these trips that he met mother. He was in Carthage, Missouri when Mr. Rose, a department store owner, introduced them at a dance and apparently that was it for life. They were married in May 1903 but not until my grandfather Moore had him investigated by his attorney Allen McReynolds to be certain that he was good enough for his daughter. On one of his train trips that his glasses flew out the window of the train and he never wore glasses again. Our family still has a box of the beautiful lace from Dad's salesman samples.

Frank and his new bride went to St. Louis where Frank formed a partnership with his best man and longtime friend in the knit underwear manufacturing business. This business venture was not a success and was soon dissolved. But most of the family and friends had visited them to attend the World's Fair and Exposition of 1904.

The young couple moved to Carthage and lived on Grand Avenue across the street from Mrs. Hitners parents at 1163 South Grand. Their first child Frances was born in this house. Just a year later, Frank Hitner and Frank Payne purchased the Humphrey Mercantile of Webb City. Humphrey's was a well-established, booming department store. But that soon changed as the mining industry took a dive around 1918. Webb City's population dropped significantly, and Frank Payne decided he wanted to either sell the business, close the business, or Frank could buy him out. Frank Hitner decided to buy him out. Payne went on to California, became associated with J. C. Penney Company and Payne died a millionaire.

Humphrey's department store had been expanded into a very complete department store with ready-to-wear (men and ladies) piece goods, shoes, toys, and a dime store in the basement. A quote from the *Daily Sentinel*, "We will endeavor to make Humphrey's store such an institution that no one will need to go out of the city or send out of the city to buy a single article."

I was no doubt a nuisance to all the personnel as I played with the little carts (trays) as they sped on wheels on the wires with money and tickets from the various counters up to the office on the balcony. I recall how much I must have bothered Florence as I insisted on operating her typewriter, etc. and playing Dad's office, which was also on the balcony. Dad worked insistently on promotions which were for the benefit of the store and Webb city. The Sales Day one Saturday out of every month is an example. The slogan "Get down and Come in" with big signs suspended across the street drew farmers into town. Livestock Sales were held in a large barn on North Allen Street and housewares were auctioned off in a nearby building. Every effort was made to retain the rural business around Webb City rather than let it go to Joplin and Carthage. Many times, Mother, Frances and I joined Dad at dinners sponsored by Schools, Churches, and organizations in the surrounding areas. Dad was an Elder in the First Presbyterian Church, Director in the Y.M.C.A., Officer in the Elks Lodge, Vice President of the Chamber of Commerce and an officer in the Jasper County Fruit Growers Association. His death was probably attributed to over-work in his effort to make the store and the town continuing to grow. He was working and making a trip to St. Louis when he should have been in bed resting. These were the days before Sulfa and other drugs and he passed away from what was known as "Flu Heart".

Frank Hitner always had time for his family. He purchased our Saxon Six and the 1918 Buick touring cars. We would always walk down Liberty Street to Daugherty Street, climb on the streetcar and go to Carthage on Sunday afternoons to visit our Aunts and Grandmother Moore. Francis would always get car sick and had to ride on the platform on the back of the streetcar. Dad would usually have to carry me home on our return as I would be sound asleep.

Dad was a big baseball fan and on a nice day would take off work from the store, load up a bunch of us boys in the Buick and take off for Lakeside Park between Carthage and Webb City. This was a good ball diamond and a real treat after the places we usually played ball. He was a left-hander and would pitch for both sides and umpire at the same time. He had as much fun as any of us.

Frank Ewing Hitner passed away at 9:00 p.m. on January 29, 1923, from heart trouble pneumonia and is buried in Park Cemetery in Carthage, Missouri.

Chamber of Commerce Resolution:

> Frank Hitner has been since the forming of the Chamber of Commerce an active and faithful member and has been a leading business man of our city, a man of high integrity, a man active in church work, a man imbued with local pride and self-sacrifice.

Why would God see fit to take such a relatively young man who had so much left to accomplish? With his faith, he would have understood.

Humphrey's Department Store>>

Hitner, Robert Moore

Baseball has been a favorite pastime of kids for many years. Quite a few years ago, I received a memory from Robert Hitner where he recalled playing baseball with friends. Here is his memory.

We all have had our Huckleberry Finn years and memories of the years that go back to our boyhood. Those years for me were spent in Webb City, from 1911–1935.

Our home at 308 South Liberty Street was only a couple of blocks north of a group of former mines that had been located south of the city (Sucker Flat), now King Jack Park. The alkaline residue from the mining activity kept grass from growing around the mining areas. This made a great baseball field, and the baseballs didn't bounce on the surface. The ball would scoot through the infielder's legs, resulting in many unexpected errors. Joplin and Carthage had never encountered such a baseball diamond. That wasn't the only problem for the visiting team. Right in the middle of the centerfield was a shaft of which you couldn't see the bottom. We, local outfielders, played immediately in front of the shaft hole so we could play the ball to the left or right, whichever was necessary, and knew where the hole was located at all times. It scared the visiting teams just a bit to know that hole was behind them if they played in front, so they played it to the right or left which resulted in errors as the ball always seemed to go the other side than what they had played it, and it rolled to distant confines of the outfield with no fence. Our home field advantage was considerable.

Generally we played baseball in the street. If you have the occasion to drive south on Liberty Street, notice the way the street gutter is indented in front of the property at 308 South Liberty Street. When the street was laid out and the gutter poured, my dad had the indenture made for parking off the street. My ball-playing buddies, and I had a better use for it. It made a great three-man site for a sophisticated variation of pepper baseball. The space was just right for a batter to hit the ball to two fellows covering the area, which was about five feet deep (front to back) and ten or twelve feet long. The proper lines of boundaries were made when they poured the concrete for the gutter. These boundary lines indicated foul balls at the sides and type of base hit in between. They provided many hours of pastime when there were only two or three fellows available for a game. It was excellent for the development of agility, plus practice in handling the baseball, and helped the batter perfect his ability to hit the ball where he wanted to place it.

Back at Sucker Flat, there were huge chat piles resulting from large stones that were ground up extracting lead and zinc, leaving a residue of stone, gravel, or chat. There were millponds some two hundred feet across and very deep. The bottom was very flinty and sharp from the crushed rock. The water was quite alkaline in content, which was hard on the eyes. We were not allowed to swim in those ponds, so when we returned home after a hot and sweaty baseball game with our red eyes, it was a dead giveaway that we had been swimming, to say nothing of our cuts and bruises. It was very dangerous swimming in the millponds, but I'm afraid we regularly skinny-dipped, to our parents' displeasure.

Wintertime brought just as much pleasure with the snow-covered mountains of chat. We could drag our sleds to the top and slide down at a very high rate of speed. The danger was trying to miss the really large stones left from blasting, which were covered with snow. It was a real problem if you hit a stone at a high rate of speed, but it was a great sport!

It is sad that most of the chat piles are gone. I'm glad that I grew up in the area before they hauled off the chat piles and leveled the land. Look at all the fun the kids of today are missing with their sleds on the slopes when it snows.

My dad owned Humphrey's Department Store, two hundred block of North Main Street in Webb City. I, no doubt, was a nuisance to all the personnel, as I played with the little carts (trays) as they sped on wheels on wires, carrying the money from the various cashier counters to the office on the balcony. I recall how much I must have bothered Florence, as I insisted on operating her typewriter, etc., and playing in Dad's office on the balcony.

I did eventually mature, and I worked at the Webb City Bank with Mr. Will Burch and Mr. Lee Daugherty. They were both great men. The Burch family and the Daugherty family owned property out west of town where the Joplin airport is located.

I did love the game of golf. After I balanced my window at the Webb City Bank, I headed for the golf course and played until dark. One Fourth of July, our foursome played fifty-four holes of golf. That is a lot of golf! Webb City was the best place for boys to grow up.

More memories of Robert Hitner.

Chat piles and traveling—Webb City, in those mining days between 1910 and 1920, was surrounded by mammoth chat piles on all sides, not only south of town toward Duenweg but also between Carterville and Webb City and around Alba and Oronogo. The sale of chat was a big business. Train loads of gravel went all over the country. The automobile was just beginning to take hold. Hard-surfaced roads were nonexistent except for a few brick and block streets in the city. To drive across the country, the roads were either single-lane dirt roads or at best gravel or creek-bed rock. The roads were called highways, were unmarked except for the roads between such cities as Joplin and Kansas City. Some highways were marked by symbols painted on telephone poles, such as a connected JH for Jefferson Highway. If you missed a symbol, you might be several miles down the road before you realize you aren't seeing the symbols anymore. That entailed turning around and going back until you found a highway sign.

The narrow roads sometimes created a problem when you met another car going in the opposite direction. You had to pull over to the side and negotiate the thick gravel and hope you didn't overturn. Tires weren't much larger than a bicycle tire. And of course, they were all made with an inner tube which frequently blew out, which could also upset the automobile. Most cars traveling very far had several tubes tied to the side in case of blowouts.

It was a two-day trip between Joplin and Kansas City. If you drove the Kansas route, it was one day between Webb City and Kansas City, and Fort Scott was where you stayed overnight and continued your trip to Kansas City the next day. Or if you drove the Missouri side of the state line from Webb City, you stopped at Nevada and hoped you had good weather to continue on to Kansas City the next day.

Driving across country from Kansas to Colorado in the summer was a hot, dusty, disagreeable trip. I recall for the first time seeing my mother drink a beer as she was about to pass out on such a journey. That had to make quite an impression, as it is my only recollection of my mother and alcoholic beverages. In fact, I recall no other instances of alcohol being consumed in front of Frances and me. Uncle Harry brought home a bottle of wine for my dad when he served in World War I, and that bottle of wine resided in the dining room cabinet for medicinal purposes until it finally reached the finish, and there were flies in the bottom.

The chat piles around Webb City are now practically all gone. I grew up and moved away before the chat piles were hauled off and the land leveled. Look at all the fun that Webb City kids are now missing when it snows, and they can't ride their sleds down those slopes of gravel.

Memories of Robert Hitner: walking the streets of Webb City, 1900s—In the early 1900s, Webb City was indeed a rough mining town. Business houses lined both sides of Allen (Main) Street from one end to the other. I was always instructed to walk down the west side of the street because the east side was composed of bars, pool halls, movie houses, and pawnshops. It still seems strange, after all these years, for me to walk down the east side of Main Street.

My father's store, Humphrey's Mercantile, was north of Bradbury's Drug Store on the northeast corner of Daugherty and Main Streets. Roy Teel's Drug Store was on the northwest corner of that same intersection. Roy Teel would buy my production of lead soldiers, which he used as premium giveaways with his ice cream soda. That intersection of the streetcar line was the one that took you to Carthage, Joplin, and north or south Webb City.

The post office was at the corner of Liberty and Daugherty Street, and Mr. Thomas, my barber, was across the street near the Blake movie house. Runt Magill's Newstand was at the northeast corner of Webb and Daugherty Streets, and every day, as I picked up the mail while working at the Webb City Bank, I would stop by Runt's, and we would flip a coin for a Coca-Cola.

Webb City Post Office

Webb City Bank

While I was the assistant cashier at the bank, I was also the treasurer of the school board and president of the junior chamber of commerce. One of my duties at the Webb City Bank was to go over to the Conqueror First National Bank in Joplin for change and currency. A garage owner in Carterville would come by the bank and pick me up, and away we would go. Can you imagine taking that kind of risk today?

The Merchant & Miners Bank stood on the corner of Main and Daugherty Street, southwest corner. Zaumzeil Jewelry was next-door to the south. The streetcar came from Carthage, crossed Webb City to the large barns and "round table" at the west end and exited town on South Madison Street. It went to Joplin and on into Picher, Oklahoma, etc.

There were fond memories of the central school, which was later replaced by Smith Brothers Shirt Factories using the same bricks from the schoolhouse. A fine new library was built at Liberty and First Street by a government grant from Andrew Carnegie. I worked there too, filing books on the shelves.

My other employment in Webb City included a trainee program with S. H. Kress and Company, Allen (Main) Street, for a lucrative salary of $13 a week. Besides training, I was allowed to sweep out daily, trim the windows, stock the shelves in the warehouse, pull the shipments upstairs on the hand-powered elevator, and take the merchandise down to the girls daily at the counters. The windows were trimmed by stacking glass shelves and glass vases some six feet high on which to display all kinds of merchandise. Sometimes a streetcar would come down the street, and my window would wind up on the floor in a heap of broken rubble.

I recall one morning, after an unusually rough Halloween night, I reported to work at the normal 7:00 a.m. to find such a situation, plus all the windows had been soaped and had to be washed.

The job as assistant cashier at Webb City Bank was a considerable promotion, however, which paid $125 a month. Mr. Will Burch and Mr. Lee Daugherty were officers and great gentlemen to work for. The Burch and Daugherty families owned property out west of town that is now the Joplin Airport.

The Webb City golf course out on West Broadway and the Schifferdecker Course in Joplin were two excellent courses, although the Webb City course had sand greens in those days. After I balanced my window at the bank, I headed for the golf course and practiced or played until dark. One Fourth of July, our foursome played fifty-four holes of gold in Joplin with a beer at every three holes as the stakes. The Easter sunrise service was always held on the ninth hole of the Webb City Course.

The Life of Robert Moore, written by Robert Moore Hitner, September 25, 1991, includes Robert's research of the history of Jasper County, Carthage, Missouri, and Lakeside:

> By 1900, Robert Moore was one of the most prominent and successful businessmen in Carthage, Jasper County, Missouri and the entire Tri-State area. He was also recognized to be a dedicated family man, a religious and loyal citizen. He was born on May 2, 1846 at Millers Run, Washington County which is in western Pennsylvania about 20 miles south of Pittsburgh. The family moved to Monogahal, Pennsylvania which was about 20 miles east, when he was 14 years of age. He worked there three or four years at Alexander's store.
>
> He did not enlist in the Pennsylvania Volunteers as did his brother Joe, whether because he was too young or whether he was not accepted due to his poor health. At any rate, after the Civil War brothers Robert and Joe went on to buy a farm in Johnson County near Warrensburg, Missouri. It was there that he met and married Sarah Elizabeth Winkler who had been born in Warrensburg Missouri on November 10, 1850.
>
> Jasper County was ready to "explode" right after the Civil War. It was first settled about 1832 among tribes of Seneca, Shawnee, and other friendly Indians. The initial town of Sarcoxie was named in honor of an old and friendly Chief of the Shawnee.

Jasper County was organized January 29, 1841 and Carthage was designated the County seat because of its geographical center of the county and for its "park like" qualities. It grew steadily until the Civil War. Since Jasper was one of the counties bordering Kansas and near the Confederate States, it was occupied and raided alternately by forces from the North and the South and at all times by gangs of Guerrillas. Therefore the towns were burned, farms destroyed and citizens robbed, raped, pillaged and killed so much that by the end of the war, Jasper County was in every sense of the word a depopulated county. There were only a few homes left in the county. *The Kansas City Star* reported, "Jasper County dropped in population from 7000 to 200, Carthage from 600 to 5. Travelers in 1866 recalled no fields nor crops...only blackened chimneys shown against the sky."

In early 1865, roving Federal patrols from Mount Vernon found deer drinking at the rain-filled drinking troughs in the ruins of downtown Carthage. Men who had occupied troops from the North and the South had seen the beauty in the land of Carthage and they proceeded to return to Jasper County to settle. Here was a place to live with ample fresh running water, ideal climate compared to where they hailed from, rich farming land, other natural resources and great industries.

Lead and Zinc had been found under the ground throughout the county in great abundance although more in the southwest corner of the county. The three mile region around Webb City was said to have more lead and zinc than anywhere in the world making millionaires of many of the citizens. White limestone quarries around Carthage were shipping throughout America some of the finest building material in the world. Rich farms were producing grain for local milling and several different kinds of fruit was produced for shipping. As examples, strawberries were shipped from Sarcoxie at the rate of 200 to 375 carloads per season. Jasper County apples and peaches were being compared with the finest throughout the land. Carthage, in fact, had everything going for it. According to the booklet, "*Carthage and Jasper County*" printed in 1887 stated Carthage "*now stands as a city of eight thousand population and acknowledged Queen of Beauty of the State and of the great Southwest.*"

Jasper County in 1870 had 14,928 people but by 1880 numbers doubled to 32,019. In 1870 the Moore brothers chose an excellent time to come to Jasper County and establish the lumber business. You have to agree that they picked the right place at the right time. They opened their first lumber yard in Granby, Missouri and eventually had 18 lumber yards operating all over the Tri-State area with their main office in Carthage, Missouri.

Cousin Eb Smith came to Carthage from Pennsylvania and went to work for the Home Lumber Company in 1885, "piling boards." He served in Sales, as bookkeeper, and ultimately manager of the operation for many years after the death of

Robert Moore. The *Carthage Press* quotes Eb Smith in an interview November 22, 1938 as follows, "*There was not a day we didn't have one to five carloads of lumber floating down the Mississippi on log rafts with the sawed lumber stacked on the logs. It was floated down to St. Louis or Hannibal. Some of the first lumber was hauled from Sedalia, Granby, and Pierce City before the Frisco Railway was built into Carthage.*"

Grandfather Moore (Robert) was involved in many businesses, industries and investments. He continued to be President of the Home Lumber Company until his death. His brother Joe left the lumber business to join his nephew Frank Moore at the Carthage Foundry plus his numerous other enterprises. Robert Moore was Vice-President and later President of the Carthage National Bank which was later known as the Bank of Carthage until his passing in 1915. He was President of the Peoples Ice Plant which made an important product in those days before electric refrigeration as everyone used an ice-cooled ice-box. He was President of the Carthage Superior Bed Spring Factory which was the largest of its type in the country at that time.

Robert was a Director and one of the nine founders of the Jasper County Electric Railway which connected all the important towns of the Tri-State area with 30 miles of rail which was instrumental to the development of the region. The "streetcar line" also established Lakeside Park on Center Creek between Carthage and Carterville. The river was deep at that point which made it excellent for swimming. Located on one side of the river was a Bath House, a roller coaster, Baseball park, tennis courts, and a wrought iron bridge crossing the river. On the south side was a Ferris Wheel, Merry-go-round, concessions and a Dance Pavilion up on the hill. Many pleasant memories are associated with Lakeside Park.

Grandfather Robert Moore was always a dedicated family man, an Elder and active in all interests of the Presbyterian Church. At the *Carthage Press* he was a man of high integrity, good judgement and fine Christian spirit." To quote Reverend McCaugherty in the final services "*he had lived a strong, active cultural and consecrated life and just as he passed the meridian and as shadows were lengthening toward evening the light went out suddenly.*" He passed away the night of March 9, 1915 about 9:30 p.m. from the second heart attack of the evening at his much loved home place at 1163 Grand Avenue, Carthage, Missouri.

Hewlett, Wade

Joe Hewlett sent a wonderful letter relating his father's youth in the west end of town. Joe is married to Patty Wise, and his father was Wade Hewlett. Joe gives the West End Pharmacy credit for him being around today. Here is his story in his own words:

My father, Wade Hewlett, was born in Webb City on February 16, 1917, at 104 North Oak Street. He later moved to 1201 West Daugherty. In notes left by my father, any kid that lived on the west side of town was one of the west end kids. My dad was friends with Harold Dowell, Leroy Smith, and Jack Mayfield. Dad and Harold worked at the West End Pharmacy for Bob Burris, while Leroy worked for his dad at Smith Paint Store, just a couple doors up from the pharmacy.

In 1938, my dad worked at Berrian's Grocery,1001 West Daugherty, for Carroll and Bess Berrian. The Berrians were wonderful people. He worked there in the daytime and in the evenings at the pharmacy, where he was a soda jerk and carhop, along with Harold Dowell.

My mom had just graduated from Monett High School and moved to 1227 West Broadway. She worked with Helen Hoerning at Hoerning's Hardware and Lumber, 1003 West Daugherty, just two doors down from Berrian's Grocery. My mom and Helen would walk from the hardware store across the street to the West End Pharmacy, heading east on Daugherty. As they would cross the Frisco train tracks, my father and Ralph Platter, the butcher at Berrian's, would slip out the side door and throw rotten potatoes at the young ladies. The potatoes would splatter on the pavement and get all over their legs. Of course, when they turned around, no one was in sight!

My father mentioned to Ralph that he thought my mom was cute. This led to my dad wanting to meet my mom. In 1940, they started dating, were married the first of September, and I came along in 1942.

So the West End Pharmacy played a big part in me being here. Thank God for rotten potatoes, Berrian's Grocery, and the West End Pharmacy.

I'm sure there are still some west end kids that remember the west end!

A special thanks to Joe Hewlett for taking the time to share his dad's memories.

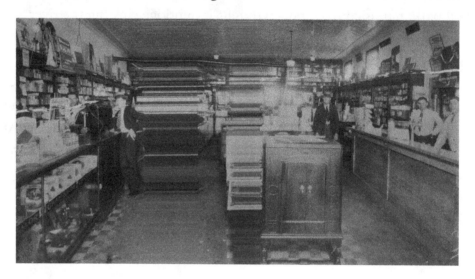

Hughletts and Polens

When Bob Polen took Minnie Ellison to be his wife in 1915, little did he know of the struggles to come in the future. The economy of the nation was at an all-time low. Jobs were scarce, and times were rough. He had farmed the family homestead until 1920, and then he went to work in Antioch, Nebraska, in a potash plant, but the plant closed because potash was cheaper in Germany.

The Polens had a little candy store in Antioch, but people didn't have money to spend, especially after the potash plants were shut down. But Bob had a family to take care of, he needed the work. He did contract work with an irrigation system at Bridgeport, Nebraska, until he heard about the dam being built in Arkansas on the White River. So he moved his family to Arkansas. As luck would have it, they delayed that project. It wouldn't be in effect for another twenty years.

Bob went to work in the lead and zinc mines in Lawton, Kansas, in 1923. For the next few years, life was quite a struggle, and Bob did mining, insurance work, and grew wheat. The Depression was bad, and work was hard to find, but Bob was one of those who could work in almost any field.

In 1931, he moved his family of six children—Charles, Jack, Bill, Marguerite, Alma, and Mary—to Asbury, Missouri, and he worked as a blacksmith. He also did work as a grain elevator operator and a bookkeeper.

Finally in 1938, after twenty-three years of moving from job to job, Bob bought some grocery supplies from Harold Coleman and opened a grocery store in Asbury. Life seemed to take on a more stable atmosphere. Minnie became well known in the area, as she taught the women how to can corn in tin cans instead of glass jars. The corn canned in the tin cans lasted longer and tasted better.

Meanwhile, back in the 1920s, Dr. William Stone, over at Glen Elm (Stone's Corner), had opened a little grocery store on the southwest corner of the intersection. His wife, Ora, ran the store while he took care of his veterinary business.

Bob Polen's daughter, Mary, had married in 1938 to Bill Hughlett (in later years, he became our Jasper County tax collector). Mary and Bill had purchased the Stone Grocery Store and were operating it. But Bill was going to do his patriotic duty during WWII and joined the navy. So Mary's parents, Bob and Minnie, purchased the store from Bill and Mary. With two stores to run, Bob and one of his children would run one, and Minnie, with the help of another one of their children, would run the other. This went on until they could sell the store in Asbury.

The store at Stone's Corner had living quarters above and add a bonus of indoor plumbing. Although Bob was embarrassed that a customer in the store could hear the gush of water that revealed what he was doing upstairs!

Later Bob and Minnie bought some land a little ways to the south of the store and moved three houses there. They lived in one and used the other two as rentals. That property stayed in the family as it was the home of their grandson, Steve Hughlett (Steve's Transmission).

After Bob and Minnie retired in 1957, their son Bill (the son they bought the grocery store from when he went into the service) and his family took over Stone's Grocery. And I finally got an answer to my question—yes! The name of Glen Elm was changed to Stone's Corner because of Dr. Stone and his veterinary office and grocery store.

I can't finish this story without further mention of Bill and Mary Hughlett. They were such a special couple. They raised six children: Bill Jr., Steve, Mike, Joe, David, and Elaine. Bill and Mary cared for people, and in turn, people cared for them. And even though he was an elected official in the '60s, Bill was still a highly respected person. At both of their funerals, the number of people who turned out to pay their respects attributes to the many peoples' lives they touched in some way!

Hulett, A. A.

When Colonel A. A. Hulett passed away on April 30, 1917, all businesses closed from 2:00–4:00 p.m., on May 1, in his honor. The colonel lived at 510 South Madison.

Hulett, Harry B.

At an April 2, 1931, birthday celebration for Webb City, Harry Hulett spoke about his first view of Webb City. He said he remembered his first view in 1877, as he fought the mud from Thom's Station (Fourth Street) to the Buffalo House on Webb Street. He said that as the sun came up the next morning, and he looked out the window, there were only a handful of buildings that made up the town of Webb City. In later years, he followed Spracklen by organizing the second city band with uniforms.

RESIDENCE OF A. A. HULETT.

Humphreys, Henry C.

The year was 1890, and forty-nine-year-old Henry C. Humphreys moved to Webb City with $4,000 worth of merchandise to start a business. He settled in a store located on northeast corner of Allen (Main) and Church Street across from the infamous Newland Hotel (southwest corner of Allen and Church Streets). Within the first year, his business had brought in $17,000. Henry's business continued to grow, and after nine years of success, he needed a building as impressive as his business.

The building he chose was the largest and most imposing building in the city. It was the Hatten-Raymond Block located at 201 to 207 North Allen (Main) Street, two stories high. A. D. Hatten and his friend Otto Raymond had built the building with their earnings from the mines. It was the second brick business building to be built in Webb City. It was built in 1887, and Humphrey was going to make it into the showplace it was built for.

Henry's business continued to grow and was reported to have made as high as $300,000 annually (that was a lot of money in the early 1900s). Humphrey's Department Store was the most extensive business of its kind in this part of the country. The company employed thirty-five to forty employees on the average.

Henry also owned other businesses and residential property in town. He was very active in real estate. But Henry was never too busy to help out in the community. He was always concerned with the city's welfare.

Henry Humphrey was born in St. Louis, Missouri, on August 14, 1841. Henry's heritage is from good stock as his ancestor John Humphrey assisted in establishing American independence while serving his country. Henry's relatives were natives of Virginia, back many generations. Henry's parents, Thomas Keyes Humphrey and Helen Cordell Humphrey moved to Missouri in 1834. They had eight children, of which Henry was number 5.

While attending Westminster College in Fulton, Missouri, the Civil War began. As much as he enjoyed education, the call to protect the South was a stronger pull, and he enlisted in Company H, Fourth Missouri Calvary, Confederate Service under Colonel John Q. Burbridge, who was attached to General Marmaduke's brigade. His service to his country was not an easy one as he traveled all over Missouri and Arkansas and was severely wounded and lost two fingers while assisting General Price on his raid. He was taken prisoner twice, with the last one resulting in him being confined in a penitentiary at Alton, Illinois. After finally being released, Henry went back to his family farm and joined in the farming for about three years. He was restless and tried his hand at merchandising in Lebanon, Missouri; Raymore, Missouri, and other cities, plus throwing in some farming along the way. He didn't do this rambling alone as he took a bride, Sarah Higgins of St. Louis, in 1878, and they had four children: Cordell Humphreys, born in Lebanon, Missouri; George Humphreys, born in St. Louis County in 1881, died at the age of twenty-two; Euola Humphreys, died at the age of two; Pearl Humphreys Graham was born in Raymore, Missouri. In 1899, at the age of forty-eight, Henry found himself in Webb City with $4,000 worth of stock. The rest is history. He continued to buy real estate as land was a great investment.

Henry was a Democrat but refused to be caught up in any political races. He was a Presbyterian and an active member of the Odd Fellow Fraternity.

Henry's son Cordell followed in his father's footsteps and became a prominent Webb City real estate broker.

HATTEN & RAYMOND BUILDING.

Inman, John Henry

Inman owned a dry goods store in the west end for twenty-six years; he died in his son's home at 1128 West Broadway. John was eighty-two years old, March 9, 1939. Inman had served on the city council to help the west end community. He belonged to the West End Booster Club and the Emmanuel Baptist Church. His wife's name was Chloe; daughters were Mrs. H. C. King and Mrs. Earl Van Hoose. His sisters were Mrs. M. Duncan and Mrs. Addie Horton, and his brother was Tom Inman. John Inman took pride in his west end community.

Jones, W. Alton

As I was doing some research for a friend, each person I interviewed would mention W. Alton Jones. As soon as the name was mentioned, I would recall that he is a member of the R-VII Hall of Fame. The more I talked about him with each interview, I got that itch to share his story once again with my readers. He was quite a remarkable fellow. Most of my information came from Bill Kamler, Columbia, Missouri, in 1999, right before Jones was added to the hall of fame. Kamler had a lot of respect for Jones. The website for W. Alton Jones was also a wealth of information.

W. Alton (Pete) Jones was born April 19, 1891, on a forty-acre farm near Webb City, the seventh child of a seventh child. Being raised by a wonderful mother whom he worshipped, Pete was quoted as saying, "Any good in my life is due to her. One thing she impressed upon me was to always to tell the truth. If I have established a reputation for anything, it is integrity. I have always believed in laying it on the line. This won't qualify me as a star diplomat, but it enables me to sleep soundly."

Pete began his working career at an early age. When he was six years old, he would get up before dawn, finish his farm chores, and get to school earlier than the other students. He used this time to sweep the floor and scrub the chalkboards which earned him $2 a week. As he grew older, he worked in a grocery store as a clerk and delivered newspapers. When he worked for the local bottling company, he earned 60¢ for each twelve-hour day. That's only 5¢ an hour, but he could drink all the soda pop he wanted.

Pete had a goal in mind, which included a Vanderbilt education. So after his graduation as an honor student in 1910, Pete headed for Vanderbilt. After the first year, Jones had to return home to help support his family. He didn't let that stop him as he continued his education through correspondence while working full-time.

At the age of twenty-one, in 1912, Jones went to work for Cities Service (gas company) and, within two years, was promoted to the Joplin office. Being a bit more financially secure, in 1914, Jones proposed to and married his childhood sweetheart, Nettie Marie Marvin.

Jones made quite a name for himself at Cities Service as he continued to climb the ladder of success. In 1921, he was transferred to New York becoming a member of the executive committee within one year. By 1927, at the age of thirty-six, he was named the first vice president, and by 1940, W. Alton Jones was made the president of Cities Service.

During WWII, Jones put all of his efforts into the home front by serving as chairman of the Petroleum Industry War Council and president of the War Emergency Pipelines, Inc. He was responsible for the speedy completion of the Big Inch and Little Inch pipelines, which allowed large volumes of fuel and oil to reach the East Coast during wartime, thereby enabling industry to produce war materials and supplying the Allied Forces with needed petroleum. This created a major impact on turning the tide of the war in favor of the Allies. In fact, Jones received the Presidential Certificate of Merit.

Kamler stated, "Mr. Jones had a magnetic personality and a remarkable capacity for making friends from pipeline workers to heads of state. He became a close personal friend of President Eisenhower." In fact, Jones was on his way to join President Eisenhower for a golfing vacation in 1962, when his plane crashed, and he was killed.

The integrity of Pete Jones, along with his sense of responsibility and concern for his fellow man, characterized his life. Jones established the W. Alton Jones Foundation in 1944. Throughout his lifetime, he continually added to the foundation. He left his estate "to promote the well-being and general good of mankind throughout the world."

For many years, he served on the board of trustees of Presbyterian Hospital in New York. During that time, he subsidized numerous interns and resident physicians who, without his aid, could not have completed their work. Maurice Clark recalls that the foundation was responsible for the addition being built at Jane Chinn Hospital in Webb City. Kamler said the Jones Foundation had given several large gifts to the University of Missouri to establish the very first endowed chair in the school of medicine in1964. This chair is the W. Alton Jones Distinguished Professor and Chairman of Surgery.

Nettie Marie Marvin Jones, Pete's childhood sweetheart and lifelong companion, continued to carry on the philanthropic vision of her husband with energy, discernment, and compassion for twenty-nine years, until her death in October of 1991.

What an impressive representative of Webb City. I would like to thank all who have contributed to this information to help share the talents and ambitions of W. Alton Jones.

Jones, W. Alton

I received a letter from Bill J. Kamler in Columbia, who has taken the time to share some information about a famous Webb City citizen, W. Alton Jones. Here is his letter.

While there have been several Webb Citians in this century who have contributed greatly to our society or have excelled in their fields, I would have to consider W. Alton Jones to be one of our most distinguished citizens.

Mr. Jones was born in 1891 near Webb City. After graduation from the Webb City High School, as an honor student, he attended Vanderbilt University. He started work in 1912 with Cities Service in Webb City and was promoted to the Joplin Office two years later. In 1921, he was transferred to New York. He became a member of the executive committee of the company in 1922. He was named the first Vice-president in 1927 and President in 1940.

He was chairman of the Petroleum Council during World War II and was largely responsible for the speedy construction of the Big Inch and Little Inch pipelines. These pipelines had a major impact on getting larger volumes of fuel and oil to the east coast during the war, thereby allowing industry to produce war material and supplying the Allied Forces with petroleum. Prior to their completion, many oil and fuel tankers were subject to U-boat attacks and it was difficult to obtain fuel where it was needed. These were mammoth projects, which involved construction over more than half the length of the continent, employing thousands of workers and to my knowledge, was completed in only nine months. The results had a major impact on turning the tide of the war in favor of the Allies.

For many years, he served on the Board of Trustees of the Presbyterian Hospital in New York. During that time, he subsidized numerous interns and resident physicians who without this aid could not have completed their work. When the W. Alton Jones Foundation was established in 1946, one of its purposes was to aid in the establishment and support of programs of medical research and education. Mr. Jones had a deep concern for the welfare of his fellow men and possessed the rare ability to recognize the talents of others and an eagerness to provide the right environment for all the full realization of those talents.

Mr. Jones had a magnetic personality and a remarkable capacity for making friends, from pipeline workers to heads of state. He became a close and personal friend of President Eisenhower, but tragically he was enroute to join President Eisenhower for a golfing vacation in 1962, when his plane crashed and he was killed.

I had heard of W. Alton Jones when I was growing up in Webb City, but frankly, only knew a vague story that he had given several large gifts to establish the very first Endowed Chair in the School of Medicine in 1965. This chair is the W.Alton Jones Distinguished Professor and Chairman of Surgery.

The most recent chairman is Dr. Donald Silver, who retired in July. My position as a surgery supervisor at the University Hospital in Columbia has allowed me the opportunity and good fortune to work with Dr. Silver, who for 23 years has represented the Jones Chair at the University with honor and provided outstanding leadership in that capacity. Dr. Silver became a very knowledgeable student of the life and work of W. Alton Jones and I found it interesting that he was always proud to maintain on his letterhead and to sign all of his official correspondence as the "W.Alton Jones Distinguished Professor and Chairman of Surgery." He also maintained a display case in his office of various memorabilia of Mr. Jones and information regarding the chair.

I hope this information is of some interest to your readers. And I hope that the people of Webb City can take some pride in learning about one of their own from out of the past, as well as this association with the university, which is a part of their heritage and history that most may not have known about.

Thanks so much, Mr. Kamler, for taking the time to share such a wonderful memory with us. There have been many who have left our city to go on to make a name for themselves, and sometimes, they are forgotten. Thanks for shining the spotlight on a great man who deserves to be remembered.

In a 1908 annual, under the name of Alton Jones is a little verse:

He dares to do what he thinks is right:
Whatever he does, he does with his might.

Note: There's an Internet website about W. Alton Jones and Nettie Marie Jones located at: http://www.wajones.org.

Knell, Emma

In the year 1882, a young upholsterer named Edward Knell moved his family to Carthage from Davenport, Iowa. He started a partnership with George C. Howenstein, and they purchased the

Hurley and Dingle funeral business. Knell showed an immediate interest in the surrounding community and jumped in to assist in any way. His first community act was to establish the Carthage Merchants Association.

In 1884, the partnership of Knell and Howenstein dissolved, and Edward Knell became the sole proprietor of the funeral business, which became known as Knell Mortuary at Third and Lyon. Feeling a need to give his best to the community, Edward went to Cincinnati, Ohio, and graduated from the Clark School of Embalming in 1887. Knell was the first embalmer in Jasper County and went on to design the first funeral chapel.

In 1902, Edward Knell established the Knell Fair, which was held on the Knell farm on the northeast edge of Carthage in the Spring River bottoms. The first action consisted of building a large grandstand to hold five thousand spectators and a half-mile running track for horse racing. The Knell Fair was later called the Jasper County Fair and then the Southwest Missouri Fair.

Edward's daughter, Emma Knell, took over for her father as the fair manager in 1909. The fair became noted as the second largest fair in Missouri, second to the Sedalia Fair. Emma managed the fair until 1926. Then Emma retired as she made some great changes in her life.

After graduating from high school, Emma had entered the undertaking business with her father, with his blessings. He felt it was important to have a female in the business to take care of the women clients. Emma was only the third woman in Missouri to receive a license to embalm.

In 1924, Emma was approached by Jasper County's presiding judge, J. F. Lee, and asked if she would consider running for the Missouri legislature. Having never given such a thought to her future, it took Emma by surprise. But she was persuaded to participate in the campaign. She kept a very low profile and relied on newspaper advertisements and word of mouth from those who had worked with her in the community.

The forty-six-year-old Emma Knell won the election. She was the third woman elected to the Missouri House of Representatives and the first woman from the Missouri Ozarks. Knell was a natural, and she loved working as a legislator.

One of the first major campaigns that Knell took on was to save the Webb City Tuberculosis Hospital, which was in danger of being closed due to lack of funds. That hospital was a necessity for the poor miners. At the time, each Jasper County miner (patient) received $5 from the state, and Knell proposed a bill that would give each patient $10 a week. Meanwhile, Senator A. L. McCawley introduced a bill in the senate asking for $12.50 per patient. Both bills passed. Knell asked the House of Representatives to accept the senate bill for the higher amount. When the bill was due before the governor for a signature, Knell approached the governor and told him of the situation at the Webb City Tuberculosis Hospital and asked him to let his conscience be his guide. The bill was approved and signed that very day.

At the end of Knell's first term, the Democrats decided to give Knell a little competition in the next election and nominated Martha Taafe to run against Emma Knell. Taafe was active in her community, and the Democrats felt pretty confident that she would be a worthy opponent against Knell. This was something new for Jasper County—an election that put woman against woman.

But Emma had also been involved in her community. Not only serving as general manager of the fair, Emma served on the Carthage School Board and the Carthage Park Board.

Knell had served a wonderful term as representative, and she had lots of backers to tell of her accomplishments. And her actions were the best advertising campaign of all. Knell defeated Martha Taafe by nearly three thousand votes.

Having a woman in the House added a softer side. Someone to show an interest in issues such as treatment for the crippled children, pensions for schoolteachers, and a state song. Her second term was just as rewarding as her first had been.

Emma decided not to run for re-election in 1928 but took two years off before running for her third term. She stated that she felt more confident and was ready to do all she could for the county. Having won the election, Knell took on the project of requiring all schools that receive state aid to fly the United States flag.

Knell did not seek a fourth term. Emma Knell returned to the family mortuary business. At the death of her brother, Emma became the president of the company in 1943 at the age of sixty-five. Finally deciding it was time to slow down a bit, Emma sold her interest in the family business to her nephews, Robert and Frank Jr. Emma stayed on as vice president until 1957, when she retired at the age of seventy-nine.

Emma passed away in September of 1963, age eighty-four. It was reported that Emma Knell remained firm in what she felt was right, worked diligently, and fought for a strict economy. Knell was a very distinguished lady who represented the Ozarks with dignity.

Lawyer, Frank G.

Webb City's greatest blacksmith, horseshoeing, carriage and wagon works.

Frank G. Lawyer, owner and manager of the livery stable on the corner of Daugherty and Tom Streets, came to Webb City in 1892. He was married in 1888 to Ms. Laura M. Henderson in Iola, Kansas, and they had four boys and one girl. The family resided at 305 South Webb Street.

Lawyer was raised on a farm in Kansas and knew his trade well. He established a good trade. His business carried a full supply of needed items for all seasons. His livery stable was 20×50, two stories high. He was noted as being a good-natured gentleman and courteous to all he had dealings, something that costs little but is of permanent nature. Lawyer was an active member of the Methodist Church and a member of the Modern Woodmen of America.

Lewis, Joseph Freemont

"Bernita and Fern Lewis dedicated their lives and intellect to Webb City's children."

Joseph F. Lewis chose his career early in life, and it paid off well. Joe was a mine operator. He built his beautiful home at 103 South Pennsylvania Street for his family's comfort, but it was a definite tribute to how well he was doing in his business.

Joe Lewis moved to the Webb City area in 1884 when he was twenty-two years old. He married Elizabeth Anne. He and his wife, Elizabeth, had two daughters, Fern and Bernita. Fern graduated in 1912 and became a schoolteacher. Bernita graduated from Webb City High School in 1917 and followed in her sister's teaching footsteps.

The girls never married but dedicated their lives to their profession. Bernita outlived the rest of the family and continued to live in that big family home. They may not have had children, but many children have fond memories of those two special teachers who influenced many lives.

Joseph owned and operated the J. F. Lewis Mine on Sucker Flat. According to mining lore, a piece of lead ore weighing several tons was taken from the J. F. Mine and was the largest piece of ore taken from the ground up to that time. It was purchased by the old Commercial Club and sent to the Columbian Exposition at Chicago in 1894.

Joseph was a member of the Presbyterian Church and the Webb City Masonic Lodge 512, AF and AM.

Joseph Lewis is buried in the Webb City Cemetery. He passed away on July 27, 1939.

Lewis Home at 103 South Pennsylvania

Lively, Melvin Roscoe

At the northwest corner of First and Oronogo, 705 West First, stands a beautiful blue house that can't help but be recognized as one of Webb City's historical homes. This beautiful home, at the turn of the century, belonged to Melvin Roscoe Lively and his wife, Alice.

Born May 11, 1869, in Hancock County, Illinois, Melvin Roscoe Lively received his education in rural schools. He attended college in Carthage, Illinois, for one term and another term at LaGrange, Missouri. He then went to Valparaiso, Indiana, where he graduated in 1884 with a degree. Going to Chicago, Lively went to work for a law firm, McClelleand & Monroe. He worked there for a year and a half for knowledge and experience. He was admitted to the bar by the supreme court.

Melvin came to the Webb City area in 1890 after first trying his legal business in Carthage and Kansas. Finally settling in Webb City, Melvin's law practice met with imminent success, not only here but in Carthage and Joplin as well.

As director of the Oakwood Mining Company, the Moore-Veatch Realty Company, and the Webb City Smelting Company, Melvin's importance in the community increased.

The Lively family was well known in Kentucky with Melvin's grandfather William Lively, who was born just south of Louisville, Kentucky. William did a little pioneering in Indiana where his son, Lewis, was born on the family farm, close to Terre Haute.

By the time the Civil War erupted, Lewis was in Illinois. When the call came to enlist, he joined with the Fourth Illinois Cavalry and was ordered to the front. As he was about to take passage on a steamer boat in Quincy, Illinois, his horse fell, and Lewis sustained injuries that kept him from serving in the war. He received an honorable discharge from the service, but he was always a little ashamed and very disappointed at the turn of events in his life.

Lewis married Mary Jane King from Illinois, and they had four children: Argil J., Minta, Harry Bryant, and Melvin Roscoe.

Melvin Roscoe and Martha Alice Nichols were married May 24, 1887, in Kankakee, Illinois. They had one daughter, Lorraine. Melvin and Alice were very active in Webb City's social scene. They also were quick to volunteer their time to help the community.

That beautiful house at First and Oronogo stands as a monument to the couple who built it. It has been cared for and holds a piece of history in its heart.

Lively home, 705 West First Street

Long, Henry

"Henry Long had a long streetcar career."

In 1888, just twelve years after Webb City was established, a young man named Henry Long left his home in Hamilton, Ohio, and came to this prosperous mining community in Southwest

Missouri. Twenty-year-old Henry had many dreams and plans for his future. He settled in Joplin on November 10, 1888, and immediately went to work for the Joplin streetcar line, working on the horse-drawn streetcars.

On September 1, 1891, Henry went to work for the Southwest Missouri Electric Railway Company. In 1896, Henry was a motorman for the first streetcar out of Carthage on the new and just-completed White Line between Carthage and Carterville. In those days, an extra motorman was needed to watch the trolley. On this memorable trip, his brother, Louis Long, accompanied Henry. It was not uncommon for families to work together on the streetcars, brothers, fathers, and uncles.

Railway work was not easy work. Employees worked hard and long hours. There were employees on call to take care of problems like breakdowns, derailments, and accidents. Many men worked seven long days a week without vacations.

These two brothers, Henry and Louis, not only worked together, they only lived two blocks away from each other. Henry lived at 928 West First Street, and Louis lived at 917 West Third Street.

When Henry passed away, on March 25, 1920, at the age of fifty-two, he had the distinction of being the oldest motorman in point of service on the line after twenty-eight years (that was twenty-eight years with the Southwest Missouri Railway Company, but he had been in the railway business for thirty-two years.) Upon his death, his brother, Louis, acquired that honor for twenty-six years.

Besides being well known from working on the streetcar line, Henry was also a member of the Modern Woodsmen of America and the Royal Neighbors Fraternal Lodge.

Henry G. Long and his wife, Emma, had one son, Roy L. Long, and one daughter, Viola Long. Here is a well-known young man who came to this area from Ohio and became a permanent resident of Webb City. Thanks to Fred Rogers for sharing this information about one of Webb City's special citizens of the past.

A note from George Rainey:

> I read with interest the story on Henry Long. I didn't know of him. My stepfather Elmer Long was Louis' son. He lived at 917 West Third with my mom until he died. The corner of 3rd and Madison was known as "Long's Corner". 917 was the only house on the block at that time. My mom was secretary of the SW Mo. Railway Association for many years. She had the yearly meeting at her home. When she died I gave all the pictures and minutes to the streetcar at King Jack Park. Roy Long and Elmer were good friends and cousins. Elmer had retired from the U.S. Navy. Roy was the projectionist at the Fox Theatre.

Lowe, Joseph R.

Joseph R. Lowe was born in Barren County, Kentucky, on February 9, 1851. Joseph was the youngest of seven children, born to Caleb and Polly (Crabtree) Lowe. Caleb and Polly raised their family on a farm in Kentucky.

At the age of twenty-five, J. R. Lowe decided to give up farming and try his hand at iron. He arrived in Webb City on October 10, 1876, just prior to the establishment of the city. The young lad had a total of $25 in his pocket, which he had saved to make this great venture in his life.

For several years, he labored in the mines. Finally deciding that even though he was successful, this wasn't what he wanted to do the rest of his life. Then on May 2, 1881, Lowe entered the retail business. He became partners in the Hancock & Howe Furniture Store. The name of the business changed to Hancock & Lowe. After eight years, he sold his interest to J. W. Aylor.

His next venture was in the partnership with a Mr. Verbrick, and they opened a furniture store under the name of Lowe & Verbrick. In 1889, the company was incorporated, with Mr. Lowe as secretary and Mr. E. T. Webb (son of founder John C. Webb) as president. The name of the store changed to Lowe Furniture Company. As time went on, Mr. Lowe bought up all the stock from others in the company and became the sole owner. The business flourished and became one of the largest furniture stores in the area.

As what seemed to be the practice in those days, Joseph started an undertaking business in with his furniture business. Later he sold the furniture store, and it became known as the Webb City Furniture, located at Daugherty and Tom. He later sold the undertaking business to J. T. Steele, which became the J. T. Steele Undertaking Company at 111 East Daugherty.

J. R. Lowe lived at 309 West Joplin (Broadway) up until his death in March of 1928. Mr. Lowe married his lovely bride on March 16, 1870, while in Barren County. Ms. Almyra Huckebey was a native of Kentucky and the daughter of William Huckebey.

J. R. and Almyra were not blessed with children, but they were active in the community, with such activities as membership in the fraternal order of Woodmen of America of the World. He was a member of the Methodist Church and a Democrat, although not an active politician.

After his retirement from the furniture business and funeral business, J. R. just couldn't handle being idle, so he opened a small store close to his home on Broadway, at the alley. He operated this small store until his health gave out.

Upon his death, in 1928, the seventy-seven-year-old J. R. made a request that two members of each of the Protestant Churches in the city be honorary pallbearers. I guess he wanted to cover all his bases. Better safe than sorry! Those honorary pallbearers were A. F. Davis and J. H. Billings, Emmanuel Baptist Church; A. R. Haughawont and W. B. Finney, Nazarene Church; D. C. Morris and Walter Ragland, Christian Church; A. G. Young and E. E. Wood, Presbyterian Church; J. H. Inman and C. T. Sanders, First Baptist Church; and O. J. Gosch and R. B. Dodge, First Methodist Church. The active pallbearers were J. J. Stansberry, John Richman, E. T. Webb, W. E. Patten, M. Beckman, and W.C. Knight.

Malang, John M.—"Father of the Good Roads Movement"

When you hear stories about the good ole days, one thing that wasn't considered great was the road system. Those old cars with the narrow wheels would make some pretty deep ruts, and on muddy days, many a vehicle got stuck in the mud up to the rim of the tires. Something had to be done, and they chose the right man to do it—John M. Malang Sr.

John was born September 29, 1866, in Nashville, Tennessee. Coming to this area in 1878 with his parents, they settled in Tanyard Hollow. John didn't get a lot of education. He started working the mines as a young lad and later became a mine operator.

John left the mining business to become partners in the Joplin Transfer Company.

At the age of twenty, in 1886, John married Anna, and they had a farm out on West Seventh Street. During several election campaigns, John, being a staunch Republican, would get into some strong debates with some of the attorneys, which was good practice for him, as he ran for the state senate in 1908 and won.

After leaving the senate, John became the superintendent of the Joplin Special Road District in 1914. His first project was the eighteen-foot-wide concrete highway from Webb City to the Kansas State Line. This was the first concrete road in the entire state.

In 1919, the McCullough-Morgan Law went into effect (of which John was the author), and it provided for the appointment of a state superintendent of highways. You know the old saying "Don't make a suggestion unless you are willing to do it!" Well, John was appointed and was also ex-officio secretary of the highway board.

He quickly went to work on developing the first Missouri road plan, which he entitled "Lift Missouri Out of the Mud." In 1921, his new campaign was called "Farm to Market," and he worked on linking rural counties with the arterial highway system.

John Malang not only designed the main network of roads in the state, he also supervised the construction. He constructed a scenic route from Joplin to Neosho, a shortcut from Joplin to Seneca and a cutoff between Highways 16 and 38 for Pierce City, Sarcoxie, and Wentworth.

He was working on another bond issue for the highway improvement when he passed away of heart complications in a hotel in Kansas City. His funeral was attended by more than one thousand people. They ranged from miners, highway workers, to politicians, lawyers, friends, and relatives. The ceremony was held in the Elks Club at Fourth and Pearl Streets.

The funeral procession went down the first highway made of concrete for which John was responsible for obtaining. He is buried in Mount Hope Cemetery where his tombstone looks out over that very same highway (although throughout the years, it has been widened).

A special commemorative plaque was installed at the capitol building in Jefferson City, in remembrance of John M. Malang, "Father of the Good Road Movement." The plaque was dedicated on January 11, 1930, just a few hours before John's loving wife passed away to join him.

Next week, we will learn more about John's personal life and his family.

The family of John M. Malang—Anna and John Malang were married in 1886 at the St. Peter's Catholic Church in Joplin. Anna had lived in this area since 1879. She moved here from Nashville, Tennessee, with her parents when she was thirteen years old. She was born in 1867.

John was also born in Nashville, but he was born in 1866 and came to this area in 1878 when he was twelve. Being born a few months apart from each other and in the same territory made it seem like fate that they should be married.

John and Anna had three sons: John M. Malang Jr., Benjamin Malang, and Edward Malang. John Jr. married Gwendolyn Bosserman in 1928. She was the daughter of Mr. and Mrs. A. G. Bosserman. John had attended Kemper Military Academy before being employed by the highway department in Cassville, following in his father's footsteps.

Benjamin Franklin Malang was born in Joplin in 1889. He married Bertha Toutz, and they lived in Webb City most of their lives. Benjamin helped his father with work on the Missouri highways. Later he became an advertising salesman. Ben and Bertha had two sons, Warren Malang and Ben Malang Jr.

Edward W. Malang married Ella Woods in 1908, and they had two children, Jack Malang and Opal Malang Thompson.

Anna was by John's side throughout his many accomplishments in life, as he served on the United States Senate and as he developed the Missouri road systems. She was always there to take care of him after his long journeys to campaign for the different bond issues.

John passed away on September 13, 1928. It was a sad day for the state of Missouri because they lost a dedicated worker. But it was an even sadder day for Anna because she lost her lifetime companion. It seemed that Anna lost her will to live after John was gone. Her health continued to deteriorate, and just as they had been born a few months apart, they departed this world a short time apart. Anna died January 11, 1930.

On the day of her death, there was a dedication ceremony in Jefferson City to honor John M. Malang. The sons sat at the hospital with their mother and listened to the radio. Anna died a few hours later.

John had a brother named Frank A. Malang. Frank was as dedicated to his work as John. Frank was a contractor and builder. He was so dedicated to his work that he just didn't have time to think about getting married. Before being a contractor, Frank (or Dutch, as his friends called him) was in the mining business. Frank built a lot of houses along South Main past Thirty-Second Street.

In 1930, at the age of sixty-one, Nina Barlow stepped back into Dutch's life. Nina and Dutch had been high school sweethearts. Nina Burress wouldn't wait around for Dutch to make up his mind with what he wanted to do with his life, so she married another fellow and went on with her life. When she became a widow, Nina decided to find her long-lost love, and believe it or not, she swept him off his feet again. But this time, he was smart enough to know that he had better marry her while she was close at hand. They were married on December 27, 1930.

Frank moved Nina into one of his new stone bungalows being constructed at 2930 Main Street. But their happiness was short-lived. On May 6, 1934, Frank had been over to check on his Tourist Hotel at 3125 1/2 Main, and he was walking back to the house when a hit-and-run driver killed him. But at least he had found some happiness the last few years of his life.

Additional information about the Malangs—Frank Malang gave the property (three lots) to St. John's when it was located at Conner and Ivy. The only provision was that the hospital pay $40 per month, for life, to his niece, Maggie Mullins.

At the time of John Malang's death, there was approximately 651 miles of hard-surfaced pavement in Jasper County, which were constructed largely due to Malang's efforts.

Manker, Charles Morrow and Alice Lillian

Marriage benefited all of Webb City.

Charles Morrow Manker and Alice Lillian McCorkle were married June 27, 1888. Both of these civic-minded people were an asset to the community. To have them married was beneficial to all concerned.

Alice was an active member of the Presbyterian Church and a charter member of the Civic Club. She was a leader in the movement, which resulted in the establishment of the Webb City Public Library and served as a member of its board for years. Alice was also active in the Women's Study Club and Social Club.

Charles (C. M.) was the first Republican mayor in Webb City. He was active in business, religion, and politics. He was employed at the Center Creek Mining Company in the office but eventually gave that up to devote time to the insurance business. Charles's father, S. L. Manker, had a hardware store at 111 South Allen (Main) Street that Charles helped him with. Charles, along with Will S. Stewart, helped organize the home telephone system.

Also Charles was one of the original founders of the Spurgin Grocer Company. After helping to organize the Merchants & Miners Bank, Charles became the first cashier, and later its president.

Besides being busy with business, Charles was active in the community. He was treasurer of the local school district, head of the YMCA, and an elder in the Presbyterian Church and Sunday school superintendent.

As mayor of Webb City, Charles was a credit to the city as well as to himself.

Charles had several sisters, including Mrs. A. A. Hulett, Mrs. W. S. Chinn, Mrs. T. I. Bennett, and Mrs. Tom C. Hayden (some very influential names in our community). Alice and Charles had two daughters: Florence Manker married James Gilbert Cox, and Marguerite Manker married Beverly Bunce.

It's great when a couple can both be actively involved in the community together. Webb City has been very fortunate to always have someone to show interest and to help our city grow and prosper. We owe our forefathers (and foremothers) a lot!

S. L.'s son, C. M. Manker (Charles), became quite an asset to Webb City as he was talented in so many different areas. He often helped his father in the hardware store. He was associated with the Center Creek Mining Company (the first mining company of Webb City). He eventually left the mining business to devote his time to the insurance business and the Building and Loan Association. He went into business with his brother-in-law, W. S. Chinn, under the firm name of Manker & Chinn Insurance. Charles wore many different hats as he was also a notary public, one of the original founders and secretary of the Spurgin Grocery Co., president of the Newland Hotel Company, helped organize and owned one-half interest in the Webb City Electric Telephone Company (later known as the home telephone system). This telephone company operated lines in Webb City, Carterville, Prosperity, Duenweg, Galesburg, and Oronogo. He helped organize the Merchant & Miner Bank and served as one of the first cashiers, eventually becoming the bank president. He was treasurer of the school district, head of the YMCA, and an active member of the Presbyterian Church.

In 1892, Charles was elected mayor of Webb City, having the distinction of being the first Republican mayor of the city. It was stated in the *Webb City Gazette* that Charles Manker filled the position of mayor with credit to himself and the city. He was very well known and well liked. All of his business partners and associates held him in high respect.

Charles married Alice McCorkle, daughter of Andrew McCorkle, one of Webb City's first mine operators. Charles picked the perfect mate as Alice was just as involved in the city as he was. She was a leader in the efforts to establish the Webb City Public Library and served as a library board member for years. In fact, the library was built on her parents' property which was right behind the house Alice grew up in. Alice was active in the Women's Study Club and Social Club, along with being a charter member of the Civic Club. Besides her church duties in the Presbyterian Church and raising two daughters, Florence and Marguerite, Alice was one busy lady. And she also attended many civic celebrations and activities on the arm of her ever-so busy husband, Charles.

What a wonderful and active family the Mankers were. I'm amazed the name of the city wasn't changed to Mankerville, as the family helped organize and operate so many important affairs in our city.

Webb City is honored to have had such a wonderful family as pioneers of our community. They helped to build a great city, and we are indebted.

1894 photo of Spurgin Grocery Wholesale, later Webb City Wholesale Grocery, located at Church and Tom until the building burned, and the business was relocated at the Power House at Broadway and Madison.

Manker, S. L.

Born on May 13, 1829, in Cincinnati, Ohio, S. L. Manker began his life in a pleasant community and enjoyed a wonderful boyhood. As he grew, he kept hearing of the newly developing country to the west, and his curiosity got the better of him. He and his wife, Sarah, ventured to Pontiac, Illinois, for a couple of years and then decided to take the plunge. He crossed the Father of Waters and Big Muddy and located in Frankford, Missouri, a year later, moving to Holden, Missouri, and finally in 1877, S. L. Manker and his family settled in Webb City, a town that had been incorporated in 1876.

S. L. and Sarah had a good-size family which included four daughters and one son: Mrs. A. A. Hulett, Mrs. Tom (Gladys) Hayden, Mrs. W. S. (Minnie) Chinn, Mrs. T. I. Bennett, and C. M. Manker (who married Alice McCorkle). Each child married into well-known families of the area.

The Manker family had a beautiful home on the northeast corner of First and Liberty Streets, and they were active members of the Presbyterian Church.

S. L. opened the first hardware store in Webb City, which was located just two blocks from his home. The store at 111 South Allen (Main) Street was deemed as the largest hardware house in Southwest Missouri. His son-in-law Colonel A. A. Hulett joined him in the hardware business, and his son, C. M., helped with the business as much as he could. Manker, Hulett & Company was a hardware store that covered any hardware products you may need, along with mining supplies and groceries. The business was established in 1877 and became quite successful.

Martin, Walter and Alma

Have you ever noticed those pinched high-top shoes in most old photos? Can you think of anything more uncomfortable looking other than the corset of days gone by? When I think of old uncomfortable shoes, I remember a *Little Rascals* episode where the kids earn some money to buy their mom a new dress and new shoes. With the amount of money they earned, they couldn't afford much. That Sunday morning, as the mother walked to church wearing her new clothes with pride, she couldn't stand up on the shoes, and they were leaning to the side with each step! Now that is a mother who puts her children's feelings ahead of her own feelings.

Webb City has had a few shoe stores in the past, and one in particular belonged to Walter Lee and Alma Martin. They had a pretty good business going in Webb City. This couple had purchased the B. B. Allen Shoe Store from Mr. B. B. Allen himself. The store was located at 112 North Allen Street (Main).

Each month, Walter would send his payment to B. B. Allen in San Diego, California. Mr. Allen would respond with comments. One letter from Mr. Allen had the following statement:

> I am much pleased to hear of your good looking store. I hope you have not made it so attractive that your old patrons will avoid you thinking it too *stylish*. There be a few in this world that are not at home unless surrounded with plenty of dirt and antiquated methods. They argue that someone must "pay the freight!"

Well, Walter must have a shrewd business person as his shoe store continued to thrive. Business was so good that the couple decided to build a new house. They were living at 421 North Pennsylvania, and Walter began planning and designing the new house. They purchased land at Ten South Roane, and in 1916, they built *and paid* for the new residence.

All work makes for a dull boy, so Walter kept busy with the Masonic and Scottish Rites, the Shriners, and the local Blue Lodge. Alma was busy with the Belle Letters Club, the Century Club, and the Women's Club. They both enjoyed membership at the Oak Hill Golf Club and the Presbyterian Church.

Later on in years, Walter was offered an opportunity to become a traveling shoe salesman with the New York Shoe Company. He decided it would provide him and Alma a chance to see the world. They sold the store and hit the road. They traveled a lot and took many pictures. They really enjoyed going out to California. They had a special friend they liked to visit out there. His name was Will Rogers, and he never met a man he didn't like!

Around 1924, Walter and Alma decided they were ready to settle down again. They bought a house in Joplin, at 602 North Byers, and Walter went into business with his brother. Edward Martin, John F. Martin, E. A. Martin, and V. C. Martin, along with Walter, founded the Martin Transfer Company. Each brother had a business of his own and then combined interest in the Transfer Company. Later they bought the Joplin Transfer and Storage Company. Walter was secretary for the Transfer Company and also served as district agent for the National Life Insurance Company. His office was in the Frisco Building.

When Walter passed away in 1938, women were just beginning to prove to the male population that they weren't as helpless and defenseless as the men always told them they were. Alma became the vice president of Joplin Transfer and Storage, and she did a mighty fine job. And when it came to time to sell, she handled that pretty well too.

After working so hard, Alma decided to enjoy her remaining years. She spent each day either traveling, playing golf, playing cards, or just visiting with friends.

Those old shoes may have been uncomfortable for the women, but they sure made Walter's life a little better!

Matthews, C. E.—"Helped Build Webb City"

C. E. Matthews was born in Huron County, Ohio, February 4, 1854. His parents were Francis and Mary Matthews, who were from England. C. E. Matthews was trained and educated to be an engineer. He followed that line of work for a while, and then he started working for S. A. Brown & Co., lumber merchants of Chicago in 1882.

Matthews was sent to Webb City to manage the company's lumberyard in this area. Matthews prove to be quite efficient in that capacity. He married Nellie O. Forbes of Carthage, Missouri. They had one son, D. Frank.

Matthews must have enjoyed the lumber business. He eventually had his own lumberyard after partnering up with Joe Stewart in 1884 and eventually bought out Stewart. Matthews had seventeen lumber plants. The office was located at the corner of East Main (Broadway) and Walker Streets. The lumberyard covered an entire city block. Matthews owned and managed this business. He was also the president of the National Bank of Webb City. He was president of the Webb City & Carterville Machine Works. History books state that Matthews was a solid substantial citizen of Webb City. He took great pride in claiming to help build the city. Any movement to help the city or district found Matthews at the wheel. His beautiful home, still standing at Second and Liberty Streets, was a symbol of his success. That same home was later the residence of Mayor Don Adamson, president of Merchant & Miners Bank of Webb City.

Additional information: Matthews Lumber Co. was previously known as the Burgner, Bowman Matthews Lumber Co. At one time, the lumber company owned sixty-five lumberyards in Missouri, Oklahoma, Kansas, and Arkansas.

Matthews was active in mining enterprises. He was associated with W. W. Wampler in the development of the Osceola Mine, north of town, in 1905. He was associated with the Little Mary Mine, Neck City, along with George Washington Ball, Tom F. Coyne.

C. E. Matthews passed away on February 1, 1929, in his home at 221 West Second Street from kidney disease. The disease drained him for the last three years of his life. He was three days shy of being seventy-five years of age. His funeral was held in his family home on his birthday. He was buried at Park Cemetery in Carthage, Missouri.

Matthews, Norval

Tracing the Matthews family: part 1—William Matthews, born in Virginia, served four years in the Revolutionary War under the command of General Greene. He fought in the Battle of Bunker Hill—a great beginning to a family genealogy.

William had a son, Benjamin, who was born in Virginia in 1800. Now Benjamin had the pioneering fever, so he left Virginia and traveled to Tennessee. There he met and married Louise Anderson in 1835.

Still having the pioneering fever, Benjamin and Louise and their three small children left Tennessee and headed west to the area known as Lawrence County in Missouri. They settled in an area that would later be known as Mount Vernon. The year was 1846, and times were tough, but the family built a log cabin and welcomed another addition to the family, Isaac. Not long after Isaac was born, the family went to Tennessee but only stayed one winter before heading back to Lawrence County and their homestead.

There were five more children born to this union. Each of the last six children was born on the Matthews homestead. The one-room log cabin had a stick and clay chimney. The family used oxen and horses to work their land and an old bull-tongue plow helped with the planting. They cut their wheat with a cradle.

The area was abundant with wild game for food. There was turkey, deer, prairie chickens, quail, and plenty of fish. Ben hunted game with a powder-and-ball rifle with bullets he made himself.

Eventually Ben sold some of his land, which was some of the first original lots where the town now stands. He even helped to clear the trees and stumps where the town square is today. A small town was born, close enough to the Matthews homestead for convenience but not too close to take away from the privacy.

Meanwhile, Isaac's sister Mary had married a young man named Marion Ham. Marion had a sister who caught Isaac's attention. Isaac and Axie were married in Marion and Mary's log cabin, and the two couples lived together for several years. Finally Isaac bought the cabin from Marion.

That log cabin became the homestead for Isaac and Axie and their ten children. The names of the children were Charles, Minnie, Effie, Dora, Onie, Lulu, Ben, Ethel, Norval, and Cecil.

Norval was born on July 15, 1885—one hundred years ago—in the Matthews log cabin, which was located where I-44 passes by Mount Vernon.

After five years of living out of a suitcase, Norval Matthews landed in Webb City: part 2—Norval Matthews, born in Mount Vernon, attended a one-room schoolhouse in Lawrence County. His high school days were in Mount Vernon where the entire school population consisted of only 125 students. Most children, in those days, dropped out of school in the eighth grade to help out with the family income. Norval was one of the fortunate to receive an education.

At the age of twenty-six, Norval was employed in the vocational division of Curtis Publishing Company (publishers of the *Saturday Evening Post* and the *Ladies Home Journal*). For five years, Norval and his wife, Marie Etter (whom he married September 18, 1921), lived out of motels as they traveled the Midwest.

During this time with the Curtis Publishing Company, Norval claimed that two people influenced him the most; one being Cyrus H. K. Curtis, publisher of the *Saturday Evening Post*. "Mr. Curtis," according to Norval, "was one of the most conscientious I have ever met."

The other influential man was Norman Rockwell. Rockwell was at the height of his career when Norval Matthews met him. Norval's comments about Rockwell were, "I was young and very impressionable. He told me about his life and how he started painting. I was impressed with his ideas and how he reached the top of his profession."

Living without a home was too much for the newlyweds, and after five years, they decided to come back home to Webb City. Here Norval started his own business, Matthews Coffee Company. In August of 1931, at 1001 West Daugherty Street, Matthews Coffee Company debuted selling coffee to institutional facilities.

During the war, when it seemed that it would be impossible to get coffee, other products were obtainable to replace this major product. Firms began to rely on the coffee company for this additional merchandise, which carried on after the war. Also during the war, Crowder Camp was a welcomed account for the coffee company.

Norval M. Matthews retired from the coffee company in 1968, leaving the business in the good hands of his son John Matthews. Norval's intentions were to go fishing every day, but plans do change.

Norval Matthews, the writer, the dreamer: part 3—After retiring in 1968, Norval planned to go fishing every day, but he didn't know what destiny had planned for him.

In 1964, when the Jasper County Junior College District was formed, Norval was one of the six trustees elected and, later re-elected, in 1968. Governor Hearnes appointed Norval as a member of the board of regents to control the senior college program.

In 1972, Norval Matthews was re-elected as a member of the board of regents of Missouri Southern State College for a five-year term. Norval said that the establishment of the college and his election to the board of trustees was probably the greatest thing that ever happened to him.

In 1968, Norval was elected the district governor by district 611 of Rotary International. Norval had been active in Rotary Club for fifteen years, even serving as president. During his year as governor of the Rotary District 611, Norval and his wife, Marie, traveled twenty-seven thousand miles by automobile and eighteen thousand miles by plane.

Starting with his retirement, Norval began working on his lifelong dream of writing a book. It was entitled *The Promised Land.* The School of the Ozarks, Point Lookout, Missouri, published the book for Norval.

Norval then began his second hardbound book, *Discovering the Ozarks*, which required many hours of research also. While doing his research, Norval took on another huge project—attending college. In 1972, Norval held the title of the oldest freshman at the age of seventy-six. He took some writing courses and became a member of the writing staff for *The Chart*, MSSC's very own newspaper.

Before the printing of *The Promised Land*, Norval did a book for his granddaughter entitled *Four Grandfathers.* It told about the Matthews side of the family that spanned the entire history of the nation, dating back to when the first Matthews came to Virginia in 1776.

Norval and Marie put a lot of work into the research and writing of *Discovering the Ozarks*, as requested by the American Heritage Publications. In 1973, Norval sent the manuscript to the publishers, and they wanted some changes. They wanted him to revamp it to more of a vacation land guide, leaving out all the history and special memories of the people Norval had interviewed. Norval felt this would rob the book of its true value, so he withdrew it from the publishers. The University of Oklahoma Press expressed an interest in scheduling it for some future publication date. That's where it was at the time of Norval's death in 1977.

October 15, 1980, was the dedication date of Matthews Hall at Missouri Southern State College. It seems appropriate that Norval Matthews would be honored with a building in his name, considering his proudest achievement in his life was associated with the organization and development of the college.

Norval Matthews made quite a contribution to our area, and it was stated quite well in reminiscence printed by *The Chart*.

His is not a solitary dream. Others shared the dream, but few worked as hard as he to make it come true did. And even fewer worked as hard as he to make it grow did. The dream was a four-year college "for the boys and girls of southwest Missouri"—a dream that became Missouri Southern State College. The dreamer was Norval Matthews.

A special thanks to those who remembered Norval Matthews so well and especially to John Matthews, who has deep roots in Webb City of which to be proud.

Note: *An Amazing City* by Norval Matthews has been reprinted by the Mining Days Committee.

Additional information on Norval Matthews: When he had been informed he had a terminal illness, Mr. Matthews had said, "Well, it's not like having the measles, is it?" Then he added, "I've got work to do." That was Norval Matthews who, after retirement from business in 1966, lived a lifetime.

McCorkle, Andrew

The city of Webb City was incorporated in December of 1876. John C. Webb had uncovered a large chunk of lead a couple of years before the city was established. The miners had already moved into the area in large numbers, seeking the riches that were being promised.

John C. Webb had moved to Jasper County in 1856 and built his log cabin at what is now the northwest corner of Broadway and Webb Streets in 1857.

There were only a few neighbors located close to the Webb's 320 acres. To the west was William A. Daugherty, who had purchased 260 acres in 1870. His home is still standing today and is owned by heirs to the Corl family. Eventually Daugherty would own over 4,000 acres of mining and agricultural land in Jasper County.

To the east of the Webb land was the Carter farm, located where the city of Carterville was established. W. A. Daugherty purchased the Carter farm, and he established the city, naming it after the original owner of the land.

To the south of the Webb land was eighty acres owned by Andrew McCorkle, a former resident of Wisconsin, who had moved to Jasper County in hopes to help his wife overcome the ill effects of tuberculosis. His brother-in-law had served in Jasper County during the Civil War, and he had written to Andrew of the wonderfully sunny and warm climate. In 1862, his brother-in-law was killed in the Battle of Prairie Grove in Arkansas.

Andrew McCorkle built his first house on the southwest corner of what is now Webb and First Streets. The year was 1870, and Andrew set aside six lots to build his one-and-one-half-story home. He had a separate log kitchen, a log smokehouse, and the beginnings of an orchard.

In 1875, the city was platted. McCorkle's first addition to Webb City was surveyed August 30, 1876. A mining boom was underway, and the Frisco Railroad began laying tracks into the city. Andrew continued to assist in the development of the mines.

Andrew had no idea that the country in which he had moved his precious wife to help her tuberculosis had a killer in its midst, and that killer was—tuberculosis. Not only did his wife eventually die of the dreaded disease, but he also lost his son to tuberculosis. Charles died on October 26, 1884, from tuberculosis he contacted in the mines.

After his wife's death in 1879, Andrew made a trip back to Wisconsin in search of a mother for his thirteen-year-old daughter. His first wife had died in Wisconsin at the age of twenty-two, and now his second wife had died at the age of thirty-seven.

Andrew married Deborah Shea on September 15, 1880. She was a schoolteacher and the sister of Margaret Shea, who was married to Andrew's brother, Robert.

Deborah nursed Andrew's son, Charles, in the later part of his tuberculosis up until his death in October, and then she delivered a son, Willie, in December of the same year, and the poor baby died of tuberculosis within two months of his birth. They had another son in 1887, Arthur Vincent McCorkle.

In 1899, as Andrew continued to increase his wealth in the mining business, he decided to build a new home. A more majestic home to represent his wealth, but he loved the location of his present home and couldn't find a new location that satisfied him. So with the help of sturdy horses and large logs, the original home was moved to the south, and McCorkle began to build his new home.

It was a two-story home, with a full basement and full attic. The beautiful woodwork made the home sparkle. The front wraparound porch with decorative railing seemed to beckon you to come in. By building up the dirt around the base of the home, it appeared to sit on a hill, which gave it a hint of grandeur.

Andrew McCorkle died in 1904, at the age of seventy-six, leaving the house to his son Arthur, daughter, Alice Manker, and his wife, Deborah. He was buried in the Oronogo Cemetery, but in 1906, when the new Mount Hope Cemetery was established, they removed his casket from Oronogo to Mount Hope in an honorary location (all noted past residents were moved to a dedicated area).

Arthur married Edna Prickett in 1927 and had two daughters, Mary L. McCorkle Marx and Margaret E. McCorkle Lewis. When Arthur died in 1952, he left the house to his wife, Edna. She sold the house to James and Orpha Watson in 1953.

The Watsons owned the home for one year, in which time they took off the round copper dome roof of the front porch, removed much of the brass door fittings and the lightning rods from the roofline. They then sold the house to Robert and Marie Kissel in 1954. The Kissels lived there until 1963 when Marie inherited a beautiful home in Joplin, and they sold the house to Richard and Helen Woodworth.

After the children left home, the Woodworths sold the family home to their daughter and son-in-law, Jeanne and Stan Newby. They raised their three children in the old family home, and when there was only the two of them left at home, they decided to sell. They found a wonderful young couple who loved antiques and needed a place to display them. Brian and Terry Berkstressor have made great improvement to the McCorkle home which celebrated its one hundredth birthday in the year of 1999.

The home has a new family, John and Hillary McCaw from California, who fell in love with the beautiful McCorkle home and have taken the time and energy to improve the home even more. The love of the home shows through the years.

McCorkle home at 106 South Webb, 1906>>

This is the McCorkle home as it looked in 1963.

McNair, James

Born in North Carolina, December 12, 1833, James McNair was the son of Daniel and Ann McNair, both natives of Glasgow, Scotland. James's grandfather Hugh McNair arrived in this country just prior to the Revolutionary War, at which time he enlisted. He served throughout the entire seven years of the war with honor and distinction. At the end of the war, he returned to his native land of Scotland and brought his family back to the land he had fought so valiantly to free.

In 1835, Daniel took his family to Charleston, Tallahatchie County, Mississippi, and then moved to Tennessee in 1852.

It was during this time that young James, then nineteen years of age, caught the gold fever and headed west. He got as far as Bates County, Missouri, when he fell ill, and it took him two years to recover. Still determined to try the goldfields, James joined in with a cow herder named Henry Riggs and worked his way to Sacramento.

James returned to Tennessee in 1859, and realizing it was time to get serious and think of his future at the age of twenty-six, he began the study of medicine. When the first shot was fired in the Civil War, James cast his lot with the north and enlisted with the First West Tennessee US Volunteers. Due to illness, James was discharged in the fall of 1864 and, in 1865, was elected a member of Tennessee Legislature. He was elected a delegate to the Southern Loyalists Convention, which met in Philadelphia, where he urged the extending of the right hand of fellowship to the defeated states. During the Civil War, James married Patience Flippin, a charming belle from Tennessee.

In 1869, the McNair family moved to Missouri, with James employed with the St. Louis–San Francisco Railroad. In 1874, the railroad company moved the McNair family to Oronogo, Missouri. The very next year, John C. Webb laid out the town of Webb City. McNair moved to the uncharted town and proceeded to build the first house for Webb on the corner of what would soon be Tom and Daugherty Streets.

When Webb City was incorporated in December of 1876, James McNair received the honor of being the first mayor of Webb City. He held that position for only one month and two days before being offered and accepting the position as the first postmaster on January 13, 1877. James Smith was appointed to fill the vacancy of mayor.

Patience and James McNair had five daughters: Annie, Minnie, Jessie, Callie, and Myrtie.

McNair, J. E.

James E. McNair, the first executive officer of Webb City, was a native of North Carolina and of Scotch descent. He was born December 13, 1833. His father was a Revolutionary patriot, having served in the Continental Army during the entire seven years of hostilities. Mr. McNair's boyhood was spent in the South, having lived in Mississippi and Tennessee before the War Between the States. In the spring of '52, he caught the gold fever and started to cross the plains en route for California. Arriving at Bates County, this state, he became ill and was obliged to leave the party of overland tourists and remained in that county until 1854, when he had regained his health. Still determined to go to the goldfields, he hired Henry Riggs as a cowboy and crossed the plains that summer, helping to drive a herd of cattle to Sacramento. He returned to Tennessee in 1859 and began the study of medicine. Mr. McNair had been brought up an Andrew Jackson Democrat, but when Fort Sumter was fired upon, he cast his lot with the north and enlisted in the First West Tennessee US Volunteers.

On account of sickness, he was discharged from the service in the fall of 1864 and, the next year, was elected a member of the legislature of Tennessee. In 1865, he was elected a delegate to the

Southern Loyalists Convention, which met in Philadelphia, and there urged the extending of the right hand of fellowship to the defeated states.

During the war, he was married to Ms. Patience Flippen, a charming Tennessee belle. In 1869, he came to Missouri and worked for the St. Louis–San Francisco Railway in the capacity of a bridge carpenter, coming to Oronogo in that railway's employ in 1874. In 1875, when John C. Webb laid out the town of Webb City, Mr. McNair came to the place which then was only represented by the surveyor's pegs in the ground and built for Mr. Webb the first house. On January 13, 1877, after having served the city as mayor for one month and two days, Mr. McNair was appointed postmaster of Webb City, which office had just been established, and resigned his position as a member of the board of trustees. F. Ball was appointed trustee to fill the vacancy and (Vice Chairman James Smith) filled out the remainder of the term as president of the board. During the administration of Messrs. McNair and Smith, order was established and the preliminaries of the founding of a city government gone through with.

Meinhart, Ernest M. and Julius Meinhart

Ernest M. Meinhart immigrated to the United States from Germany in 1865, settling in Chicago. He married Ms. Minnie Mueller, also from Germany, in November of 1868, and they had six children. At the time of the great Chicago fire, the Meinhart family moved to Kansas, and Ernest found employment as a stage driver. Later, with a desire to stay closer to home and family, Ernest took up a new profession—selling wallpaper and paint. He opened a store in Atchison, Kansas, which he operated until his death in 1908.

One of those six Meinhart children was named Julius E. Meinhart. Julius attended public schools and Monroe Institute before heading out into the world to find his fortune. At eighteen, he tried the trade of drapery work and hanging shades with the S. A. Orchard Carpet Company in Omaha, Nebraska. Deciding that drapery was not his line of work, he decided to be a traveling salesman for paint and wallpaper company in Chicago, known as Lartz Wallpaper Company and the Colt Manufacturing Company. After twelve years, he still hadn't found what he wanted be when he grew up, so he tried his hand at retail sales of wallpaper by opening a store in Leavenworth, Kansas. Leaving that line of work, he decided on working with cut flowers, and it seemed he had finally found that niche in life that he had been searching for.

Julius married Ms. Margaret Foster on June 30, 1890, and she was by his side as he made these numerous changes in his life. Margaret died in Leavenworth on November 18, 1900, leaving Julius with two small children, Ruth and Foster.

Julius made one more move with his children. They came to Webb City in February of 1910, and Julius bought the Brenneman Florist and Green House. Brenneman Florist had a reputation of being the largest greenhouse in the Jasper County area and a very productive business.

Changing the name from Brenneman's Florist to Webb City Greenhouse, Julius continued the business for twenty years. Julius was an active resident in the community, a member of the Knights of Pythias, Elks Lodge, Order of Maccabees, Security Benefit Association, and the Fraternal Aid Union. He was also a member of the Lutheran Church. Julius married a second time, a lady named Grace.

At the time of this death, on April 28, 1929, Julius was only fifty-eight years old, but he had accomplished more goals and fulfilled more dreams than most people who live to be older. At the time of his death, Julius resided at 416 South Pennsylvania Street (where the special Road District is located now and before the construction of MacArthur Drive).

Here was a man who wasn't afraid to search for his happiness and was smart enough to realize that Webb City was his pot of gold at the end of the rainbow.

Meinhart Nursery, located where MacArthur Drive and Pennsylvania is located today. Across the street from the house to the right is the location of today's Praying Hands. The house still stands today at Fifth Street and Pennsylvania Street.

Miller, Dr. Darrell and Peggy

Boy, did your article in the *Sentinel* bring back memories with the mention of Dr. Darrell Miller. My folks were friends with Darrell and Peggy. I'm not sure how that happened, but it might have been Darrell and Dad were Lions. The Millers were about the only family in town that had an inground swimming pool. In my eyes, that made them really rich. The other thing was Peggy Miller was quite a tole painter. Of course, she had items all over her house, and I believe she taught classes in her home. She could take an old camelback truck and make it into a true centerpiece of attention. I think my sister may still have one of Peggy's trucks.

The Millers would always spend the summer in Estes Park, Colorado. Peggy would paint the rest of the year to take items to Estes Park to sell. Several years, they ran an ice cream parlor just off the main street in Estes. And I believe several years, Darrell ran a canoe rental business on the Elk River here. They had two daughters and a son. The oldest girl, Becky, I think, was a teacher, but she moved to Australia, probably in the 1970s. Laura, the youngest, became a flight attendant for TWA back in the days when that was a glorious job. Ned was the only one to marry, and he became a teacher. Darrell and Peggy divorced, and both left this area. Mom and Dad kept some contact with them for several years, but last I heard was Peggy was in Arizona, and Darrell was in Southwest Missouri—Stella or Granby? I'm not sure, but I think Darrell and Dr. Jack Snider went together and built the Madison Plaza at Sixteenth and Madison, where they both had their offices. Janice peek

Hello, Yes I do have his number. I was thinking about this because there are so many that have passed away that use to be an everyday face in the business community. I am one of the Parish twins and my grandparents and parents owned the Webb City Cafe when it was on the corner of main in front of Buds Barbershop. Virgil Rogers just passed away a few months ago. He was the Banker at WC Bank. There use to be a Webb City Bakery and the man that was the baker us kids called him Frankinstein because he was so tall. I can not remember his name. Don Meridieth use to give us candy from the Ben Franklin. My sister Sharon, myself, Tom Maxwell, Jim Maxwell, Jeff Grosse and a few others worked for Katerine Patton two summers. We worked for the neighborhood youth program cleaning and clearing the King Jack Park where the Chamber of Commerce is now. After having a heart attack, and with Gods grace surviving it, I realize how precious the past is and every generation should be interested in knowing it. I remember my mother telling us If you are ever feeling lonely, or you are ever feeling small, Remember that you matter to the One who made us all! It is nice to honor those who are memorable while they are still living, and you do such a great job. Thank You, Love, Karen.

Miller, Max and Maxine

Max Miller and Maxine Etter both graduated from Webb City High School in 1923. They were married on March 24, 1927. This couple really enjoyed music in their lives. Max was a singer, Maxine sang and played the piano. Many of the Webb City youth became a big part of the Miller family. They may not have had children of their own, but their music family was large, and their hearts were full.

Maxine was very proud of her parents and family. She wore the Etter name with pride. She was a great mentor to this author. She gave sage advice and shared many historical details.

Milton, William B.

It's been stated that a lot of our pioneers came from the great state of Tennessee and settled in the Jasper County area. One such pioneer was William B. Milton, who was raised in Tennessee but was actually born in Virginia in 1838. His parents were going into unchartered territory when they moved west into Tennessee. That same pioneer spirit is what moved William and his Tennessee wife, Nancy Dennis, when they moved farther into the unknown west as they settled in the Preston Township of Missouri, just north of Alba.

One source says they arrived in the area in 1861. Another says they came just after the end of the Civil War. Either way, they were one of the first settlers of the Jasper County area.

Being a farmer, William found the area to his liking. His farm consisted of about four hundred acres. But produce wasn't the only thing William and Nancy grew as they had a family of eight children, five boys and three girls. Robert L., John V., Andrew Jack, William A., (another source calls him Link), and Edwin J. (Squeaky) were the boys. Samantha Ellen, Millie, and Julia were the girls.

Life on a farm in those days wasn't easy (not that life on a farm is necessarily easy today, but it was quite a trial in the old days). Most of the farming was done with a horse or mule pulling a plow. The Miltons had to raise what they needed to survive, such as chickens for eggs and food, cows for their milk. The garden contained the vegetables that would be canned and eaten all winter.

Not everyone had an icebox, so milk was kept cold by lowering it into a well, or if you were lucky enough to have a freshwater spring running through your land, it did an excellent job of keeping things cold.

Large families were an asset because everyone had chores to do on the farm: milking, gathering eggs, plowing, canning, butchering, weeding the garden, feeding the animals, chopping wood for the heat stove and the cookstove, cooking and cleaning. Washing the clothes was a time-consuming process, as the water was to be boiled out on an open fire, and clothes were draped on anything available. Some folks were lucky and had a clothesline strung from the house to a tree.

Many times, extra money was made by taking eggs, butter, and milk into town to sell. Those folks living in the city had to buy their necessities at the general store. They welcomed those fresh eggs, butter, and milk. After selling the eggs, milk, and produce, supplies needed for the farm were purchased or bartered. You didn't need a lot of money, but you did need to work hard. And with a large family, you could get a lot more accomplished.

William B. Milton passed on in 1918 at the age of eighty-eight. He left quite a heritage as those eight children grew and married and had children of their own. Most of them stayed in the area. Some inherited the pioneer spirit and traveled west to California, but some of those travelers returned home after they retired. After all, when you're ready to relax, there's no place like the Ozarks, especially Jasper County.

R. L. Milton, son of William B., made quite a name for himself in the mining business. In August of 1901, W. M. Wigginton and R. L. Milton conceived the plan of organizing a company to devote its energies exclusively to the building of mining plants. The Wigginton & Milton Company built many of the mines in this area.

Before the formation of the Wigginton & Milton Company, most mining plants were built on the same basic plan without any attention being paid to the property itself. That often created a poorly arranged plant, resulting in a financial loss because of the inconvenience and resulting increase in labor. Wigginton & Milton was determined to reduce mine plant building to a science, to individualize the needs of each mine, and to secure the best possible results from the investment of the mine owner. Their motto, "What's Worth Doing is Worth Doing Well," resulted in mining plants that were well-constructed symmetrical buildings.

R. L. Milton left his mark on the mining territory of Jasper County. He passed away in 1939 at the age of seventy-seven.

Moore, George W.

"W. C. forefather and wife were popular."

George W. Moore was born September 29, 1871, in Dallas County, Missouri. He was married June 19, 1891, to Ms. Ida Watson.

George was one of our most popular forefathers of Webb City. After serving on the city council in Aurora, George moved to Webb City and served on the council here also. He was elected mayor in 1904 and re-elected in 1906.

A Republican in a Democratic city, George was a faithful servant to the people, not to his political party. A lot was accomplished while George was in office. He was highly motivated and very energetic.

George and his wife, Ida, were well thought of. Both possessed good personalities and pleasant dispositions. There were no social functions that didn't have their names on the guest list.

George's occupation was ore purchaser for several different companies and president of the Webb City Smelting and Manufacturing Company.

George and Ida Moore, royalty of Webb City—As you drive down Madison Street, you see the gradual transformation from residential to commercial. At Ninth and Madison was a beautiful home that could easily be described as a mansion, carried the address of 903 South Madison. This beautiful structure has a historical background, as it was the residence of George W. Moore and his wife, Ida. Their first residence in Webb City was 732 West First Street, according to the 1906 Webb City Directory. They purchased the Madison Street mansion from C. C. Howard in November 1908, right after Howard's completion of the building.

George was born in Dallas County, Missouri, on September 29, 1871, to Alexander A. and Louisa (Richey) Moore. Both of George's parents came from the state of Tennessee. The family settled in Joplin in 1873, moving to Aurora in 1882. George attended public schools in Joplin and Aurora. Unfortunately, he was forced to go to work and earn a living at the age of fourteen.

A year later, George became an ore purchaser for W. J. Lanyon of Aurora. He also took on the Lanyon Zinc Company. In 1908, he became associated with the American Metal Company and the Bartlesville Zinc Company of Bartlesville, Oklahoma, which was owned by Lanyon Starr Smelting. Then in 1909, he organized and became president of the Webb City Smelting and Manufacturing Company. George was the ore buyer for all of these companies. That's a lot of companies to handle at one time, but George did an excellent job, and all companies were well pleased with his expertise

The Webb City Smelting and Manufacturing Company was an extensive manufacturer of pig lead. The main office was in Webb City, but there were branch offices in Joplin and Galena. Although George was interested in mining, he did not take an active part in the working of the mines that he connected with.

This energetic man carried this enthusiasm into the community also as he served on the Aurora City Council in 1896 when he was twenty-five years old. When he moved to Webb City, he served several terms on the city council until he was elected mayor in 1904 and re-elected in 1906.

Being only the third Republican elected as mayor of Webb City, it was surprising when the normally Democratic Webb City voted for the man instead of the political party. And that is the way George served the city. He was a servant of the people.

As mayor of Webb City, George made many major improvements. Twenty-one blocks in the business district and a number in the residential area were paved with vitrified brick, along with the first streetlights being installed.

George negotiated a deal with the Alba Streetcar Franchise, which obligated the company to move the streetcar tracks from Main (Broadway) to Daugherty and to build a viaduct between Webb City and Carterville at a cost of $100,000. The company also put down $7,000 of paving when they removed the tracks, did $2,000 worth of sidewalks between Carterville and Webb City, and double-tracked West Daugherty Street and paved five blocks of Daugherty. What a contract.

George and Ida were very popular in the community. They did lots of community work and were highly respected. Every social event had the Moore's on the guest list.

G. W. Moore time line:

1871—September 29, George Washington Moore was born in Dallas County, Missouri, to Alexander A. and Louisa (Richey) Moore.

1873—The Moore family settled in Joplin, Missouri.

1882—The Moores moved to Aurora, Lawrence, Missouri, after 1882 and remained there until 1897.

1885—George W. Moore quit school to help family with finances.

1891—June 19, George Moore united in marriage with Ida Watson.

1895—April 16, daughter, Nanna Mae Moore, was born.

1896—George began his career as an ore purchaser at Aurora for W. J. Lanyon Zinc Company.

1896—At age of twenty-five, George served a term in Aurora's City Council, being the only Republican elected to city council.

1897—Alexander Moore purchased a farm north of Carthage, 1907. Alexander died at his Carthage farm at the age of sixty-seven.

1897—George and Ida Moore moved to Webb City.

1900—George elected to Webb City, City Council, served on council till 1904.

1903—Member of the first class of twenty-five men who were initiated into the order at rites held in the old Blake Theater on Daugherty Street.

1904—George was elected as mayor.

1906—Re-elected mayor of Webb City, a Republican in a Democrat town.

1906—October 14, son, Clyde Earl Moore, was born.

1908—George became connected with the American Metal Company. Became in charge of ore buying for Lanyon Starr Smelting Company with plants in Bartlesvill and was president of the Webb City Smelting & Manufacturing Company's Lead Plant.

1908—November 21, purchased a new home at 903 South Madison from W. W. Howard. Moved in December 1, 1908.

1909—George Moore organized and was president of the Webb City Smelting Company.

1909—July 27, George's son, Clyde, age eleven, died in Colorado Springs while on vacation.

1926—July 28, George's daughter, Nanna Mae Moore Merrell, age thirty-one, died.

1946—August 27, Ida Moore passed away in Joplin.

1954—August 4, George W. Moore (age eighty-two) died in an automobile accident in Lamar, Colorado, while en route to Colorado Springs for vacation.

Moore, Harry C.

His legacy reigns that he was a backer of the Republicans, the Presbyterians, the Elks, and a master hunter.

Harry's father, N. T. Moore, was born near Winchester, Adams, Ohio, on October 5, 1835. As soon as he finished school, he began teaching which was his life's desire. He chose to give up his precious career to join with the Fifty-Ninth Ohio Infantry to serve in the Civil War, from 1861–1865. As soon as the war ended, he returned to his favorite career of teaching. He married Sarah Louise Manker, who was born in Thincastle, Brown, Ohio, on August 5, 1844.

N. T. traveled with his teaching career, and they were in Butler, Kentucky, when their son, Harry C. Moore, was born on October 9, 1878. N. T. and Sarah moved to other places, such as Kentucky, Indiana, Arkansas, and Mountain Grove, Missouri. They finally retired in 1911 in Webb City, Missouri.

Harry C. Moore, after graduation, became a clerk with the Kansas City, Fort Scott, and Memphis Railroad Company in Mountain Grove. He had a desire to make more money, so he changed careers by moving to Webb City and starting work with W. F. Spurgin as salesman and bookkeeper for nine years. When Spurgin united with the Interstate Grocery Company, Harry stayed with them until 1901. He then went to work for the Pacific Coast Borax Company of Chicago as a traveling salesman. While traveling, he begin to think about opening a business of his own. He sent his resignation to Chicago and headed back to Webb City where he bought out Walter Spurgin's grocery business.

While traveling with the Borax Company, Harry met a young lady and her family in Dallas, Texas. Harry married that young lady, Mae Chapell, on June 8, 1906. They had three children: William Chapell Moore (April 29, 1907); Harry Claude Moore Jr. (March 12, 1909); and Dorothy Louise Moore (May 21, 1910).

Murratta, James—Murratta Drug Store

Susan A. Murratta was born in Springfield, Kentucky, in 1831. At the age of fifty-four, her husband passed away, and being very adventurous, she made the move from Kentucky to Jasper County in 1886 with three of her four children. In 1893, they moved to Webb City.

Susan's son, James, who was twenty-eight years old at the time, was a druggist at Murratta Drug Store located at 110 North Main street. He had two sisters living in the area, Mrs. Belle Yankey and Sue Murratta. They bought a home at 404 North Ball Street. Life seemed to be going pretty well for the prosperous family until July of 1903, when some fireworks exploded at the drugstore and badly burned James's face. He never really recovered from that accident.

In 1908, at the age of seventy-seven, Susan passed away, and James continued on with the drugstore. He also belonged to the Masons Scottish Rites, Elks, AF and AM, and Knights Templar. But his health did not seem to improve. Then in 1911, the doctors decided they needed to amputate James's foot. It took two surgeries from which James did not recover. He died at the young age of forty-six.

INTERIOR JAMES MURATTA'S DRUG STORE.

Murratta Drug Store 110 North Main Street

Nesbitt, Fred H.—Captain

Veteran of three wars—Fred was born January 5, 1878, in Mantene, Illinois, son of A. R. Nesbitt. Nesbitt moved to Webb City with his parents in 1890 at the age of twelve. Fred worked with his father as a contractor. At the time of his death, March 12, 1844, he was a purchasing agent for the Eagle-Picher Company.

During his high school years, he interrupted his education to serve in federal service in the Spanish-American War on May 4, 1898. He served as a corporal in Company G, Fifth Missouri Regiment, with his service ending November 9, 1898, at which time he returned to Webb City to complete his high school education.

Before serving in World War I, Fred served with the Southwest Missouri National Guard and went to the Mexican borders as a company commander. In World War I, Fred served as captain and commander of Company A, 130th Machine Gun Battalion, 35th Division, made up mainly of Webb City, Missouri, and Kansas men they served in Europe. He saw action in Vosges, St. Mihiel, Meuse-Argone, and Verdue sectors. He was advanced to major after the war (but still carried the name of captain until his death). A long-time friend and fellow veteran of the Thirty-Fifth Division was United States Senator Bennett C. Clark. Fred was also active in the American Legion.

Fred Nesbitt was connected with the Tri-State Zinc and Lead Producers' Association in the Picher area. He was active in the organization's accident-prevention campaign in the mines. Fred was also instrumental in establishing the mineral museum at Schifferdecker Park in Joplin. He collected mineral specimens and assisted in obtaining necessary funds to meet incidental expenses in starting the museum.

Fred Nesbitt's family home was at 1401 West Broadway in Webb City. His wife was Eva, his daughter was Helen Nesbitt Hatten, whose son was Coyne Hatten.

Fred passed away on March 12, 1944, and is buried at Mount Hope Cemetery with a bugler and twenty-one-gun salute by men of Camp Crowder.

*It was said that when Fred's grandson, Coyne, was younger, he was entertaining some young girls at Fred's home during the holidays. When the captain patted one of the girls on the head, Coyne said, "Say, Grandpa, cut out patting those girls on the head, I'll take care of that."

**Coyne Hatten was murdered in Webb City beside Morgan Drug store at Daugherty and Webb Streets.

***Fred Nesbitt received a letter from citizens of Webb City, soon after the WWI, requesting him to run for county sheriff, stating that the times called for 100 percent Americanism. The letter was signed by the following Webb City citizens: J. A. Daugherty, Frank L. Gass, A. D. Hatten, S. W. Bates, R. E. Harrington, T. E. Coyne, C. R. Chinn Jr., W. C. Burch, W. F. Gill, G. R. Mosley, Stonewall Pritchett, R. L. Morton Jr., J. M. Hirons, Harry B. Hulett, George W. Hall, Roy R. Veatch, Fred Black, B. F. Hall, Frank L. Forlow, Morrison Pritchett, Walter Ragland, George W. Jones, Alvin D. Hatten, W. A. Corl, E. E. Spracklen, A. G. Young, J. D. Corl, Thomas E. Parker (a list of very impressive citizens).

Newby, Milton

Milton and Nancy Jane Newby decided to make the journey to Jasper County and settle near Carl Junction.

Just a few short years later, Katie Jane Fullmer, daughter of Daniel and Caroline, married John Cyrus Newby, son of Milton and Nancy, on October 5, 1890.

Katie and John lived on a farm and raised twelve children. The children remembered that there was never a dull moment in their large happy family. They didn't have a lot of luxuries, but they were never hungry or without shelter.

Those children were Ruth Jackle, Lucy Yearwood, Gladys Frazier, Marion Newby, Daniel Newby, Grace Klein, John Cyrus Newby Jr., Myrl Newby, Alvin Newby, Helen Kelley, Lois Lammlein, and George Newby.

Here's a memory shared by one of the grandchildren of Milton and Nancy Newby.

"At the end of the day, after chores are done, we take the spring wagon and ride the one mile to Grandma's. The mile seems extra long because the horse has worked all day, and Daddy won't push it faster than a walk.

"As we near the big gate at the road, the children hop off the wagon to open the wooden gate. Mama and Papa drive on up the lane, and we children race to see who can get to the house first.

"Grandma and Grandpa have just finished milking, and you can hear the deLaval cream separator working in the smokehouse. The cellar is just off the smokehouse, and the dirt walls are lined with rows of canning jars filled with blackberries, jams, jellies, beets, yellow tomato preserves, and lots of other goodies. Strings of last year's red peppers and dipper gourds hang on the walls.

"Several tabby cats are waiting patiently to have their wooden bowls filled with milk. Grandma draws up a fresh bucket of water from the well, we all take a drink with the dipper made from the gourds. In another bucket, Grandma puts a jar of milk, along with some freshly molded butter, and lowers it back into the well. Everything keeps fresh and cool down in the well.

"As it begins to get dark, the mosquitoes chase us all indoors. Grandma lights the kerosene lamp on the kitchen table. The table is already set for breakfast with the plates turned upside down. The plates remain upside down until after Grandpa blesses the food.

"The living room floor is covered with a rag carpet. Grandma has just finished cleaning the carpet, swept up all the old straw and put fresh straw underneath.

"Back in the kitchen, everything feels so homey. There in the corner is the wood and coal cookstove. The stove is polished nice and shiny black. In the cupboard drawer, Grandma keeps her box of soda cards—some have pictures of dogs. On Sundays, sometimes Grandma lets the children play with the cards. She also has some paper dolls and paper furniture that she got from Arbuckle Coffee. And she has so many delightful trinkets that she got out of boxes of Victor Toy Oats.

"As Grandma and Mama talked about how many eggs their hens laid, Grandpa and Papa talk about their crops. And a quiet evening draws to an end. Grandma gives the children a half-gallon syrup bucket filled with fresh milk to take home with them, and they can't wait to get home to drink that cool fresh milk."

What a pleasant memory. Everything seemed so calm and simple. No stress of the fast-paced life of modern days.

Nilson, Sven

In 1890, a small grocery store opened in the north end of town. At the corner of Allen (now Main street) and Galena, this small grocery store carried anything you could possibly need, from country produce to flour, meal, feed, butter, eggs, vegetables, bottled and canned goods, meats, fruits, preserves, sweets, and anything a good table would require.

Can't you almost imagine in your mind the wonderful smells that would greet you as you opened the door to enter the friendly atmosphere of S. Nilson Family Groceries? Sven Nilson himself would greet you, with his smiling face and his Swedish accent. His partner in business and marriage was Ida M. Peterson Nilson. They had been married since 1881, and they had a beautiful daughter, Ms. Anna, who can occasionally be seen in the family grocery store helping out the business.

Being the good honest Swedish native, S. Nilson has earned his reputation of being honest, thrifty, frugal, fair and square. This fine reputation has resulted in his prosperous business that requires two delivery wagons to respond to customer needs.

It would be great in this day and age to dial 140 and have that sweet Swedish voice ask what he can do for you. After giving your order to S. Nilson, in a matter of minutes, the wagon would be rushing to bring your groceries. And it would be added to your tab at the end of the month. You could trust that S. Nilson would supply you with the best possible merchandise at the lowest possible price.

Additional information on Sven Nilson: Sven was born May 3, 1857, in Sweden. He came to America in 1869. He lived in Chicago for about one year before heading to Jasper County. He landed about nine miles northwest of Webb City and proceeded to farm. Sven married Ida Peterson on May 30, 1881. Ida was from Georgia City, Missouri. Their one child, Anna, attended Webb City College at the age of sixteen. Sven's second wife was Ada Aylor, who died March 9, 1926, while staying in her winter home in West Palm Beach, Florida. Sven died December 2, 1937.

S. Nilson Grocery, 1894, at 314 North Allen (Main) Street

Oldham Family

John William Oldham was born in Clay County, Illinois, to Daniel and Mahala (Sims) Oldham, who had previously lived in Kentucky. John was a farmer and loved it. He married Rebecca Dudman, who hailed from Illinois. Rebecca's father was William Dudman. Rebecca died in 1889, leaving two sons and two daughters: George L., Alva, Sallie E. Smith, Minnie B., Garrett.

Alva Oldham, having been raised on a farm, enjoyed working in agriculture. He purchased the J. H. Ralston property in Union Township, Jasper County, in 1909. One hundred and sixty acres brought in plenty of harvest, which included hay, grain, and fruit with five acres of strawberries. The land also allowed him to have lots of stock of cattle and pigs. But the greatest benefit of his land was when he drilled down about 225 feet and found a rich vein of lead ore.

In 1890, Alva married May Sims, daughter of Frank W. and Minnie Perry Sims, and they had four children, Ernest, R., Hugh D., Virgil T., and Cecil E.

Virgil T. Oldham, born 1902, opened a service station in Webb City at northeast corner of Broadway and Webb Streets, behind Webb City Bank. He owned and operated that service station for forty years. Virgil passed away in 1981.

Judge Woodson Oldham helped Virgil run the service station.

O'Neill, James—Colonel

He was born in New York on October 31, 1836, to poor immigrants from Ireland. At an early age, James began to show a talent at succeeding in most anything he attempted. He received his education in the schools at Liverpool Village in New York. His father, Peter O'Neill, came to America from Ireland in 1828 when he and his wife, Hanna (Walsh) O'Neill, and settled in New York. He began working at the early age of twelve. His first business adventure was driving along the waterway of the Erie Canal for $9 a month. At the end of three years, he was given a position on a freight boat and was a valued employee.

At the age of twenty-nine, James took his hard-earned savings and headed to the Pennsylvania oil region to invest in land. It was a wise decision on his part; the land proved to be rich in petroleum.

In 1879, at forty-three years of age, James O'Neill came to Jasper County to invest once more in land, only this time he was investing in lead and zinc. He also bought 1,500 acres in Kansas to become involved in coal mining. He purchased land in Newton County for mining and farming.

As if he wasn't busy enough keeping track of all of his investments, James O'Neill decided to take on a new business that all his friends considered a hazardous undertaking—the Webb City Waterworks. He had to invest a lot of money with only a small amount of return possible. Well, his foresight paid off. As the community developed, so did the waterworks, which became a necessity for both the city and the mining industry. O'Neill also started the gas service in Webb City. The big day for Webb City, the day they piped in natural gas from Kansas was a celebration. They set up some four-inch pipes that were in the air about eighteen to twenty feet high on some prairie land between Jefferson Street and Madison Street, just south of First Street. As the gas was turned on by a valve at ground level, the gas escaped with a tremendous roar from the upright pipe and was ignited by a roman candle. With an even more terrific roar, it lit up the prairie for miles around, and Webb City had natural gas for 25¢ a month.

Being the smart businessman that he was, James O'Neill owned all but one-twentieth of the stocks associated with the water company. His son-in-law George H. Bruen was the secretary, and Henry O'Neill was the vice president, with James as president.

To add to his list of accomplishments, James was half-owner in the Webb City Ice & Storage Company. He also built the famous Newland Hotel. And he was involved in many organizations in the community. He also started the first gas service in Webb City and the first ice plant.

James was married to Lucy Bachelder (from New York), and they had two children: Grace, who married George R. Regdon in Pennsylvania, and Jennie, who married George H. Bruen in Webb City. James's second wife was Ora Hubbell of Cedar County, Missouri, and they had one son, Robert Newland O'Neill. Their home was located on the southwest corner of Pennsylvania and Joplin (Broadway) Street.

I think James O'Neill rightly qualifies as an honored forefather and ancestor of Webb City history. If we had more dedicated people today who were concerned with Webb City's future, we would see a flourishing metropolis. We do have those who are concerned, but only a handful can't accomplish something that needs the support of the entire town. I would like to see our city working together as a unit instead of being torn apart by opposition.

Additional information: The O'Neill Building was the home of the Water Department, 9 1/2 South Webb Street. The waterworks system cost O'Neill $100,000 in 1890. James O'Neill had the title of colonel, but I don't know how he came by that title.

O'Neill built a beautiful home on the southwest corner of Pennsylvania and Broadway Streets. His son-in-law and daughter Jennie and George Bruen built the house next-door to O'Neill at Sixteen South Pennsylvania, and George was O'Neill's right-hand man in all of O'Neill's business ventures.

O'Neill was known as Colonel O'Neill, which title he acquired by virtue of his popularity among the citizens of Webb City.

At one time, O'Neill took it upon himself to help those in need. He donated money and then started helping with donations of coal for those who couldn't afford the necessary coal to keep their families warm. He set out about ten carloads of coal for those in need. He not only gave away the coal but supplied transport of the coal from the wagons to the homes. Many said they were in such dire need that it saved their lives. The greatest part of the story is that most of the people never knew it was the colonel who saved them. When mines would be shut down and men were out of work was when O'Neill took it upon himself to help the poor and needy. He recalled that he had lived in poverty and knew the anguish and pain of no food, shelter, or heat.

O'Neill loved the children of Webb City. He became friends with them all. When O'Neill became ill, the children knocked on the door of the O'Neill home and inquired about their friend. At his funeral, there were many single flowers from each child or from a poor family that had been befriended by the colonel. This man, who started out his life in poverty, became one of the wealthiest residents of Jasper County. Not only responsible for the city's water and gas supply, he owned a large number of buildings on Main Street, many mines, thousands of acres of land in Missouri and Kansas. But he was wealthiest in the number of friends he had. His last mining action was with Sucker Flat, renewing life into a once famous tract.

The death of Colonel O'Neill—O'Neill died in November of 1907. His body was placed in a temporary vault at Mount Hope Cemetery as they waited for his mausoleum to be constructed. It was later determined that O'Neill was to be buried in his hometown of Liverpool, New York, and his mausoleum was built there, and his body was shipped there.

The colonel's funeral was at his beautiful home.

Water Department 9 1/2 South Webb

O'Neill home, southwest corner of Broadway and Pennsylvania

James O'Neill also built this Newland Hotel in the middle of town. He didn't have enough land available to build the hotel, so he went to the neighboring businesses along Allen (Main) Street and asked the owners if he could buy the area above their buildings. They kept ownership of their two-story buildings, and O'Neill built a third floor, and he owned the third floor. He had one building that he owned the first and second floors, and that was his entry and dining room for the hotel, and the stairway took the customers up to the third floor to their rooms. Smart man!

Palmer, Ernest Jesse—Botanist

A great botanist, Ernest Jesse Palmer who was a professor at Harvard, became well known when he wrote a couple of books. One was called *Catalogue of Plants in Jasper County*, and he cowrote *A Catalogue of All Known Plants of Missouri.*

We've had a few inventors from Webb City and some wonderful artists who still reside in Webb City. There are musicians, actors, singers, and businessmen who have made a name for themselves and still call Webb City their hometown.

And as Webb City continues to grow, there are many who have made their fame and fortune elsewhere, but who have decided to settle in Webb City and call it home. It doesn't matter if you were born here or were a transplant, Webb City is proud to have such wonderful citizens.

Additional information on Ernest Jesse Palmer: He once maintained a herbarium in Webb City that contained twenty thousand species. He published a book of poetry in 1958 when he was eighty-three years of age.

Parker, Charley

Charley Parker was born in St. Charles in 1853. As early miners journeyed to Webb City to make it rich in the mines, Charley joined them in 1877. But Charley didn't plan on making it rich in the mines; he had his mind set on owning a business. So at the young age of twenty-four, Charley opened a saloon to help quench the thirst of the miners.

Business was good to Charley, and he became quite wealthy, just as he had planned to do. But Charley didn't forget how it felt to be without, so he shared his wealth with the poor. He gave out free meals to the down-and-out miner and helped many a young family get started with a roof over their heads.

Before Charley passed away in 1911, at the age of fifty-eight, bad luck had found him. Charley died in poverty. I wonder if any of those who Charley had befriended with a meal, home, or just some spare change was there to give Charley a helping hand?

Charley's wife left him and married W. B Daniels, and her new husband took her away to California. His only daughter went to California with her mother, leaving Charley alone. He did have a brother, Tom Parker, who was well known in the real estate business, but he passed away a few years before Charley.

Charley lost quite a bit of his property, and it was tied up in the supreme court. Then he got sick. He had some liver ailments and other complications, and he was in Jane Chinn Hospital for a couple of weeks before he passed away, November 14, at the age of fifty-eight.

At one point, he was worth over $75,000, and then everything went downhill. At his death, he was penniless. And he was alone. The mortuary received notice that no near relatives would be in town for the funeral. A simple funeral.

Patten, William E.

William E. Patten was born October 1, 1860, in Sullivan, Indiana. During the 1870s and 1880s, Patten roamed the west. He drove cattle from Texas to the northern markets, dabbled in many trades as a carpenter, butcher, plasterer, roofer, blacksmith, and lead mining in Colorado. While in his twenties, he settled in the mining boom town of Prosperity, Missouri. He became a business partner with R. B. Dodge, and they invested in several mining challenges under the name of Dodge & Patten Mining Company.

In 1891, at the age of thirty, Patten married Rosa DeJarnett on March 4, in Carterville. They had three sons: Cecil Patten, Russell Patten, and Lester Patten; one daughter, Creola Patten Bonell, and raised one grandson, R. L. Patten Jr.

Patten moved to Webb City in 1901 and continued his mining ventures. He and Dodge were associated with the Dominion Mine, the Avondale 1 and 2, and he also owned the Nearby Mine. His name was also included with the Eleventh Hour Mine.

Business was such a success that Patten and Dodge were looking for ways to invest their money, and they established the Merchant & Miners bank in 1905. Patten served as vice president and member of the board for many years. Not knowing much about the banking business, Dodge and Patten included L. J. Stevison and C. M. Manker in the organization of the bank.

Patten's money was invested in real estate, not only in Webb City and Joplin but in the Rio Grande Valley.

Patten built a magnificent home at 106 North Pennsylvania in 1908 to reflect his success in the area. Quite an improvement from the young couple that used empty powder boxes for chairs when Patten was working for Ben Aylor at one of his mines as a steam engineman, operating water pumps on the night shift. While the mines were shut down at night, Patten would pump water from the mines. He tried to convince Aylor to install lights (a new idea at the time) so he could see at night while he worked the pumps. The conservative Aylor suggested that Patten slow the pumps down, go to sleep, get up early, speed up the pumps, and lower the water level before the miners arrived for work.

Patten claims that this procedure helped him make his fortune because he earned enough money to feed his family and had plenty of time during the day to prospect unlike other miners who worked all day and didn't have time for anything but work. If they did any prospecting, it was without a steady income.

That 1904 Rambler, which carried the notoriety of being Webb City's second automobile, was unique as it had an entrance door in the backend and a central carbide generator piping gas to each headlight. The car carried hampers on the side for picnics.

W. E. Patten spent many an evening reading his Bible, and he served as superintendent of the Methodist Church having contributed large sums of money for the construction of the church at Broadway and Pennsylvania, where Patten could see the church from his front porch. Patten died in January 1945, at the age of eighty-four.

Thanks, Leslie Patten Brown, for sharing this wonderful information about your great-grandfather W. E. Patten.

Patten is giving a ride to these children in honor of his daughter, Creola's, birthday.

Left to right starting with
the back row is:

(1) unknown (minister's daughter), (2) Josephine Pritchett, (3) Ruth Robertson

Middle row: (1) Marie Lambert, (2) Mary Chenoweth, (3) Marguerite Smith, (4) Mary Robertson, (5) W. E. Patten, (6) Grace Webb, (7) Margaret Burgner, (8) Creola Patten (birthday girl), (9) Russell Patten, (10) Maurice Craig

Front row in back of driver: (1) Marguerite Robertson, (2) Bill Robertson, (3) Unknown

Photo: Webb City's second car. A 1904 Rambler being driven by owner, W. E. Patten.

Patten Home, 106 North Pennsylvania

Pence, Perly—Doctor

Those of you who grew up in the Webb City-Carterville area will recall the name of Dr. Perly Pence. He was not only a local doctor, he had his hands in many business operations. He also had a pilot license, and his favorite hobby was flying. Here is a story about one of Dr. Pence's other jobs.

As I have mentioned many times before, when a highway comes through, it's for progress and convenience, but there are usually changes made to accommodate these ribbons of concrete designed for man to get from one place to another in less time. And over time, we seem to forget what used to be located in the area before the highway.

Such is the case of Highway 71, which was changed from a two-lane road to the divided highway of today. The interchange at the Carterville exit brought about many changes. How many of you can still recall the Ozark Quail Farm that sat on the south side of Highway 71 just east of Johnstown?

Perly Pence was one who knew the importance of advertising. If you don't advertise, people don't know what you're selling or where you are located. Perly was doing so well with the quail farm that the Ralston Purina Company featured it in a bulletin sent out to other breeders as an example of success.

I guess we could add author to Dr. Pence's list of accomplishments, as he put out a small book on raising game birds. He shared all of his secrets about the art of raising quail and pheasants.

Of course, Dr. Pence didn't handle this quail farm all alone. There would have been no time left for doctoring. So family members helped. There were Ward and Mary Ijams (Perly's sister), and Perly's son, Burnace. And I'm sure the days were long, and work was hard.

According to the book, it was necessary to turn the eggs in the incubator five times a day. There were thousands of eggs at his farm, so I'm sure that took some time. I would think that Burnace and his aunt and uncle had to be seeing those eggs in their sleep.

The bulletin from Ralston Purina states that "The owner of Ozark Quail Farm is Dr. P.M. Pence, a lover of wildlife and a true sportsman. The farm is managed by Ward Ijams—a man of Indian descent and who has a way with wildlife." This bulletin, published in 1952 or 1953, locates the farm "down in the busy Tri-Sate Area of Missouri where lead and zinc is the principal industry."

One of the things Dr. Pence wrote about in his book was the vanishing bobwhite quail. Have you heard the cheery whistle of the bobwhite lately? Those of us who live in the city are deprived of that joy.

Dr. Pence said in the early days of settlement in the area, farmers had crisscross rail fences around small weedy fields, and that was the perfect habitat for the quail. They thrived in poorly tilled fields, gardens, and orchards. The pioneer farmers briar patch gave a safe refuge from weather and predators. But in this modern day of farming, with tractors and power machinery replacing the walking plow and horse, many of the favorite habitats of the quail have disappeared. Most of the farmers have removed old stumps, briars, and brambles and have clean farms that are more productive.

Thus, the bird country of old primitive America had been systematically destroyed by the industrial activity of civilized man in his struggle to produce profitable farm products and livestock. "The tragic end of the Bobwhite Quail is near."

He encouraged people to think of the benefits of controlled quail farming. He raised them for food, for stocking farms, and for breeding. He sold them (quail and pheasants) to individuals who came to the farm to buy for their own freezers. He also sold them to restaurants and even supplied them with stickers to put on their menu—great advertising strategy. He sold them to hunters to stock their hunting area. What an unusual business venture, and what an unusual man who seemed to have the Midas touch.

There is nothing left of the quail farm to trigger our memories, but the next time you take that exit ramp on the south side, when you get to the top of the hill, take a look around and imagine that quail farm. It's another missing piece of history that can only be visited through pictures, stories, and memories. Share them with your kids (the story about the quail farm is located in the business chapter)!

Perly M. Pence, 1907–1984. He practiced in Carterville for thirty-two years, retiring in 1974. He married Flora Dills on October 31, 1932, Perly's twenty-fifth birthday; pretty smart to get married on your birthday so you will never forget your anniversary! They had four children: Burnace, Robert, Carole, and Sue. A person from our past, Dr. Pence is remembered as the special person he was.

Perry, W. H. "Bill" II

As you know, I love going back in time. I enjoy hearing stories of long ago and what life was like in the olden days. Bless his heart, W. H. Perry took the time to write his lifetime memories, and occasionally I will pick up one of his books and take a trip down memory lane with him. He did such a great job of detailing everyday happenings, and I would like to share a few with you.

Many of us know that we live in a wonderful time era where we have electricity and many modern conveniences. Alas, that was not the case in the good ole days. W. H. stood for William Henry, but let's call him Bill, tells of playing baseball in the middle of Pennsylvania Street between Third and Fourth streets (a good wide street), and they were often interrupted in their playing as the ice wagons would be making their rounds delivering ice to each and every home. With only one ice plant in town, the Interurban Ice Company in the northeast part of town held a monopoly as each household needed a block of ice to keep their food cold. They delivered the ice in specially made wagons pulled by mules. As they approached each house, there would be a 9"×12" card in the window or on the door with numbers printed so the deliveryman would see the number and cut a portion of ice to match the number. Most folks ordered five, ten, fifteen, or twenty-five pounds of ice. The lady of the house would make sure her card was in the screen of the front door. The iceman had a three-hundred-pound block of ice, and he would use an ice pick to score the ice so it would break into the size needed. He used ice tongs to carry the ice to the house.

Bill said the iceman had a leather jacket to protect his back from the ice as he slung it over his shoulder to carry the heavy blocks. There were always small slivers of ice left on the floor of the wagon after chipping out the block, and while the ice was being delivered inside the house, the kids would rush to the wagon to grab those wonderful slivers to put on their tongues. The iceman would come back and shoo the kids away. In the meantime, the mule would automatically move to the next house without the driver even stepping in the wagon. Having made the same stop day after day, the mules knew when to stop and when to go.

Bill recalled that the block of ice would be set inside their icebox, and the ice would slowly melt. There was a small shallow pan under the block of ice that would catch melted ice drippings. The pan had to be regularly emptied, and this was a chore Bill's mom and dad would forget, and it would run all over the floor, and they would have to mop up the water. So Bill's dad decided to fix the problem. He drilled a hole in the floor and put a funnel in the hole to allow the water to go underneath the house. Bill, being about four or five, marveled at his dad's ingenuity.

As a youth, Bill and his friends loved to play tennis, but Webb City did not have a tennis court, so the neighborhood boys took the situation into their own hands and built their own tennis court on the east side of Pennsylvania on a vacant lot. He said they would play tennis for hours. Ironically Bill, along with his wife, Marion, in later years would donate money for the city to build a beautiful tennis court in King Jack Park.

Bill was born on a cold day at 6:00 a.m. on January 9, 1918, and his name was William Henry Perry Jr.

Bill's father and grandparents moved to Webb City in 1906 when William H. Perry Sr. was nineteen years old.

Bill and his sister grew up at 310 West Fourth Street.

Bill was an entrepreneur starting at an early age. The family did not have much money, and Bill was always figuring out a way to earn a little cash. His mother taught him to bake, and he would make gingerbread, frost it, and sell it door-to-door while it was still warm. He started a little pop stand where he sold pop and candy bars, Hershey, Milky Way, Snickers, etc. He would buy a case of flavored pop, twenty-four in a case for 80¢, and the candy bars were the same price, a case of twenty-four for 80¢. He would sell them for 5¢ each and double his money. He said the name of his business was Ye Olde Poppe Stand.

One wintry day, Bill decided to go out shoveling snow to earn some money. He recalls that one contrary old lady agreed to pay him 10¢ to clear about fifty feet of sidewalk, but when the job was finished, she said Bill had misunderstood her, and she did not want her sidewalk cleaned. He did not have nice memories of that lady!

Bill tried his hand at selling magazines door-to-door, *Pictorial Review, Liberty, Grit, Ladies' Home Journal,* etc. He also sold White Cloverine Salve, which healed the smallest cut to anything else that needed healing. He felt he was doing something great for mankind!

Herrod's Grocery Store, during the Depression, would hire boys to put flyers in every mailbox on Saturday morning to announce the sales of the day. Bill was paid 50¢ to get up at four in the morning to have the flyers distributed. One cold morning, the other boys went out in the chats and burned all their flyers instead of delivering them. Bill told his dad, and his dad went to talk to Al Herrod. His dad talked Al into letting him deliver the flyers all over town for $2.50, which was welcomed money to a family suffering from the Depression.

Another moneymaker for Bill was when he played in the Webb City city band. He received $2 every Friday night when the band played from eight o'clock to ten o'clock at the Memorial Park on Daugherty Street. They also marched in parades and, once a year, would play at the TB Hospital.

They practiced on the third floor of the Roney building. So the young man who felt he didn't play a clarinet very well, played in the city band from 1925–1942, when the band was disbanded due to the war. Bill said he never played his clarinet again after that.

What wonderful memories Bill wrote concerning growing up in Webb City. And I only touched on a few of those memories. Are your memories preserved for the next generation?

Pritchett, Paul—Doctor

Doc and Thannie—Reverend Joseph H. Pritchett and his wife, Mary, were very proud of their four sons. Each one had chosen a noble profession. One son, F. Morrison Pritchett, came to Webb City in 1900 as a promising new attorney. His brother Stonewall soon joined him, and they set up office together since Stonewall was an attorney also.

Both of these young men were considered good catches for the ladies of Webb City. Well, it took fifteen years before Anna snagged Morrison as her husband.

Both Morrison and Stonewall served in the position of city attorney. Morrison was also the assistant county prosecuting attorney. Stonewall and his wife, Margaret, eventually left town to investigate the new territory to the west. That left the legal business to Morrison.

In the meantime, their younger brothers had also chosen professions of importance. J. Thomas Pritchett had followed in his father's footsteps and became a minister. Thomas located in Kansas City.

The fourth son, Paul, became a doctor and moved to the area where his brothers had found so much happiness—Webb City.

Many of you probably still remember Doc Paul Pritchett. Doc came to Webb City in 1908 with his bride, Thannie. They came from the new territory known as Oklahoma.

Thannie's father, Perry Thinsley, a carpenter, a construction man, had helped develop the town of Sulpher, IT (Indian Territory, that's what it was known as before it became Oklahoma). He built the first church and the first schoolhouse because it was a new town. They lived there until Oklahoma became a state in 1907.

The young couple married and headed off into the wilderness, Webb City, Missouri. Life and times were hard for the young doctor and his wife. They didn't have much money but had lots of work. Thannie helped out as much as she could. She was right beside Doc on his house calls and helped out in the office.

One time, Doc was away at the hospital when a lady went into labor. Thannie went to the lady's house and delivered the baby. She had seen Doc do it often enough that she didn't have any problems.

Doc and Thannie had two daughters of their own, Marjorie and Helen. Doc passed away in 1952, and Thannie continued to help people whenever she could. Her motto was "to think of others." Dr. Pritchett and his wife, Thannie, at one time or another, touched many living in Webb City.

Thannie just passed away on April 7, 1991, in Arizona. She had lived to be 104 years old. She had witnessed Webb City in its glory, and she was there during the struggle to survive after the mining era. No matter what trial she was put through, she kept smiling with a twinkle in her eye. She had many accomplishments.

The Rev. James Kellett summed it up pretty well at Thannie's funeral when he said, "On April 7, Marjorie and Helen lost their lovely mother. The Central United Methodist Church lost its oldest member, and the United States of America lost a piece of living history."

Pritchett, Thannie

The Dr. Paul Pritchett's wife—I was reading a letter about a dear lady that many will remember—Thannie Pritchett, who passed away in 1991 at the age of 104. She recalled what it was like being married to a doctor (back when doctors didn't make a lot of money). She said she would go on calls with her husband and assist him in delivering babies. She said the sad part was walking into a home that may only have a bed with bare slats covered with cornstalks. She said they wouldn't even have a piece of cloth to wrap the baby. She would go home and tear up one of their sheets and bring it back for the baby.

Thannie grew up in Indian Territory before it was Oklahoma. That brought back to my memory stories that I have heard about the Indian Territory. I think the most popular story of that era was the Big Oklahoma Land Run, also known as the Cherokee Strip Run of 1893. The Cherokee Outlet was the last frontier, a land of lush grass and fresh streams, five million acres of "promised land" is the way Jessy Mae Coker described it. She said over thirty thousand people crowded into Arkansas City to sign up for the race. Men stood in line for three days to register. On the day of the run, she said there were covered wagons and buggies as far as the eye could see. There were buckboards, carts, bicycles, and thousands of men on horseback, all waiting to make the run for land that most had already looked over and set their minds to have.

At noon, the signal sounded, and all you could see was a cloud of dust as horsemen vanished. Jessy's fiancé, Walter, was in that cloud of dust ahead as he hurried to lay his claim. Her mother was also forging ahead in the crowd as she wanted land to live near her daughter. In the middle of the night, Jessy's mother showed up to say that she had claimed her land, but with all the fighting for land, she felt she wasn't safe staying on the land by herself for the night and gave up. In the meantime, Walter staked his claim and held tight, only to discovered that the land he claimed was on school land, which had to be purchased (not free land). With no money to purchase the land, Jessy, her mother, and her fiancé, Walter, headed back to Kansas with nothing more than memories of the land run.

What was most interesting about the folks that shared their stories of getting the free land in the land run was that they kept that land in their families for several generations. That land had become a part of their souls, and they weren't about to sell it.

One lady said her husband made the run, and they moved onto their land in October of 1893 with three children, the oldest was nine and the youngest five weeks old. Their land was one and a half miles from the Cimarron River. She said her first home didn't look like much as it was a soddy, then they built a log home, and finally they had a nice wooden-framed home. In March 1894, they had their fourth child, and in July, just one year after the land run, her husband died of cancer. There she was with four children, ages ten years to four months, and all alone. She had to keep the farm active to keep the land from being contested. She said she plowed, planted, and harvested, and she received a patent on the land signed by Teddy Roosevelt. She raised her family on that farm and at the age of eighty-eight in 1955, she was going to pass that farm on to her children as it was a part of their heritage.

Back to Thannie Pritchett. Thannie and her husband, Paul, lived at 927 West Second Street, and in 1928, their office was located in the Humphrey Building, and in 1947, it was above the Haynes Drug Store at 101 1/2 West Daugherty. Now I don't know which office she was in at the time, but she recalled a crowd gathering on the street below outside of their office. She leaned out the window and saw Harry S. Truman standing on the end of his wagon, making a speech right there in the street. When he finished his speech, he went upstairs to their office and sat down to talk with them. Thannie said, "Long before the White House and the vice presidency, of course, Truman had started in local politics, splitting his time between campaigning for county judge and running a haberdashery in Kansas City, quite a bit north of Webb City." Thannie also recalled that she didn't really get into politics, but she did remember voting for a long list of candidates for state offices as soon as it was legal for women to vote, although she couldn't recall a single name of those she voted for. But how neat to know that President Harry S. Truman had once sat in their office and talked to her and her husband on a summer afternoon.

Obituary/Eulogy of Thannie Pritchett

Thannie Pritchett was born on October 9, 1886 at Henry's Crossroads near Knoxville, Tennessee, the next to the youngest of four children that were born to Perry Thinsley and Lydia (Bryant) Thinsley. She passes away on April 7, 1991 at more than 104 years of age.

She experienced the American frontier, and her strong character reflects a hard but happy childhood. She lived in "Indian Territory" before it was Oklahoma. She saw pristine rivers, virgin forests, and untainted nature. It was her privilege to know the hearty men, women, and children who were settlers to a new and unforgiving land. Many believe that it was her era that most shaped the American character at it's best. Strength, will power, courage and tenacity were not mere virtues but necessities to survive.

People, in common, believed in hard work, earning your own way, honesty, helping your neighbor, taking care of your own, commitment in marriage, love of family, and in love of God. In some ways, the values of that time seem as pristine and unspoiled as the land.

Thannie was married to a physician, Dr. Paul Pritchett. In her own words "the best thing to me that God ever let loose..." The two labored side by side when medicine was a struggling ministry. They knew calls for help through long night hours. Thannie spoke of delivering babies in those days: "We'd get there and the only thing in that house would be a bed with bare slats covered with corn shucks. There'd be nothing to wrap the baby in… I'd go back home and tear up our own sheets and take them back to the baby." In the absence of her husband, Thannie even delivered a baby herself. She declared, "There wasn't much to it."

Thannie said, one day she was working in the office and a crowd gathered below. She leaned out the window to see "Harry S. Truman, who stood right there on the end of a wagon and made a speech, right there in the street. He saw our office was open, and when he finished his speech, he came right upstairs and sat down to talk to us." Long before the White House and the vice presidency, of course, Truman had started in local politics, splitting his time between campaigning for county judge and running a haberdashery in Lamar, about 20 miles north of Webb City. Politics didn't really light her fire, although she does remember voting for long lists of candidates for state offices as soon as it was legal for women to vote. "Now, you know I can't remember a single name," she said, "But I'm kind of old now!" (104 years).

Thannie was a wonderful mother to daughters Marjorie and Helen. Her own words concerning them are: "Good girls? Lord yes, I'd like you to find some better children than I had." Although busy keeping the office of her husband, she was attentive and caring to her own children. She was a vital part of the Methodist Church and was always in the kitchen preparing dinners on special occasions, and she was very involved in Eastern Stars. She believed in doing for others: "If you want to keep going, you've got to keep your mind on something besides yourself. Think about others."

Mrs. Pritchett's dear husband, Paul died in 1952. "I've been a widow for an awful long time now," she said, smoothing the coverlet on her lap. "I was in my 70's when my husband died." She paused to reflect. "You know, I don't think I've ever been mistreated or misused. But I do believe most everybody would be happier if they understand they can't have every little thing they want." She is survived by her two daughters, Marjorie Dallas and Helen Pederson of Sun City, Arizona, two grandchildren, seven great grandchildren and two great, great grandchildren and by many other relatives and friends.

It was not this minister's privilege to meet Thannie Pritchett, but I would like to have sat down with her for a talk and a cup of coffee. She said, "I still enjoy a cup of coffee just straight." That's also the way she'd talk to you, "just straight!"

On April 7th, Marjorie and Helen lost their lovely mother. The Central United Methodist Church lost its oldest member and the United States of America lost a piece of living history.

Reverend James Kellett

Purkhizer, Leonard L.

Little Alice came to the big mining town of Webb City as it was just beginning to develop in 1877. Her family came from Tennessee, where she was born in 1863. As Alice grew along with the mining town, she fell in love with J. M. Purkhiser. They had a large beautiful family; one daughter, Callie, and four sons, Leonard L., Thomas S., William P., and Roy H. This family was raised in the family home at 101 South Roane.

J. M. Purkhiser had been a jigman in the mines.

William Purkizer married a couple of times in his life and had a successful career as an insurance salesman for Hiron & Hiron Insurance Company. His life ended rather tragically in 1939.

Thomas married Anna S., and they lived a couple of houses from Thomas's parents at 107 South Roane, later moving to 908 North Hall. And after his death, Anna lived at 523 North Pennsylvania. They had a son named Howard.

I don't have much information on Callie or Roy.

My main topic of this story is Leonard L. Purkhiser. Leonard married Mary Anna Reigle in 1928. They lived at 912 West Second Street and had a daughter, Carolyn. They were most remembered by their business, L. L. Purkhiser Ice Cream Company. Ice cream parlors were plentiful in Webb City, so to make a success of that business was a constant effort. But it paid off for Leonard. He had a couple of locations for his business, once at 110 North Main, and later at 209 North Main.

The memories of L. L. Purkhiser Ice Cream Company are sweet memories. Many sundaes, cones, and malts were tasted there.

Rogers, Fred and Della

Many cars with a variety of license plates pull into King Jack Park every day to check out the Praying Hands, the Kneeling Miner, the plaque on the history of Webb City, and the Southwest Missouri Railway Monument.

Have you taken a close look at the Southwest Missouri Railway Monument? It is really an impressive memorial to the mode of transportation that was the heartbeat of this area during the mining era.

Fred (Fritz) Rogers, who is well known in Webb City for his work on the restoration of streetcar 60, was also responsible for the monument that stands in memory of a bygone era. Rogers had a knack of getting things done without having to spend much money. He really became a pro at this during the restoration of the streetcar.

Having been in the salvage business, Rogers was knowledgeable about the procedures in procuring needed materials. This was the knowledge Rogers used when he went to the Conner Hotel as it was being prepared for demolition and talked to the necessary individuals about some of the beautiful art panels that were being removed from the grand old hotel. One evening, about 5:00 p.m., Rogers went down into the basement of the Conner Hotel to talk with the contractor. The French

Renaissance design art panels had already been removed and were being placed in crates to be stored for future use. Arrangements were made for the Southwest Missouri Railway organization to buy two of the panels at $250 each. The contractor told Rogers that the panels would be on the north side of the building whenever he was able to make arrangements to haul them. The next morning, at 6:00 a.m., the Conner Hotel collapsed prematurely.

When Rogers went to pick up the panels, he was told that he could have them as a donation instead of paying the $250. The panels were stored at the airport until the site could be prepared for them.

Rogers knew he needed money to finish this project he had started, so he advertised that names of those donating $100 would be put on the plaque of the monument. He earned $7,000 to complete his project.

The Missouri Army National Guard moved the panels for Rogers, and a company in Carthage supplied necessary equipment for lifting the panels. Support of the citizens was what helped Rogers complete his task.

Arrangements had been made for Rogers to remove the actual Southwest Missouri Railway sign from the north side of the powerhouse. Being an actual part of the building, Rogers was to pay $250, plus replace the bricks where the sign had been. As Rogers thought about this task, he wasn't feeling too good about it. Jack Dawson suggested to Rogers that they could make a sign that would look just like the original. So that project began. They made a cement form, constructed letters out of Styrofoam, and glued them into the form. Cement was poured into the form with the Styrofoam staying intact. After the cement dried, they burned the Styrofoam, which caused it to melt right out of the concrete block. Many people have thought that sign really did come from the powerhouse. They did an awesome job of reproducing it without damaging a historical building.

As the monument came together, more structural support was needed for the upright concrete and marble. Ironically Rogers used three old streetcar bumpers for the props.

As mentioned earlier, Rogers restored streetcar 60 and put in many hours installing the streetcar tracks that go around King Jack Park. Before the arduous work began on installing the tracks, a fifty-year agreement was drawn up with the city. This agreement allowed the streetcar association to place the tracks in the park and gave it a twenty-foot easement on both sides of the tracks. Rogers says that agreement has an option for renewal after the first fifty years.

Fred Rogers has journals that record every movement made in building of the streetcar monument—the laying of the tracks, the restoring of the streetcar, the building of the depot, and even helping Jack Dawson with the Kneeling Miner Statue. It's recorded that Rogers helped Nancy Dawson keep mud mixed as Jack Dawson's magic fingers formed the Kneeling Miner. Rogers also built the base for the statue.

The Highway Department was going to demolish a wonderful depot, which was situated in Carterville. It had been a wait station for the streetcar line, and it would be an added attraction in King Jack Park, so Rogers asked the Highway Department if he could have the depot. With the help of some comrades—Bud Veatch, Roy Ross, and Harry Hood—Rogers removed the roof, windows, and rafters of the original depot. It was impossible to move the cemented rocks that formed the walls, so they built the rock portion of the building with new rock and donated cement. The old parts of the original depot were put into place, and the depot (now dubbed as Sucker Flats depot) that now houses the Webb City Area Chamber of Commerce is a quaint addition to the park.

Fred Rogers retired from his salvage business in 1973 and began his volunteer work. For the past twenty-eight years, Rogers has become a permanent fixture at King Jack Park. He has been injured many times, gotten ill—you name it! But his love for the work he has done is obvious in the notes he has kept in his journals.

He says he couldn't have accomplished any of the work if it wasn't for the support of the citizens of Webb City and his faithful friends from the streetcar association. He is proud of the fact that he very rarely spent a lot of money on any project. He relied on donations and volunteers, like himself, who wanted the best for Webb City.

Anytime a building was being torn down, you could bet that Fred Rogers was there to see what he could salvage for some future project.

We salute you, Fred Rogers, for the many sacrifices and your dedication to the history of Webb City.

Roney Family

Charles Roney was born in 1838, Franklin County, Ohio. He was the father of William Thomas Roney and Charles B. Roney. In 1870, Charles and his wife made the journey from Ohio to Missouri in a covered wagon with his eight-year-old son, William Thomas Roney. Seven years later, Charles B. Roney was born.

Both of these industrious young men took charge of their lives and became very successful. In 1882, at the age of twenty, William opened a mercantile establishment in Smithfield, west of Carl Junction. Later he moved his store to LeHigh and finally settled in Carl Junction. Settling in this area as a young man, in a new frontier, William experienced many changes throughout his life. When he first arrived with his parents, they settled on a farm north of Carl Junction. At that time, there was no Carl Junction. In fact, there wasn't a Joplin or Webb City. Oronogo was called Minersville, and Sedalia was the closest shipping point, and all merchandise had to be shipped overland.

At the time of his death in 1934, William Thomas Roney was truly considered a pioneer, not only in settling a new territory but also in establishing a business. He had served as president of Citizen's Bank in Carl Junction, president of Roney Mercantile Company, and vice president of H&D Motor Company of Joplin. He was a pioneer settler, a farmer, and a successful businessman.

Charles B. Roney served with his brother as secretary of the Roney Mercantile Company and also started his own business, Roney Funeral Home. Charles was very involved in the community. He was mayor of Carl Junction, served on the school board, sexton of the city cemetery, and a member of the Masonic Lodge.

It's men like these that helped Jasper County get organized and helped the small communities develop into cities. They were always willing to get involved. They knew that everyone had to chip in if anything was to get accomplished.

Every city in Jasper County had men like the Roneys. But as the years have passed by, those men and women have become a dying breed. People are too caught up in their own lives to consider volunteering for community activities, and as a result, it's the community that suffers. Without volunteers, there can be no city celebrations, parades, and community dinners.

Roselle, Arthur and Alice

Many times, I have mentioned the first brick home in Webb City which was built by our founder, John C. Webb, with the help of McNair. The home was located on the west side of Webb Street, between Broadway and Daugherty Streets. Later 112 North Webb was the location of the *Daily Register*, the Civic Drive-In, and then, Myers, Baker Rife and Denham CPAs and the law firm of Myers, Taylor Whitworth and Associates. It has also been a health clinic and doctor's office.

Larry Larsen tore down the original Webb house in 1936 to build the present building, which first housed the Civic Drive-In Restaurant.

John C. Webb had built his new house in 1882, north of the location of his original log cabin that he had lived in for almost twenty years before he discovered lead. This house was his symbol of success, but he didn't get to live in it very long before his death in 1883. His daughter, Mary Sue Webb Burgner, lived in the home after the death of her father. She also did not live in the house very long.

In 1891, a gentleman by the name of W. A. Snodgrass established a newspaper in Webb City known as the *Daily Register*. He housed his business in the old Webb-Burgner house at 112 North Webb Street. The paper was a highly thought of institution, doing a weekly edition on each Monday.

In the meantime, an up-and-coming young man by the name of Arthur B. Rozelle was making quite a name for himself in the newspaper business. In 1882, at the age of twenty-two, Rozelle founded a newspaper in Iowa which he operated for about ten years before selling it and heading south to Missouri. In 1892, in the little town of Tarkio, in Northwest Missouri, Rozelle started a new newspaper which he operated for about six years before being lured to Lamar, Missouri, in 1898 where he purchased the *Lamar Leader*. While in Tarkio, Arthur participated in a bit of politics as he was appointed Missouri's labor commissioner under Governor L. V. Stevens for one term. In 1899, Arthur married a young lady named Pauline Stone from St. Louis, who was the cousin of Missouri senator W. J. Stone. Pauline passed away in 1901. Rozelle was once again lured to another town, this time Webb City. Rozelle purchased the *Daily Register* from Snodgrass in 1903.

Rozelle was a man of modern thought, and one of his first business decisions upon arriving in Webb City was to do the unthinkable, and he hired a young lady as a reporter. Ms. Alice C. Cresswell, daughter of Judge E. Cresswell, had moved from Nashville, Missouri, to Webb City two years earlier. Desperately seeking an opportunity to become a reporter, Alice dropped out of high school to take on this new position with an established newspaper. Do not think ill of this young lady as she continued her education by attending night classes at the Great Western Normal School and Business College, located at College and Austin in Webb City. She not only finished her high school classes but went on to finish two years of college.

Alice was driven by a need to succeed, and she moved up the career ladder very quickly, from reporter to city editor to business manager within five years. The twenty-three-year-old dynamo then took a major step in her career when she married forty-eight year old Arthur Rozelle in 1908, promoting her to copublisher of the *Daily Register*. Alice Rozelle was one of very few women publishers in the state of Missouri. But all of this excitement was shared with the excitement of being Mrs. Arthur Rozelle, married to a man she had grown to love and admire while working side by side in a business they both loved.

The *Daily Register* reported on the mining activities in the area and kept the couple busy, but not too busy to start a family. Their first child, a baby boy, died at the age of seven months. A year later, a daughter, Alice, was born. Then after only four years of marriage, tragedy struck the couple once again as Arthur became quite ill as a result of blood poisoning from carbuncles. Alice was pregnant with their second daughter, trying to take care of a small child, run a newspaper, and be at the side of her dying husband.

Arthur was a well-loved citizen of Webb City, and knowing he needed peace and quiet to recover, Mayor W. V. K. Spencer ordered the streets near the Rozelle home to be roped off to cut back on traffic and noise that might affect the slightest chance the editor had for recovery. Children were cautioned not to shoot firecrackers before the Fourth of July and avoid all excessive noise. Despite the precautions, Arthur Rozelle passed away on June 28, 1912 at the age of fifty-two.

There was such a large turnout for the funeral of this highly respected man that the Southwest Missouri Electric Railway provided a streetcar to carry mourners from the Methodist Church to the Mount Hope Cemetery. In the paper, it was stated, "If everyone for whom Arthur had done some loving kindness brings a single blossom to his bier he would sleep beneath a wilderness of flowers." And that is just what happened. Everyone remembered Arthur Rozelle with a blossom, even small children who knew him remembered him by placing a blossom on his grave.

Arthur left his business in good hands, as Alice was a pioneer among women. A widow at twenty-seven, with one young child and another on the way, a business to run, and a reputation to uphold. But life went on.

Alice was now publisher and editor, and she took on this responsibility with a strong desire to succeed. At the height of the newspaper's success, under Alice's charge, the *Webb City Daily Register* had a circulation of twelve thousand and was published with eight to sixteen pages, six days a week.

In 1918, the mining industry dwindled, and Alice closed down the newspaper but kept the title in hopes of a revival of the mining business, which would create a need for the *Register*. In the meantime, she kept busy doing freelance writing, advertising promotions, and reporting for other area newspapers.

Many of you may remember that the daughter, born after Arthur's death, was Nadine Rozelle, who married P. Don Crockett, one of Webb City's finest mayors. The home that was mentioned at 423 North Roane has been in the family since 1901. Eminger and Elija Jane Cresswell, parents of Alice Rozelle, built three houses on Roane when they first move to Webb City, with the last being completed in 1906. They had planned on using all three as rental houses, but plans change, and they decided to live in one. Their daughter, Alice Rozelle, lived there, as did her daughter Nadine, and then the daughters of Nadine and Don Crockett live there, making it four generations. Alice Cresswell Rozelle lived to the age of eighty-seven, having lived in that house for seventy-one of those eighty-seven years. Nadine Rozelle Crockett lived to the age of eighty-two and had lived in that house all of her life.

Arthur and Alice Rozelle left their mark in Webb City. Both were well thought of, and both were masters in their trade. Arthur left his business in good hands as Alice was a strong pioneer of women in business. At her death, in 1972, Alice C. Rozelle was given the title of Dean of County's Journalists.

A special thanks to Alice Crockett Ladd for helping fill in the blanks on this wonderful couple that Webb City claims as part of its heritage.

Sauls, Thomas E.—Centenarian

Thomas E. Sauls was born in 1803. By the time he reached the age of twenty-five, many new things were happening in this great country. One of those happenings was the discovery of lead. This lead was a novelty for Americans who were only familiar with copper at that time. This new discovery captured the attention of many young men who headed west to make their fortunes. The great gold rush for California had not yet occurred. And heading west meant going as far west as Tennessee or Missouri.

In 1828, a young Virginian by the name of Thomas Sauls had learned of the wonderful lead mines of Missouri. He was determined to reach this new phenomenon and cast his fortunes with the other dreamers of America.

To get from Virginia to Missouri, when railroads were unknown, and most of the roadway was a trackless wilderness, was no small task. But young Sauls had the true grit, and one bright summer morning, with all his worldly possessions wrapped up in a yellow cotton handkerchief, he started walking west.

Thomas Sauls was quoted as saying, "I shall never forget the look of sadness, which overspread my mother's face, when I bid her goodbye. She said she would never again meet me on this earth." And she was not mistaken. She died just a few years afterward.

During his journey, Thomas first had to walk north across the Appalachian Mountains to Pittsburgh, Pennsylvania. There he obtained a canoe and, putting his luck in God's hands, set himself afloat down the Ohio River with its rapid current. He stopped in Illinois, and for fifteen years, he put his body and soul into mining.

As word spread about the ore strikes in Southwest Missouri, Thomas once again set out on foot in search of fortune. He arrived in the Six Bulls country, later known as Southwest Missouri, and noticed that the few miners who were obtaining mineral had no way to smelter the ore. The Granby Company backed him as Thomas Sauls constructed the first lead smelter. Known as an air furnace, it was located about two miles south of Parr Hill on Shoal Creek. His only competition came a few years later when Captain Livingston started one on Center Creek. But there was enough business for both furnaces.

It wasn't just the smelter furnace, however, that carried Thomas Sauls' name into history. Thomas was a dedicated military person, having served the government in the Mexican War, the Civil War, and the Seminole Indian War. This is quite an accomplishment, but there's more!

Thomas E. Sauls went on to have the title of centenarian in Webb City, and later in Jasper County. When someone lives for more than one hundred years, that is amazing, but when you add the special contributions of serving in three wars and being a mining pioneer, it adds to the glory.

In November 1904, when Sergeant Thomas E. Sauls was 102, it was reported that he walked to the polls unassisted to vote for the president of the United States, a habit he had established during every election since he was of voting age. He was also one of the few to be able to say that he had personally met and shaken hands with all but two presidents of that time, President Washington (died before Sauls was born) and President Roosevelt (who was elected when Sauls was too old to travel).

Sauls received many honors in his life, one of which was a visit to the Missouri House of Representatives in 1904, where he received three hearty cheers from the assembly. In 1906, during the last year of his life, Judge C. E. Elliott of Oronogo held an honorary celebration for him at the Newland Hotel in Webb City (the judge and Sauls had served in the Civil War together in the same regiment). Sauls' health, however, was failing, so instead of him going to the celebration, the celebration came to him to his home on North Liberty. Sauls' bad eyesight prevented him from seeing his friends, but he managed to recognize everyone by the sound of their voice.

So it seems that Thomas E. Sauls was a walking history book. He lived through much of the United States history and participated in it as well. Can you imagine how much United States history that Thomas E. Sauls experienced from 1800–1906. I think he could have written a great book about the changes in his lifetime. He was a great forefather in Webb City's history.

Thank you, William H. Perry, for sharing this information on Thomas E. Sauls.

Schars, H. K.

H. K. Schars' beautiful home was located at 503 South Madison Street and became the home of Tom and Sharon Taylor, and they had it looking more beautiful than it did in 1909. Through modern progress, the homes on the five hundred block of Madison were being torn down, and the Schars home was looking at being one of those demolished. But the contractor of the new shopping center had some foresight and moved many of the beautiful historical homes to an area west of Third and Madison.

H. K. Schars was the manager of the Forest Lumber Company, located at 307 North Allen (now Main Street). Forest Lumber Company was established in 1894, but Schars didn't take over management until 1906 and did an excellent job.

Schars had an ability to make and retain friends, especially among the influential people of Webb City and Jasper County, which was an asset for the lumber company. Coming from the state of Michigan, Schars was able to learn firsthand about the lumber business in a state where many of the world's largest lumber interests were located.

Forest Lumber Company handled lumber, timber, building materials of all kinds, lathe, shingles, roofing, and everything the builder or contractor would need. And the success of the lumber company was evident in the beautiful home that Schars could afford to live in.

Home of H. K. Schars, 503 South Madison

Schooler, Isaac

Not all politicians fit the stereotype.

Some of the people in our country have forgotten just how lucky they are to be living in this great United States. Sure, there are days that you get disgusted with politics and those in charge, but we still have it better than a lot of other countries.

One of the things that made our country so great is the fact that an ordinary fellow can be in an authoritative position. It once was an honor to hold those positions, but lately, those honors have been tarnished.

In 1857, Isaac and Sarah DeHart Schooler moved into Jasper County. Isaac was the son of John Schooler, who was an Ohio state representative. Following in his father's footsteps, Isaac became involved in his community and became a judge. His farming was his life, but being a judge was very important to Isaac.

Isaac and Sarah had two sons who followed their father and grandfather's lead. John N. Schooler became a member of the eastern Jasper County legislature. John was a Republican and an honorary member of the thirty-second general assembly of the state of Missouri. The second son, William R. Schooler, became a judge, just like his dad.

In 1869, Isaac's brother, Samuel, moved to the Jasper County area. He served the county as tax collector. Samuel's son, E. Lee Schooler, did not follow along the political path of his family; instead he became very active in the mining industry, for which Jasper County was well known. Lee was the superintendent of the American Zinc and Lead Smelting Company, Carthage Lead and Zinc Company, Victor Mining Company, Ashcraft & Reynolds Mining Company and handled many mining enterprises for Allen Hardy.

Some have the opinion that only lazy men seek an office of politics, but those particular individuals have never felt the frustration or the exhaustion of being a politician trying to help the ungrateful. Now I admit there are a few out there who give their positions bad reputations, but politicians should not be categorized. Stand behind your representatives. Vote in the election.

If you have had a politician in your family history, be proud and let the world know that your ancestor helped to build this glorious country we live in.

Slaughter, Melville S.—Doctor

We've had many stories on the ancestors of Webb City, but this time, we are going to pay tribute to one of our legends!

The *Webster Dictionary* states that a legend is "a notable person whose deeds or exploits are much talked about." Well, this definitely fits the description of our subject, Dr. Melville S. Slaughter.

Melville S. Slaughter came to Missouri from Iowa where his family was some of the original settlers. His grandfather J. F. Slaughter was born in Ohio in 1820 but became one of those first settlers in Jasper County, Iowa, where he married his wife, Malinda. They lived on their farm until their deaths in 1901 and 1902.

Malinda came from a family of longevity as her father lived to eighty, and her mother lived to be seventy-eight. Malinda herself lived to be ninety-three.

J. F. and Malinda had a son named Z. T. Slaughter, who was born in Jasper County, Iowa. He married Margaret Wagner, who moved from Pennsylvania with her parents to the wild area of Iowa. She met and married Z. T. in August of 1861.

Z. T. and Margaret had seven children, one of which was Melville. Melville had five brothers and one sister. Growing up on a cattle ranch didn't change Melville's dream of becoming a doctor. He attended Iowa State College at Grinnell and then transferred to the School of Osteopathy in Kirksville, Missouri. He graduated in June of 1907. That was quite a year for Melville because he not only graduated in June, but he opened his first office in the McCorkle building on Main Street of Webb City. He then married Myrtle V. Shreve in September. Myrtle was from Trenton, Missouri, and her father, David G. Shreve, was a railroad conductor.

Melville and Myrtle had one son, Melville Scott Slaughter, born January 2, 1910. But that's not what makes Dr. Slaughter a legend. His fame comes from the fact that many of Webb City's citizens born from 1907 up until the 1950s can claim to have been brought into this world by Dr. Slaughter.

Dr. Slaughter stayed in Webb City even when the mining business left, and Webb City was on shaky ground. His office was located in the Wagner Building at 205 West Daugherty. His home was at 208 North College Street and also the 815 West Fourth Street.

Another step in his fame is that he served on the Webb City School Board from 1921 until 1943, a total of twenty-two years. That was the record until last year (1994) when Terry James was re-elected, and he now holds the honor of serving on the school board the longest (does that make Terry James a legend in his own time?).

Dr. Melville Slaughter also served on the city council but did not enjoy the politics involved. He was also a member of the Yeomen of America and the Elks and, for many years, served on the Webb City Commercial Club.

Another claim to fame for Dr. Slaughter was the organization of the first official high school football team on September 28, 1908, with Dr. Slaughter as the coach. After the first season, it was stated that Webb City had too strong of a team. Then it was stated:

> Owing to the fact that the other high schools had formed an agreement not to play the Webb City team, it was necessary for the Webb City team to get games with teams farther from home, which were stronger than any of the teams of the surrounding towns. In all of the games, Webb City carried their share of victories and closed the season very successfully.

There have been many great doctors in Webb City and the surrounding area, and I don't mean to diminish their good works as I brag on Dr. Slaughter. But he holds a special place in my heart as he delivered my husband, Stan Newby, on May 28, 1948, and that must be Stan's claim to fame!

A note received after this article appeared in the paper:

> *Dear Ms. Newby, Your recent column in the Sentinel was passed on to me by my cousin Mary Curtis James Browning. I enjoyed reading about Dr. Slaughter. My family thought he was the finest doctor who ever lived. My mother Lorraine Carmody Terry was working as his receptionist when she met my father, Paul Terry in the early 30's. He must have been one of those doctors who are excellent at diagnosing and also skillful with their treatments. The only time I remember seeing him was in about 1944 when mother was bitten by a dog. She went back almost daily for several weeks. The bite was quite severe and this was surely before antibiotics. At that time, Dr. Slaughter was perturbed about daylight savings time. That is relevant to nothing at all, just my recollection of him. You may get more input on him since the paper has been published and perhaps enough material for another column. I always enjoy the clippings I get*

*from your paper and look forward to more in the future. Sincerely, Karen Terry Perdue.
P.S. I am first cousins to that "living legend" Terry James!*

815 West Fourth

208 North College

Smith, Fredrick—Judge

Before the Civil War had even begun, Missouri was being torn apart by violence and disorder as proslavery forces tried to win Kansas and Missouri to their side.

Missouri, from the very beginning, claimed to be neutral but stayed in the Union, which made some proslavery forces feel that Missouri was sympathizing with the North.

After the war broke out, most of the Missouri population stayed loyal to the federal government, largely due to the activity of strong unionists like Francis P. Blair.

The state convention, which first met in 1861, voted against seceding from the Union. But as usually happens in wartime, nothing stays the same. The governor, C. F. Jackson, was a Southern sympathizer, and it didn't take long for the convention to depose the governor. They set up a provisional government headed by H. R. Gamble.

This next part is from the memories of a Confederate Civil War vet named Frederick A. Smith. It was in the spring of 1861, as near as Smith can recall, when the event took place. The state legislature, harassed by Union forces, had fled to Neosho and had set up temporary headquarters in the old log courthouse. General Sterling Price's army was camped in the vicinity, and young Smith, a member of a volunteer company from Charlton County, was also a soldier in Price's army.

"I wasn't a member of the legislation, of course," said Smith in a 1930 interview.

"Before the war, we had organized a mock legislature in Charlton County, and I was the one who wrote and introduced the resolution for the secession of Missouri.

"Well, while the legislation was in session at Neosho, a man named Andy Campbell, told Price about my writing the resolution in Charlton County. The result was they asked me to write a similar one. I did and they passed it!" Neosho was declared the Missouri State capital.

What an important episode in the life of young Smith, but the resolution was ineffective as Missouri was kept in the Union. But Smith, at the age of twenty-one, had already led a full and active life, having survived many battles such as Carthage, Springfield (Wilson Creek), Cross Hollows, Pea Ridge, Pittsburgh Landing, Corinth, and Vicksburg.

Smith was taken prisoner near Steelville, Missouri, as he was trying to make it home. He had been one of only thirteen to survive the battle at Vicksburg. His captor was General Mullins, who just happened to have been a prisoner of war under Smith's custody and, as soon as possible, ordered Smith's release and escort home.

After the war and a little moving around, Smith received a grant of land in Oronogo, Missouri, and he settled down for many years. In 1935, at the age of ninety-five, Smith was recognized as the only remaining Civil War vet in Jasper County.

In his long life, Frederick Smith had the distinction of being a city marshal in Pierce City, a sheriff in Lawrence County, and a long-time justice of the peace and lawyer in Oronogo.

The last ten years of his life were spent in the home of his son, Paul Smith, 1305 West Sixth, Webb City. But he passed away in the Confederate home in Higginsville, Missouri, after residing there only a few months.

Having been born in Keytesville, Missouri, in 1840, Frederick Smith had been a lifelong resident of Missouri. He received an honorable grave in the Confederate cemetery in Higginsville, and he was buried in the gray uniform of the Confederate soldier.

What a surprise to find out we had such a legendary figure living in Oronogo and Webb City. And to find out that for a short time, Neosho was our acting state capitol while the legislature hid from Union forces.

There were more heroes in the Smith family as A. Chester Smith served our country in World War I, and his son, Chester A. Smith, served in WWII and was held a prisoner of war by the Germans for fourteen months.

You know the Smith name is one of the hardest names to do genealogy on, along with names like Jones. But Greg Smith has quite a legacy in his great-grandfather and a name to be proud of. Thanks, Greg, for taking the time to share this wonderful information and memories of Judge Frederick A. Smith

Snodgrass, Hamilton

William Snodgrass was born in Tennessee, and his wife, Elizabeth S. Gray, was born in Pennsylvania. They both came to live in Indiana with the migration of their families. In 1854, William's family moved again to Fort Dodge, Iowa, and in 1868, they moved again to Jasper County, Missouri, settling on a three-hundred-acre farm southwest of Carthage.

William and Elizabeth's son, Hamilton Snodgrass, was born in Randolph County, Indiana, on August 23, 1833. His education was in a small log cabin not far from his home. He also attended school in Iowa. He married, August 17, 1865, at age thirty-two to Menttis E. Karr in Webster

County, Iowa. Mentiss was the daughter of Moses and Elizabeth Shaeffer Karr. When Hamilton's parents decided to move to Missouri, 1868, Hamilton and Mentiss went with them.

Hamilton was in the grocery business, and he settled in Webb City, August 6, 1877, where he started a grocery store. Hamilton and Mentiss had three children: Ida C. Snodgrass married Jesse Zook of the newspaper business; Dicie F. Snodgrass married Walter L. Spurgeon of Webb City, a grocer; and William A. Snodgrass married Jessie Motley in 1895.

William A. Snodgrass became interested in the newspaper business, and he and his father, Hamilton, purchased the *Webb City Register* in 1895. Born in Jasper County, William graduated from Webb City High School. He began his newspaper career under Jesse A. Zook, editor of the *Webb City Register* and his brother-in-law. Willian served on the school board.

Spracklen, Edwin E.

As you sit and gaze at some of the old photos in your family album, the name at the bottom of the photos jumps up at you. It is a beautiful script, and it says "Spracklen." The signature of the best! A photograph by Spracklen was a piece of art. Edwin E. Spracklen was an artist in his profession.

Edwin E. Spracklen was born December 7, 1853, on the Isle of Guernsey, British Channel. His parents were Samuel and Elizabeth (Evelich) Spracklen of England. The family moved to London, Ontario, Canada, when Edwin was only six years old.

While in Canada, Edwin attended a common school. As a youth of nineteen, Edwin crossed the border and went to Chicago, Illinois. After training in the profession of photography, Edwin went on the road as a traveling photographer. He traveled around thirty-two of the states of the Union doing stereoscopic views.

In 1880, Edwin found himself in Webb City, and he liked what he found. He sold his traveling outfit and settled down permanently. His first place of business was in a building at the corner of Allen (Main) and Main (Broadway) Streets. He was in a building owned by Dr. Donohue. He kept his business there for eighteen years.

Then in 1901, Edwin purchased a lot at the northwest corner of Webb and Daugherty Streets. He built a business block to hold his photo gallery, and he leased out the rest of the building. Edwin was a highly artistic photographer, and his fame grew.

It's not very often that a politician is highly thought of, but Edwin was able to accomplish the unbelievable. He was mayor of Webb City in 1898. He won the campaign on the Law and Order Proposition. To show how unique Edwin was, he actually tried to fulfill every promise he made to constituents. He worked diligently to accomplish the Law and Order Proposition. Edwin served on the city council for six years, school board for three years, and park board for six years.

He was not only politically involved, Edwin was involved socially as well. He belonged to the Commercial Club, chamber of commerce, Masons, Woodmen of the World, and served as a colonel in the Eighth Missouri Uniform Rank. Edwin had served as a bugler in the seventh Battalion Light Infantry of the Canadian Forces.

In 1884, Edwin married Mollie Rice of Jasper County. Mollie was the daughter of Joseph and Flovilla Rice. Edwin and Mollie had six children born to their union. Marvin R. Spracklen was a corporal in the Thirteenth Engineers in World War I. Bernard B. Spracklen (Bun) married Mary Alice Sportsman. E. E. Spracklen (Jack) served in the First World War as a lieutenant and brevet captain. Mary Elizabeth Spracklen became Mrs. Mary Ball and the mother of Harry Raymond Ball. Maurine Spracklen and Grace Spracklen were both schoolteachers. Marvin, Maurine, and Grace never married but lived in the family home at 204 North Webb.

The name of E. E. Spracklen will continue to live on as we preserve the precious photographs that he took. Photographs that immortalize the image forever also immortalize the image of the photographer.

I would like to give a special thanks to Wally Spracklen for the information about his grandfather E. E. Spracklen. Wally is the son of E. E. Spracklen, who was the son of E. E. Spracklen. Wally also had a brother named Edwin E. Spracklen. So the name lives on in generations as it does in photographs.

During a fifty-fifth birthday celebration for Webb City, Spracklen described his first view of Webb City in 1880. He recalled that the only way out of town on the south side was through a farm fence. There were only two brick buildings and lots of tents. There were no trees—all prairie land, except for John Webb's orchard. Spracklen was a noted photographer in preserving Webb City's history.

204 North Webb

Starkweather, Bert

Born in Lawrence, Kansas, April 20, 1865, his parents, John M. and Mary J. Moore Starkweather, moved to Kansas in 1862 from Albany, New York, and Independence, Missouri. John died in 1871, and Mary passed in 1883.

Bert had been employed in a local clothing store as a clerk, but when he was eighteen, and his mother passed, and he was on his own. In 1885, he made the decision to head to Pueblo, Colorado, to work in a clothing store for four years. The year 1889 found young Bert in Webb City, Missouri, clerking for the well-known Humphrey's Company. He worked there for five years and went to work for Sam Morris.

Wanting to own his own store, Bert Starkweather and a friend, John T. Albert, opened a firm under the name Starkweather & Albert in the Stevison Building, 216 North Allen Street. In 1910, they moved to new location and, in 1911, opened a second store in Independence, Kansas. Starkweather was a member of the Presbyterian Church.

Starkweather passed away January 18, 1950, in his home, at 215 South Liberty Street, following a three-year illness. He is buried in the Webb City Cemetery. No wife or children survived him, just his business.

Starkweather and Albert, 216 North Allen (Main) Street

Starr, Jess

In May of 1865, in Vermillion County, Illinois, "a Starr is born!" Jesse G. Starr's parents were Simon P. and Maria Starr. Jesse was one of six children, and he was industrious from birth. By the time Jesse was eleven, Simon made a major decision in his life to move the family to Pittsburg, Kansas. Being a farmer and merchant in Illinois, Simon continued that profession in Kansas and was quite successful.

Jesse couldn't wait to finish school, to head out into the working world. At the age of fifteen, he got a job with the Lanyon Smelting Company in Pittsburg. He made good money for a young lad, $1 a day, which was high pay in 1880.

Throughout the next nine years, Jesse gradually made his way up the ladder through promotions. In 1889, he was transferred to the S. H. Lanyon Company in Aurora, Missouri. His new duties included being in charge of the ore buying.

Jesse made the move to Aurora with his new bride, Myrtle Spicer Starr, a native of Pittsburg, Kansas. They stayed there for about eight years when Jesse moved his wife and daughter, Elsie, to Joplin. He was now working with Lanyon & Sons Smelting Company. Then in 1906, at the age of forty-one, Jesse, along with E. V. and Dee Lanyon, organized the Lanyon, Starr Smelting Company. They built a large plant in Bartlesville, Oklahoma. The business was exceedingly prosperous with Lanyon as president and Jesse Starr as vice president and in charge of the ore buying.

A year before the organization of the Lanyon, Starr Smelting Company, Jesse had been instrumental in organizing the Conqueror Trust Company, of which he became a chartered member and vice president.

When the smelting company closed down in 1910, Jesse then devoted all of his time and energy into the trust company. Jesse's partner in the trust company was William Houk who was president of Conqueror Trust Company until his death in 1927, at which time Jesse became the president.

In 1928, Conqueror Trust Company consolidated with First National Bank, and Jesse Starr continued to serve as president. He sold his holdings in 1929 and established the Starr Investment Company with the following officers: Jesse as president and J. W. Ratcliff as vice president. When the company incorporated, it became the Installment Finance Company, with Ratcliff as president and Starr as vice president.

In 1929, Jesse sold his holdings in the Quinton Smelting Company in Quinton, Oklahoma. There was a large gas well and additional acres used for leasing of gas. The holdings sold for $2 million.

By this time, Jesse felt he had earned some time for rest and relaxation. He spent the winter months in Ephraim, Florida, where he kept a summer home and in Miami, Florida, and he owned apartment houses and business lots.

Jesse Starr was not born with a silver spoon in his mouth, and his success was not accidental. He worked long and hard to obtain his status as a millionaire. He did it without stepping on people; in fact, he was a highly respected individual in the community. He contributed to many charities, and he was active in the community. He belonged to the Masonic Lodge and the Rotary Club.

Now you may be wondering why I would give so much time and attention to someone from Joplin, but there is a connection with Webb City. You see, Jesse's daughter, Elsie, married Roy Teel, owner of the Teel Drug Store in Webb City. And she was the mother of Bob Teel.

Stevison, Lewis J.

The parents of Lewis Stevison were John W. Stevison and Lucinda Howe Stevison of Jackson County, Ohio. John W. Stevison, a farmer, served in the Civil War. His son, Lewis, was born November 3, 1861, in Jackson County, Ohio. The parents died in 1902 and 1894.

Lewis attended school until he reached the age to be able to work, and he was pulled from school to be a farmer. At age nineteen, Lewis went to work as an Ohio coal miner for three years, at which time he went to work in the coal mines in Pittsburg and then Fort Scott, Kansas. In 1886, Lewis J. Stevison arrived in Webb City, Missouri, to begin working in the mines as a pulley boy receiving a dollar and a quarter to pull buckets of ore out of the shafts. It was hard work, eighty feet below ground, but Lewis persevered and managed to save some of his hard-earned money. When he had saved enough money, Lewis bought an interest in a mine and earned enough money that he felt he was ready to take on a bride.

Lewis J. Stevison and Mary P. Hatcher, daughter of H. E. and Melissa Hatcher, were married February 3, 1887.

In 1890, after his mine ceased to produce ore, Lewis, along with Joseph Aylor, Will Coil, and Mack Bergner, leased some lots on the Eleventh Hour land and struck pay dirt. He kept buying interest and working in other mines and finally found himself beyond the reach of poverty and close to reaching the millionaire mark.

In the fall of 1900, Stevison, along with Charles Moore of Joplin, leased some lots in the Conner Lands, south of Webb City. They developed the mine, taking out ore worth $20,000 within a short space of nine months. Then they sold the mine for a tidy sum of $33,000.

In 1901, Stevison secured a lease on the L. H. Baker land, along with a lease on forty acres of the Musslemand Property on which he opened mines on both properties, each bringing in a profit until 1904. In this same time period, he bought seventy acres of the Smallhouse Fee at Neck City and organized the Reliance Mining Company, capitalizing at $300,000, and the company's three properties paid in dividends amounting to $270,000. In 1904, 1905, and 1906, Lewis Stevison, along with James Stewart and a few other prominent men, purchased a mine in Duenweg, Missouri, which proved profitable.

In the spring of 1905, Stevison, along with others, organized the Merchants & Miners Bank of Webb City with a paid-up capital of $50,000. They opened the bank in an old building on Main (Broadway) Street, meanwhile buying a lot at the corner of Daugherty and Allen (Main), where they built a magnificent building which became the home of the Merchants & Miners Bank.

In 1906, Stevison organized the Stevison-Rogers Land and Zinc Company which controlled several hundred acres of rich land and some very good mines.

Lewis and Mary Stevison had six children: Edwin F. Stevison, born April 20, 1888, graduated from Webb City High School, 1907, entered the University of Michigan, and while sailing with some friends at Ann Arbor, the boat overturned, and Edwin died May 12, 1908; Elmer G. Stevison was born March 20, 1891, graduated from Webb City High School, graduated from University of Missouri with the class of 1909; Earl C. Stevison, born July 6, 1893, graduated from Webb City High School and from the Welch Military School in 1911; Clara Stevison, born May 28, 1894, died May 1, 1902; Harold Stevison, born April 27, 1903; and Mary Louise Stevison, born May 26, 1905.

Stevison belonged to the Webb City Lodge 512 of the AF and AM; Chapter RAM; Joplin Commandery, K. T.; and the Webb City Lodge BPOE. He was a Republican. Mary Stevison was a member of the Eastern Star and belonged to the Christian Church.

This brief history of Lewis J. Stevison's career shows clearly that our nation offers every opportunity to men to rise by their own efforts to positions of influence and affluence. He started at the bottom of his chosen career and worked himself up through the ranks with hard work and smart investments. What an inspiration to all.

304 North Ball Street

This is one of my favorite stories of homes in Webb City. Most of the time, we are disappointed when the older homes are left in disrepair, and they remove a front porch or an upper floor. This particular home at 304 North Ball was one of just the opposite. The original home was a single-story home, and the owner, L. J. Stevison, added a second story to his family home after he struck ore. L. J. Stevison came to Webb City in 1886 and acquired a job as a pulley boy, pulling buckets of ore out of the mine. He made $1.25 per day, and within five years, he had saved enough money to get married and start a mining operation of his own. He leased the Eleventh Hour Tract. A neighbor lady recalled the excitement of the day when Stevison rode into town at a fast gallop, stopped in front of the house, and, while running into the house, shouted, "Hey, Molly, we've struck it rich!" He soon added the second story, and the home represented his success.

304 North Ball

A memory from a friend, Bob Chancellor—"I was intrigued by your item on the Stevison house because that is the block I grew up on. We lived at 315 North Roane, which took up the northwest quarter of the block. The big house was on the southeast quarter, and another Stevison lived on the northeast quarter, I think it was one of the sons from whom we bought our house. I think our house was built by the Stevison on the northeast corner for one of his children. The big house we always referred to as the Troxel house, for some years, it was vacant, then Steven Troxel and his mother moved into it. She was a Stevison, I believe, and Steve Troxel still lives in the area and may still live in the house.

"I remember the big house had a greenhouse attached at the back, at the basement level. When the house was vacant, we still could slip into the greenhouse as a hiding place. There also was a huge barn behind it and a concrete block mulch pit, which was another great hiding place for playing hide-and-seek or kick the can. The northeast corner was our playground. It had a low concrete block wall all around it, which was a great place to sit and talk and to watch pickup baseball games which, we played in the middle of Ball Street.

"In the alley behind our house (315 North Roane), there was a spectacular wall along the back line of the lot and the alley, topped with large mineral specimens. According to Google Maps, that wall is still there and worth looking at. Our yard had a large vacant side yard, enough for football, and lots of trees." All gone now, probably due to Dutch elm disease.

Thank you, Bob, for that trip down memory lane. It was very descriptive, and we almost felt like we were there with you!

Stewart, Joseph C.

Joseph C. Stewart was born in Blair County, Pennsylvania, April 19, 1844, of thrifty Scotch Irish and German ancestry. His parents were Robert and Charlotte Flack Stewart, early pioneers of Pennsylvania. Joseph finished school at the age of sixteen. His first jobs were those of store and post office clerk, as well as working for the railway station. Within a year of graduation, the Civil War began. As a dedicated American and believing that all men are created equal, Joseph served two years as a soldier, enlisting in a Pennsylvania regiment.

A young man with a lot of ambition, Joe was a little restless as he searched for what he wanted to do with his life. He decided to try his luck in the goldfields of Montana in 1867. He had moderate success in the goldfields, but hardships along left him with not much money. He made a trip back home to Pennsylvania to get the feel of home before he ventured off again. This time, he headed for Webb City, Missouri, to find out about mining, arriving in Webb City on February 1, 1877. Webb City was in the early beginning days of development, with a few houses and businesses scattered about. Without much money, Joseph C. Stewart found work with his uncle, S. L. Manker, in a grocery store, and then he tested out the mining. He worked in the lead smelter until he had enough money to invest in a business; nothing could stop him.

Investing in the Center Creek Mining Company, Joseph Stewart started out as the assistant superintendent and soon became the general manager, a position he carried for quite some time. The Center Creek Mining Company was capitalized at $1,500,000 of which one-third was treasury stock. With time, Joseph and his brother William C. Stewart held the controlling interest. The company was invested in 160 acres of Webb City land, a 40-acre tract north of Carterville, and 10 acres on the south of Webb City. These extensive tracts of land were remarkably rich in high-grade ore, and according to history, John C. Webb made his discovery of mineral upon the 160 acres of

Webb City land first described. Joseph purchased some of the land, and it had a continuous output of valuable ore, nearly $9,000,000. Joseph and his brother organized the Exchange Bank in 1878, and Joseph acted as president until it merged with the National Bank, which eventually merged with the Webb City Bank in 1906. William and Joseph started the Stewart Brothers Lumber Company (later bought out by the Matthews Lumber Company). The Stewart brothers still had a lumberyard in Joplin, Peabody, Lincolnville, Kansas. Joseph also owned farming acreage in Kansas and Missouri. He was the organizer of the Webb City Iron Works, becoming president and the heaviest stockholder. This business eventually merged with the Webb City and Carterville Foundry and Machine Works.

Joe bought up mining property in Missouri and Kansas. He started out with almost nothing but soon proved to be a self-made successful man.

In 1879, Joseph C. Stewart, at the age of thirty-five, decided to get married. He married Hortense D. Street, who was born in Salem, Iowa, in 1850. Hortense was twenty-nine at the time of their marriage, but she had been busy with her education. She had graduated from Monticello Seminary in 1871 and began her teaching career. She taught school in Lincoln, Nebraska; Council Bluff, Iowa; and also in Webb City, Missouri.

Being active in the community was important to Joe. He was a member of the Presbyterian Church. He was a chartered member and first officer of the Masons, Wilmot Chapter, RAM, president of the school board. He was a pronounced Republican and was one of the delegates to the national convention which met in Chicago in 1888, which nominated General Benjamin Harrison for president. Joseph refused to enter the political field to run for office. He did, however, serve four years on the Webb City School Board, serving as president in 1899. Joseph was a member of the Webb City Lodge 512, AF and AM, and past commander of Ascension Commandery, Number 39, Knights Templar of Joplin. He was an active member of the Webb City Commercial Club.

Joe and Hortense had three children: Cora Latta Stewart, born in 1884, married to Thomas McCrosky; Robert F. (named after his grandfather), born in 1886; Joseph Edgar Stewart (named after his father), born in 1891.

Cora Latta Stewart married Thomas J. McCroskey, and they settled in Knoxville, Tennessee. Robert F. Stewart became a lawyer after graduating from the University of Michigan in 1910. Robert and his wife, Dorothy D. Doane, built a beautiful home at 805 West Fourth Street and, in 1923, moved to Los Angeles, California. Joseph Edgar Stewart moved to St. Louis to finish his training as a physician. He became very well known in his field.

Joseph and Hortense had a beautiful home on the northwest corner of Broadway and Liberty Streets, 301 West Broadway. After Joseph C. Stewart passed away in 1906, at the age of sixty-two, Hortense stayed in the home until the 1920s when she went to live with her daughter in Tennessee. She sold the house to John T. Steele, who turned the house into a funeral home. When Hortense passed away in 1926, at the age of seventy-six, she was brought back to Webb City, and her funeral was held at the Steele Undertaking Company in the home she lived in for over forty years and loved so much.

Hortense was active in the community, just like her husband. She was a member of the Civic Club, the Princella Club, Women's Study Club, Social Club, and an active member of the Presbyterian Church.

Cora Latta Stewart McCroskey died in Knoxville, Tennessee, at the age of fifty-five, March 7, 1939. She was a graduate of Webb City High School, class of 1908.

Joseph Edgar Stewart, a prominent physician in St. Louis, Missouri, died a few days before his sister, Cora, on March 5, 1939, at the age of forty-eight. Both died of heart ailments.

Joseph C. Stewart was considered an acknowledged leader in all business and public enterprises. His judgment was highly regarded. It was a lucky day for Webb City when Joseph C. Stewart, noted pioneer miner, decided to try his luck at mining in a little town in Missouri where his uncle, S. L. Manker, had settled.

305 West Broadway Street, home of Joseph
and Hortense Stewart until 1920.

Became Steele Mortuary, owned by John T. Steele.
Became Hedge Lewis Mortuary 1947.

Stewart, Robert F.

Robert F. Stewart, firstborn son of Joseph C. Stewart was born in 1886. He graduated from Webb City High School in 1903. He went to college at the University of Missouri for three years and took a year off to work with his father before switching to the law department of the University of Michigan, from which he graduated with the class of 1910. Robert returned to Webb City to start his legal career with a brilliant young lawyer, S. E. Bates. Their office was in the Wagner Building

Robert F. Stewart married Dorothy Doane on June 25, 1910 in Kansas City, Missouri. They built a beautiful home at 805 West Fourth Street. Dorothy was the daughter of L. F. Doane, a prominent architect, well known for his work in Kansas City. L. F. Doane passed away in 1903.

Being active in the community sat well with Robert's career. He was a member of the Presbyterian Church, a staunch Republican, a member of the BPOE (Elks), the Masons, the Phi Alpha Delta, the YMCA, and the Webb City Commercial Club. Robert served as director of the Webb City and Carterville Foundry and Machine Company and secretary and treasurer of the Center Creek Mining Company. Well thought of in the community, Robert had a host of friends and was a great leader of the city.

In 1923, Robert and his wife, Dorothy, moved to Los Angeles, California, to work as a trust officer at the Bank of America. Robert passed away in June of 1934, at the age of forty-eight. He had two daughters and two sons: Elizabeth H. Stewart; Mary D. Stewart; Doane Stewart; and Robert F. Stewart.

Stewart, James P.

A native of Blair County, Pennsylvania, born March 24, 1845, to Matthew and Mary Cryder Stewart. James was a year younger than his cousin Joseph C. Stewart, listed above.

Starting early in life working on the farm, James headed out into the working world at an early age as a clerk in a general store owned by Henry Thatcher in Martinsburg, Pennsylvania. He moved on after a year and found employment with E. B. Isett Iron Works in Sabbath Rest, Pennsylvania, doing clerical work and being assistant manager. With the onset of the Civil War, James, being devoted to the Union, signed up under the Company G, Twelfth Pennsylvania Volunteer Cavalry. He was released after thirty-five months, with honors of never being wounded or taken prisoner.

Returning home after the war, James engaged in merchandising in Sinking Valley, Pennsylvania, forming a partnership with D. P. Tussey. Two years later, he sold his interest in the business to Mr. Tussey and left with his cousin Joseph Stewart to try his hand at mining for gold in Montana. After three years and bad health, James returned home to Pennsylvania and started back in the mercantile business, venturing into steel and ironwork. He went to Charter Oak, Iowa, and organized the H. M. Moore & Company Bank, serving as a clerk for a year.

In 1888, James made the move to Webb City, Missouri, where his cousin Joseph had organized the Exchange Bank and was serving as president. James worked as a cashier until the bank merged with the National Bank, and he served as cashier of the new organization until 1910. At this time, he was elected president of the Mineral Belt Bank.

James was of the Democratic Party but not too active, spending his time on his work. James had married in Altoona, Pennsylvania, on December 7, 1877, to Kate A. Moore. She is of the Presbyterian faith.

In Webb City, James held the reputation of being courteous and obliging.

The J. P. Stewart home was located on the northwest corner of Pennsylvania and First Streets.

Thirty-Two South Pennsylvania, 1888

Stone, William Ernest

William Stone was born in England in 1889. His brother W. T. Stone had moved to America and became a veterinarian. William followed him, and at the age of twenty-three, in 1912, he married Anna D. Davis of Oronogo. They owned a small neighborhood grocery store before moving to Webb City and opening Stone's Grocery & Meat Market on East Daugherty Street. They were in business for several decades. William was active in the community, serving on the board of directors at the Merchants & Miners Bank and on the school board

William and Anna gave the ultimate sacrifice for their country with the deaths of their two sons during WWII. Both were air force pilots and died within five months of each other. The only other child was Mary Stone Osborne. She was a dedicated Webb Citian who was active in many Webb City projects and a dedicated volunteer.

Tappana Family

The Tappana family legend tells of the first Tappanas to come to America. It seems that there was much religious turmoil in Spain during the early 1800s. Lands were being taken from families, wars were numerous, and many lives were taken. So the head of the Tappanas brought his family, consisting of two sons and one daughter, to America for safety. Then he went back to Spain, close to Madrid, to try to recover the family land. It ended sadly as he was beheaded. But his family was safe here in America.

One of his sons, Charles E. Tappana, who was born in 1836 in Spain, married Mary Sigler from Peoria, Illinois. They lived in Granby, where all eight of their children were born: Arthur E., Don Carlos, Leslie V., Claude Leroy, Floyd L., Walter, Audra, and Katie May.

Arthur E. lived at 831 North Oak in Webb City. He had been a grocery man most of his life. Arthur married Mary Francis Vaughn. They had two daughters and one son: Lorraine, Christina, and Arthur Charles.

Don Carlos was born in 1877 and married Ollie McAboy. Don Carlos had an excellent career of repairing sewing machines at a time when Webb City had several factories to keep him in business. They had three daughters (I only have their married names): Mrs. W. F. Collier, Mrs. Edith Miller, and Mrs. Wendell Dooley. Don Carlos was an active community person. He served as the city assessor from 1930 to 1936. He was also a justice of the peace.

Leslie V. married Maude Sutten. They had five sons and one daughter: Burl, Herman A., Don A., Leslie (Jobe), Vernon, and Betty Lou. Their family home was at 804 North Madison.

Claude Leroy (Roy) was born in 1881 and was employed by the Southwest Missouri Railroad Company as a conductor for eighteen years. Then he started his own collection agency. He worked for the Webb City Post Office for seven years, then opened a small grocery store in Brooklyn Heights. Roy was married to Alte Lee Hutchinson in 1909. They had two sons, William and Robert, and one daughter, Geraldine. Their son Robert[*] was a World War II casualty as he fought for his country. Robert was also a songwriter with several published songs before his death.

Floyd L. (Dude) was born in 1884. Floyd was also a justice of the peace. He didn't have any children.

Walter Tappana married Lena Toutz from Webb City. They had five sons and three daughters: Walter Levis (Buck), Truman, Paul, Eugene (Gene), James, Pearl, Mary, and Mrs. Dan White.

---

[*] Robert Lamont Tappana graduated from Webb City High School in 1939. He died September 8, 1945 (age twenty-three), while serving on the staff of the Admiral Chester Nimitz.

Audra Tappana Cole had four daughters and three sons: Tressa, Crystal, Mrs. Aloe Yates, Mrs. Valentine Shuey, Floyd, Edwin, and Harlen.

The other daughter of Charles and Mary was Katie May, who was born in 1874 but died at a young age on October 10, 1888.

The first generation of Tappanas was born in Granby. Similarly the second generation was all born in Webb City. Now the number of Tappanas has continued to grow, but space limits the naming of them all. There are still third and fourth-generation Tappanas in the area. The Tappanas have been in Webb City since Charles and Mary moved here in 1887.

Tappana was a royal name in Spain, with much land and a castle. The Tappanas have a heritage to be proud of. We in Webb City are proud of their American heritage, as they have a part of Webb City's history, and you can tell they have added to the population growth.

A special thanks to the many family members who helped me fill in the blanks and told me of the family legend. You have plenty to be proud of.

Teel, Roy—Teel Drug Store

Susan A. Murratta was born in Springfield, Kentucky, in 1831. At the age of fifty-four, her husband passed away, and being very adventurous, she made the move from Kentucky to Jasper County in 1886 with three of her four children. In 1893, they moved to Webb City.

Susan's son James, who was twenty-eight years old at the time, was a druggist at Murratta Drug Store, located at 110 North Main Street. He had two sisters living in the area, Mrs. Belle Yankey and Sue Marratta. They bought a home at 404 North Ball Street. Life seemed to be going pretty well for the prosperous family, until July of 1903, when some fireworks exploded at the drugstore and badly burned James's face. He never really recovered from that accident.

In 1908, at the age of seventy-seven, Susan passed away, and James continued on with the drugstore. He also belonged to the Masons Scottish Rites, Elks, AF and AM, and Knights Templar. But his health did not seem to improve. Then in 1911, the doctors decided they needed to amputate James's foot. It took two surgeries from which James did not recover. He died at the young age of forty-six.

Roy Teel then purchased the Murratta Drug Store, and the name changed to the Teel Drug Store. Many memories of the Teel Drug Store have been shared. It seems that Roy Teel is most fondly remembered by Troop 25, of which he was made an honorary member. This honor was bestowed upon him for his kindness and a little for his generosity toward the troop with free ice cream.

The Teel family moved to Webb City from Illinois during the early days of mining development in the area. The children consisted of Catherine, Bob, Lee, Flora, Florence, Elizabeth, Maude, and Roy.

Roy not only was known for his drugstore, he also operated the Roy J. Teel Real Estate, Loans and Insurance, located at 117 East Broadway. A man of many talents.

Teel Drug Store, corner of Daugherty and Main

Tholburn, Walter

Twenty-seven-year-old Joseph Tholborn, along with his young wife, Mary, and their new baby, Walter, born October 23, 1846, left England for the land of milk and honey. Joseph knew the decision to leave his homeland was a major stepping stone in his life, but as soon as he arrived in the United States, he had an even greater decision—where to settle in this new land?

The Tholborns landed in New York, and tragedy struck as Mary passed away. So Joseph and little Walter went on to Canada and Wisconsin but couldn't find the comfort they were seeking. Venturing farther west, they arrived in Cole County, Missouri, in 1852, when Walter was six years old. Jefferson City seemed to be a good place to raise a young boy, but when he was twenty years old, Walter wanted to travel. He headed to Newton County, Missouri, and dabbled in agriculture. While he was there, he met and courted the young and lovely Hila Katherine Harris, and they were married in 1870. With a family to consider, Walter decided to change from agriculture to the mining industry.

In 1872, Walter got the opportunity to work in the Murphy & Davis Smelter, so they moved to Joplin, Missouri. After five years of working in smelting, Walter figured he would like to try his hand at actual mining, so he went to work as superintendent of the North Creek Mining Company. It was impressive that Walter started out this new part of his career as superintendent.

It didn't take long for Walter to make a name for himself, as he started the first steam concentrator works in this part of the country. Walter found himself being sought after by many different mining companies and settled for Short Creek Mines, which were owned by Pat Murphy and Salem L. Cheney. Cheney couldn't help but notice that Walter had another talent, and that was agriculture so convinced Walter to manage the Cheney Farms, which Walter really enjoyed.

Torn between his two loves of agriculture and mining, Walter made a big decision that mining was where the money was, so he moved his family to Webb City, which was in its seventh year of the mining frenzy.

At the age of forty-one, Walter made a big move in his life once again and sold all of his mining properties and went into a completely different walk of life—he opened a livery barn. Walter really liked his new business, which seemed to be financially profitable. But the hands of fate can deal you a mighty blow, and three years later (1900), a fire burned down the livery barn. Walter lost all of his stock and equipment, along with the barn, and Walter found himself completely wiped out, with no money and no business.

This might have been more than the average man could handle, but Walter went to work for the Interurban Streetcar Line as a motorman. As soon as his life was stable once again, Walter made yet another career change as he became a salesman for a powder company.

Walter had enjoyed a pretty diversified and challenging life, and as he neared the age of sixty, he couldn't resist another change in his life. In 1906, Walter had the opportunity to become postmaster of Webb City. Now his life was complete, and he felt contented to sit back and enjoy this new career.

Walter and Hila raised their family of two boys and two girls at 109 North Oronogo. The children's names were Joseph Oliver Tholborn, Cora Tholborn, Ethel Tholborn, and Walter (Harry) Tholborn. Joseph and his wife, Anna Lee, lived in Kansas City, where Joseph worked for Frisco Railroad Company. When he retired, they moved back to Webb City and lived at 810 Broadway. Cora married W. E. Moore, who was a cashier at the Webb City Bank, and Ethel married a well-known businessman in Joplin named E. A. Mattes.

Walter's son Walter (Harry) Tholborn, who was named after his father, was married to Maude, and they had three daughters: Dorothy, Vivian, and Josephine. The family resided at 421 South Madison. Harry began his career at the post office alongside his father. Not content with only one career, Harry began breeding pedigree Jersey cows and became well known in this field. Not to be idle, Harry served as county assessor, was the mayor of Webb City in 1928, and when he passed away in 1946, he was serving as the president of the Webb City School Board.

What a great family to have in Webb City. The Tholborns were an asset to our community and worth mentioning as part of the builders of our past.

Thralls, Richard

Richard Thralls, at the young age of seven, came to Missouri with his parents, Charles Jacob Thralls (Kentucky) and Susan Cameron Thralls (Kentucky) in 1869. His father died within two years of arriving in Bates County, Missouri. Richard attended school until he was fourteen years of age. He helped with the farm for the next four years, and when he reached the age of eighteen, his ambition to do something with his life encouraged him to move on. He leased 160 acres of land and went to work. Working his land from 1880–1903 in Butler, Missouri, Richard built up a prosperous business as a dealer in meat and in livestock. Still having that spirit of adventure,

Richard disposed of his interests and moved to Webb City, Missouri, and embarked in the retail grocery business.

He opened a store in the west end of Webb City for five years and moved on to a new location at 202 South Allen Street. Being organized and self-motivated, Richard had an immediate success in his business.

Richard married Ella Evans, October 25, 1887, in Butler, Missouri. They were the parents of three children: Zoe, born in Butler, December 6, 1888; Vance, born February 9, 1890; and Mabel, born May 22, 1892.

The description of Richard Thralls in the *History of Jasper County* states, "He is industrious, enterprising, and energetic. He was active in the development and promotion of the mercantile interests of Webb City and numbered among the most leading grocers of the city."

His daughter Zoe Thralls went on to be as ambitious as her father and left her own mark in history.

Thralls, Zoe

I have often touched a bit on the name of a lady that I have a great admiration for—Zoe Agnes Thralls.

I've known for a long time that Zoe had published a geography book, *The Teaching of Geography*, and wondered, exactly how do you write a geography book? I wasn't making fun of Zoe, just intrigued at how you would become an author of a geography book.

Let me start off by telling you a little about Zoe Agnes Thralls. She was born in 1888 to Isaac Victor (Richard) Thralls and Helen (Ella) Evans Thralls. They moved to Webb City from Butler, Missouri, in 1903 (Zoe would have been fifteen). She had a brother, Vance (a grocer), and a sister, Mabel (Goldsberry). Their family lived at 124 North Liberty.

Zoe graduated from Webb City High School in 1907. She went on to Springfield to attend the State Teachers College as her desire in life was to become a teacher. In checking her education, I found out that Zoe also went to the University of Chicago.

When listing her teaching credits, it is obvious that this lady was going somewhere in life. In a time era when most administrative positions were held by men, Zoe was the principal of a junior high at the State Manual Training Normal School, Pittsburg, Kansas. She was also the professor of geography at the Normal School, Pittsburg, Kansas.

I then started researching the book that I knew Zoe had written and was surprised to find out that the one book was one of many. I know it may seem boring to list all of her books, but she has a wonderful accomplishment of publications. There are probably more than the ones I have found (her books are selling on the Internet). The earliest printing I found was:

The Geography of Pennsylvania, published by MacMillan Co., New York, in 1927.

She coauthored a book with Edwin Redder in 1931, a 441-page book, *Geography in the Elementary School*, published by New York/Chicago Rand McNally & Co.

In 1932, an article by Zoe Thralls is listed in the *NEA Journal*, "The Theme of Modern Geography."

In 1938, she wrote *The British Isles*.

Making a Living in Our Southland, 1940

The World: Its Lands and People, 1948

"The Globe Is an Essential Geographic Tool at Every Level" was another entry in the *NEA Journal* in 1957.

Her most well-known book was *The Teaching of Geography*, published by Appleton-Century-Crofts, Inc. in 1958 (339 pages). She was quoted, "This book comes from a long career in elementary, high school and college teaching." She dedicated the book to Edith Putnam Parker, an inspirational teacher.

The World Around Us was a 480-page book published in 1961.

At the age of seventy-four, in 1962, Zoe was an editorial consultant, along with Dorothy Furman and Elizabeth Nichols, for the *Scholastic Hammond World Atlas*, which contained maps, facts about the world, and instructions on "How to use a Map."

Back here, on the home front, Zoe was listed in the *1947 Webb City Annual*, as one of the "noted Missourians" from Webb City High School. She is listed as an author and a geographer. And to think, at that time, she was only halfway through the list of publications she would eventually finish in her lifetime (that I am aware of!). Zoe passed away in 1965.

In 2005, Zoe A. Thralls (who would have been 117 years of age had she still been living!) was nominated to be featured in the National Council for Geographic Education's "Historic Women in Geography Education" calendar.

Here is definitely a hidden forefather or lady of distinction from the history of Webb City who seems to have been forgotten by us, but not by the Internet which offers her books for sale still today!

Her entries in the *NEA Journal* are still on file at the University of Missouri and other noted locations.

I want to give a special thanks to this lady who dedicated her life to teaching.

Zoe Agnes Thralls was admitted to the Webb City RVII Hall of Fame in 2013.

Toutz, Robert

Throughout the pages of history about the United States, you read where people came to the United States seeking fortune, fame, or freedom. As they gathered in this vast country, they usually sought out others from their own homeland. The Irish, Swedes, Germans all did this. They even formed little colonies to feel closer and not so far from home.

One such gentleman, Robert D. Toutz, had a dream to come to America. His goal was accomplished at the age of sixteen, when he reached the shores of the United States. The year was 1879, and Robert arrived first in Bloomington, Illinois. Later he ventured into Jasper County, settling in Carthage.

Feeling more at ease with other German families, it only seemed natural that Robert should marry Elizabeth M. Gentes. Elizabeth's family had come to the United States from Germany in 1866, when she was only four years old. The Gentes family consisted of five children: Jacob J., Daniel, Lena (Tappana), Anna (Ruitt), and of course, Elizabeth (Toutz).

Robert and Elizabeth moved their family to Webb City in 1891 and bought a house at 315 West Austin Street. All of his children were raised in that house. Robert and Elizabeth both passed away in their family home, Robert in 1936, and Elizabeth in 1929.

Robert was involved in the community by serving on the city council and the board of education. Elizabeth was known for her involvement with the War Mother's chapter.

Robert was a mine operator. He operated the Richland Mine and the Marguerite Mine near Carterville, and he was the mine superintendent for the American Zinc Lead and Smelting Company and the C. T. Ore Mines.

Robert was responsible for the land being donated for Memorial Park. His son Robert Jr. became well known in the area as the director of the Webb City Municipal Band, which played every week at the Memorial Park.

All the children in the Toutz family were musically inclined. The children were: Robert Jr., Carl, Otto, Earl, Alfred, Caroline, Lillian (Davis), Bertha (Malang), and Gladys (Olson).

If you close your eyes, you can just imagine the sound of the band playing on a warm Saturday evening. Young couples walking hand in hand, children running and playing. Those were the good ole days!

Memorial Park Band stand

Troup, James R.—Baptist College

One of the prominent and substantial citizens of Webb City, Jasper County, was James R. Troup, who resided on a farm of 190 acres just beyond the city limits, where he was engaged in agricultural pursuits for many years. He owned the land upon which Prosperity now stands and opened the rich Troup Mines. The birth of Mr. Troup occurred in Monroe County, Missouri, and he was a son of Jacob and Catherine (Willis) Troup. The father was located in Monroe County in 1832. He moved there from Franklin County, Virginia. He became widely known and universally respected and was a leader in the Baptist Church. His death occurred in 1864, at the age of seventy-seven years. The mother of our subject was a native of Franklin County, Virginia. She died in Missouri, when her son was sixteen years old.

James R. Troup was reared and educated in Monroe County, Missouri, and there became prominent in public affairs. On May 8, 1867, he came to Jasper County, Missouri, and bought forty acres of land at Prosperity, which proved rich in mineral deposit. Mr. Troup took an active interest in this locality and soon became identified with its political, religious, and educational affairs. An active Democrat, he exerted a great influence and took a leading position in every campaign.

He was connected with the Baptist Church since youth and was one of the founders of the Webb City Baptist College, which was established in 1895. He was a member of the board and its treasurer and devoted time and money to it. He had a controlling interest in its faculty, and his liberality in this connection was well known. For many years, he had been a deacon in the church and was deeply interested in the work of the Sunday school, for a long period, acting as its superintendent. The college stood as a testimonial to his devotion to his church and the cause of education. The building was one of the finest in this section, costing $40,000, and accommodating a large number of pupils.

Mr. Troup was married in Monroe County, Missouri, to Ms. Lucy Jane Greening, who was a daughter of James Greening, formerly of Kentucky. The children born to this marriage are Emma J. of Webb City; Thomas of Joplin Township, engaged in farming and drilling; Oscar H. of Webb City; Maggie, wife of Albert Litt, in the oil business, in Webb City; Cora, wife of A. S. Kerr, a successful miner of Joplin Township; and Walter. Mr. Troup was a man of large means and of advanced ideas. He did much to promote the interests of this section of the state and was one of the best-known and most highly esteemed citizens of Jasper County.

Webb City College

VanHoose, James

Kentucky is a mighty "perty" state, and it seems quite a few early pioneers to Jasper County originated from the blue grass state. James H. VanHoose, at the age of twenty-five, in 1891, decided not to follow in his parents' footsteps and left farming and moved to Webb City, Missouri. James was the fifth of fifteen children. His father was one of twelve, and his mother was one of fourteen, so he had plenty of kinfolk that he left in the hills of Kentucky. James was seeking the dream of becoming wealthy in the mining industry.

James had the opportunity to open a wholesale and retail coal business which proved profitable. He took on a partner, L. B. Hare, who eventually sold his share to George W. Moore. Moore was mayor of Webb City, very outgoing and well thought of in the area, which was the same description given of James. After Moore retired, James became sole proprietor once again.

In 1905, James joined Ben Aylor and other well-known men in establishing the Merchants & Miners Bank of Webb City. He went on to serve as a member of the board with Aylor, L. J. Stevison, W. E. Patten, R. B. Dodge, J. G. Wilber, W. R. Robertson, George Hardy, and C. M. Manker. A very influential group of men.

Bank owner Ben Aylor and James VanHoose went into partnership in 1907. Their office was located to the rear of the Merchants & Miners Bank at 108 West Daugherty, and they handled mining leases, along with city and county properties.

James married Maude Ray in 1893, and they had three children: Harry Orval, born in 1894; Charles (Earl), born in 1896; and Alton (LeRoy), born in 1901. Their home was located at 923 West First Street. James was dedicated to the community and served on city council, attended church at The Church of Jesus Christ of Latter-Day Saints at Third and Liberty Streets, and belonged to the Elks Club and the Knights and Ladies of Security.

James's first son died at the age of nine. His other two sons became as well known around the town as James himself. Earl was associated with the banking business, working with the First National Bank of Webb City until it merged with the Webb City Bank. He then joined with the Merchants & Miners Bank as an assistant cashier until he succeeded G. Everett Hough as the executive vice president until 1936.

Following in his father's footsteps, he started his own business, operating an auto financing business out of his home at 105 South Ball. He attended the Presbyterian Church, served as vice president of the chamber of commerce, and belonged to the Elks Club.

Earl married Louise Inman in 1915, and they had two daughters, Betty Lou and Joan VanHoose.

When the Blake Theatre burned in 1931, Earl was prominent in financing the building of the new Civic Theatre, which was a community project. Citizens could buy a seat in the theater for $100, which helped raise some of the financing needed. Larry Larsen, who had acclaimed fame across the United States in the building of theaters, designed the Civic with designs of the new era. Lighted marquees and bright neon lights lit up Daugherty Street, creating a festive mood. The building was completed in 1933.

James's other son, LeRoy, was the personal director of the Webb Corporation, working with C. H. Bentley. LeRoy married Louise Clark, daughter of Dr. A. Benson Clark, in 1923. They had two daughters and a son: Martha Jean, born in 1924, who died at the age of three from scarlet fever. Their other daughter was Jane Clark VanHoose, born in 1926. Their son was James Benson VanHoose, born in 1934.

Jane VanHoose married Bruce Benson, and they had four children: Susie, David, Van, and Lori. James and his wife had four children: Scott, Gregory, Jeff, and Mary Lynn.

Jane and Bruce Benson have been very active in the community, and when you think of Jane, you automatically think of dancing. Many a youth learned to dance under her guidance. The names of Jane and Bruce together bring to mind Webb City's very own Fred and Ginger, as they have taught many couples the magic of ballroom dancing. And then the name of Bruce brings to mind the sounds of music as he has played many tunes with his bands.

Jane and Bruce raised their children at 809 South Madison, in the home of Jane's parents, LeRoy and Louise. It had been a gift from LeRoy's parents, James and Maude, around 1920. It was quite a house, as it was brand-new and came with gaslights.

James had such a generous nature about him that Jane says she has many letters written to him throughout the years, thanking him for helping someone in need.

Another piece of trivia on the VanHoose family is the fact that between LeRoy and Earl, they had three daughters: Betty Lou, Joan, and Jane, and all three were King Jack queens, and LeRoy's son, James, was the editor of the *King Jack*.

James H. VanHoose was a great forefather and asset to the Webb City community, and the generations that followed him have seemed to carry on that same tradition. A personality worth imitating.

Waggoner, William Winston—Doctor

Born in 1862, this Webb City physician made the move from St. Louis to Webb City in 1901. He was a graduate of the University of Cincinnati. He did post-graduate work at the University of Heidelberg, Germany.

The doctor married Pearl Wilson of Hartville, Ohio, whose father was C. T. Wilson of Lamar, who was the prosecuting attorney of Barton County.

Dr. Waggoner died December 15, 1936, at the age of seventy-four. His wife passed away February 23, 1935. Dr. Waggoner was a member of the Webb City Lodge, Elks Club, Methodist Episcopal Church, and the Jasper County Medical Society.

The children of the doctor and Pearl were Virginia Waggoner, who married Frederick Baxter. She was a WCHS graduate. William W. Waggoner, born April 17, 1909, at Lakeside, who married Mary Louise Burch on August 25, 1940, in Carterville. W. W. was an army veteran of World War II. He was an insurance salesman (1948–1974) and was a 1927 graduate of Webb City High School. He was a member of the Webb City Masonic Lodge 512, Royal Arch Chapter of Joplin Lodge, Webb City Rotary Club, and American Legion of Webb City. He was a member of the First Presbyterian Church. They lived at 818 South Jefferson. Their daughter was Nancy Waggoner Bittle, a 1968 graduate of Webb City High School. Bruce Reed Waggoner, a WCHS graduate. Bruce lived at 116 North Roane in Webb City.

Dr. Waggoner was a member of the Webb City Lodge, Elks Club, Methodist Episcopal Church, and the Jasper County Medical Society.

The original post office building became the Waggoner Building after the new post office was built.

The Waggoner Building became home to many doctor offices and business offices.

Wallace, William S. (Wallace Brothers)

William was the oldest of the Wallace brothers who owned and operated the Wallace Hardware Company of Webb City, Missouri. He began his career in 1898 and was well known in the business community.

Born in Morgan County, Illinois, on the July 30, 1869, to Richard M. and Ellen J. (Potter) Wallace, he was moved, at age five, to Bourbon County, Kansas, as his father was in the merchandising business. Nine children joined the family after William's birth.

Following graduation at age eighteen, William apprenticed himself to a carpenter and enjoyed that trade for twelve years. While being a carpenter apprentice, William married Louise Chimpky on July 27, 1887, in Fort Scott, Kansas. William journeyed to Jasper County in 1898, landing in Webb City, Missouri. Continuing his trade of carpentry, William built some houses and important buildings in the area until the mining bug bit him, and he started mining from 1904–1906, at which time he withdrew after experiencing a considerable loss in that field.

William had enough finances left to open a hardware business in November of 1907, at 211 North Allen Street (age thirty-seven). He continued to put his earnings back into the business and developed the leading retail Wallace Hardware Company. His two sons joined in the business, Richard L. Wallace and Elbert N. Wallace.

William and Louise had four children: Richard L. Wallace (September 23, 1888), who married Ida Mayer of Carthage on December 4, 1910; Lula Pearl Wallace (July 25, 1890), who married D. C. Mallory, an attorney in Webb City, Missouri; Grace May (May 15, 1892), who died in infancy; Elbert Nelson Wallace (February 23, 1893).

Wampler, Wilson W.

W. W. Wampler had his home built on the southwest corner of First and Oronogo Streets (702 West First Street). It still stands today, minus several distinguishing architectural features.

Mr. Wampler was an active member of the Presbyterian Church. He was an elder for twenty-four years, clerk of session, trustee, Sunday school teacher delegate, and a member of various pulpit committees. He died on January 30, 1939, at the age of seventy-eight, after a seven-month illness. He was said to have lived a long life with many good deeds. He was buried at Mount Hope Cemetery.

Wilson married Maggie, and they had two sons: Oliver Wampler and Clarence Wampler. Wilson was the director of National Bank and a mine operator. He had two brothers, Ben and W. A., and two siters, Mrs. Arlin and Mrs. Katie Palmer, and five grandchildren.

Wampler was the retired director of the National Bank. He was involved in several mining operations. He moved to Webb City in 1889.

Ward, Orin

At a young age, Orin R. Ward went to work in the mines, as many young men in Webb City area did. Orin was fortunate enough to escape the mines when he went to work for Wells Fargo.

Cargo would come into Webb City by railway. Orin would meet the trains and load the cargo onto his Wells Fargo wagon to be distributed to various locations.

The west end of town was the hustle and bustle of the railway. Along with Wells Fargo, there were many liveries, such as the Frisco Livery located at 214 North Madison, one-half block west of the Frisco Depot. The Frisco Livery featured carriage and baggage transfer. They boarded horses and stored wagons and buggies. If you weren't traveling by railway, you could catch a jitney and ride by wagon for 5¢.

Orin married Sophia Brannon on November 14, 1907. Sophia was the daughter of Benjamin and Rebecca Mosses Brannon. The other Brannon children included Annie, who was married to L. M. Long; Kate married Byron Wells; and Birdie was married to Charles O. Connelly.

Not long after their lives were just getting settled, tragedy struck for Orin and Sophia. The mining job that had given Orin his start as a teenager took his life away. Orin got consumption from working in the mines, and even though he had changed occupations, the consumption still took his life away at the early age of twenty-eight.

Sophia and Orin had a son named Kenneth. While Kenneth was at the CC Camp in New Madrid, Missouri, he met the love of his life, Ms. Vivian Simpson. So he brought Vivian (Pippy, as family members knew her) back to Webb City. This was Vivian's first time to be away from her loving family, and she was homesick.

In 1942, Kenneth built Vivian a home of her own at 708 West Eleventh. Except for the year Vivian and Kenneth went to Lawrence, Kansas, to work at the Rocket Powder Plant during the war, they have lived in the home Kenneth built for his bride.

Many young people can remember gathering around the old pump organ with Uncle Kenny and Aunt Pip to sing songs (of course, Vivian says she "had a voice for calling pigs, not singing!"). There were many hayrides where once again, there was singing and laughing. A good time could be had by all.

Kenneth worked at the Webb Corp for thirty-four years. His roots were deep in the Webb City soil. Even though Kenny has left this world, his home holds many loving memories of him.

A special thanks to Vivian Ward for sharing these wonderful memories of her husband and family.

Watson, Judge Ray

M. H. (Marcella Hayden) Watson and his wife, Kate Graham Watson, moved to Webb City in 1885. They had a large happy family of four boys and two girls: Claude, Frank, Ray, Dorsey, Ethel, and Valeria. All the children were model citizens of Webb City and left fine legacies, but today's story is about one particular family member—Ray E. Watson.

Ray was raised in a family that wasn't afraid of work. His father worked in the mines, and his mother baked bread and other delicacies that she sold to help support the family. Ray followed in his parents' footsteps. After graduating from Webb City High School in 1910, he went to the University of Missouri School of Law. To support himself while at the university, Ray worked at the bookstore on campus, and then during the summer, he worked in the wheat fields of Kansas, along with some of his friends, Jack Spracklen, W. Alton Jones, and his brother, Dorsey Watson.

After graduation from law school in 1916, Ray stayed on at the bookstore to save some money to prepare for his future law practice. Upon returning to Webb City, Tom Roney gave him some space in his law office to commence his law practice.

But things weren't meant to be; World War I changed Ray's plans. He entered the US Army Training School, and in November of 1917 was commissioned as second lieutenant and ordered to France. He served in active duty from January 1918, until February 1919, when he was wounded in both legs by machine-gun fire.

In recognition of his extraordinary heroism, the US government awarded Ray with the Distinguished Service Cross and the Purple Heart. From the French government, he received the French Croiz-de-Guerre, which read, "An officer of admirable courage. Although severely wounded, he remained in command of his platoon. With coolness and an absolute disregard of danger, under heavy machine gun fire, he repulsed the attack of the infantry of the enemy."

After returning to Webb City, in 1920, Ray helped to organize Battery G of the 203rd Coast Artillery of the reconstituted Missouri National Guard. He accepted a captain's commission and became the battery's first commanding officer.

The year 1923 was a good year for Ray, as he was promoted to major and became colonel in 1933. Also in 1923, he married his sweetheart, Hazel Gist of Joplin. Of this union, there were two daughters, Lois Watson Spracklen and Frances Watson Lewis.

Ray E. Watson ran for the office of city attorney and lost his first race, but he was undaunted as he said, "You must be defeated to appreciate winning!" Moving on in his political career, he was elected prosecuting attorney in 1930, a position he held for four years. A quote from the *Kansas City Star* states:

> Ray Watson's record as prosecuting attorney stands as one of the most enviable in all of the history of the county. Within a period of only about two years, he handled seventeen capital crime cases and did not lose a single case. During a wave of crime, which swept the county soon after the depression struck, Watson assumed the role of investigator as well as prosecutor. He was "on the scene" in every crime inquiry.

Ray's career moved from prosecuting attorney into the office of judge of division 1 of Jasper County circuit court, where he served for twenty-one years and eight months until he retired.

When he was up for re-election in 1940, he was out of town with the national guard, which was federalized fifteen months before Pearl Harbor. He won without even campaigning. When he returned to the bench in 1942, he earned the reputation of being a tough but fair judge.

Watson was involved in the community and served in a leadership role in many organizations, such as the board of governors of the Missouri Bar Association, Jane Chinn Hospital, and Jasper County Board of Jail Visitors. He also supported many civic organizations such as the Masonic Lodge, Elks Lodge, IOOF Lodge, and the American Legion.

He devoted many hours to the hospital board throughout the years. He was instrumental in securing grants from the W. Alton Jones Foundation to build two additions to the hospital building. There was an ulterior motive behind his desire to help maintain a good hospital. He felt that the dedicated nurses who took care of him during WWI kept his wounds from becoming disabling. Since Ray couldn't return the favor to the nurses personally, he would help someone else, thus creating a chain of goodwill. After more than twenty-five years on the hospital board, he was elected president emeritus.

When Ray Watson walked down the streets in Joplin or in the square in Carthage, many called out a greeting to judge or colonel, but in Webb City, the greeting was simply Ray. And that was what he wanted. He treated all people with the same respect and dignity, no matter what might be their walk in life. He was constantly being asked for his advice or guidance while at the post office, in a restaurant, or even at home, and when those asking offered to pay for that advice, he never accepted the money. The biggest contribution of his lifetime was his one-on-one with the citizens of Webb City that he considered his friends.

An editorial in the *Webb City Sentinel*, after Ray's death in 1979, at the age of eighty-seven, summed up his life pretty well:

> SMALL TOWNS HAVE BEEN KNOWN *to point with pride to sons and daughters who left home and became successful in their chosen fields. Quite rightly so. We reflect in their*

glory. Less often do we recognize that those who "stayed home" are the ones who make the greatest contribution to our quality of life. They support and give leadership to our civic institutions, our schools, our churches, and our businesses. The Webb City community has been a better place to live and raise a family and our lives all enriched because Judge Ray E. Watson "stayed home".

Judge Watson's service in the Armed forces in two wars, his decorations of bravery, his repeated election to public office as prosecutor and judge, his service on many "Blue Ribbon" committees and his service to his church attest to his dedication and service to the welfare of his fellowman. With Judge Watson, his family always came first, but he was a member of many families: a lawyer, a soldier, a jurist, a church and civic leader. Each of these "families" has suffered a great loss but none greater than the Webb City Community. We point with pride that he "stayed home." He will be missed.

What a wonderful tribute to a wonderful man! I would like to thank Lois Spracklen for the information she supplied about her father. She has a wonderful heritage of which she and Frances Lewis both have a right to be proud.

Watson home, built 1906. Been in the Watson-Spracklen family since 1938.

Before becoming the Watson home, this beautiful home belonged to the Orr family.

Watson, Claude L.

Claude L. Watson was noted as one of the most active and intelligent promoters of Jasper County.

Marcellus (M. H.) and Kate Graham Watson were married April 6, 1879, and had six children: Claude L. (1880), Frank (1887), Ethel (1889), Ray E. (1891), Dorsey (1894), and Valeria (1898). Claude was the oldest and had a head start on the rest of the family. He attended the first school building in Webb City, a one-story frame school located on Webb Street between Broadway and First Streets. As the schools improved throughout the city, after graduation, Claude found himself teaching but decided that wasn't the profession for him.

Claude had an interest in real estate, but before he could really get his feet wet, he had the opportunity to run for the political position of city clerk. After winning the election in 1904, young Claude enjoyed his term in office but soon developed an illness that required him to work outside. The most prominent employment for Claude seemed to be millwork. After a couple of years, Claude decided to get back into real estate, so on July 1, 1909, Claude organized and incorporated the Claude L. Watson Real Estate and Investment Company.

Having been married since 1901, Claude and his wife, Lutie Cresswell Watson, welcomed a new addition to the family the same year that Claude opened his new business. On October 26, 1909, R. E. Watson was born.

Claude's business grew steadily, and Claude became noted for his expertise in property within in the city limits and farmland as well.

But Claude's notability seemed to come from the fact that he was associated with Webb City Theosophical Society and had a fondness for good literature. Claude had a prized collection of over a thousand volumes of books in his own private library at home. He became a lecturer for the International Philosophical Society and continued in that service for twenty-five years.

Webb Family

Much of the information toward the Webb family was gathered by Don Freeman, who lives in the E. T. Webb home and has been able to get it registered on National Historic Registry. He has dedicated himself to gathering all the info he can on E. T. Webb, John C. Webb, and other family members. E. T. was so involved in many businesses and boards, it is hard to imagine being able to gather all the info.

John Cornwall Webb was born March 12, 1826, in Overton County, Tennessee. He was the second child in a large family. His father was Elijah C. Webb.

Elijah C. Webb was an early pioneer to the state of Tennessee. His family was long-time residents of North Carolina. Elijah's father, Benjamin C. Webb, had fought in the Revolutionary War. Born in North Carolina, Benjamin had immigrated with his wife to Tennessee and died there in 1825.

Farming was the occupation that Elijah was familiar with, and when he moved his wife, Martha Johnson, to Tennessee in 1826, it was natural for them to continue their farming tradition. The farm life they provided for their family was a good solid foundation. The children were raised in a spiritual home and attended school in a little log schoolhouse with split-log benches. Education was very important to the Webb family.

In 1849, at the age of twenty-three, John C. Webb found the love of his life, Ruth F. Davis, and they were married. They bought a little farm of their own, and life was pretty content for about six years. Then in 1855, Elijah and his brother, James C. Webb, with the family pioneer spirit in their blood, decided to make a change in their lives as they uprooted their families and moved west to the new frontier. Missouri was that new frontier of which they had heard stories.

The two Webb families settled in an area about three miles east of what would later be known as Joplin. They had good land at the head of Turkey Creek. To this day, there is a Webb cemetery called Harmony Grove located on that original homestead land.

A year later, in 1856, John C. and Ruth Webb joined the family in Southwest Missouri. They stayed a short time on the Webb homestead as they contemplated where they wanted to start their own family homestead.

John found a beautiful site to build a home. Any direction you looked, you could see green meadows. The wooded streams carried lots of cool clear water, and the hills of the Ozarks could be seen in the distance. So in 1857, John invested a few hundred dollars and applied for two hundred acres in Center Creek Township, which later changed to Dubuque Township, and then in 1873 changed to the Joplin Township

Ruth F. Davis Webb was married to John C. Webb in June 1849. She passed away March 24, 1876, just nine months before the town of Webb City was incorporated.

Ruth and John had four children: Mary Susan Webb Burgner, John B. Webb, Elijah Thomas Webb, and Martha Ellen Webb Hall.

John C. Webb was a Methodist and a Democrat and cast his first vote for president in 1848, voting for Lewis Cass. He was a member of the Masonic fraternity. John served in the Civil War with the Confederate Army in response to call from Governor Jackson for volunteers to defend Missouri.

In 1877, John C. Webb married Mrs. S. M. Couchman. There were no children in this union.

In 1882, John C. Webb and his son Elijah T. Webb established the Webb City Bank.

On April 13, 1883, John C. Webb passed from complications of his health. He had bronchial trouble and Bright's disease. He had only been married seven years.

Interesting notes about John C. Webb—In the 1850 Overton County, Tennessee Census, John C. Webb is listed as newly married and unable to read or write. John C. Webb and his wife moved to Jasper County in 1856. In the 1880 Jasper County, Missouri Census, John C. Webb is listed as a capitalist. The definition of a capitalist is a wealthy person who uses money to invest in trade and industry for profit. A person who has capital especially invested in business, broadly described as a person of wealth. A person of investments.

Webb served in the Civil War under General Sterling Price. His family moved to Texas during the war for safety from the dangers to civilians in this area.

The following information is about the extended Webb family.

Those of us who have lived in the city most of our lives find it hard to imagine what it must have been like for John C. Webb and his wife, Ruth, to come to this area in 1856 and only see land as far as the eye could see. It must have been a beautiful sight because Webb decided that this was where he wanted to raise his family.

Webb was the modest unassuming citizen and familiar friend to the last, apparently unconscious of the wealth which was his, and caring nothing for the distinction it might afford (*Encyclopedia of the History of Missouri*).

Webb, Erasmus Thomas E. T., son of John C. Webb—Elijah Thomas (E. T.) Webb was born in Overton County, Tennessee, on August 24, 1851. His parents, Ruth and John C. Webb, moved to Missouri in 1856 to join E. T.'s grandfather Elijah C. Webb, who had made the move one year before.

In 1874, E. T.'s father, John C. Webb, founded Webbville, which was platted in 1875 and incorporated as Webb City in 1876.

E. T. attended common schools. At the age of twenty-six, after his father founded the town of Webb City, E. T. attended the State University of Columbia from 1877–1879. He then went to Gem City Commercial College in Quincy, Illinois, where he graduated in 1879 at the top of his class.

When he returned home, he started working as a deputy collector for the county collector's office in Carthage, Missouri. He held that position for two years.

In 1882, E. T. and John C. Webb went into partnership and established the Webb City Bank, which was located on the southeast corner of Webb Street and Main (Broadway) Street in Webb City's first brick building. E. T. started out his banking career as a cashier and worked his way up to president of the corporation. The bank was a privately owned bank from 1882–1890, when it became incorporated. E. T. continued to serve as president. He was noted in the *1900 Webb City Souvenir* as president of the Webb City Bank.

E. T. built a lovely home on the southwest corner of Liberty Street and Joplin (Broadway) Street in 1881. Three years later, 1884, E. T. erected a piazza (porch) on the east and north sides of the residence, according to the *Joplin Globe*.

Behind of Webb's home was a large carriage house which held the horses and buggies. Webb donated the land behind his house where his carriage house was located to build the Central Methodist Church. His wife donated all the lighting fixtures for the church (1909).

E. T. Webb donated the land in which the YMCA building was built.

E. T. became nationally known for his extensive art collection on display in his beautiful home at Liberty and Joplin (Broadway) Streets.

Mrs. E. T. Webb supplied all the light fixtures for the ME Methodist Church, 1909.

(*The Biographical Record of Jasper County*, Hon. Malcolm G. McGregor, 1901).

My favorite researcher, Don Freeman, who has my gratitude, has searched the dusty files and archives to come up with some interesting history from the past, and he has shared them with me.

Webb Hall, Martha: daughter of John C. Webb, wife of William E. Hall—Martha was born in 1853, and she was four years old when she and her family moved to Jasper County in 1857.

Martha married William E. Hall in 1871 when she was eighteen years of age.

After her husband, William's, death in 1907, Martha and her son moved back to Hallwood Farm. The farm had a fifteen-room mansion, well furnished. A showplace. Martha died in a horrific fire at the farm in 1916.

Hall, William E., son-in-law of John C. Webb—As you may recall from previous articles, I'm always trying to figure out just how the different streets received their names. Well, I think I may have figured out who received the honor of having Hall Street carry their name!

William E. Hall was a name known to many in Jasper County. His parents, Winston and Jane Robertson Hall, were married not too long after their families moved to Jasper County. Both families were well known in North Carolina. Arriving to this area in 1838 and 1840, it wasn't long before the young couple was married.

Winston and Jane settled in a very comfortable hand-hewed log cabin upon a tract of unimproved land. Even though the area was highly populated with Indians, the young couple had a fairly uneventful life other than the normal hardships and trials of frontier life. They eventually accumulated 140 acres and lived there until Winston's death in 1863.

Their son, William E. Hall, born in 1845, grew up on the land his parents had cultivated and made into an impressive farm. He worked the farm during the summer and attended school in the winter. When his father passed away, William was eighteen years of age and the oldest; therefore, he took upon himself the responsibility of caring for the farm. This role brought out his best and showed his strength of character.

Not long after taking on this great responsibility, William took on the challenge and cast his lot with the Confederate Army. He served under General Shelby, General Standwaite, and later General Cooper.

Receiving his honorable discharge at the end of the Civil War in 1865, William joined his mother, who was then living in Texas. He made a short trip back to Jasper County and married Ms. Margaret C. Glasscox, and they returned to Texas to take care of Jane Hall. Jane passed away in 1869, and a year later, William's wife, Margaret, died. William immediately returned to the familiar territory he called home, Jasper County.

Having found a favorable career in stock industry, William would buy cattle in Texas and drive them back to Jasper County. A very profitable enterprise for a young man of twenty-five.

Having finally settled down near what would soon become Webb City, William visited often with John C. Webb, a farmer whose family had been in the area as long as the Hall family.

In May of 1871, William E. Hall married Martha E. Webb, daughter of John C. Webb. They lived on a farm that was next to the Webb farm in Mineral Township. In 1874, William was elected to the office of township assessor, then in 1878, two years after the establishment of Webb City in 1876, William was elected to the office of county collector. Finding the commute to be too much of a hardship, William and Margaret moved to Carthage to be closer to the courthouse. At the end of his term, William took up an interest in farming and mining. In 1883, they moved to their eight-hundred-acre farm and lived there until 1889, at which time they moved back to Carthage. Although William still managed his farm, a farm that was well stocked with cattle and horses. Many of the state's finest trotters and saddle horses came from the farm of William E. Hall.

In 1894, Jasper County established the United Confederate Veterans Camp. Since W. E. Hall was one of the first to enlist in the regiment that the county sent to the front, it was only right that William held the honor of being elected as treasurer, and he held that position until his death in 1907.

Being the son-in-law of the founder of Webb City, and owning land close to the Webb farm, leaves no doubt in my mind that Hall Street is named after William E. Hall.

And what a distinguished gentleman he was!

1845—William Hall was born in Jasper County, Missouri.

1863—Joined the Civil War and served under General Shelby, General Standwaite, and General Cooper. Honorably discharged in 1865.

1865—Married Margaret C. Glasscox. She died in 1870.

1871—May, married Martha E. Webb

1874—Township assessor

1878—County collector; moved to Carthage

1883—Purchased an eight-hundred-acre farm outside of Carthage he named Hallwood Farm

1889—Moved back to Carthage but still managed the farm, well stocked with cattle and horses.

1894—Established the United Confederate Veterans Camp

1907—William Hall passed away.

A letter received from Colleen Belk of Joplin gives a genealogy record of the Webb family. Colleen was active in the Joplin Historical Society and helped to catalog most of the cemeteries in the area.

Dear Mrs. Newby

A lady called me and told me you had an article in the paper (Webb City) about the Webb family…that is my family line…have been researching it for several years and along the way have made contact with 8 other researchers of the same line…from offshoots in Tennessee and North Carolina. I am descended directly from Mary Anne Webb Terry, a sister of John Cornwall Webb, the founder of the city.

We have traced back to William Warren Webb, who died an old man (I have the estate) in 1783, Orange County Virginia. Had a large family. Then one of his sons, James Crittenden Webb, migrated to North Carolina. Had a large family, I have his list of children. One of his sons, Benjamin C. Webb born in North Carolina and his wife Jane Coffey (daughter of Reuben and Sally Scott Coffey) migrated to Overton County Tennessee (died in 1824, I have the estate).

Two of his sons, migrated to Jasper County in the 1850's: Elijah C. Webb, father to John C. Webb and my great, great, great grandfather, along with James C. Webb, the father of Jane Chinn.

Also from Tennessee came Thomas C. Webb who lived where the Mt. Hope Cemetery is now located, and Solomon H. Webb. So, four lines of the same tree came here. Since my Great Grandparents Erasmus Webb and Eliza Jane Terry Webb were cousins, I'm also descended from the above listed Thomas C. Webb. We also have the female lines of the family tree.

The Harmony Grove cemetery east of Joplin, is the Webb family cemetery. All four lines are represented there and the parents of John C. Webb are there (died 1859). John Cornwall Webb was named for his maternal grandfather, John Cornwall Johnson who was the son of John Boswell Johnson, a Revolutionary War veteran.

John C. Webb was originally buried in Harmony Grove Cemetery in 1883, but after the formation of Mount Hope Cemetery his first wife; a son and John C. Webb were removed to Mt. Hope.

John C. Webb had a younger brother, William J. whose first wife died young, leaving three little girls. The young wife was a dark eyed German (Schubert).

Regards, Colleen Belk.

Colleen has since passed away. I really appreciate her letter; it is nice to have this information directly from the family.

Webb, Thomas Hall

"Founder's grandson dies."

In researching history, it is so wonderful to stumble upon the genealogy of a family. It seems to complete a story and make it so much more interesting. Genealogy is becoming more and more popular as the years go by. Some may not be interested at all in their family lineage, but let me tell you, when you get bitten by the genealogy bug, it bites hard, and you can't seem to get enough information.

I received a phone call that there has been a loss for our city. It seems that the last remaining direct descendent of our city founder has passed away. He was John Cornwall Webb's great-grandson, Thomas Hall Webb.

John C. Webb's family is traced back to William Warren Webb, who lived in Orange County, Virginia, and died in 1783 after a very long life. One of his sons from his large family, James Crittenden Webb, migrated to North Carolina, and he also had a very large family. James's son, Benjamin C. Webb, migrated to Tennessee, along with his wife, Jane. Benjamin was a participant in the Revolutionary War.

Two of Benjamin's boys, Elijah C. Webb and James C. Webb, decided to migrate to Jasper County in 1855. They settled on a farm just east of what would one day be Joplin. Elijah had left grown children back in Tennessee, and it wasn't long before they decided to join their father in his adventure to this new land.

John C. Webb and his wife, Ruth, lived on Elijah's farm when they first moved to Missouri in 1856. But within a year, John had located the site where he wanted his farm. It was beautiful land where any direction you looked, there were green meadows. The wooded streams carried lots of cool clear water. The hills of the Ozarks could be seen off in a distance.

John's younger brother, William J., who was nine years old when his parents moved to Missouri, grew up on the Webb Farm, east of Joplin, but when the town of Webb City was formed, he moved into town and started a blacksmith business.

Two of John's cousins, Thomas C. Webb and Solomon H. Webb, also moved into the area. There were several branches of Benjamin Webb's family living in Jasper County.

John C. Webb and Ruth had three children: Elijah (E. T.) Webb, Martha Ellen Webb Hall, and Mary Susan Webb Burgner. The children lost their mother in 1877, just one year after Webb City was incorporated, and John died in 1883.

John's only son, E. T., had one son, Ernest Webb, the father of Thomas Hall Webb, who just passed away. Thomas and his wife, Sally, have been living in Texas. They visited Webb City several years ago, and he recalled days of his youth visiting his grandparents in their grand home at the southwest corner of Broadway and Liberty Street. Thomas has a stepdaughter, Lee Anne, and sister, Alice, who also live in Texas.

There are many Webbs still living in the area, and some are related to the brothers and cousins of John C. Webb, but this is the end of the direct line of our founder.

Our sincere sympathy to the family of Thomas Webb. He will not be forgotten as Webb City strives to keep recalling the glorious history that has made our town such a great place to live.

A special thanks to Rusty Stanford for keeping me informed.

A letter was received from *Alice Spradley*, Thomas Webb's sister, dated August 24, 1999, in which she corrects some of the above information.

Dear Jeanne Newby

The enclosed article concerning my brother in particular and the Webb family in general was much appreciated by the family. I apologize for being so tardy in writing about the column. Truly, I did not discover the error that I would like to correct until very recently, when I re-read the article.

You say in the column that my brother has a sister, which is correct and therefore negates the next paragraph, which indicates there are no remaining direct descendents of John C. Webb. In fact, there are eight of us living now. I am Alice Webb Spradley, the great granddaughter of John C. Webb and the granddaughter of E.T. Webb. I have three children in their 40's. The eldest is Ernest (Webb) Spradley, then Charles D. Spradley and a daughter Alice Spradley Alex. Webb has a daughter, Rachel Hay Spradley; Charles has two sons, Walter Bowles Spradley and Martin Webb Spradley; Alice has one son, Ronald Marshall Alex, Jr.

My children and I have always been proud of our Webb City heritage and have been pleased to see the Webb house, the Methodist Church and other things of note when we have been there for my brother's funeral (1998) and my mother's funeral in 1968. I would like, for the record, it be noted that there are direct descendents who wish to keep in touch with this part of our heritage always.

Also, I would note the headline to the article, though it doesn't really matter… my brother was the great grandson of the founder. It is true, of course, that my brother is the last of the direct line to carry the Webb name as a surname.

Thanks again for your attention to this. Please include it somewhere in the records of your paper. I'll send a copy of this letter to the library, where other records are kept.

Alice W. Spradley
Dallas, Texas

Whiteley, W. M.—Doctor

Dr. W. M. Whiteley hailed from the state of Wisconsin, graduated from the University of Michigan in 1874, and settled in Joplin in 1875. He married Ms. Evadney Myers of Joplin, and they were content with their lives until 1879. Dr. Whitely saw an ad stating that the fairly new town of Webb City was in need of doctors. He moved his wife and family to Webb City and set up practice. His three children were Albert, Daisy, and Nora. Once again, the call to come to Webb City seemed to echo through the air.

Dr. Whiteley's father-in-law, Edward Myers, had a busy life. Edward was born in England and made the trip to New York City in 1847 at the age of twenty-three. He acquired employment in a clothing store on Chatham Street as a salesman. Later he worked as a clothing salesman in St. Louis, then headed on to California to follow a dream. He stayed in Sacramento for thirteen years, working in the hotel business and the clothing business. He traveled considerably from New York to Oregon and San Francisco, always staying in the clothing or hotel business. Then the theater called his name, and he became Professor Myers, the "American Magician." This new profession took him all over the west as he gave his exhibitions. He retired from show business and settled in Joplin. He opened an auction business, which failed, and he headed to Webb City in 1882 and engaged in a new clothing store and saloon. Not one to handle leisure time too well, Edward's active mind was constantly on the move. He began to fiddle with gadgets, and he invented a safety attachment for railroad cars. The attachment kept the railroad cars from leaving the track. He also invented a safety switch. Both inventions were deemed very valuable. What a special man Edward Myers was. With his travels and varied employments, he was a very interesting person to talk with, and he had an inexhaustible amount of stories to share.

It is amazing what each person brought with them that added to the character of Webb City.

Wise, Hal—Newspaper Man

Ann Francis, daughter of Robert Jesse and Olive Cox Dale, was born on March 24, 1851. She was the fourth of nine children. On March 25, 1871, Ann Francis married Andrew M. Wise (on her father's fifty-first birthday). To this union were born three children: May Wise, Hal M. Wise, and Orville Wise.

Only seven years after their marriage, Andrew died an early death, leaving a very young widow with three children to raise alone. The year was 1878, and Ann Francis, being of strong pioneer blood, managed to raise those children in such a manner that they were pillars of the community.

The middle child, Hal M. Wise, started at a young age to be involved in the community. In the early 1890s, football was just beginning to be played in the local high schools. Hal was going to school at Carthage and played on the first football team.

Their coach was a new teacher who had been a football star at the University of Missouri. He got the boys interested in playing the sport of football, and they became one of the best teams around, having to play such teams as Drury College.

Besides playing football, Hal was the editor of the *Carthage Press,* until he started college at the University of Pennsylvania in Philadelphia.

After graduating from the university, Hal worked for the *Philadelphia Inquirer.* In 1904, Hal was working for the *St. Louis Post-Dispatch.* He covered the world's fair in St. Louis. In 1905, he was given a special assignment to do a series of features in Oklahoma and Texas.

In 1906, Hal has an opportunity he couldn't pass up. He and an old publishing comrade, James E. Stickney, purchased the *Webb City Sentinel.* After eight years, James sold his interest in the *Sentinel* to a cousin, Walter Stickney. Walter lost interest after a couple of years and sold his share of the paper to Hal. As sole owner of the *Webb City Sentinel,* Hal was able to do things his own way, and the newspaper flourished. Hal had a wonderful way with words, and his feature articles showed just what a dedicated and loyal citizen Hal was to Webb City.

Hal wrote a feature article on the twenty-fifth anniversary of his being the editor of the *Webb City Sentinel.* I would like to quote from that article a paragraph that shows Hal's dedication to the town of Webb City.

> The Sentinel has urged for 25 years and will urge again, that we of Webb City look upward; not compare ourselves with bigger towns and lament "what a dinky town with is, what a dumbbell I am to stay in Webb City"…but to buy stock in ourselves, to believe in our own stores and shops, our own shows and parks, our schools and churches; to believe in hometown trade and traditions…and that our town is the best town on earth. (*Webb City Sentinel,* March 19, 1931)

Wise wedding—I want to share one of my favorite honeymoon stories of a Webb City family. Hal Wise, editor and publisher of the *Webb City Sentinel,* asked Ms. Gladys Warthen to marry him, and she said *yes.* Even after she found out his plans for the wedding and honeymoon, she still said yes!

Hal took his lovely young fiancée east to Galena, Missouri, in Stone County. They were wed in the Methodist Church in Stone County at three o'clock on Sunday afternoon, February 8, 1909. The very next morning, bright and early, Hal took his young bride on a very unusual honeymoon. They took a four-day boat trip down one hundred miles of the James and White Rivers. About three years earlier, Hal had built a log cabin, which he named the Hello Bill cabin, at the mouth of Indian Creek.

Hal had a dream to spend the first two weeks of his married life in front of the big stone fireplace in the humble cabin, with bare necessities, just as his grandparents did when they first came to this area. The romantic Hal had pioneer blood flowing through his veins, and his charming wife was very adventurous and, after surviving their honeymoon, could handle any obstacles in their future lifetime together.

Hal Wise on his honeymoon, 1909.

Gladys Wise on her honeymoon, 1909.

Wilhite Brothers

At the turn of the century, as big beautiful homes were frequently built in Webb City, there was a great need for talented housepainters and wallpaper experts. The Wilhite brothers, J. Frank and Harley S., came to the bustling town of Webb City and immediately developed a good reputation for a job well done. Frank owned the business, and Harley worked for him. One of the best indicators of a good company is repeat business, and that's just what the Wilhite brothers had.

In many old homes in this area, as old wallpaper is removed, writing can be found on the wall, stating, "Wallpapered by the Wilhite Brothers," accompanied by the year. Then a little farther down is writing that says, "Stripped and re-wallpapered by the Wilhite Brothers," and gives a date, a few years later. The Wilhite brothers not only had repeat business, they were proud enough of their work to sign it!

Being the smart businessman that he was, Frank knew his business needed to change with the times, so in 1921, as more automobiles appeared on the streets of Webb City, Frank advertised his business as handling signs and automobile painting. He would put on new tops, cushions, side curtains, seat covers, and upholstery. He advertised that he would do "anything to doll up your car"!

While Frank took on the mysterious automobiles, Harley stayed with the house painting and wallpapering business. Harley later married Edna Hamrick, and they lived at 325 South Webb Street.

Meanwhile, Frank married his wife, Goldie, and they lived next-door to Harley at 323 South Webb Street. Frank and Goldie had three sons: Robert F., Hugh, and Charles. Robert married Mabel Johnson, and they lived at 321 South Webb Street. Hugh married Pauline Girton, and they lived at 315 South Webb Street.

Now that's a close family. They took up four houses on the same block. I think they should have changed the name to Wilhite Street.

As the boys grew up, they began to help with the company. Eventually it became known as the Willhite Brothers Sign Company. The shop was located at 301 East Broadway, the corner of Hall and Broadway.

The Wilhite Sign Company in Joplin is the original sign company that was located here in Webb City. Their ad declares that it was established in 1921.

I had the privilege of talking to Mrs. Mabel Wilhite a few years ago, and she was very proud of the Wilhite name and that the business could have lasted as long as it has. The Wilhite name will always be associated with signs and homes of Webb City.

Veatch, Snowden H.

Snowden and his wife, Mary Rice Veatch, moved to Webb City in 1890, and Snowden built the S. H. Veatch Milling Company. The mill was located on the northeast corner of Madison and Austin. Veatch had accumulated knowledge of the milling business by working many mills in his lifetime. Getting his business off to a good start, Veatch sold his prosperous company to Ball & Gunning in 1900. Veatch moved to Alba and started yet another career operating a grain elevator. Added to his many accomplishments were operating a coal yard in Alba as well as an icehouse. Veatch became well known for his strawberries that he grew and shipped to all places. Snowden and Mary had nine children, with only four making it to maturity. Their son H. C. Veatch became an important part of Webb City.

Veatch, John Crebbs (J. C.)

J. C. Veatch worked with his father at the S. H. Veatch Milling Company until his father sold it in 1900.

Veatch took on many challenges after the milling company, such as grocery store, pool hall, but centering his career in real estate. He married Dona Sala in 1903 and raised a family of five children. Active in the community, J. C. was a member of many organizations, such as Modern Woodmen of America, AF and AM of Webb City, Elks Lodge. Cecil J. Veatch carried on the Veatch name in Webb City history.

Veatch, Cecil J. "Bud)"

A Webb City graduate, Bud Veatch found joy in life and in his career. He worked for the Missouri Conservation Commission until he joined his father's real estate business in 1944. Veatch really became a very well-known name in real estate in Webb City. Veatch was very active in the community, making himself well known along with Fred (Fritz) Rogers in the great hunt for streetcars. They worked together in the restoration of Old 60, the streetcar that can be found at King Jack Park. Veatch and his wife, Vella, had three daughters: Cecilia, Jeanneane, and Janette. Many generations of the Veatch family have made Webb City their home, and they have left their mark.

Zaumseil, O. C.

O. C. Zaumseil married his sweet wife, Anna V. Stewart, in 1908, in his parents' home at 22 South Pennsylvania that he inherited and where he raised his family. The Zaunseil Jewelry Store was located at 12 South Allen Street before Minerva Candy Company. The jewelry store relocated to the Unity Building, 114 North Main, before Drachenberg was located there in 1939.

Zook, Jesse A.—Webb City Register

Sidney Smith once said, "Whatever you are from nature, keep to it; never desert your own line of talent. Be what nature intended you for, and you will succeed."

Jesse Zook took that path in his career. He measured his own ability and went straight on to becoming a fine representative of a self-made man.

Jesse was born in Muncie, Indiana, on May 19, 1863, to John W. Zook. At the age of six, he traveled with his parents to Carthage, Missouri, where he attended school. Seeking the printer's trade, Jesse found employment with a printing office as a "printer's devil." He mastered every mechanical detail of the printer's trade with enthusiasm that was part of his natural nature.

At age twenty-four, Jesse took on the challenge of being on the editorial staff of the *Joplin Herald*, edited by Kit Carson. He held that position for thirteen years. Moving on with his career, he became editor and part owner of the *Webb City Register* from 1902–1906, at which time he sold his interests back to the newspaper and headed back to Joplin.

By combining his interest of the mining world with his love of writing, Jesse was empowered as he became the special correspondent of zinc and lead statistics. He wrote for the *Eastern Metal Journals*, making his articles be of importance to the industrial world in governing zinc metal prices.

Work was not his only interest as he married Ida E. Snodgrass, daughter of Hamilton Snodgrass of Webb City, on November 6, 1887. The young couple had four children: Dixie Zook was born December 26, 1888; Hamilton Zook, born November 25, 1890; Jesse Zook, born May 10, 1894; and Wesler A. Zook, born October 23, 1903, with Wesler being the only surviving child.

CHAPTER 7

Webb City Legends and Tales

Stories handed down through generations.

The James Gang

Legend has it that the James boys, Jesse and Frank, hid out in the Ku Klux Klan cave at Belleville (northwest of Joplin) and a cave over by the Grand Falls in Joplin. Many of the caves in the four-state area (especially down around Pineville) claim fame to having been the hideout of the notorious outlaws.

Well, it seems that the James boys and the younger boys didn't have to put up with such uncomfortable lodgings while visiting (or working) this area. They had friends in the area that they rode with when they were members of the Quantrill's guerrillas.

On one occasion, it seems that the James gang had entered a bank in Joplin owned by John H. Taylor with the intentions to hold it up. But Fletch Taylor, brother to the banker, recognized his comrades from the Quantrill raids. He greeted the boys as if they weren't doing anything out of the ordinary and invited them back in the office to meet his brother. Jesse signaled for the men to put away their guns. A grand evening followed where Fletch entertained them with dinner and visiting a few saloons and resorts. When he introduced the gang members, they assumed different names. From then on, John Taylor's bank was protected, and the James boys had a place to stay while in town.

The reputation of the James boys seems to be mixed. There are those who seemed to worship Jesse and Frank. Stories were told about their Robin Hood robberies of stealing from the rich to help the poor. Many stories followed about the robbing and plundering.

One story tells of an elderly lady who had put Jesse and Frank up for the night, and she told them that the banker was coming the next day to take her home away because she couldn't pay the mortgage. As Jesse and Frank were getting ready to leave the next morning, they gave the lady enough money to pay off her mortgage.

Now that seems like a mighty nice gesture for those notorious scoundrels, until you find out that they waited in the woods outside the lady's house, and after the banker collected the money, Jesse and Frank robbed the banker and got their money back. The lady had her mortgage torn up, and they recovered their money.

There may have been a few heroic stories, but the gruesome stories of robbing and plundering far outnumbered the good stories, and some stories never existed but were told often. One old-timer who watched the filming of the Jesse James movie in Pineville stated, "The James gang were 'skonks.'"

With the many trips that the James gang made between Joplin and their home in Clay County, it's quite a wonder that there weren't stories of them visiting the quaint area of Webb City, except for the fact that Webb City wasn't incorporated as a town yet! So maybe they did visit a few of the folks who lived in this area.

There was a saloon in Joplin located at Seventh and Main, on the west side of Main. In that saloon, there hung a picture of Jesse James. Next to the picture was a bullet hanging by a string with a sign that claimed, "This is the bullet that killed Jesse James."

Well, it seems that about a dozen times a day, that bullet was cut down and slipped into a pocket and carried away as a souvenir. The porter would receive his signal and head to the back room where he would proceed to pour another bullet in the mold he kept for just such occasions—and another bullet was hung on the string by the picture.

History and stories shared by old-timers make life so interesting. I guess I am the old-timer sharing stories now!

Stories from Local Books

Many a tale has been told of Webb City during the mining era. The new town of wooden buildings, dirt streets, and no law to speak of brought many a wild night. As the wooden buildings were eventually replaced with brick (to reduce the fire hazards), a pattern emerged. The east side of Allen (Main) Street housed the many saloons, pool halls, and gambling houses. The area from Allen (Main street) heading east to Carterville on Daugherty Street was referred to as "Red Hot Street." Some history trivia say it was Daugherty Street, and others say it was Broadway Street. Since it wasn't official in the city, it is hard to prove.

Dolph Shaner noted in his book *The Story of Joplin* that at one time, Carterville was "dry" (no liquor sold), and Webb City remained "wet," which created quite a bit of foot traffic as miners wandered across Ben's Branch to have some fun. Shaner noted that when the Carterville miners staggered, crawled, and/or were carried back to Carterville, as the Webb City saloons were closed at midnight, they woke up the town with their yelling and shooting.

Carterville citizens decided they needed to band together to establish some law and order in their town. Squire Campbell, a deacon of the ME Church South, headed the movement. To avoid fatalities, no guns were allowed to be used. The men who were deputized by the marshal carried wooden hammer handles to be used as billy clubs. The miners said they were using pick handles and, therefore, dubbed the Carterville lawmen the pick-handled police.

The first Saturday night, the organized lawmen caught the miners off guard, and there were some miners who spent the night in jail. The next Saturday night, the miners were prepared and fought off the new lawmen, took their billy clubs, and ended the pick-handled police league.

Webb City's east side of Allen Street continued to flourish as the miners spent all their hard-earned money on the "evils of the devil." Many a rough group from other towns entered Webb City on a Saturday night to have some shooting practice. Citizens were afraid to be out at night, and the wicked seemed to be taking over the town.

Norval Matthews stated in his 1976 commemorative booklet, *City of Webb City*, "*In spite of the efforts of church people and law enforcement officers, Webb City at this adolescent period of her existence at times became a rip-snorting, rioting, mass of lusty humanity.*"

Eventually peace and harmony rested on the streets of Webb City. There were still saloons, pool halls, and gambling, but the law seemed to have more control.

According to Marvin VanGilder's book *Jasper County, the First Two Hundred Years,* one of the favorite pastimes from pioneers days into the first quarter of the twentieth century was footracing. A big event in Joplin, it didn't take long for the practice to head over into Webb City. VanGilder told of a Webb Citian named Robert "Buckfoot" Boatright who developed footracing into a fine art. The reputation of Boatright, a saloonkeeper, included his shenanigans as the leader of a band of miners and businessmen who were dubbed the Buckfoot Gang. They had a footracing scam that netted them close to $3 million from unsuspecting gamblers. There was a racetrack in the northeast part of Webb City that the Webb City Athletic Club used to stage their footraces. This group had no shame as they had fixed races, paid off winners with satchels full of newspaper instead of money, or held the money in a wall safe for safe-keeping, only to open the safe later and find it empty. Law officials stated that the safe had a false back, and as soon as the money was put in the safe, the men in the next room would remove it.

Boatright eventually opened a commercial gymnasium in the upper rooms over a pool hall on Allen (Main) Street. The building was located on the southeast corner of Daugherty and Allen. There were many stories about the new establishment, but nothing documented. Bets on boxing matches, footraces, and other gambling activities were rumored to have taken place. During a rather questionable footrace scam, Boatright left the area by dark of night, and according to VanGilder, he subsequently died in Kansas City following a workout at a gymnasium.

Decent ladies did not walk on the east side of Allen Street, as it was a sure way to ruin your reputation. When the first opera house of Webb City was built (1883) on the southeast corner of

Allen (Main) and Main (Broadway), the Middlewest Building, it was very important that ladies be let out of the buggy directly in front of the opera house or cross the street and enter into the opera house without coming in contact with the activities of the east side of Allen Street. The opera house was upstairs and the downstairs had businesses that also needed to be avoided by the genteel ladies.

By 1937, Webb City had gained the reputation of being a "decidedly church town," according to Ms. Henrietta Crotty, in her book *A History and Economic Survey of Webb City Missouri.* She states that "Webb City has twenty active churches which have a morally uplifting effect on the community." In her survey, M.s Crotty doesn't mention how many of those notorious saloons, pool halls, or gambling houses still existed on Main Street.

A 1947 directory lists twenty-three churches, six liquor stores, two pool halls, and only two taverns. Some of the taverns weren't listed but existed!

But the shoot-'em-up days that existed in Webb City's early days soon gave way to civilization. There were still occasional swindlers in the midst, but on the whole, Webb City didn't take too long changing into the wonderful safe community we all remember as kids! Of course, even into the '60s, we (kids) were still forbidden to walk on the east side of Main street! Old habits die hard!

Brunnelle, Emma

Moral of this story: Don't go into marriage "blindly."

Life had been rough for *Emma Brunnelle.* Her husband had left her a widow at thirty years of age, with two sons to raise. It had been really hard for her to leave the boys with her mother in LaPlata, Missouri. She came to Webb City where the mines were making men rich. Maybe she would find her a rich young man to take care of her. Right now, she would have to be happy to have her job as a chambermaid working at the *Webb City Hotel* for $2 a week, plus a room to sleep in and food to live on. But as she lay her head on the pillow each night, she said a little prayer in hopes that someday, her prince would come along to rescue her.

One day, the town was all abuzz with the story of a blind man who claimed to have been robbed by the newsboy on the train. He was temporarily put up in the Webb City Hotel, while the sheriff investigated his accusations. It didn't take long for the old blind man—*Fleming* was his name—to be taken by the charms of the young widow. Truth be known, it didn't take the young chambermaid long to be entranced with the stories Fleming told about his mines in Colorado, which he claimed brought him about $1,000–$1,200 a week.

On September 12, 1883, Emma Brunnelle and Fleming took the trip to Carthage to exchange wedding vows. Emma's prayers had been answered. Her rich man had come along. Even though he was a mite bit older than she would have preferred, he would still be able to give her a secure home for herself and her two sons, ages fourteen and nine. Her search for a husband had taken a whole four months, but her search was ended—or was it?

Fleming promised Emma that they would go to Jefferson City for their honeymoon, then on to Florida to spend the winter, and then to Colorado to check on his mines.

Only one day of marital bliss, Fleming abandoned his young bride and just disappeared. Emma had the sheriff and some of the miners out searching for her husband. Knowing him to be just a helpless blind man, she couldn't imagine him just up and leaving her. But he had done just that—up and left. Emma's dream had turned into a nightmare. Not only did she lose her husband, but also she had already given her notice at the Webb City Hotel; therefore, she was unemployed with no money. You see, since Fleming had been robbed, he had talked her into giving him her savings until he could collect some funds from his mines in Colorado, at which time he would pay her back.

She finally found a job as a waitress, and she once again began her search for the man of her dreams, the one who would take care of her for the rest of her life. Only this time, she would make sure she saw the money first before she fell for the stories being told.

Young Lovers

Pansy Brasuer was so much in love. Whenever Chandos McMullen walked into the room, her heart would beat a little faster, and she had difficulty breathing. This must be true love, and she wanted to share it with the world. But alas, her mother did not approve of the courtship of Pansy and Chandos. She was very boisterous in her declaration that Pansy would never marry that Chandos. So Pansy and Chandos decided to take care of the situation and elope!

The year was 1903, and the young couple carefully planned their elopement. Chandos would sneak over to Pansy's house late in the night. Pansy would be watching for him and would tiptoe out to meet him in the yard. As luck would have it, Pansy's mom got wind of the elopement, and she had plans of her own to put a stop to this insanity. She locked Pansy in one of the bedrooms that didn't face the yard where young Chandos would be making his appearance.

Poor Pansy worried and fretted because she had no way of letting Chandos know why she had been detained. Meanwhile, Chandos patiently waited outside for the love of his life to join him. He never doubted for a moment that she wouldn't be there.

As daylight dawned, poor Chandos knew there was trouble somewhere as his true love had not appeared. He decided to go over and see Pansy's best friend, Nellie Pratt. He told Nellie about his and Pansy's plans and how Pansy had not joined him, and he was worried about her. Nellie investigated and found out what Pansy's mother had done.

To make her mother happy, that very morning, Pansy and Chandos, through tears of love and sadness, said their goodbyes to each other. Pansy promised to obey her mother and never see Chandos again.

As soon as Chandos left, Pansy was whisked away to the Frisco Depot to be sent to distant relatives in hopes that she would forget her sweet Chandos. Pansy's mom felt confident that the situation was well in hand.

The old adage "absence makes the heart grow fonder" came into effect with full force, as Pansy pined away for her Chandos. She was able to come home for an occasional visit during the next year, and she was good at hiding from her mother that she still carried a torch for Chandos. With the help of her best friend, Nellie, Pansy and Chandos were able to meet secretly to declare their love for each other.

Meanwhile, young Chandos had kept pretty busy working at the Hoffman Bros. Music House, located in the Blake Theatre on Daugherty Street, as a piano tuner. He was happy while at work because other than Pansy, music was what made his life worth living. Another reason Pansy's mother did not approve. She did not want her daughter to marry a musician.

Chandos began to write music in his spare time. Some of the local theaters even featured his music. He was getting to be quite well known and well liked around town. The story of Chandos and Pansy's romantic dilemma was often discussed with sympathy for the young couple.

In the last part of October 1904, Pansy came home for one of her visits. Her mother gave in to the idea of Pansy and her sister, Lalah, taking the train to St. Louis for the girls to attend the world's fair. Most of the folks on the train were heading to the fair also; it was such a festive occasion.

When they were halfway to St. Louis, Pansy confided in her sister that she had a surprise. It seemed that the day before, on October 23, 1904, with the help of her best friend, Nellie, Pansy and Chandos had exchanged their vows in front of Nellie's father, Justice of the Peace T. B. Pratt. Nellie and another friend, Fred Baker, stood in as witnesses.

After telling Lalah about the wonderful union with the love of her life, Chandos joined them from another part of the train, and the happy trio went on to St. Louis to enjoy the world's fair.

Lalah made the trip back to Webb City alone, as Pansy and Chandos traveled on to Tampa, Florida, to visit Chandos's family and take up residence, as Pansy was sure her mother would never speak to her again.

Back here in Webb City, Lalah got off the train with lots of stories to share, and she was telling anyone and everyone of the marriage of Pansy and Chandos. Many of the young couples' friends were glad to hear that they were finally together, and nobody would be able to separate them again! Nellie Pratt was the heroine of the day, as she was the one that helped to bring a happy ending to a local love story.

Sill, Katie

I have two stories about a lady named Katie Sill. I haven't been able to connect them in any way to see if it's the same lady. Both stories tend to compliment the lady as a very sympathetic and generous woman, so I am thinking they are of the same lady.

One came from the *History of Jasper County*. It tells of a pioneer settler of Jasper County named Mrs. Katie Pennington Sill, who was renowned for her cooking talent. Her most noted talent being in her biscuits, which old settlers often claimed were so good they just melted in your mouth. Katie and her family had settled in Jasper County in 1840, when Katie was about thirteen years old. In those days, young ladies were taught to cook at an early age to help around the house. And it helped to catch a good man!

During the first year of the Civil War, which started in 1861, many soldiers stopped by the farm of Katie Sill to enjoy some of her good biscuits. Katie served both the Union troops and the

Confederates, even though she was a Southern sympathizer. Her family tried to remain neutral so as not to be involved in the conflict.

At first, feeding the many soldiers didn't bother Katie. She enjoyed watching those men devour her cooking and listening to the raves of her biscuits, but by the time the second year of the war came about, Katie was finding it hard to feed her own family, let alone all the soldier passing through.

One day, a troop of Confederate Scouts stopped by, and as they dismounted, they asked Katie to make them some biscuits. As Katie pulled the first batch from the oven, the aroma that filled the air had the men smacking their lips in anticipation, when suddenly, a bugle call sounded from a short distance away. Looking up over the hill, a regiment of Union Calvary could be seen approaching at a quick gallop.

The Confederates realized that if they tarried to eat the biscuits, the Union would overtake them, so they quickly mounted and rode away. Katie worked fast and threw the biscuits in a cradle and covered them with a blanket. The Union soldiers stopped to water their horses, but they did not notice the biscuits in the cradle, and Katie's family enjoyed a wonderful meal, thanks to the biscuits that had been baked for the Confederate soldiers.

By my calculations, Katie was about thirty-four years old when she was baking those biscuits during the Civil War. And she would have been about sixty-four years old in this next story. A very nice lady who lived out by the Sill Farm supplied this information to me.

Many a wagon train pulled through this area on the way west to make their fortunes or just to take advantage of the land being given away. Most families started out with a covered wagon full of all their belongings. But as the trip usually was more of a hardship than anticipated, some or all of those belongings were sold along the way or stolen. Sometimes possessions were left along the side of the trail to lighten the load or make room for a sick or injured person. Katie had a visitor one day. A visitor that left a very precious bundle.

A wagon train was heading past Katie's farm, located just north of what are now Highways 96 and 43. A lady driving a covered wagon pulled out of the wagon train and stopped at Katie's house. The lady, who was only known as Mrs. Ritter, was in a very emotional state. Not only was she very pregnant, but her husband had just died, and she needed to make arrangements to bury him.

Katie helped the young lady make all the necessary arrangements, and they had a proper funeral for the young man. Katie felt so sorry for this young couple who had headed west to find a pot of gold at the end of the rainbow, only to have all their hopes and dreams shattered by the unexpected call of the angel of death.

The whole ordeal must have been too much for the young woman as she went into labor, giving birth to a very healthy little boy. Katie helped nurse the young lady back to health, and she really enjoyed having the baby around. The little baby boy was named Arthur, and he was such a good baby.

Before long, another wagon train was passing through town, and the young lady wanted to continue with her journey as she and her husband had planned. But she didn't know how she would be able to handle the wagon and take care of the baby all by herself. She talked with Katie and finally asked the question that changed Katie's life drastically. Would Katie please take care of the baby until a home could be established in California, and then the baby would be sent for? Well, being the sweet generous-natured woman that Katie seemed to have been, it didn't take long for her to make up her mind.

That little baby boy, Arthur Ritter, grew up in Jasper County. His mother was never heard from again. It's not known if something happened to her on the way, or if she just decided that the baby was in better hands. Arthur never knew his birth mother, but he had the loving arms of Katie Sill to guide him in his growing years.

Arthur had a son, Paul, born in 1911 at the same Sill Farm that Arthur had been born. Katie was eighty-four years old by the time Paul was born. She never knew too much information about Arthur's mother, so genealogy research is almost impossible. But you know, if Katie hadn't taken that young baby in, there may have been an even shorter genealogy. What a special lady!

Sterett, Wayne and John Wolf

Condensed version of Wayne Sterrett and John Wolf's journey, from Branson to New Orleans, by canoe in 1915.

On October 4, 1915, after traveling from Webb City to Branson by train, Wayne Sterett and John Wolf headed out on White River in a little canoe. Their destination was the grand town of New Orleans. Each week, Wayne Sterett would write a few words about their adventures on the water and send it to the *Webb City Sentinel*. At the end of each article, he would give the information of which town they would be in next, and he always asked them to send *Sentinel*s to that next address so they would have news of home.

I want to take this time to relate the wonderful adventures of Webb City's very own Tom Sawyer and Huck Finn. Now Wayne Sterett had graduated from Webb City High School in 1910 and had continued a study of science and electricity. He dabbled a little in some newfangled inventions, and then he got this crazy idea to take a trip to New Orleans by canoe.

Not being a shy person, Wayne made many friends as he traveled along, and he asked many questions, which the folks who lived along the river seemed more than happy to answer. He said that he had many wonderful Southern stories, but we don't have any record of them—too bad!

The boys never paddled on Sundays. They always tied up their canoe, changed into clean clothes, had a good dinner, and went over their Sunday school lesson, just as if they were at home.

On the first report, Wayne said they had traveled 225 miles shooting the white rapids through the Ozark Mountains and had only spent 33¢ so far. They had dined on such wonderful delicacies as frog legs. Wayne used the rest of the frog for fish bait and caught a five-and-a-half-pound catfish. He had a huge frying pan, but it still took two batches to fry up that fish. The boys said the hunting and fishing was splendid. There were plenty of squirrels, ducks, geese, and turkey, not to mention an abundance of nuts and pawpaws. In spending the 33¢, they gave a woman a quarter to bake them some fresh bread, and they spent 8¢ on a peck of sweet potatoes.

Because of a flood in August, many pumpkins were growing along the bankside, and Wayne stewed it in the evening, wrapped it in a blanket, and had it for breakfast the next morning.

What was interesting was the many commercials that Wayne included in his reports, such as, "We bought our clothing at Humphreys and we both think they are the best outing clothes that we have ever seen." He also bragged on the canoe when he stated, "If we had any other kind of boat it would have taken a little over twice as long, Robert Stewart and Beverley Bunce are the Webb City agents for these canoes, which are the best in the world."

Wayne mentions the town of Buffalo, Arkansas, and he said:

> They claim to have a hundred or more people but I believe that they must have counted the pigs and chickens. One grocery store man had his chickens penned up on the porch in front of the store and you had to go to the back door to get in. Another had a general merchandise store and hotel combined with pigs running loose in the store.

The water was so clear that the boys could watch the bass swim under the canoe. They experimented fishing with a wooden minnow. At night, the owls and wolves made so much noise there was no chance of sleep. Traveling along the river was magical, as the beauty was overwhelming.

The houseboats along the river were homes to the many families that were crawfooting for mussels. They looked them over for pearls and then sold the shells to the button factory at Augusta. A powerboat would run up and down the river buying the shells.

One month after leaving Branson, the duo reached the end of the White River and turned their canoe into the Mississippi River. Quite a change, as the waters turned muddy.

One day, they were caught in a rainstorm, and everything got wet. As the sun set, a heavy fog settled on the water. The river was two miles wide, and it got dark before they could reach the shore, and then they couldn't see the shore. They just let the boat float along on its own. After a while, they could hear voices and hollered for them to show a light, which they did. They were able to pull up alongside a houseboat. When they climbed aboard, they found out the owners of the houseboat were in as sad a shape as they were. They couldn't find land either, and they had no furniture or supplies on the boat. They just drifted along until they drifted into a pocket of the river and tied up to an old fallen tree. They went on shore and made a fire to fry some bacon and make coffee. After dinner, they climbed aboard the houseboat again as a strong wind sprang up. The next morning, they floated into Greenville, Mississippi, where one of the men in the houseboat had some family. The boys ate some good Southern cookin'.

Wayne commented that even though it had been many years since the Civil War, the South had not recovered, and it was very evident.

When the boys reached Vicksburg, Mississippi, John Wolfe decided he was homesick and abandoned ship to return to Webb City. Wayne Sterett sent a postcard to the *Sentinel* that read, "I am the captain, the mate and the crew. The cook and pilot too. John is homesick for some of the folks around Webb City and is going back home. I am going on, so send me some Sentinel papers to Natchez, Miss."

In his next report, Wayne said that some of the nicest people that he had ever met were from the South. He noticed that all of the post office clerks had been women, then he went on to make an unusual statement.

> Another thing was that there are so many pretty girls down here. One thing that I do not like is that nearly all of them paint their cheeks. The day that John went home his lips were both sore and swollen: I bet that face paint is poison, but I can not figure out how he came to get it on his lips. I intend to be very careful not to get any on my lips, (before coming home.)

Before leaving Webb City, Wayne bought some big fishhooks, and he received quite a bit of teasing, but he was determined to use them. This is his fish story:

> I had one of those fish hooks baited and hung to about twenty-five feet of line weighted with lead and tied to the back of my canoe. I had forgotten about it, until a big catfish came along and began to run up stream at about ten miles an hour, pulling and the canoe with him and turning around several times. I felt like I did not know whether that fish had me or I had the fish. I worked him to the top once but I could not begin to hold him as he was nearly as large as I was. I was going to let him run until he got tired and then drag him out on a sand bar. He ran for about three miles and we met a steam boat and he headed straight for it, so I had to cut the line and let him go.

Now that's a fish story!

Wayne thought about the hunters back home as he would come upon bunches of wild geese with five hundred to two thousand geese making enough noise to hear for miles.

When Wayne finally reached New Orleans after forty days in the canoe and spending only $17, he immediately checked into the YMCA, which was set up like a hotel. The first thing on the agenda was sightseeing.

The return trip home was aboard the Natchez Steamboat with first-class treatment all the way. His canoe was sent by freight to Webb City. As he traveled along in comfort, Wayne couldn't help but think about the forty days and 1,300 miles he had just traveled. An old steamboat pilot said that due to the currents and channels, Wayne had traveled nearly 2,000 miles instead of 1,300.

What an adventure, for two young men, in a time era when only small towns were few and far between along the river. What a story they had to share with their grandchildren. And it was well documented in the *Sentinel*.

A special thanks to Tom Hartman for sharing the 1915 newspaper articles with us.

Wayne Sterrett, the water traveler—The same story as told above, but in Wayne's own words as he sent the story to the *Sentinel* in 1915.

Wednesday, 1915—**REPORT # 1**

Dear folks at home: Well, I suppose that you are all wondering why we have not written before. The reason is that there has been so many things for us to see that I have not had time.

Well, we stayed at Branson and Hollister all day Monday [Branson was just a small fishing town in 1915] and got our boat unpacked and our baggage so we could handle it without much trouble. A mouse had gotten into our box while it was at the depot in Webb City and caused us a little trouble. (Wish some one would send an old tabby cat down there.)

It took us all day to paddle through Lake Tanycomo, all dead water with the wind against us. I will not describe the lake or the lauches and club houses on the lake as I suppose many of you have been there. We carried our luggage around the dam at powersite on a wheel barrow.

The next morning, Wednesday the man in charge gave us permission to go through the power plant as I was an electrician. The next day we got out in the current of the river and since then we have been shooting the rapids o White River as it winds around the Ozark Mountains. That night John killed a big bull frog and we ate his hind legs for supper and I used the rest of him for fish bait. I set eight bank hooks and caught one catfish. I weighed him and he weighed five and a half pounds. I bought the largest frying pan that the Lindsay Hardware store had. Well, we had to fry twice to cook all of that fish. We sure filled up on fish all day.

The next night I caught another not quite so large but he filled the pan once; we also got two bass. The hunting and fishing here is splendid at this time of the year. The woods have lots of squirrels and duck, geese, and turkey are flying south. We have had nuts and pawpaws. It took us two weeks to go from Powersite to Cotter, Ark., a distance of 225 miles. We have never paddled more than four or six hours a day and we always tie up on Sunday. We had intended to travel faster, but there are too many interesting things in the Ozarks to see. People do not need to go hungry down here. We only spent thirty three cents for eats above Cotter. We gave a woman a quarter to bake us some bread and eight cents for a peck of sweet potatoes.

On Sunday we tied our canoe up, put on clean clothes, had a good dinner and went over the Sunday School lesson just like we were at home.

We saw a man that said he had helped Claude and Fant Balland Ed Flournoy, as he called him. He said that he had often helped them fish and hunt; they called him Kit Karson, but he always let them have the honor for all he did for them. We have seen very few people above Cotter, but lots of animal life.

I have been stewing pumpkin while writing this. It is done so I will turn in and wrap up in my wool blanket till morning. We have cots inside a small tent, we cover the cots with oil cloth before spreading our blankets. It is so much warmer down here than it is at home.

We bought our outing clothes of Humphreys at home and we both think they are the best outing clothes that we have ever seen.

I will mail this somewhere below here in a day or so. Our next address will be Batesville, Arkansas. Send us a few copies of The Sentinel to that place. Yours Truly, WAYNE STERRETT, JOHN WOLF

Wednesday, 1916—REPORT # 2

John Wolf and Wayne Sterrett floating down rivers to New Orleans, write the Sentinel above Newport, Ark., again, interestingly, as follows:

Well, I mailed that last letter at Buffalo which is one of the great mant towns that are on the White River below Cotter. There are a dozen or more of them. They claim to have a hundred or more people but

I believe that they must count the pigs and chickens. We took two men from Carthage across the river. They sure looked a couple of Miss Nanceys down here. Then we went up to the town of Buffalo. One grocery store man had his chickens penned up on the porch in front of the store and you had to go to the back door to get in. Another had a general merchandise store and hotel combined with pigs running loose in the store. Some of the buildings were on pegs so that the high water would not get them. Most of the houses around in the hills were log houses. We have been in many of them, and now whenever I hear anyone say that they were raised in a log house in Arkansas I know just what it is loke. At one house we got some home grown, home cured tobacco and let me tell you whenever you smoke that kind you sure know that you have been smoking something: granger and cotton boul twist are not in it.

We have met some of the nicest people down here that we have ever met. People in Arkansas will be Arkansawers but I will always take off my hat to man, woman or girl from Arkansas.

When we first started White River was very low, but you can not imagine how terrible the high water was last August. A man in one of the houseboats said it looked like a cyclone had struck it. We saw a houseboat turned upside down on the bank and nearly buried in gravel. Another upside down in the river. We saw boats that had been twisted around trees. Immense sycamore trees have either been uprooted or laid flat, sometimes for miles along the banks. White River was 53 feet eight inches above normal, higher than it was ever known to be before.

Field after field all along the way has been laid in waste. We saw a woman gathering nuts, who said they had lost nearly everything they had. Lots of these people will have to live through the winter by hunting and fishing.

Of course there is a funny side to everything. People down here plant pumpkins in the cornfield. Well, the high water washed the pumpkins away, and the drift wood along the river is full of nice ripe pumpkins.

I never saw as many bass before as I have seen in White River, the water is clear and you can see them all around the boat. I have been learning a great deal about them and how to catch them with a wooden minnow. I have learned that it is not the man that can throw the most line that catches the most but the man that keeps himself and his lineout of sight and drops the bait in the proper places, that is at the ledges of the rocks and under the willows.

We have been making six or seven miles an hour with our little Old Town canoe and are in a more thickly settled part of the country than we were. One night the owls and wolves kept us awake most of the night.

Our next address will be Augusta and then Devils Bluff. Be sure and send us some copies of The Sentinel. Better send to Devils Bluff for the current of this river carries us at a pretty fast rate. We have been through three government locks, have passed several steamboats and government boats. Yours truly, WAYNE STERRITT, JOHN I. WOLF

P.S. Went from Batesville to Newport, 65 miles by water in 8 hours.

Titanic Slim Thompson

We live in an age when a sense of humor is in great demand. If more people had a sense of humor, we would not be hearing about road rage, bar fights, etc. If we could learn to laugh away our frustrations, life would be a paradise.

I came across a story about a young man in the early days of Joplin and Webb City. This young man had such a determination in life that he could accomplish anything he set out to accomplish. If someone was better at a certain sport, then he would practice and work at it until he had mastered the sport in question.

With such a great determination and such a talent to succeed, this young man was destined to become famous. And famous he did become! It may not have been a good famous, but he was well known.

As a young boy in Cassville, Titanic "Ti" Slim Thompson discovered that he had a talent for throwing a baseball farther than any of the other boys in town. Being an adventurer, Ti headed to the big town of Joplin. He was amazed at the number of men who associated at the saloons each night. He also watched and noticed that as the men drank, they became more willing to place bets on what they thought were sure wins.

This was the beginning of Ti's unusual profession. Titanic became a professional swindler. His talent for pitching baseballs became the first of his bets. He would bet anyone who was willing to participate that he could throw the ball the farthest. He was able to make a little bit of money, but before long, none of the men were willing to bet as his reputation was spreading around town. So he had to come up with something new—and he did!

He was constantly working on new schemes to hook the men into a bet. There was a bartender from Texas named Gooddee who had to take a lot of harassment from the men because he had not been to school and could not even spell *d-o-g*. So Ti took the bartender aside and worked with him for weeks, teaching him to spell two words, *hippopotamus* and *rhinoceros*. When he felt his pupil was ready, Ti began to work on the men in the saloon.

He calmly made a remark that maybe Gooddee was not so dumb. Maybe he could spell a really big word. The men were inquisitive and asked, "Like what?" And Ti led them along and suggested that maybe the bartender could spell the name of some big animals like hippopotamus and rhinoceros. The men were willing to take Ti up on this bet, and they all sauntered up to the bar where Gooddee was working, and Ti said, "Hey, Gooddee, can you spell *hippopotamus* for us?"

Well, the bartender was proud of what he was about to spell, so he squared up his shoulders, and in a voice that announced his confidence, he spelled *r-h-i-n-o-c-e-r-o-s* instead of hippopotamus. Okay, so Ti didn't win all of his bets. He knew that this loss was due to him overcompensating, he should have taught Gooddee only one word, not two.

But most of the time, Ti was a winner. Like the time he bet that he could make a cat pick up a Coke bottle and carry it for thirty feet. The men accused him of having a trained cat, but Ti assured them that he could do it with an old alley cat from out back. The bet was on, and a cat was brought in from the alley. First he wrapped his handkerchief securely around the Coke bottle. Ti picked up the cat by the tail. When a cat is suspended in this position, its claws will grab at anything it can reach, and so Ti hung this poor cat by the tail over the Coke bottle, and its claws grabbed that handkerchief and actually picked up the bottle. Ti then proceeded to carry the cat for thirty feet, and the cat held onto the bottle the entire way. Chalk another one up for Titanic.

One time, Ti bet that he could throw a pumpkin onto the roof of the eight-story Conner Hotel. This seemed like a sure bet to those within earshot because they knew he could not get a good enough momentum on something as big as a pumpkin. So the crowd headed outside to see Ti lose another bet. Well, the older Ti got, the trickier he became. Outside Ti had a small pumpkin that was practically petrified from being dried out, and it was about the size of a baseball (remember, Ti could outthrow anyone with a baseball). Ti picked up that little pumpkin and easily threw it onto the roof of the Conner Hotel.

While traveling by streetcar to Commerce, Oklahoma, with some friends, they saw a farmer working in the fields not far from Commerce. The question came up that they wondered what the farmer might be planting. Ti simply stated that the farmer was planting hemp. Well, his audience said that nobody planted hemp around this area, and he was wrong. They took him up on a bet and decided that the next morning, they would walk out to the farm and ask the farmer what he was planting. Sure enough, bright and early the next morning, the guys walked out to the farmer's field and asked what he was planting, and he replied, "Hemp!" The guys paid Ti, and it wasn't until later they found out Ti had went out in the middle of the night and bribed the farmer into saying he was planting hemp.

There were many more stories about Titanic and his unusual profession. The last bet that many remember Titanic being involved with was in Kansas City. While standing by a large lake, Ti commented that he could drive a golf ball across the lake. This was a feat that was humanly impossible to accomplish, so everyone was willing to take him up on the bet. The only thing Ti requested was that he would get to choose the date. They all agreed, and it was on a really cold day that Ti made his decision to drive that golf ball across the *frozen* lake. Many say that golf ball is probably still going!

Ti made a lot of money in his lifetime, but he had to leave many a town late at night and in a hurry as he swindled many people. Some with a sense of humor could enjoy someone like Titanic Slim Thompson, but unfortunately, even in those days, there were many without that sense of humor (especially those who lost money!).

But he had to have been an interesting person to be around. And even though he stood over six foot, he had a slight resemblance to a little leprechaun and just about as sneaky.

Willard, Dell and Mabel—Old-Fashioned Romance

Mabel McMillan had been hired to collect payments for Sedgwick's. Her older sister, Vern, was married to the undertaker, Willie Mills. Mabel would drive out in a horse and buggy to Alba, Neck City, Purcell, and Oronogo to collect payments on furniture. She would even locate men in saloons, and she would have someone go inside to request that the person meet with her outside, and they were usually good at paying this pretty young bill collector.

On one occasion, Mabel took her mother, Sarah, her sister, Vern, and Vern's young son along to keep her company during the long route. As they were headed back to the Webb City, the horses spooked for some unknown reason, and the horse and buggy, along with all occupants, wound up in the ditch. Nobody was injured, although a stick came close to going in Sarah's eye. This bedraggled group was sure happy to see a beer wagon come along. The driver helped them up onto the wagon, tied the horses to the back, and drove them into town.

Now Mabel had a close friend, Josie Beasley, who lived on a small farm where the Carterville Dump was located on Dump Road. Josie was a bit of a matchmaker. It seemed that the menfolk in her family had been working with two young men in the mines, Dell and Jess Willard. So Josie told Mabel all about this wonderful young man named Dell Willard.

Josie had a plan for Mabel and Dell to meet. She knew that Dell and Jesse had volunteered to help dig a grave, so they made plans to attend the funeral. First they had to forge excuses to get out of school for the funeral. Having accomplished this feat, without complication, they moved on to step 2—getting to the funeral. Of course, there was the usual girlish chatter that goes along with the excitement and the anticipation of meeting a handsome young man. They were so busy talking, they weren't aware that the funeral procession had slowed down to make a turn into Carterville cemetery. The buggy in front of them had almost completely stopped, and they hadn't. The girls' horse kept right on going until his head was right between the couple in the buggy ahead of them.

Not long after this eventful meeting, Dell and Jess both took with smallpox. They didn't have a mother to take care of them, so they were sent to the pesthouse, located on East Street and Aylor Avenue. Jess seemed to recover quicker than Dell, so he would take notes written by Dell to the corner fence and put them under a rock where notes from Mabel would be waiting to be returned to Dell.

When their lives seemed to finally be on a normal routine, Saturday nights would find Dell heading to town for a shave and haircut at the barbershop, and then on to the funeral parlor to visit with Mabel. As most romances go, there are always those embarrassing moments that we have no control over. Mabel's nephew came up to the smitten couple and cried, "Aunt Mabel, I wet my pants, that just what I done!" Being the normal teenagers that they were, they both pretended not to hear the poor uncomfortable little chap.

The inevitable finally came, and Dell proposed to Mabel. Mabel readily accepted to be the wife of the man she loved. She went to her mother and informed her that Dell was going to ask for her permission to marry, and she didn't hesitate to let her mother know that she had better say yes because she was going to marry him anyway. She was such a headstrong young lady in love. Sarah McMillan agreed to the nuptials, but it was reported later to Mabel that her mother cried as she made the wedding dress for her sixteen-year-old daughter.

The wedding was on March 27, 1907. Mabel and Dell Willard were in heavenly bliss but a little dismayed when the local paper came out with the following dismal report:

> From Morgue to Matrimony, Miss Mabel McMillan became the bride of Iridell Willard. From undertaker's clerk to bride is the somewhat happy step taken by Mrs. Iridell Willard, who until last evening was Miss Mabel McMillan in the employ of Sedgwick Undertaking Company, at least up to a few weeks ago, when she resigned her gruesome position to make preparations for her marriage. Justice of the Peace Jones, performed the ceremony at the home of the bride's parents, 311 East Daugherty, remaining for the wedding feast which followed and which was attended by a large number of friends of the bride and groom. The groom is a hoisterman at the Oseola Mine.

Needless to say, Mabel was not happy about the way her marriage was presented to the community. But that had no reflection on their marriage. Mabel and Dell had forty-six years together before Dell passed away due to a heart attack. Dell was always proud of his wife and his home. They had two children, Byron and Dell (Pat) Willard.

A special thanks to Pat and Laura Willard for sharing this story with us.

CHAPTER 8

Buildings and Landmarks

The Zinc City sign erected on West Daugherty to be seen by
passengers as they arrived at the Frisco Depot.

The Zinc City

Webb City was the center of the lead and mining district of Southwest Missouri. There was more lead and zinc mined within a radius of three and a half miles than any other similar area in the world. From 1894–1904, the mines produced $23 million worth of ore. During the First World War, at Webb City's mining peak, there were over fifty mines in operation around Webb City.

The wooden buildings were soon replaced with brick, some three stories high. Webb City boasted of paved streets, electric lights, good waterworks, a complete sewer system, two telephone companies, and the best-equipped interurban electric railway in the west, connecting Webb City with the surrounding towns in every direction. There were eighteen churches of different denominations, a reliable fire department, an opera house seating 1,500, and many beautiful homes. There were two railroad depots, four banks, and a YMCA.

Many businesses were established during the beginning years of Webb City, some of which are still in existence today. The *Webb City Sentinel* was established in 1879, the Webb City Bank (Mid-Missouri Bank) was established in 1882 by John C. Webb and his son E. T. Webb. The Webb Corporation incorporated in 1895.

After World War I, the mining industry declined because of the low price of ore and the discovery of Oklahoma ore pockets. Webb City's enterprising citizens, led by the chamber of commerce, turned to industry and brought many factories into town. Webb City had a leather factory, shirt factory, shoe factory, cigar factory, box factory, and a casket manufacturer. In 1920, Webb City attained the distinction of increasing her industries more than any other city in the United States, with an increase of 250 percent.

Another prominent feature in Webb City's growth and national recognition was the gravel industry. Countless tons of gravel, chat, and sand have been shipped to every state in the Union for building roads, forming ballast for railroads, as well as concrete and stucco construction.

Webb City put great energy and zeal into establishing one of the best school districts in the state. From the very beginning, the citizens of Webb City have shown loyalty to their schools by voting for the money necessary to keep pace with progress in education and the rapidly increasing demand for teachers and larger buildings.

As we take this journey into Webb City's past, we see the building blocks that have formed this wonderful community. Webb City is a town that is noted for its amazing school system, continuing growth, community pride, great leadership, and proud heritage.

Building Names

In this day and age, we live in a society controlled by numbers. We have numbers to associate with almost everything we come in contact with each day. We have account numbers, invoice numbers, addresses, phone numbers, fax numbers, Social Security numbers, pin numbers, charge card numbers, e-mail numbers, etc. And when we call a place of business, we are only one of a many number of customers, and they do not know us, and usually we do not know them. Now let us take a trip back to those good ole days where a customer was so important and a treasured asset.

In the late 1800s and the early 1900s, life seemed so much simpler than today. You could call your favorite grocery store, give your name and the list of groceries needed, and felt assured they would be delivered. You did not have to give your life's history. He knew who you were and where you lived. He wanted your business. He not only delivered, but when you paid your bill on payday, he gave you a sack of penny candy in appreciation. Of course, there were grocery stores on just about every block, and that was some stiff competition.

In looking at the advertisements of businesses in those days, it was interesting to note that some did not list an address. Small towns knew where every business was located and, for that matter, where everyone lived. My favorite saying noted, "In a small town, you don't have to use your turning signal because everyone in town knows where you are going."

Many doctors and lawyers had their offices on the upper floors of buildings, and they would just list the names of the buildings and maybe a room number. For instance, an office may be located in room 2 of the O'Neill Building. People who were familiar with Webb City knew the O'Neill Building was located at Nine South Webb Street where the water company was located. The building was named after Colonel James O'Neill, who established the city's first water system.

We will play a little game, a name game. I will mention the names of a few buildings, and you see if you can recall where they are or used to be located. Some are pretty easy, but a few may take some concentration. There was the most commonly known Wagner Building, the Ryus Building, the McCorkle Building, the Zinc Ore Building, the Dermott Building, the Coyne Building, the Wright Building, the OPCH Building. I have more to list, but take a moment to see how many of these buildings you have located so far.

Some of the easiest names to locate or remember are the Unity Building, the YMCA Building, the Webb City Bank Building, the National Bank Building, the Blake Theatre, the city hall building, or the Humphrey Building.

The Wagner Building was well known for all the offices located on the upper floors. There were many doctors, lawyers, and general offices for businesses located on the edge of town, such as the Webb City Brick Company. The Wagner Building was previously referred to as the post office building. It was the first official Webb City building built specifically for the post office. The Wagner Building was next-door and eventually took over the PO building. Some ads for this building were listed as room 10 of the Wagner Building or the PO building, or next to the PO building, or the Wagner Building next to the Elks Club. Now that I have mentioned the Elks Club, some of you are more likely to recall the location. It is the half-block of buildings located on the northwest corner of Broadway (then known as Joplin) Street and Webb Street. Later fame of the building was due to dances on the second floor.

The bank buildings had plenty of offices for professionals. The Webb City Bank Building was on the northwest corner of Main (Allen) Street and Broadway (which was known as Main) Street. Did that get you confused? The street names were changed in 1922.

The National Bank Building was in the one hundred block of North Main, west side by the alley. You may recognize it as the present home of the Roderique Insurance Company. The Unity Building was home to the Merchants & Miners Bank and many professional offices. It was easier to say Unity Building than Merchants & Miners Bank Building.

Buildings like the Dermott Building, the Coyne Building, McCorkle Building, Donehoo Building, and Ryus Building were named after the men who built them. The Dermott is located on the northwest corner of Main and First Streets. The McCorkle Building was located on the corner of Church and Main Streets. McCorkle was a mining tycoon. The Donehoo Building was located on the northeast corner of Church and Main Street. It burned in 1982 and was the home of the *Webb City Sentinel*. Donehoo was a doctor. The Coyne building is at 109 West Broadway, and Coyne owned a lumberyard and was very active in the community. The Ryus Building was at 122 North Webb Street.

Many of the buildings have their names and dates built into the building, like the Zinc Ore Building, Eight South Main, present home to the *Webb City Sentinel*; the Dermott Building located on the northwest corner of Main and First Street; and the Century Building, Thirty-One South Main.

The Humphrey Building, the second brick building in Webb City, was located in a half-block section of the two hundred block of North Main. The first brick building was the Wright Building, where the chamber of commerce now stands in the old service station. The Wright Building was the first home of the Webb City Bank and later home of the Wright Jewelry Company.

Take a ride and search out the famous buildings of Webb City and don't forget the Middlewest Building, One South Main Street, originally home to a beautiful opera house.

Some of the buildings known by name in Webb City:

> Aylor Building, (Odd Fellows Hall) 208 North Main
> Stevinson Building, 214–216 North Main
> Blake Building, replaced by the Civic Building, 217 West Daugherty (opera house)
> Middlewest Building, 1 South Main (opera house)
> Morris Opera House, 111 North Main
> Corl Book Store, 10 South Main; later address change with addition of small restaurant, became 10 1/2 Main. Wanglin Book Store in 1909 (10 South Main).
> Humphrey Building, 201–207 North Main
> Zinc Ore Building, 8 South Main
> McCorkle Building, 14 South Main
> Ryus Building, 122 North Webb Street
> Coyne Building, 110 West Broadway
> Dermott Building, 34 South Main
> National Bank Building, 108 North Main
> Unity Building, 114–116 North Main
> Parker Building, 106 North Main
> Webb City Bank Building, 100 North Main

Century Building, Tom Hayden Building, Clark and Dodson Building, 25, 27, 29 South Main Street, mostly referred to as the Century Building.

McLellan Building, 1904

Sutherland Building

Frisco Depot, Daugherty and Madison

Church

First church in Webb City—The first work for Webb City was begun by a little band of Presbyterians—W. A. Wheatley, C. S. Manker, and Van Pelt, who, with their good workers, organized a union Sunday school at Webb's Hall in the latter part of 1876. The Sunday school from the first day was a success, not only in point of number but in the interest manifested. W. A. Wheatley was its superintendent. The attendance grew so rapidly that it was necessary to secure a larger place of meeting, and permission was given to use the new schoolhouse that recently had been completed. And here the work was carried on during 1877–1878. At the time the Sunday school moved to the schoolhouse, it numbered over two hundred regular attendants, the primary class, in charge of Mrs. W. A. Wheatley, containing forty-two little tots. The matter of organizing a church was now agitated, and from this union Sunday school grew later the First Presbyterian Church of Webb City, which was organized March 27, 1877, with eight members.

Messrs. Wheatley, Manker, and Van Pelt, who had taken the initiative in the organization of the Sunday school, were elected the first session of the new church. During the remaining '70s, the church did not have a regular pastor, but the Rev. D. K. Campbell of Joplin preached to the congregation, which grew slowly but surely, every Sunday afternoon, until after he closed his ministerial work in Joplin.

In 1879, the society, which now had grown to twenty-six, purchased a building on Allen Street, which had been erected for a saloon, fitted it up for a church, and there worshiped until the latter '80s. During the pioneer days of Webb City, the church exerted a great influence. Its choir—the famous Stevenson-Wheatley quartette, consisting of W. A. Wheatley and wife, and Professor J. M. Stevenson and wife—won great distinction, singing at all of the principal gatherings over the county.

In April 1879, the Ozark Presbyterians met in the Webb City Church. One other little incident might be mentioned which shows the influence that the church exerted on the community. During the winter of 1877–1878, there was a great amount of sickness in Webb City, due partly to the inclemency of the weather and partly to the lack of proper shelter, and quite a number died of pneumonia. Mrs. Wheatley and Mrs. Hull, both active workers in the church, were ministering angels who went out and helped care for the afflicted. Many a sickroom was cheered by the kindly attentions of these two church workers.

In those days, there was no undertaker in Webb City, and when death entered the home of a friend, they came and, with loving hands, helped prepare the body for burial. Thus as they performed these kindly acts of love and tenderness, they reflected credit on the church, whose deaconesses they were.

Cemeteries

Mount Hope Cemetery—The area of Mount Hope Cemetery was known as Pilot Grove Thomas C. Webb, a cousin to founder John C. Webb. Tom brought his wife from Tennessee, and he found this beautiful land with rolling hills and plentiful trees. Thomas could stand at the high point of his land and see all over the area for miles. This young couple in their twenties had many plans and dreams for Pilot Grove.

During the Civil War, vigilantes were very active along the Missouri-Kansas lines. The sad part is those who were just defending their property were often killed. Thomas was one of those brave property holders that were killed defending his property and family. That left Mary a young widow. Mary kept the Pilot Grove Farm going and raised her children alone.

She divided the land among their children. One of those children was Erasmus Webb, who married his second cousin Eliza Jane Terry. Erasmus and Eliza had three children: Jesse Thomas Webb, John Edward Webb, and Clementine Webb. Erasmus died in 1888, leaving Eliza to raise the children alone. Eliza married William Alonzo Bigger. The land on the hill became known as the Bigger Place, but old-timers still referred to the hill as Pilot Grove.

In April of 1905, eleven Joplin and Webb City businessmen incorporated a business and purchased the seventy-seven acres of the Bigger Place from Eliza for $11,550. The businessmen made the cemetery a tribute to the wonderful families that helped build Webb City. They contacted family members and arranged to have the bodies of those glorious families moved to Mount Hope Cemetery. The top mound of the cemetery holds well-known families such as the Webbs, McCorkles, Stewarts, Chinns, and many more families.

Entrance to Mt. Hope Cemetery, Joplin, Mo.

Mausoleums

You might want to take a peaceful walk through Mount Hope Cemetery, it is so relaxing. The landscape architect, Sid Hare, designed natural-looking circular roads that were around the beautiful plants and trees. The cemetery is known for the architecture of its mausoleums—nine of them to be exact—that dot the landscape. Each mausoleum seems to carry a family story.

The practice of building mausoleums started in 353 BC, when King Mausolus passed away, and his wife, Artemisia, built a mausoleum in memory of him. Artemisia was also his sister.

In 1804, Paris established the Pere Lachaise Cemetery, which included many acres to allow the construction of fanciful mausoleums.

In 1861, as Queen Victoria mourned the death of Albert, she changed the looks of cemeteries. She turned the cemeteries into parks with incredible statues, as if in an art gallery, in hopes that those who were visiting their loved ones might absorb a bit of culture.

Spain followed suit and started community mausoleums with many wall vaults.

New Orleans is well known for its above-ground mausoleums. Most people think the mausoleums were placed in New Orleans because of the flooding, but really it was based on the mausoleum craze that was spreading across the United States.

Many of the protective and benevolent associations, such as the Elks, built society tombs, with multiple crypts for their members. The only problem was there were more members than crypts. So after a reasonable time, the bones were swept up and placed in an ossuary, and someone else from the association would be placed in the crypt of honor. An ossuary is a receptacle made to hold ashes or bones, usually large enough to hold thousands at a time.

In rural America, a movement was started to turn cemeteries into wonderlands, with statues and architectural designs. Private mausoleums were a wonder to see as families tried to outdo one another. Cemetery promoters would push the idea of mausoleums and how it was easier on the family to leave their loved ones in a vault. Some of the first mausoleums were not built to the best of quality, and cemeteries had to spend their profits on maintenance. But with time, the architecture and designs were of better quality.

Webb City Mount Hope Cemetery's first mausoleum was built by the Rogers family in 1905. The ninth mausoleum was completed in 1928 by the Kenneday family. The other families and individuals who have mausoleums in Mount Hope include the Schermerhorns, Schiffer, Orrs, Austin Allen, St. George Noble, Prehms, and Amsel Taylor Blackwell. The mausoleums all have bronze doors and a stained glass window in the rear. Other than that similarity, they were unique in their architectural design.

When Colonel James O'Neill passed away in November 1907, his body was placed in a temporary vault at Mount Hope Cemetery as they waited for the building of his mausoleum. It was later determined that his body would be shipped to his birthplace, Liverpool, New York, where his stately mausoleum stands among six tall pine trees. His resting place would have made a fine addition to the nine mausoleums in Mount Hope, but he is at rest in his home state. It was noted that O'Neill left enough money for the perpetual care of his mausoleum, and there are still sufficient funds available today.

Not everyone can afford a mausoleum, but most still want a special monument to grace the grave of their loved ones. Some gravestones are pretty elegant and leave a bit of class in place of the mausoleum.

Peace Church and Cemetery

Peace Baptist Church was the second organized church in Jasper County. The church was organized by Elder Greenville Spencer (killed for preaching against slavery, who had also erected the first church building in Jasper County, Freedom Baptist Church). Early preachers at Peace Baptist Church were Reverend Richardson, Reverend Cy Pearson, Reverend Tooely, Ebenezer Hopkins, and David Hopkins. As more modern churches began to appear, Peace Church was not used and became neglected as was the cemetery. Peace Church Congregation was organized in 1840 at the home of E. P. Dale. In 1842, Peace Church hosted a meeting of the Spring River Baptist Association. Mrs. Jamison, granddaughter of Thacker Vivion, the county's first white settler, stated that her father was killed in 1852 while hauling logs for the building of Peace Church. The logs probably were for a school near Peace Church or for some other church building.

It is believed that the first burial was a black employee of James Elbert in the mid-1800s. The employee was a driver on a freighter carrying goods to general stores, who became ill while delivering and died on the road. Another of James's men found a peaceful place to bury him.

In 1956, area residents organized records and noted there were eight hundred graves, but that did not include those graves that had rocks that sank into the ground or were never marked to begin with.

A well-known grave at Peace Church was that of William E. Cook, Jr. (Billy), convicted of murder and executed at San Quentin gas chamber in December of 1952. Buried the first time on December 18, 1952, his body has been moved with no stone to mark the grave to keep people from desecrating the grave.

It has been noted that there are grave on top of other graves. According to Dolph Shaner, E. P. Dale, father of Robert J. Dale, assumed squatters' sovereignty to a tract of land west of Joplin near the Oak Hill Golf Course in May 1838. An old-timer states that there was a school built near Peace Church in 1843. The same old-timer says the schoolhouse burned, and the church was dismantled, and the logs of the church or the school were moved to Reverend Johnson's farm, southeast of Carl Junction, and used to build part of a barn. Robert J. Dale entered upon a tract of land northwest of Joplin on March 5, 1856. Peace Church and Cemetery were located on that land.

Several local churches are taking turns in the upkeep of the Peace Church Cemetery.

Webb City Cemetery

The first cemetery in Webb City as the city was organized in 1876 and Mount Hope wasn't established until 1905. The entrance to the Webb City Cemetery was only available through private property until an ordinance in 1897 extended the length of Oronogo Street to allow entrance into the cemetery.

City Hall

Another correction that I need to make concerns the old city hall and fire department at First and Main Streets. Through the years, we have talked about the upper floor of the city hall catching fire in the '60s, while the fire department was located in the building. A business owner located in the newly remodeled building was going through the newspaper files on the third floor of the library in the Genealogy Department, and she uncovered some very interesting information. It seems that the building did not burn; the bricks just fell from the second floor. In other words, the top floor just collapsed. Now we know the rest of the story, thanks to a patient young lady who diligently went through the newspaper films.

City hall, fire department, and police department built in 1889. Picture from the 1900 *Webb City Souvenir*, published by F. L. McInnis & Company.

Webb City College

The laying of the cornerstone in 1894 brought a parade one-mile long to celebrate the building of the new college. The first graduating class occurred May 23, 1896, with twenty-three students completing their course of study.

Sitting on eight acres—completed 1896—stone, pressed brick, iron, three stories high, heated by steam, lighted by electricity. Library had over one thousand books, land donated by Jacob J. Nelson, lawyer. Was to be named Nelson Collegiate Institute.

Hospital

Jane Chinn Hospital—The building has been turned into senior citizen housing. Located at the corner of Austin and Rose Streets.

At one time, Webb City had three hospitals. Of course, most of us remember the Jane Chinn Hospital, the birthplace of many residents of Webb City. There was even an old tradition of carrying the baby to the attic and back before taking the baby home. This was for good luck!

Jane Chinn Hospital was built and equipped in 1910, at the corner of Austin and Rose Street, at a cost of $60,000. It was a gift to the city from Charles R. Chinn and (Elizabeth) Jane (Webb) Chinn. This hospital had accommodations for twenty-three patients in wards and ten other rooms for private cases. There was a laboratory, laundry facilities, sterilizing rooms, a morgue, operating rooms, cooking facilities, and a doctor's lounge. One of the most modern features was an elevator from basement to the third floor. The building sat on a small hill without too many buildings or trees to block the view when the building was first built, and you could sit on the sunporch on the front of the building and see most of Webb City, some of Carterville. They claimed you could even see the tall buildings of Joplin by looking out the third-floor windows. The operating room was lighted at night from the ceiling by eight Mazda holophane lights, producing one thousand candle power light. It had cross lighting, which prevented shadows interfering with any operation. This allowed doctors to work on emergency cases at night as well as in the daytime. This spectacular lighting system was the envy of medical professionals throughout the nation.

The building architectural plans were drawn by Frank W. Caulkins of Webb City. John R. Thomas of Joplin was the general contractor. John R. Schwartz of Webb City was in charge of the plumbing and heating, with Fred H. Nesbitt of Webb City in charge of the masonry work. The building committee consisted of Dr. C. E. McBride, chairman; T. J. Roney, secretary; members, E. T. Webb, B. C. Aylor, F. C. Wallower. Before the building of the hospital, there was an organization known as the Webb City Hospital Association, and the members consisted of President Thomas F. Coyne, Vice President George H. Fullerton, Secretary and Treasurer F. C. Wallower; and the other directors were A. D. Hatten, J. J. McLellan, T. F. Lennan, and Charles R. Chinn.

The stone on the building came from the Carthage Stone Company. The ventilation in the hospital was perfect with each partition having its own ventilation duct connected with a vacuum fan in the attic, discharging three hundred thousand cubic feet of air per hour.

Maurice Clark recalls that the W. Alton Jones Foundation was responsible for the addition being built at Jane Chinn Hospital in Webb City.

Support of the hospital, at first, was by subscription from the miners. The miners would pay 25¢ per month, and the mine operators put in $5 per month. Eventually the hospital was supported by a tax levy and became city-owned with a hospital board for decision-making.

Jane Chin Hospital

Webb City's First Hospital—Before the Jane Chinn Hospital, Webb City had another hospital located at the corner of Webb Street and First Street, in a house built by Captain Hemenway. The hospital was established by Dr. Lincoln Curtis Chenoweth, who had been a practicing physician in Webb

City since 1888. The hospital was a temporary location until the completion of the building of the Salvation Army Hospital (1905).

Salvation Army Hospital—Dr. Chenoweth moved his hospital to the new building at 200 East Main (East Main Street was changed to East Broadway in 1920.) The building was completed in 1905 and owned by the Salvation Army under the direction of Ensign Vredenberg, who had raised the money to build a hospital.

Dr. Chenoweth was eager to move the hospital to the two-story brick Salvation Army building.

Webb City has the distinction of being one of the first cities in the west to establish a hospital to be maintained and operated by the Salvation Army. The Salvation Army continued to provide Thanksgiving and Christmas dinners to the poor as well as operate the hospital.

When Charles and Jane Chinn donated the money to build the Jane Chinn Hospital, Dr. Chenoweth was active in organizing and managing the new hospital, later becoming the director and the vice president.

Salvation Army Hospital, 200 East Main (Broadway)

Jasper County Tuberculosis Hospital—Webb City's third hospital was the Jasper County Tuberculosis Hospital, built in 1916, which was reportedly located three miles north of Webb City. The cost of the facility was $100,000. In 1937, it was described as being located half a mile northwest of Webb City. Eventually the hospital was located within the city limits of Webb City.

Once again, Dr. Chenoweth was a target player in getting the Jasper County Tuberculosis Hospital built and served on the board of directors. The hospital was definitely needed in this area. With the active mining industry, tuberculosis was a major cause of death, not only for the miners but also for family members who acquired the disease from exposure to the miners. This dreadful disease claimed its victims, the rich as well as the poor. Nobody was immune to this deadly visitor.

The citizens of Webb City donated linens and supplies. They assisted in beautifying the grounds. The patients were supplied newspapers, magazines, delicacies, and music by generous citizens. The hospital was supported by a Jasper County tax levy.

The semicircle red brick building, with its park like landscaping, consisted of 125 beds. There were sleeping porches on the front of the building to allow patients to enjoy the beautiful surroundings. The building was completed in 1916, but it was 1918 before funding was established for the new hospital. The land (forty acres) for the TB Hospital was donated by James A. Daugherty. The hospital was kept busy combating the deadly tuberculosis, trying to discover a cure, educating the citizens about preventative measures and how sanitation was a priority.

With the end of the mining era, the need for a Tuberculosis Hospital ended also. The building was converted into the Elmhurst Nursing Home. The tranquil setting was appreciated by those who became residents of the nursing home. A new building was built, and a tornado wiped out many of the beautiful old trees that had been there close to a hundred years. There is still a tranquil parklike setting, and the description says the Webb City Rehabilitation Center is located in the northwest section of Webb City.

Originally the Jasper County Tuberculosis Hospital.

Then Elmhurst Nursing Home

Webb City Rehabilitation Hospital.

Humphrey Building

The year was 1899, and Henry C. Humphreys and his wife, Sarah, moved to Webb City with $4,000 worth of merchandise to start a business in the fast-growing town of Webb City. He located a building at Thirty-One South Allen (Main) Street. Within the first year, the business had brought in $17,000. Within a few years, Henry was able to claim an annual operations of $300,000. Henry needed a building as impressive as his growing business. So when A. D. Hatten and Otis Raymond had a large strike, they took their mining profits and built the Hattern-Raymond Block, facing Allen (Main) Street from Daugherty Street, north to the alley, the north two hundred block of North Main. Henry Humphrey knew that was the building he was searching for. The building was the second brick building built in Webb City. Humphrey's Department Store became the most extensive business of its kind in Southwest Missouri. The company employed thirty-five to forty employees on the average. It was like a miniature mall as the store was divided into four buildings, with different departments in each building. There was the work clothes department with overalls, denim, and flannel work shirts, with an area for ladies to shop for their desired threads. There was the shoe department, with necessary work boots for the miners, as well as the dainty shoes for the ladies. Mining supplies were in abundance in the mining department, and household goods were always on hand in the household goods. People came from miles around to shop at Humphry's where selection was plentiful, and service was the best in the area. This building served as the US Post Office in 1891.

In later years, Dr. C. S. Bradbury opened the Yankee Drug Store in the southeast part of the building. Yankee Drug Store became the Electric Drug Store, and later Bradbury Bishop Drug

Store. There was a skating rink in the northern part of the Humphry Building during the Yankee Drug Store time. That section became a grocery store in later years, Karbe's, SavMor IGA, and Anderson's IGA.

The H. C. Humphrey Building was the second brick building built in Webb City by Hatten and Raymond.

Webb City Library

This is another of my favorite photos. It is of the Webb City Library taken about 1957 by W. Vance Langley. I am so impressed with the architecture of the buildings of Webb City, especially the library which was designed by Grant C. Miller of Chicago. Mr. Grant, at this time, had supervised the building of over fifty libraries. The Webb City Library architecture style is considered a combination of Gothic and modern. As much as possible, native materials were used in the building of the library. They used limestone boulders, gravel, and sand from the local mines for the foundation and the walls. They also used Carthage stone for the exterior trim.

The Civic Improvement Association, a group of Webb City ladies, showed determination that resulted in Webb City's dream of a library coming true. Many correspondences between the ladies and the Carnegie Corporation of New York secured a promise of $25,000 in which to build a library on the condition that the people of Webb City purchase the site and vote for a maintenance tax on the library.

By an overwhelming majority, a mill tax was voted in on the sixth day of April 1913. Thanks to many donations from citizens, the site was purchased from Mr. and Mrs. Andrew McCorkle at the corner of Liberty and First Streets.

Special attention was given to the inside of this magnificent building from floor to ceiling. The floors were covered with an ear-ever, noiseless battleship linoleum that gave the impression of walking on air. The arched walls and ceilings were painted in an exquisite manner. The tables, chairs, and shelves were made of oak. The building contained excellent systems of lighting, heating, and ventilation. The cost of the building came to $23,944. 20. Once the architecture fees were added, the building of the library, plus the furniture, used a little bit over the $25,000 donated by the Carnegie Corporation.

Webb City had its library, a building that was the pride of the community. To continue the use of natural local material, the west exterior wall, on the north end, near the door was placed a large chunk of zinc taken from a local mine. Lead and zinc were added to the exterior on each side of the front door. An arched canopy was added over the front door in 1957 (as shown in the photo).

The Webb City Carnegie Library outgrew the building, as did most of the libraries built with Carnegie funds. But instead of moving to a new location, as most other libraries chose to do, Webb City took on the challenge of preserving history. In April of 2004, the ninety-one-year-old building underwent treatment for expansion. It was an amazing building project that looks as if the new addition was part of the original building. The Webb City Library is still an architectural beauty.

Another bit of information uncovered that was very interesting concerned the library. Many years ago, whenever I was doing research on the library, I had read that the Civic Improvement Association, a group of Webb City ladies, had a dream of a library in Webb City, so they began writing to the Carnegie Corporation to secure a promise of $25,000 to build the library. That information led me to believe that we did not have a library before this organization started their campaign. But I discovered that we had a library, in a one-story wood frame building at 210 1/2 South Allen, also known as 212 South Allen (Main) Street, in 1900. I don't know if they stayed at that address until the new library was built in 1912, but it was listed in 1900.

Library, Andrew Carnegie, 1912

One of the few Andrew Carnegie libraries still in use. The new addition to the library blends in well with the existing building. The building exterior has samples of the lead and zinc mined in this area. Located at 101 South Liberty Street.

National Guard Armory

Once again, we are going to visit a beautiful building that once stood proudly in Webb City and is no longer there. Changes that have taken place are often forgotten, and we want to remind everyone of their existence.

At 109–111 East Broadway, in Webb City, once stood the beautiful Jamison Building. It was built in 1901 and was first used as a livery stable operated by the Burris family. This sturdy three-story brick building, with Carthage stone on the front and wonderful arch windows on the front third floor, was a handsome building. There was an elevator that carried items from the first floor to the third floor. That elevator carried carriages to the third floor for storage during the livery stable era. The ground floor was used to stable the horses.

In later years, the building moved up from horses to automobiles. There was a car salesroom on the first floor, and once again, the elevator was handy to move cars to the second and third floor for display.

Rex Metallic Casket Company made use of the building, which was located across Broadway, to store caskets to be shipped at a later date. Webb Corp also used the building after the casket company, as the building was in a convenient location, just three blocks down Broadway Street.

But in 1948, the building really got its distinction of importance when the Missouri National Guard leased the building.

The history of the national guard in Webb City started in January 1909. It was reorganized after World War I. The 203rd Coast Artillery, Houn Dawg Regiment, "G" Battery was under command of Captain Ray E. Watson. As Colonel Watson, the regiment served in the Aleutian Islands on the Alaskan Coast.

After WWII, early 1949, the national guard was once again organized in Webb City as Company B, 135th Tank Battalion, and later as Company B, 203rd Armor, and had headquarters in several towns, including Webb City. The commanders were Captain Mel Kennedy, 1949–1951; Captain LeRoy Skinner, 1952–1954; Captain W. Terry James, 1955–1962; Captain Jimmie C. Morris, 1963–1965; and Captain Don Miller, 1966–1967. This information was compliments of Colonel W. Terry James, retired.

In the 1947 city directory, it lists the Missouri State Guard Armory at 201 South Main Street, and records show, 109–111 East Broadway was leased to the National Missouri State Guards in 1948. I received a letter from James O. Toutz, and he remembers joining the Missouri National Guards in the spring of 1949, along with many of his classmates who were graduating. Webb City citizens recall the men doing drills along Tom Street South, weather permitting.

We would like to take a moment to thank those young men and all the others who served our country. Webb City always had willing men who served in the military.

A new site was required by the state that was to be provided by the city and be cost-free. Such a site was obtained on South Ellis Street in 1960. The unit commander at that time was W. Terry James. Before the new armory could be completed, the Missouri National Armory at 109–111 East Broadway Street burned on May 22, 1963. History notes that Sergeant E. J. Gamble entered the burning building and saved records and the history of the unit by passing his file cabinets through a window to helpers below.

The national guard under command of Jimmie C. Morris used part of the Elks Building at Webb and Broadway until the new federal armory was completed and dedicated on October 17, 1965. The Crowder Campus and the Webb City Fire Department now share the location of the previous armory.

Webb City was well represented in the wars, and there are two memorial plaques standing in Memorial Park for the servicemen lost in five wars. In the 2007 *Webb City, Carterville, Oronogo Pictorial History* books put out by the Genealogical Society, there are pictures and stories of many of the servicemen from this area. God Bless America and those who serve and protect us.

The national guard armory, 111 East Broadway

Post Office

When asked where the Webb City Post Office is located, most of us will point out the post office building with pride. That beautiful building on the southeast corner of Daugherty and Liberty Street was completed in 1916, and it has served the city well. The post office construction began in the year 1915 (which coincidently happens to be over one hundred years ago!) and completed in 1916. The building was constructed with lots of marble, which helps to keep the grand building in such great shape. Marble holds up well but does tend to wear down at times. When you enter the front door, that first step into the building has taken a bit of wear over the last ninety-nine years, and there is an indent. And the marble in front of the lobby window shows some wear. When the building was new, you went to the left to go to the lobby window. It was a small window, and the postmaster took care of your needs. As business began to expand, the service window was changed to the right end of the lobby with a large open window. Later a glass indoor and wall were added to keep the cool air from attacking the postal workers and also for security in the off hours. But most of the lobby is exactly as it was built ninety-nine years ago.

It is hard to imagine how much mail has passed through the post office in the last ninety-nine years. I know that during the 1990s, I was told that Webb City Post Office handled about 180,000 pieces of mail and about one thousand parcels per week. And that is just for our small town of Webb City. Imagine what the amount would be for the United States.

When Webb City was first founded in 1876, there was a need for a post office, and it was decided that city hall would be the appropriate place to handle something important as the mail. Now at the time, city hall was located in a wooden building on the northwest corner of Allen Street and Main Street. In today's direction, that would be the northwest corner of Main (then known as Allen Street) and Broadway Street (then known as Main Street). The present home of Mid-Missouri Bank (formerly the Webb City Bank). The city hall in 1876 had quite a bit of activity as the building held Hann Mercantile (grocery store), Hann Drug Store, and post office was well as the city business.

When the Wagner Building was constructed (1905) on the northwest corner of Webb Street and Joplin Street (now Broadway), the lobby downstairs was the new post office. What an active building for the new post office. There was a business behind the post office, not to mention the many businesses upstairs. Doctors, lawyers, and individual offices were open for business. When the present-day post office was built in 1916, this wonderful Wagner Building became the Franklin Cigar Company and the *Webb City Daily Sentinel* office was located in the rear. The second floor was the Elks Club, as many of us remember.

Webb City has three impressive buildings that served as the post office, but today's building holds such majestic classiness, we can understand why it has been a building of prestige for almost one hundred years.

Now on to more information uncovered. We have often talked about the fact that the first building actually built as a post office was the Wagner Building, northwest corner of Broadway and Webb Streets, which was built in 1905. The first post office, 1876, was Halls Drug on the northwest corner of Allen (Main) and Main (Broadway) Streets. This wood frame building held the city hall, school, church meeting, post office, and such when the city first became incorporated. It was served as the hub of the city until 1890, when it was torn down, and the Webb City Bank Building was constructed. City Hall moved to its new building at 37–39 South Allen (Main) Street, northeast corner of Allen and First Street. So where was the post office from 1895–1905? It moved across the street to 105 North Allen (Main) Street until the Hatten-Raymond Building was completed in 1887 (home of the Humphrey's Department Store, 1900).

So the post office moved around a bit before it became located in its own building in 1905. And it stayed at that location until the new federal building (post office) was built in 1916.

1603   POST OFFICE, WEBB CITY, MO.

Wagner Building/Old Post Office Building/Elks Club

The main claim to fame for the building at 102 North Webb Street seems to be that it was the first building built for the Webb City Post Office.

1908–First federal post office building in Webb City. The post office moved when the new federal building was completed, 1916, at Daugherty and Liberty.

1920—The old post office building became home to the Elks Lodge 861.

1928—It is known as the Elks Building, but the downstairs is home to the Cuban Cigar Factory 102 North Webb. The upstairs offices are home to Webb City Stone Co., Webb City & Joplin Ballast Co., A. D. Hatten's Home Land Loan Co. The Wagner Building north of the Elks building became part of the Elks Building. About this time, the *Webb City Sentinel* printing was in the back store of the post office building. Building facing Broadway (Joplin Street).

1949—It is still referred to as the BPO Elks Building with 102–106 North Webb with doctor offices, beauty shop, Rotary Club, chamber of commerce, and Lion's Club listed in this building. Numbers 106 and 108 are listed as Veatch Realty, Hiron's Insurance, and a beauty shop.

1953—Still called the Elks Building. Many a high school dance was held in this building.

1990—The Elks Lodge moved to 1010 North Madison.

The building was purchased by the Hughes family for storage.

YMCA (Young Men's Christian Association)

Let's take a step back in time to learn about one of Webb City's landmarks that have disappeared, the YMCA building.

The Young Men's Christian Association had been active in Joplin since 1891. It was making quite a good influence with the youth. In 1897, they bought an old opera house at Fourth and Virginia with plans to build a future home for the YMCA (where the *Joplin Globe* is now located). That building opened in March of 1901. About twenty years later, the new building at Fifth and Wall was built to allow more room for the growing organization. Not to be left out, in 1905, the Young Women's Christian Association was formed in Joplin, with their meeting place to be at 527 Joplin Street. In 1920, the John Wise home at 504 Byers was purchased to house the YWCA.

Meanwhile, a few businessmen took it upon themselves to organize a local chapter of the Young Men's Christian Association in Webb City, during the year of 1900. They used the second floor of the new Aylor Building, home of the Oddfellows at 210 North Allen (Main) Street. After the first year, E. T. Webb donated a lot to build a YMCA building. The building was built through private subscriptions from local residents and businessmen. The YMCA was located at 107–109 West Daugherty, just half a block west of Allen (Main) Street. It was the perfect location for those young men who were passing through town and needed a place to stay or just to bathe and get rid of the dirty travel dust. They would be within walking distance of a café, grocery store, or any other needs that might arise.

The Webb City YMCA catered to the local youth, as they had many programs to keep the young men active and out of trouble. They held Sunday services with three Bible classes. The Boy Scouts met in the building once a week. Over one hundred youth attended the gymnasium classes. The YMCA allowed the boys to have access to a library, a reading room, bathrooms, game rooms, the gymnasium, and a debate club.

The basement of the YMCA building had a unique swimming pool. The floor would slide over the pool when it was not in use and serve as a regular room. When the pool was needed, the floor would slide back to reveal the pool for the youth to exercise.

The Sunday services and Bible classes were important in this organization, as their goal was to supply the boys with spiritual, moral, and character-building influences. It didn't take long for the association to realize that their grand building was decreasing in size as more and more opportunities were offered the youth.

The first floor of the YMCA building housed businesses to bring in revenue for the upkeep of the building. Throughout the years, the businesses included grocery stores, barbershops, shoe stores, etc. In the latter years, most folks remember that Wheeler's Shoe Store and Shoe Repair occupied the space.

When you entered the middle doorway and walked up the wide stairway, the space seemed to just open up and invite into a spacious second floor. There was the main room and smaller rooms off to each side with doors that had transit windows above them. Continuing across the main room to the north, you entered the gymnasium. It was set up for basketball, exercise, and even had a piano in the corner for singing.

The YMCA was operated by a board of trustees. Over the years, as those trustees passed away, they were not replaced, and the building went into a state of disrepair. The Webb City Historical Society, under the direction of Alfred Jenkins, Fred Spille, Cecil Veatch, Sue Rose, and others that don't come to mind right now, operated and stored wonderful pieces of history for use in a future museum. As the building deteriorated, they tried to move the artifacts to safer areas, except the piano. The gymnasium floor was far too gone to move the heavy piano. The floor had begun to give way, and it was unsafe. The building was eventually demolished (1992), and a piece of Webb City's history was lost. But that doesn't stop the wonderful memories that were shared by many young men as they were taught religion, morality, and good health.

Most of us are aware of the old YMCA building that was located next to Bruner's Drug Store to the west of the building. What a unique building it was. It was built in 1901 on a lot donated by E. T. Webb, 107–109 West Daugherty. The first floor of the building held retail stores that brought an income for the YMCA organization. The funds were for the upkeep of the building and to keep the organization itself in operation. In the middle of the retail shops was a door to enter the YMCA. It led upstairs to an open foyer with rooms on each side and straight ahead to the gymnasium. It was perfect for the many opportunities that the *Y* offered to young men. The unique part of the building was in the basement. There was a swimming pool that was enjoyed by the boys, and when not in use, the floor was rolled over the top of the pool. How ultramodern was that?

The new information I found on the YMCA was the location of the organization when it was first organized in 1900, before they built the YMCA building. The Aylor Building at 210 North Allen (Main), home of the Oddfellows, was built in 1900. This building was the temporary home of the YMCA, on the second floor, for a year or two while the new building was being built.

107 and 109 West Daugherty Street

Zinc Ore Building

As the city begins making plans to refurbish the downtown area, the history of each building takes on a new light. How old is the building? What business did it house? Who built the building? These are important questions that need answers. I thought I might start with a building that has recently undergone some wonderful changes to the interior—the Zinc Ore Building. In case you don't recognize the name, I'll tell what business it houses—the *Webb City Sentinel*/Wise Buyer.

The *Sentinel* hasn't always been in the Zinc Ore Building. You see, there was a fire in December of 1882 that caused the *Sentinel*, which had been at Thirteen South Main for many years, to search for a new home, and that home became the Zinc Ore Building.

The Zinc Ore Building at Eight South (Allen) Main first appears on the Sanborn map in 1906, having been listed as a frame building in 1900. It was built by mining operator John Dermott, who used room 1 as his office, and he lived at 110 North Ball. Dermott leased out the bottom floor for retail, starting out with gentlemen's clothing, furnishings, and shoes. The third floor was noted as a lodge hall, and Bob Foos says there is evidence still there concerning the Sisters of Pythias who used the lodge hall.

Dermott's only child, a daughter named Belle, married a lawyer, Thomas J. Roney, who became a state representative of the central district of Jasper County. He used rooms 1–4 of the Zinc Ore Building.

Dermott made his money in mining, but he believed in investing his money in real estate. He built the Dermott Building in 1900 on the northwest side of First and Allen (Main) Streets. He also started the Dermott Sub-Division in 1907. He also did some real estate and business buildings in Arkansas and Oklahoma. Not bad for a poor Irish boy who came to America with his older brother at the age of seven.

Dermott passed away in 1912, with his address still listed as 110 North Ball. Representative Roney's father was James Roney, and he passed away in 1925 with his address listed as 110 North Ball. In the 1928 city directory, Thomas and Belle lived at the same address. That home stayed in the family. Chester Roney, the son of Thomas and Belle, was listed as living at 110 North Ball.

The gentlemen's clothing business stayed on in the building for a while as in the 1919 directory Sol. H Baum Clothing was the main concern. M. R. Lively still had his office on the second floor.

In the 1928 directory, the Zinc Ore Building is listed as home of Webb City Bakery. The lawyers, M. R. Lively and Ray E. Watson, had offices in the building. By this time, the Sisters of Pythias had moved to their new hall at 110 1/2 West Broadway.

According to the 1947 directory, Eight South Main had become The Gamble Store, Automotive and Farm Supplies, Appliances. Chester was married and living at 212 South Pennsylvania, and the widow of Thomas J. Roney (Belle) was still living at 110 North Ball. Lawyer Wayne Wheeling had his office in the Zinc Ore Building, as well as the Webb City & Joplin Ballast Co and the Webb City & Joplin Sand & Gravel Co.

Chester Roney had a little retail shop in the Zinc Ore Building. He sold lots of miscellaneous, and he loved to put stickers on little knickknacks that said they were a souvenir of Webb City purchased at Roney's.

Webb City Time Line

Webb City Area Time Line

1792—*Jesse Killey*, from Kentucky, arrived in the area of the Osage Indians and settled in Southwest Missouri in what would eventually become Barton County. This area was under Spanish domain and part of Louisiana.

1801—The Louisiana territory was returned to the French.

1804—March, the United States purchased Louisiana.

1805—*President Thomas Jefferson* appointed *James Wilkinson* as governor of the territory.

1807—*Lewis Merriwether* became governor.

1809—*Benjamin Howard* appointed governor.

1810—*John Walton* and *George Hornback* and families settled in the area soon to be called *Carthage*.

1811—Massive *earthquakes* shook Southeast Missouri, and the effects were felt on this side of the state.

1831—*Thacker Vivion* settled in an Indian village he called *Centerville*, but later known as *Sarcoxie*. He was soon joined by *John Fullerton*.

1838—*James Carter* moved his family to Jasper County and settled in an area that would later be known as *Carterville* and Lakeside. Lived in a log cabin until just before the Civil War when they built a frame house.

1841—*Barry County* was subdivided, resulting in the formation of *Newton* and *Jasper Counties*.

1842—Carthage founded

1844—Government survey of the area was completed, and the settlers could finally begin making proper filings to secure title to their lands. The *government land office* was in *Springfield*, which was about a seven to ten-day trip there and back, weather permitting. The price on first entries ranged from 25¢–$1.25 per acre. Usually if one of the neighbors was making the trip to Springfield, he would file for his neighbors and bring back the proper release or deed for the rightful owner.

1848—*Medoc* founded but not platted

1849—*William Tingle* and *David Campbell* discovered/uncovered one hundred pounds of Galena in *Turkey Creek* in a little valley known as *Shakerag*, which would soon be known as *Leadville Hollow* (Joplin). The same year, *Judge Cox* and his Negro boy Pete discovered lead along *Joplin Creek* in what would soon be known as the Kansas City Bottom.

1849—*Judge Andrew McKee* and *Thomas Livingston* hit pay dirt and started a new town called *Minersville* (later platted as *Oronogo* in 1856).

1850—*J. G. L. Carter*, son of *James Carter*, married *Mary Cooley*, daughter of *Judge Samuel Cooley*. They had ten children.

1853—Mining began in *Minersville* (*Oronogo*).

1856—*John C. Webb and his wife, Ruth,* moved to *Jasper County* and purchased 200 acres to begin with and later purchased an additional 120 acres, for a total of 320 acres. They built their log cabin in the location, that in future years, would be the northwest corner of Broadway and Daugherty in Webbville/Webb City. Webb cultivated 100 of his acreage.

1856—The town of *Sherwood* (been in existence since 1847 and known as *Rural*) was formally platted.

1856—*Oronogo* was platted.

1856—*Avilla* founded but not platted until 1858.

1857—*Benjamin Franklin Hatcher* moved to Jasper County with his parents. He was the nephew of John C. Webb. Benjamin married *Dora Daugherty*, daughter of *W. A. Daugherty*, in 1870.

1858—A Sarcoxie teacher, who had come from Kansas, taught his students the evil of slavery. He was asked to resign, he would not, and the same citizens gave him a coat of tar and feathers.

1860—January 27, *Preston* (east of Alba), the seventh city of Jasper County was platted by *Luke E. Ray* and *Jacob Nicholson*. *Dr. Patterson* built the first building, a general store. The town burned during the Civil War. The town was revised and replatted, September 10, 1867.

1861—*John C. Webb* answered the call of Governor Jackson to volunteer to serve in the Confederate Army.

1861—July 5, *Battle of Carthage*

1861—August 23, *Skirmish at Medoc* between Confederates and Union sympathizers en route to Fort Scott to enlist.

1862—June 18, *Coon Creek Engagement* between Confederates and Union in Northern Jasper County.

1862—Skirmish between the *Confederates* and an *Indian regiment* started at an old mill near what would soon become Lakeside, and the Indian regiment was overtaken at *Shirley Ford* on Spring River. The Confederates had a dispute among themselves and the Indian regiment escaped.

1862—November 20, a short engagement between the Confederates and Union near Carthage

1863—Fight just south of Sherwood which resulted in the Confederates sustaining severe loss

1863—May 14, skirmish at *French Point*, which was located west of Oronogo with a second skirmish on the eighteenth. The Confederates came out ahead.

1863—May 19, skirmish at Sherwood which resulted in the burning of Rader home by the federal soldiers.

1866—Joseph W. Aylor moved to Webb City and on January 21, 1866, married Ms. C. M. E. Webb.

1866—*Ulysses Hendrickson* moved to Jasper County, three miles west of Oronogo; county sheriff in 1874. In 1890, elected to the *senate for four years.*

1867—*Dr. David Whitworth* moved to Jasper County and purchased land west of the future Webb City. Served as a doctor in Webb City until 1895.

1867—The town of Preston (east of Alba), which was first platted in 1860 and burned during the Civil War, was replatted on September 10, 1867.

1868—*Granby Mining and Smelting Co.* obtained control of the mines in Oronogo. *Colonel J. Morris Young,* superintendent of the *Granby Mining and Smelting Co.* served as legislator, 1869–1870.

1869—*Joseph Aylor* and *Andrew McCorkle* began mining in neighboring towns. At this time, Aylor lived on the hill across from what would become *Mount Hope Cemetery.* The hill was referred to as Aylor Hill.

1870—W. A. Daugherty purchased 260 acres of land just west of John C. Webb (later known as Colonial Road). He soon purchased 320 acres east of John Webb from *James Gilbert Leroy Carter.*

1870—Andrew McCorkle purchased eighty acres just south of John C. Webb and built a one-and-a-half-story home at 106 South Webb Street. He would later build a larger home on the same spot in 1899.

1870—October 1, *John Cox* leased ninety acres on Joplin Creek to Moffett and Sergeant to mine (Joplin).

1871—Granby Mining Company heard about Adolph Von Wiese, a German, had discovered a use for zinc. The mining company gathered up all the "black Jack" waste that had been cast aside and sent it to Von Wiese, and the value of zinc was established and became more valuable than lead.

1871—May 7, twenty-six-year-old *William E. Hall* married eighteen-year-old *Martha Ellen Webb,* daughter of *John C. Webb.*

1872—*The Memphis, Carthage, and Northwestern* (later became the *St. Louis–San Francisco*) Railroad was built through Oronogo.

1873—A bright June morning, John C. Webb was plowing his land (between what would later be Webb City and Carterville) when he uncovered a shiny rock known as lead. He did not make it known to anyone for about four months.

1873—In October, John C. Webb and a friend named *Murrell* attempted to do a little digging at Murrell's pleading with Webb. Webb supplied the tools, Murrell brought his mining knowledge. The shaft kept filling with water, and Murrell was getting discouraged. William Daugherty bought Murrell's share for $25. Webb was also losing interest, but Daugherty knew the water could be controlled. *Grant Ashcraft* came into town. Webb leased Daugherty and Ashcraft the land, and within two days, Ashcraft had unearthed a one-thousand-pound chunk of lead. Within four days, they brought up eighteen thousand pounds. The fun began as the word spread.

1873—November 19, by court order of Jasper County, the name of Minersville was changed to Oronogo and incorporated as a town. The post office was changed from Center Mines to Oronogo at the same time.

1873—Elijah Lloyd bought a mine in 1874. He struck payload in 1882. The original town consisted of twelve blocks.

1874—John C. Webb hired *Elijah Lloyd* to survey and plot out the town of *Webbville*.

1874—*John B. Webb*, son of John C. Webb, passed away.

1874—Granville Ashcraft married *Theresa Belle Baker*. He built the first frame house on the northwest corner of Pennsylvania and Daugherty.

1874—August 12, 1874, construction began on John C. Webb's brick home at 112 North Webb.

1874—The St. Louis–San Francisco Railroad moved *James and Patience McNair* to Oronogo.

1875—September 10, *Carterville town plat* was filed. Legend has it that Carter and Daugherty flipped a coin to see who would have the town named after him and who would have a street named after him. I guess Carter won! Another associate was *William McMillan*.

1875—In the fall, the entire prairie where the town of Webbville was to be built was burnt to start planning the town. It was all prairie land with the only trees being the orchard planted by John C. Webb years earlier.

1875—July 26, the town of Webbville was officially platted and surveyed by Elijah Lloyd, recorded by James A. Bolen, recorder, September 11, 1875. Twelve blocks; John (Austin), Daugherty, Main (Broadway), Church, running north to south. Liberty, Webb, Allen (Main), Tom, and Hall running west to east.

1875—*James E. McNair* moved to Webbville from Oronogo. Built a home for John C. Webb at the corner of what would be Tom and Daugherty Streets. Webb lived there while his new brick mansion was being built at 112 North Webb Street (the first brick home).

1875—The *Transit House*, 208 East Main (Broadway) a two-story hotel, seventeen rooms, was built by Smith and Fisborn. Was later operated by Mr. Coyne in 1878. Later the location of the Salvation Army Hospital. The building was 150 feet long, 50 feet wide, two stories high, and contains seventeen rooms, well furnished and ventilated for the accommodation of the guests.

1875—*Nelse McTerron* built the first store on the southwest corner of Allen (Main) and Main (Broadway).

1875—The *Hann Grocery* Store was built on the northwest corner of Allen (Main) and Main (Broadway) being a grocery store, drugstore, and post office, and later the first city hall.

1875—*Mrs. Henderson's boarding house* was located on Allen (Main) Street where in later years, the Kress Dime store would be located.

1875—The *Columbia Building*, a grocery store owned by Mr. Spurgin, sat on the southeast corner of Allen (Main) and Main (Broadway) where the Middlewest Hotel would later be built.

1876—Webb City's First Presbyterian Church was established. A Sunday school was organized by Mr. and Mrs. W. A. Wheatley, Mr. and Mrs. C. S. Manker, and Mr. and Mrs. Hiram Van Pelt.

1876—*The Webb City Hotel* was erected by John C. Webb. It had a frontage on Webb Street of sixty feet, with a south ell eighty feet, and a north ell of sixty feet. The lower floor was occupied with an office, baggage room, sample room, parlor, dining room, kitchen, etc. The second floor consisted of eighteen rooms for the accommodation of guests. Mr. E. A. Baker took over the lease and was landlord on March 14, 1883.

1876—Four more additions were platted to Webbville.

1876—March 20, *Ruth F. (Davis) Webb*, wife of John C. Webb, passed away.

1876—October 10, *Joseph R. Lowe* moved to Webbville with $25 in his pocket.

1876—August 30, *McCorkle's First Addition* was surveyed.

1876—December 11, 1876, Webb City was incorporated under the Statutes of the State of Missouri. James McNair honored to be first mayor. The name of Webbville no longer existed.

1876—*George W. Ball,* age sixteen, arrived in Webb City, poor and penniless.

1876—*H. A. Ayre* was heading to the goldfields of California and passed through Oronogo and never made it to California. Within four years, he had enough money to buy 204 acres. Became *postmaster* of Oronogo in 1898.

1876—October, the *Coyne family* moved to Webb City. Thomas Coyne graduated from Webb City School. Sadie Coyne, in later years, married AD Hatten.

1876—November, the first Presbyterian service was held in Webb City at the A. W. Hann Grocery, northeast corner of Allen (Main) and Main (Broadway). Preached by Reverend Donald K. Campbell from Presbyterian Church in Joplin.

1876—*William Toms* built a *lead furnace* on Bens Branch between Webb City and Carterville. This allowed the lead to be melted down for easier transport. The furnace was destroyed by fire in 1880. Smelters were expensive to build and quick to burn.

1876–1877—Winter consisted of building the four-room frame schoolhouse on Webb Street, between Church and First Streets, facing east. Professor Dickey was the principal.

1876—*The Western Hotel* was built and then operated by Mrs. Pratt.

1876—*Dr. J. J. Wolf* established his office in Webb City.

1876—*Lon Ashcraft* moved to Webb City, and his first day of school was upstairs over the Hall Drug store, northwest corner of Allen (Main) and Main (Broadway). He remembered the days of *Bud Blunt and a gang of desperadoes* who shot up the town.

1876—*J. Van Buskert* grocery opened. He had moved from Joplin.

1877—Six more additions were platted to Webb City. At the end of the year, Webb City had a population of about 2,300.

1877—January 13, McNair resigns as mayor (after one month) to accept the position as the first postmaster of Webb City. *James Smith* filled the vacancy of mayor of Webb City

1877—*Pacific Hotel* was built by *G. W. Scott* at Fifteen South Allen (Main) and Church Street, northeast corner. It was a two-story frame building, fifty feet long and forty feet wide. It contained a spacious office, twenty rooms, dining room, parlor, replacing the *Scott house,* northeast corner of Allen (Main) and Main (Broadway) which had burned. The Webb City drugstore was built on the northeast corner of Allen (Main) and Main (Broadway).

1877—The *Webb City Hotel* was built, Nine South Webb Street.

1877—The first brick building was built on the northeast corner of Main (Broadway) and Webb Street, housing the first Webb City Bank and later Wright's Jewelry Store.

1877—A. H. Rogers was attending college at Harvard and went to visit *Professor Alexander Graham Bell*, who had just received the patent for his telephone invention. While there, Rogers was in the attic and spoke on the telephone with Bell, who was in the basement. Rogers always claimed to have been the first person living in Southwest Missouri to talk over a telephone.

1877—March 4, John C. Webb married *Sarah M. Canchman*. At this time, John C. Webb owned 1,000 acres in Jasper County, of which 160 was mineral land being leased out.

1877—March 27, Webb City Presbyterian Church, founding of the church

1877—April 14, *Charles (Carl) Skinner* filed a plat for a town called *Carl Junction*, with eighty-one lots, seven streets, and four alleys.

1877—April 24, petition to incorporate Carterville as a village was presented to county. Accepted on September 6, but no action or meetings on the part of the town trustees was taken until April 1882.

1877—April 30, Presbyterian enrollment of the First Presbyterian Church of Webb City.

1877—August 6, *Hamilton Snodgrass* moved to Webb City; grocery business

1877—*Charles R. Chinn Sr.* moved to Webb City and opened the largest dry goods store in the city. *C. R. Chinn and Co. Dry Goods*, 17×30-foot building with $3,000 stock.

1877—*S. L. Manker* and his wife, Sarah, moved to Webb City and opened the first hardware store at 111 South Allen (Main). *Manker, Hewlett, and Co.* mining supplies, hardware, and groceries.

1877—*J. G. L. Carter*, also known as Leroy, built a new family home at Lakeside.

1877—*Joseph C. Stewart* came to Webb City, *Center Creek Mining Co.* Opened a lumberyard with brother *W. C. Stewart.*

1877—March 27, the First Presbyterian Church of Webb City was organized with eight members.

1877–1888—*Pneumonia* claimed the lives of many due to inclement weather and lack of adequate shelter.

1877—The wood framed *central school* opened; started as four rooms, later became eight rooms.

1877—*Harry B. Hulett*, as a young boy, arrived in town with his father on the Frisco train. He said the train station at that time was on Fourth Street. They "rode into town" in a cab. They lived in a house where the Memorial Park now stands.

1878—April, *Ben C. Webb*, mayor 1878–1881

1878—February 28, Webb City became incorporated as a fourth-class city to allow a tax levy so the city would have enough funds to generate, as the city was going bankrupt. In 1879, Webb City collected the first taxes.

1878—*Hancock Second Hand Store* started with a stock of secondhand goods in which he traded his horse and wagon to obtain.

1878—*The St. Louis–San Francisco Railroad* extended from Oronogo to Webb City and Joplin (ten miles). Located on the east side of Webb City by the Center Creek Mining Company.

1878—The *Webb City Board of Education* was established.

1879—*George W. Ball* married *Martha Ann Palmer.*

1879—The Presbyterian Church purchased a worship hall at Twelve South Allen (where Minerva Candy Company was located at a later date). A one-story wood frame building that was a saloon and dance hall. The church cleaned and painted the building to be used as a church. The first building to be used exclusively for a church in Webb City.

1879—Hancock Second Hand Store changed the business name to Hancock & Laur Furniture and Funeral Co., with the addition of furniture and an undertaking business.

1879—The *Webb City Sentinel* was established as a weekly paper

1879—December 11, 1879, the *Webb City Times* was established by Milholn and Lingle using the equipment from the *Galena Messenger*, Galena, Kansas. In March 1880, Mr. Lingle bought out Milholn and had full control as proprietor and editor.

1879—*Colonel James O'Neill* arrived in Webb City. His future accomplishments will include establishing the Webb City Waterworks, half-owner of the Webb City Ice & Storage Company, and built the famous Newland Hotel. He was as also responsible for starting the gas service in Webb City. A very important citizen of Webb City.

1879—*Hendrickson Murray Hardware* opened for business.

1879—*The Frisco Railroad Depot* was built in the west end of Webb City.

1879—*E. T. Webb*, son of John C. Webb, graduated from college and returned to Webb City.

1879—*The Wright Drug Store* opened. *Charles Wright & Bros.* drug and jewelry opened with $1,200 stock. Continued in business for thirty years until Charles retired.

1879—Dr. L. Green moved from Medoc and opened a drugstore.

1880—*Edwin E. Spracklen* said when he came to town in 1880, they had to let down the bars of a farm fence on the south end of town to allow you to enter Webb City. Spracklen was a noted photographer. Elected mayor in 1898.

1880—A local promotion declared that Joplin was "The Wonder of the West," Carthage was "The Queen of the West," Sarcoxie was "The Strawberry Capital of the Nation," and Webb City was "The Zinc Capital of the World."

1880—*Jesse Frankenberger* came to Jasper County in1882 and located in Webb City. In 1898, he was elected justice of the peace.

1880—The *Webb City Cemetery* was organized.

1880—*Union Pacific Railroad and the Burlington Northern Railroad* came to town and found a home in the west end of town. The Frisco Depot was not built until 1914.

1880—*Ward & Laster Transfer Business* opened, as well as the *J. B. Overstreet Coal & Wood.*

1880—*Dr. Thomas Donehoo* purchased the Pacific Hotel at Fifteen South Allen (Main) and leased it to E. M. Fenniken.

1880—City officials were Mayor T. J. Harrington, Marshal R. F. Fitzpatrick, Councilmen D. H. Mack, John Marlsolf, John Lofter, and D. J. Horn. Clerk J. E. McNair, Treasurer C. H. Murray, Collector James N. Stephenson, city attorney W. M. Robinson.

1880—*Parker Bros. & Sinclair* meat merchants opened for business

1880—Hancock & Laur Furniture and Undertaking Company changed to Hancock & Howe Furniture and Undertaking Company.

1881—April, T. J. Harrington, mayor 1881–1886

1881—*Parker Chinn & Co.* opened for business.

1881—*The Missouri Pacific Railroad* came to Webb City and was located by Ben's Branch, between Webb City and Carterville.

1881—Webb City received its first telephone with the *American Bell Telephone Company* (*Charles W. McDaniel*). Wires were strung along trees, bushes, buildings, porches, etc.

1881—The *Webb City Foundry and Machine Shop* began (Webb Corp) in the spring by D. Fishburn & Co. In the fall of 1882, the entire business was purchased by Jno. Robison. The works are located on Center Creek Mining and Smelting Co. land near the Mo. P. and K. C., Ft. S. and G. depots. All kinds of heavy and light castings are manufactured. There is also general machine repairing business done.

1881—*Wright Jewelry* established by Will Wright, in the Charles Wright & Bros. Drug Store. He later established the Wright Jewelry in the old Webb City Bank Building (first brick building in Webb City) at Main (Broadway) and Webb Street, southeast corner.

1881—Webb City welcomed many new businesses: *Gammon & Henderson Grocery* and the *O. P. Sutherland Grocery. Allie Rice, Milliner* opened for business.

1881—Hancock & Howe Furniture and Undertaking Co. changed name and ownership to Hancock & Lowe Furniture and Undertaking Company.

1882—The *Webb City Bank* was established by John C. Webb and his son Elijah (E. T.) Webb. The first three assistant bank clerks were Clem Fishburn, W. S. Chinn, and Tom Coyne. Walter Spurgin's father made a walnut counter for the bank, lined inside with quarter-inch steel, and armed with revolvers handy to resist robbers. Extra caution was observed by making shotguns available at neighboring stores to assist the bank if robbers were trying to rob the bank.

1882—E. T. Webb built a beautiful home on the southwest corner of Liberty and Joplin (Broadway). He added the piazza in 1884.

1882—Lead ore was discovered at Troup City (later known as Prosperity), just outside Carterville.

1882—April 4, Carterville was incorporated as a fourth-class city.

1882—The Webb City Silver Cornet band was organized in the fall. There were eleven first-class instruments.

1882—December 29, *Charles R. Chinn Jr.* was born. He was president of Webb City Bank from 1915–1929.

1882—*Joseph Allen Hardy Sr.* and his wife, Emily, moved to Webb City. He opened the *Hardy & Lillibridge Mine*. He was influential in getting the Bishop Lillis of Kansas City to establish the *Sacred Hearts Catholic Church* in Webb City.

1882—The *Webb City Silver Coronet band* was organized.

1882—Saw the beginning of the existence of clubs, lodges, and organizations with the establishment of the AF and AM, 512, on April 5, 1882.

1882—The first church was built in Webb City on land John Webb had set aside for that purpose. Located on the southeast corner of Liberty and Joplin (Broadway) Streets. Webb was sick at the time, and telephone wires were run from the church to the house so Webb could hear the ceremony. The church was named Webb Chapel by the pastor, *Reverend Ben Deering*. Webb paid $5,000 for construction of the Southern Methodist Church.

1882—*Alba* was platted March 24, by Stephen Smith and a man named Johnson. The city was named after a man who operated a trading post (Alba's Station) during the Civil War. The community consisted mostly of members of the Friends (Quaker) Church. The post office was registered under the name of Breckenridge from April 1856–January 1860.

1882—New businesses: *M. M. Confectionery, Morris & Co. Clothing Store, S. A. Brown & Co. Lumber*

1883—Establishment of *the Reynolds Post, GAR.*

1883—February [March 9?], a fire burned the entire east side of Allen (Main) between Church and Main (Broadway). Fire started in the Pacific Hotel and took out six other buildings.

1883—April 13, John C. Webb passed away from consumption at 7:00 a.m., age fifty-seven. Webb was buried in the Harmony Grove Cemetery, later moved to the Mount Hope Cemetery when it was established in 1906.

1883—A slump in the mining business as miners were getting discouraged, moved away, population diminished.

1883—*Amos D. Hatten* arrived in Webb City and purchased the Center Creek Mines from Granville Ashcraft. Hatten was a successful businessman. No slump in mining for him.

1883—May, *Oronogo twister,* 7:00 p.m. Two killed and thirty-three injured.

1883—Webb City's first opera house in the Middlewest Building, built by Lester and Aylor. The opera house occupied the second floor of the building.

1883—*E. A. Baker* purchased the Webb City Hotel, Nine South Webb, and changed the name to *The Buffalo House.*

1884—February 29, Leap Year Ball given by the young ladies of Webb City.

1884—*Dunlap, Columbia & Bradford Bros.* opened for business.

1885—Carterville's paper was established, *The Carterville Mining Review,* by *T. J. Sheldon* and *W. D. Sallee.*

1885—January 17, the temperature reached seventeen below zero.

1885—New businesses: *W. F. Spurgeon Groceries, J. E. Magrader Groceries, Sheffer & Co. General Merchandise, Lowry & Dunlap Harness and T. J. Harrington's Restaurant & Oyster Parlor*

1886—April, *William Hilburn,* mayor 1886–1888

1886—*Amos A. Cass* arrived in Carterville; partner in *Weeks Hardware Co.*

1886—*Stewart & Matthews Lumber* dealers opened business.

1887—*Knights of Pythias* instituted on February 2.

1887—*Amos D. Hatten and Otis J. Raymond* built a block of buildings at 201–207 North Allen (Main) Street with money acquired in the mining industries. The block of buildings (the second brick building in Webb City) housed the *Webb City Post Office*, a dime store, clothing and hardware stores, and a tin shop in the rear, later becoming home to *Humphry's Department Store*, the largest mercantile business in the area.

1888—February 29, second Leap Year Ball was presented at the Webb City Opera House.

1888—The Presbyterian Church sold their church building at Twelve South Allen and put the money toward the new sanctuary.

1888—April, *Peter McEntee*, mayor 1888–1890

1888—*Dr. Lincoln Chenoweth* and his wife, *America Levina McNatt Chenoweth,* moved to Webb City. He had graduated from medical school in 1887, and they had married July 10, 1887.

1888—September, the Webb City Presbyterian Church dedicated their new building on the corner of John (Austin) and Liberty Street, costing $1,200 free of debt.

1888—November 8, Amos D. Hatten married Sadie C. Coyne (sister of Tom Coyne, Hatten's business partner).

1888—June 27, *Alice McCorkle* and *Charles Morrow Manker* married. Charles holds the notoriety of being Webb City's first Republican mayor. He helped organize *the Home Telephone Company* (a.k.a. Webb City Electric Telephone Company). He helped organize the *Merchant & Miners Bank in 1905.*

1888—A water system for Webb City and Carterville was built on Center Creek.

1888—*CE Matthews* opened huge lumber business.

1888—The first police judge was Joseph Fetlers. Previously the mayor handled that office.

1888—*Ben C. Webb*, husband of the future Jane Chinn, died.

1888—H. Greely Gaston opened an insurance office, later sold to Henry Hulett.

1888—The new bell was set on the roof of city hall to report the curfew, births, and deaths, time for school, etc.

1889—December 26, Webb City changed from fourth-class city to third-class city.

1889—The volunteer fire department was organized under the leadership of Colonel Henry Wonner and Tom Hayden. Before that, the city used bucket brigades.

1889—The Presbyterian built a neat wooden structure at Third and Webb, northeast corner.

1889—*The Exchange Bank* was organized by J. C. Stewart and his brother W. C. Stewart, later became the National Bank, 108 North Main.

1889—A. H. Rogers established a mule-drawn streetcar line from Webb City to Carterville.

1889—*John Dermott* came to Webb City and became a mine operator.

1889—Lowe sold his interest in Hancock & Lowe Furniture & Undertaking Co. to J. W. Aylor and went into business establishing Lowe & Verbrick Furniture Company.

1890—April, T. J. Harrington, mayor 1890–892 (seventh term as mayor)

1890—Colonel James O'Neill established the *Webb City Waterworks* for a cost of $100,000 (against the advice of friends). Built the O'Neill Building at 9 1/2 South Webb Street to house the waterworks. The black stand pipe that held 120,000 gallons of water stood grandeur on the highest point at Hall and Tracy Streets.

1890—August 19, *Dr. Charles Henry Craig* and his wife, Lucy, moved to Webb City after obtaining his medical degree in 1887. He worked at the state prison after graduation.

1890—Beginning of the formation of the *W. C. Commercial Club*

1890—The first commencement exercises were held with six graduates from central school.

1890—The *Webb City Sentinel* became a daily paper.

1890—The city hall was built at First and Allen (Main); home to city hall and the fire department.

1891—Troup City filed for a post office to keep from being incorporated into Carterville. They were denied by authorities because of the name. They filed again under the name of *Prosperity* and it was accepted.

1891—*James VanHoose* moved to Webb City.

1891—The *Newland Hotel* opened in February. One hundred rooms, hot and cold water, fireproof system.

1891—The *Commercial Club* was organized with 140 members.

1891—The organization of the *Shakespearean Conversational Club*

1892—April, C. M. Manker, mayor 1892–1894

1892—W. C. Routzong moved to Oronogo and established the *Index* newspaper. He became the Oronogo postmaster in 1893, justice of the peace in 1896, and re-elected in 1898. In 1898, he was notary public, city clerk, later becoming police judge and leader of Democratic Party. He served in the Civil War, receiving an honorable discharge. Busy man!

1892—*The Carterville Daily Journal* was established by Barnes and Wallace on Fountain Street.

1892—Finding of two adult *mastodons* and one baby in Carl Junction, thought to be at least five thousand years old.

1892—*Charles Manker* elected as the first Republican mayor of Webb City.

1892—*Bank of Carl Junction* founded.

1892—*Bank of Oronogo* founded.

1892—Central school expanded from four rooms to eight rooms. *West Side School* and *Webster School* were built. The high school classes were moved to west side (one room).

1893—A. H. Rogers discontinued the mule-drawn streetcar line and started the *Southwest Missouri Railway* by purchasing the Jasper County Electric and the Joplin Electric Railway.

1893—Webb City's first baby, daughter of Granville Ashcraft, *Bernice Ashcraft* graduated from high school.

1893—Jane Webb (later to be Jane Chinn) married Daniel F. Stewart. They built a home at 302 South Pennsylvania Street.

1893—*Chicago World's Fair.* Lead from Webb City on display, acclaimed as one of the finest displays.

1893—*Murratta Drug Store* began at 110 North Main. Susan Marratta, being widowed at the age of fifty-four, brought her three children from Kentucky to Webb City and helped her twenty-eight-year-old son, who was a druggist, open a drugstore.

1893—The new four-room schoolhouse in Johnstown was completed in time for fall classes. *J. W. Beddingfield* was the first principal.

1893—The *Exchange Bank* has a setback during the Panic of 1893 due to loaning heavily to the mining companies who were opening in the district. The bank experienced a short suspension until paperwork completed. There was no financial loss.

1893—January 15, Lowe bought out his partner, Verbrick, and the business changed to Lowe Furniture & Undertaking Company.

1894—April, J. J. Funk, mayor 1894–1896

1894—New brick central school was built in same location as the original wood frame central school had been. High school classes were moved back to central with three rooms.

1894—Cornerstone laid for the college at College and Austin Streets. Land (six acres) donated by J. J. Nelson.

1894–1904—The mines produced $23 million worth of ore.

1894—*Frank L. Forlow* opened his law practice at 112 North Allen (Main), and his business remained there until his death on March 28, 1927.

1894—*Labor Day* established as a holiday.

1895—Daniel Stewart passed away.

1895—November 22, *The Webb Corp* was incorporated under the name The Webb City Iron Works. Located next to the Missouri Pacific Railroad Depot, they invested $100,000 in erecting five buildings of brick. They are doing in excess of a quarter of a million dollars per year. J. C. Stewart was president.

1895—*Carthage Courthouse* completed.

1896—April, *F. M. King*, mayor April 1896–October 1896

1896—Competition for the American Bell Telephone Company when Charles Manker and W. C. Stewart set up the Home Telephone Company. Many businesses would have two phones, one from each phone company so all their customers could reach them by phone (in 1913, the two-phone companies merged. In 1925, Southwestern Bell Telephone Company bought them out).

1896—August 9, debut of the *Joplin Globe*.

1886—First semester of the *Webb City College*.

1896—William A. Snodgrass and his father, Hamilton Snodgrass, purchased the *Webb City Register* from his brother-in-law *Jesse Zook*.

1896—October, J. W. Frey, mayor October 1896–April 1898

1896—The Southwest Missouri Railway purchased the Jasper County Electric Railway which ran from Carterville to Carthage. They also purchased the Galena Electric Railway.

1897—*Jane Webb Stewart* married *Charles Chinn Sr.* She became *Jane Chinn*.

1897—*John Henry Etter* and his wife, *Fannie Phelps Etter,* opened a bakery at Second and Main, southwest corner. Later they are located on Daugherty Street, west end.

1898—April, E. E. Spracklen, mayor 1898–1900

1898—September, *Colonel W. F. Cody* and his Wild West Show appeared in Joplin, and people came from area towns. By 10:00 a.m., Main Street was packed as everyone awaited the parade.

1898—*Bernice Ashcraft* first baby born in Webb City and daughter of Grant Ashcraft, married *Earl A. Bunch.*

1898—Webb City had a mineral display at the *Omaha International Exhibit.* Webb City received the only silver medal awarded.

1899—Webb City's output of lead was 1,010,280 pounds; zinc was 27,252,730 pounds.

1899—Webb City had population of five thousand, purest water in the state, coming from a spring. Webb City had electric lights, large ice plant, and three railroads, finest streetcar association. There were three large hotels: The Newland, the Arlington, and the Maine. There were two foundries, huge lumberyard, milling company, nice brick city hall, two newspapers: *The Webb City Sentinel* and the *Daily Register.* Webb City Bank and the Exchange Bank, large opera house, nine churches, Baptist College.

1899—Webb City's <u>paid</u> fire department was organized under Mayor E. E. Spracklen. The city purchased the first auto fire wagon for $5,000.

1899—*Henry C. Humphrey* moved to Webb City and started a new business known as *Humphrey's Department Store,* located across the street from the Newland Hotel. He brought with him $4,000 worth of merchandise. His first year netted him $17,000, and before long, he was bringing in $300,000 annually. He later purchased the Hatten and Raymond Block (the second brick building in Webb City) at 201–207 North Allen (Main).

1899—Andrew McCorkle moved his home to the south using logs and horses to allow room to build a grand home that would reflect his mining success; 106 South Webb Street.

1899—July, *F. E. Adams* came to Webb City and bought the *Webb City Daily Sentinel.*

1899—*Webb City Gazette* was printed.

1899—The Webb City Iron Works (Webb Corp.) now covers 86,430 square feet of ground.

1900—The state supreme court decided to dispossess Webb City of five additions, placing three thousand people outside the city limits and depriving Webb City of about six hundred voters.

1900—April, S. F. Clark, mayor 1900–1902

1900—*John Dermott* built the *Dermott Building,* northwest corner of Allen (Main) and First Streets. He also built the *Zinc Ore Building* (*Sentinel* office) at Nine South Main, an office for himself and his son-in-law *Thomas J. Roney, state representative.*

1900—*Franklin School* was built located by the water tower.

1900—Webb City's YMCA was formed by C. M. Manker, and he served as the first president until his death. The YMCA met at the Aylor Building at 208 North Allen (Main) until the new building was completed in 1901, at 107–109 West Daugherty.

1900—Webb City had a population of 9,201; Carterville, 4,445; Carl Junction, 1,117; Carthage 9,416.

1900—*St. John's Hospital* in Joplin opened.

1900—The Southwest Missouri Electric Railway Company built new streetcar shops at Madison and Broadway, northeast corner.

1900—The Century Building at Twenty-Five and Twenty-Seven South Main was built.

1900—Grand opening of the Blake Opera House, at the time considered to be the largest and grandest in the area. Cost $30,000, 1,200 seats, ten private boxes. On the night of the grand opening, all seats were filled at an astronomical fee of $10 each. Later known as the Blake Theatre (it burned in 1931).

1901—YMCA building, 109 West Daugherty, was built. Retail shops on first floor.

1901—*Spracklen Photography* building was built at the northwest corner of Webb Street and Daugherty.

1901—September 6, *President McKinley* was assassinated.

1901—*Dr. William Winston Waggoner*, a recent graduate of school of medicine of the University of Cincinnatti, with post-graduate work at University of Heidelberg in Germany, arrived in Webb City. He lived at 116 North Roane.

1902—April, *D. F. Wertiz*, mayor 1902–1904

1902—Eighth grade was admitted to high school.

1902—*John Henry Etter* and his wife, *Fannie Phelps Etter*, moved their bakery to 1005 West Daugherty.

1902—The Middlewest Building, One South Allen (Main), built in 1883, underwent major remodeling, and the opera house on the second floor became a hotel.

1903—The new powerhouse made of brick and stone was built in Webb City by Southwest Missouri Electric Railway Co. The Webb City Northern Electric Railway Company was built to connect Oronogo, Neck City, Purcell, Alba.

1903—Fireworks exploded at the Murratta Drug Store and *James Murratta* was badly injured. His health did not improve, but he continued to work the store until 1911, when he died at the age of forty-six from complications of that accident. In 1911, *Roy Teel* purchased the Murratta Drug Store.

1903—Presbyterian Church built a new sanctuary at Broadway and Ball. Brick building adorned with Carthage Stone.

1904—November, Webb City's centenarian, *Thomas Sauls*, at the age of 101, walked to the polls to vote for the president, as he had done every election since he was old enough to vote. He also laid claim to that fact that he had shaken hands with every president at that time, except President Washington (who died before Saul was born) and President Teddy Roosevelt, who was serving at that time and was up for re-election. Saul was not in condition to travel to Washington, DC, to shake Roosevelt's hand. Saul passed away in 1906, at the age of 103.

1904—*St. Louis world's fair*

1904—*Mr. Barbee* suggested the plan of organizing school classes with officers.

1904—Mr. Barbee started the school newspaper *The Review*. It lasted two years and was discontinued as it took up too much schooltime, and grades were suffering.

1904—Andrew McCorkle passed away.

1904—November, Range Line School dedicated

1904—December, Joplin's new federal building completed at Third and Joplin.

1904—*George W. Moore* elected mayor of Webb City, after having served on the council for several terms. He was re-elected as mayor in 1906. He was a Republican mayor in a Democratic town, and he was a popular mayor. He bricked twenty-one blocks in the business district. First city streetlights were installed. He also negotiated the building of the Webb City–Carterville (streetcar) Viaduct (1906) that cost $100,000.

1905—May 18, Merchant & Miner Bank organized by W. E. Patten, R. B. Dodge, L. J. Stevison, and C. M. Manker. The business opened in a temporary location at 110 East Main behind Middlewest Building.

1905—*Dr. Lincoln Chenoweth* opened the first hospital in Webb City in the home of Captain Hemenway, northwest corner of Webb Street and First Street. He then closed that establishment (that same year 1905) and opened the second hospital at the Salvation Army, Two Hundred East Main (Broadway).

1905—The Webb City and Carterville Gas Company was organized by *Colonel James O'Neill.*

1905—February 12, the temperature ranged between twenty-one and twenty-seven below zero

1905—Population of Webb City was twelve thousand.

1906—*The Exchange Bank* nationalized and became known as the Webb City National Bank

1906—April, Merchants & Miners bank building completed, southwest corner of Main and Daugherty.

1906—May 8, Presbyterian Church purchased the lot north of the church building for future annex.

1906—San Francisco earthquake

1906—*Hal Wise* purchased the *Webb City Sentinel* with his best friend, *Jim Stickney.* Wise had spent the previous year with the *St. Louis Dispatch* covering the world's fair. About ten years later, Wise was the sole owner of the *Sentinel.*

1906—Mount Hope Cemetery was established, and forefathers of Webb City history were exhumed from area cemeteries and moved to the center hub of the new Mount Hope Cemetery.

1906—The Southwest Missouri Railroad Company was organized and replaced the Southwest Missouri Electric Railway Company.

1906—According to the *Annual Review*, a $75,000 viaduct was being erected by the Southwest Electric Railway Co. between Webb City and Carterville (it would end up costing $100,000).

1906—There were twenty-two major mining companies operating in the Webb City-Carterville and Prosperity field. Most had more than one shaft at each site.

1906—*The Independent Gravel Co.* was organized by Thomas McCroskey and Ben Reynolds.

1907—The telephone company built a building at 209 West Broadway.

1907—The Webb City Iron Works consolidated with the Carterville Foundry Company and the Oronogo Foundry and Machine Works (Webb Corp. the president of the business is W. R. Caulkins and vice president is C. E. Matthews).

1907—A fire destroyed almost the entire business district of Alba.

1907—*Dr. Slaughter* arrived in Webb City with his new medical degree and hung his shingle. It was the beginning of over forty years of delivering babies and doctoring the sick. Many have the honor of saying they were delivered by Dr. Melville Slaughter.

1907—October 1, the new skating rink opened in the two hundred block of North Main. A $40 bedroom suit was being offered to the first couple to be married that night at the skating rink wearing roller skates during the ceremony.

1907—The Masonic Building was completed at Nine South Webb Street. Open as retail.

1907—Presbyterian Manse built west of the Sanctuary on Broadway.

1908—April, *Peter J. McEntee*, mayor 1908—1910

1908—The *King Jack Annual* began and was referred to as a paper, semiannually presented by the seniors. The first one being in May 1908. Class of 1909 issued the King Jack II in December 1908.

1908—*Dr. Paul Pritchett* came to Webb City.

1908—The new Catholic Parish was built at Webb and Third Streets.

1908—November, *Howard W. Taft* defeated William Jennings Bryan. Taft had taken a campaign tour on a train and had stopped in Webb City and spoke from the porch of the Chapman home at First and Pennsylvania northeast corner. Later determined that he also spoke at the corner of Webb and Broadway (Joplin) from a wagon.

1909—*The Central Methodist Church* was built at Broadway (Joplin Street) and Pennsylvania Avenue on land donated by E. T. Webb. Jane Chinn donated $10,000.

1909—June, grand opening of the new *Schifferdecker Electric Park* in Joplin.

1909—The *Belles Letters Club* of Webb City was organized

1909—Population of Webb City was fifteen thousand.

1909—The Webb City Iron Works has changed their name to the Webb City & Carterville Foundry & Machine Works (Webb Corp).

1910—April, *W. V. K. Spencer*, mayor 1910–1914 (two terms)

1910—February 1, the citizens of Webb City vote to go dry 1195 in favor of selling liquor and 2,262 in favor of not selling liquor.

1910—February 11, Saturday, 3 miners killed at the Red Dog Mine. Will Hall, age thirty-two, married; Jack Gallagher, age twenty-six, married; Frank Burris age twenty-two, single.

1910—March 22, a magazine from the Rochester Mining Company containing several hundred pounds of dynamite, located one mile north of Webb City, exploded. The home of Edward Vinson was located a few feet from the magazine was destroyed. Edward, thirty-five and his wife were killed. Mrs. Ellen Allen was seriously injured and Edward's two children, ages eighteen months and a three weeks old were miraculously saved.

1910—*Jane and Charles Chinn* donated $60,000 to build and equip the *Jane Chinn Hospital,* on the southwest corner of Rose and Austin. Jane Chinn was eighty-one years of age at the time.

1910—November, *James A. Daugherty* elected to the House of Representatives from the Fifteenth Congressional District.

1910—The Southwest Missouri Railroad Company built a three-story clubhouse for the employees of the railway.

1910—*The Library and Civic Improvement Association* organized. Most instrumental in establishing the library (later known as just the Civic Improvement Club).

1911—Roy Teel purchased the Murratta Drug Store changing the name to Teel Drug Store. 110 North Main Street

1911—July 24, Granville Ashcraft (Webb City's "Man of Firsts") passed away.

1911—Construction of new high school, $90,000 on Broadway between Washington and Jefferson.

1911—Carl Junction had its first annual Bingville Celebration.

1911—The First Methodist Church dedicated, seating capacity of over 750.

1911—August, Joe Clary buried alive when the White Oak Mine on the Thousand Acre Tract caved in. Cut off Joe's air supply. Water began to seep into the dark chamber area. Joe sat there for two days feeling the water slowly rising around him. Finally rescued, he rested a day or two and went right back to work in the same mine. It was his job, he said!

191—There were seven theaters operating in Webb City: the Blake Theatre, 217 West Daugherty; The Electric Theatre, 110 East Main (Broadway); The Frisco Theater, 911 West Daugherty; The IT Air Dome; Outdoor Theater, southeast corner of Allen (Main) and John (Austin); The Ideal Theater, 104 South Allen (Main), Ideal Air Dome, Outdoor Theater, northwest corner of Allen (Main) and First Street; and the Mystic Theater, Twenty-One South Allen (Main). Known as a theater if there were live performances at any time. A theater just showed movies on a screen. In later years, the civic replaced the Blake when it burned. The Jr. Theater replaced the Mystic and the Dickenson Theater was built at Twenty-two South Main.

1912—August 7, *Prosperity* business district burns

1912—September, *President Theodore Roosevelt* stopped in Joplin to campaign.

1912—Future president *Warren Harding* was in Joplin to speak on behalf of *President Howard W. Taft.*

1912—William Wheeler opened Wheeler's shoe store in the YMCA building.

1912—The West End Pharmacy building was completed, originally a drug and grocery store, the building also served as a waiting area for the Southwest Mo. Railroad Co. (streetcar). The building was owned and operated by E. E. Fugett. Sold the business to Robert Burris in 1915.

1913—The two phone companies, Bell Telephone Company and Home Telephone Company, merged, making life easier for businesses that had to have a phone from each company to allow customers of both companies to call them. Kept the name of Home Telephone.

1913—April 6, Webb City adopted a municipal tax to finance the library.

1913—December 31, Jane Chinn passed away. One of the wealthiest woman in Jasper County.

1914—April, *J. E. Locke*, elected mayor 1914–1916

1914—Oronogo's Circle Mine declared to be "the greatest zinc producer in the world."

1914—*Webb City's Carnegie Library* was completed December 31, at a cost of $25,000.

1914—August 4, 1914, a major railway disaster on the Kansas City Southern Line at Tipton Ford took fifty-six lives.

1914—The *Frisco Depot* was constructed at Madison and Daugherty Streets. Previous location of the train station was on Fourth Street.

1915—Jasper County Tuberculosis Hospital was completed. State funds for operation did not come through, so the building sat idle until 1918. It was turned into a nursing home in 1956.

1915—Robert Burris purchased the drugstore in the west end of town and named it the West End Pharmacy. He sold it to Ed Sever and Fred Jackson while serving in WWI. He bought it back in 1920 after returning home. His brother Lewis Burris went in partnership with him.

1916—April, *W. F. Gill*, was elected mayor in 1916 and served to 1922 (three terms)

1916—April 26, *Martha E. Webb Hall*, daughter of John C. Webb, died in a tragic fire that burned her estate of Hallwood west of Carthage. Her son Ed died the next day from the fire.

1916—The mining industry reached its peak. Zinc reached a value of $135 a ton. Webb City was known as the richest zinc and lead mining district in the world.

1916—Completion of the *Jefferson Highway*. It entered Webb City on Daugherty to Devon, across Broadway, west to Main Street. South on Main to Fourth Street, west on Fourth to Madison, south to what would be the new concrete road which began at Thirteen and Madison. The concrete highway extended through Royal Heights to Broadway in Joplin. The concrete road was built by the WPA in 1918.

1916–1917—The building of Webb City's federal building (post office) at a cost of $90,000. The marble structure was completed in 1917.

1916—A. D. Hatten discovered a petrified ear of corn on his land while building his home on Ball Street.

1917—World War began.

1917—The Webb City Chamber of Commerce was organized to take over for the Webb City Commercial Club.

1917—Joseph Aylor (age seventy-seven) passed away, being worth over $2.5 million.

1918—January, campaign begins to raise funds to finance the Tuberculosis Hospital operations in Webb City. It began with a $500 contribution from A. H. Rogers, who was in California at the time, and sent a telegram announcing his contribution. The hospital was completed earlier, but state funding did not come as expected, so the hospital was idle. Funds were collected, and the hospital began operations in September.

1918—*Etter's Bakery* needed to expand. Etter built a two-story brick building with twelve rooms upstairs to rent out. He built around the existing building to allow business to continue to operate.

1918—The greatest ore strike in the tristate district was discovered in Oklahoma. The beginning of the end for Webb City's mines.

1918—Not to allow the city to die, as the miners left, the Commercial Club, the new chamber of commerce started the campaign to find industry for Webb City.

1918—May, concrete highway contract started at Thirteen and Madison extending through Royal Heights to Broadway in Joplin. Works Progress Administration (WPA) project.

1918—October, *Lieutenant Ray E. Watson* was cited for heroism in action near Nantillois, France. Watson was severely wounded in the battle.

1918—Lowe Furniture Company became Webb City Furniture Company, and the Lowe Undertaking Business 115 East Daugherty became J. T. Steele Undertaking Company at 111 East Daugherty.

1918—November 11, end of World War I. Celebrations were celebrated everywhere. Two days later, Mr. and Mrs. Samuel Schalk, 817 South Madison received word that their only son, Darrell Schalk, had died on October 3, in France.

1918—*Preble Shoe Mfg. Co.* established and began making high-grade children's shoes.

1918—*Webb City Register Newspaper* shut down, 112 North Webb Street, had been located in the John C. Webb mansion

1919—*C. H. Baker* owned a little grocery store at 618 West Fourth street.

1919—Influenza causes the schools to be closed for 6 weeks. Masks of gauze were being worn for protection by public employees such as barbers.

1919—Memorial Park built in memory of those who perished in the World War. Concerts and public gatherings were held in Memorial Park. Roll of honor board, "Dedicated to the men and women in service from Webb City, Mo and sponsored by the Wives of the Servicemen's Club." Land (one-fourth of a block) for the park was a gift to the city from Robert Toutz. His son Robert Toutz Jr. became the director of the Webb City Municipal Band, and his family participated in the band that played a free concert every week in the *Memorial Park Bandstand*. The project to build the bandstand was headed by A. D. Hatten.

1919—*Elder Garment Plant* (shirt factory) opened. Chamber of commerce raised $20,000 and purchased the lot and built the building to bring the plant to town.

1919—July 12, John C. Webb's mansion at 112 North Webb Street burned. It was being used as a storage place for J. T. Steele Undertaking Co.

1920—Webb City attained the distinction of increasing her industries more than any other city in the United States, with an increase of 250 percent. A leather factory, shoe factory, shirt factory, tobacco factory, and a box factory were established. Some of previous factories included the Interurban Ice Company, The Jersey Ice Cream and Butter Factory, The Star Bottling Works, Ball & Gunning Company, West Side Machine Shop, Webb City and Carterville Foundry and Machine Company, Rex Casket Company, Independent Gravel Company, Crocker Packing Company.

1920—A day nursery was established to take care of children of factory workers

1920—February, the Theatre and café burned at Lakeside Park as the grounds were being prepared for spring opening of the park.

1920—March 7, A. H. Rogers passed away; Southwest Missouri Streetcar Association

1920—*Ray Watson*, having returned to Webb City from the World War with honors helped to organize the Battery G of the 203rd Coast artillery of the reconstituted Missouri National Guard, becoming the battery's first commanding officer.

1920—October 18, a little change in street names for Webb City. Allen Street (north to south) became Main Street. Main Street which went east, from Webb Street became Broadway Street as did Joplin Street starting at Webb Street and going west becomes Broadway Street. John Street became Austin Street. No reason given in the city council minutes for name changes.

1920—December 28, C. M. Manker (former mayor and businessman) passed away.

1920—Webb City adopted the motto "Get Down and Come In," a real invitation to the manufacturers and farmers, in the business way, as well as to strangers in the hospitable way.

1921—The elevator was installed in the Carthage Courthouse.

1922—April, *A. G. Young* elected to a two-year term for mayor, 1922–924.

1922—The Halloween tornado struck at midnight. It first hit the Webb City cemetery and then jumped over to Webb City's northeast side, killing one and many injuries and nearly destroying that entire side of town on Hall, Walker, and Elliott Streets. Twenty-five to thirty homes were flattened. One fatality, Nancy Frad, on North Centennial Street.

1922—*Freeman Hospital* established in Joplin.

1923—October, *H. C. Humphreys* passed away.

1923—April 6, on a Wednesday morning, the *Bank of Waco* was robbed by two unmasked men at 10:30 a.m. A posse pursued as far as Opolis, Kansas, before abandoning the chase.

1923—*Sam Kallas* moved to Webb City from Kansas City and opened the Coney Island on the southwest corner of Broadway and Main. Nobody in this area had ever heard of a Coney dog. He sold them for 5¢ each, selling $500 each weekday and $1,000 per day on weekends.

1924—April, *W. F. Gill*, elected mayor 1924–1926 (his fourth term as mayor).

1925—*Southwestern Bell Telephone* company buys out the Home Telephone Company.

1925—Many passenger lines on the streetcar schedules were shut down. Freight cars still ran. The line between Joplin and Webb City was still running at half-hour intervals. The Southwest Missouri Railroad Company purchased a fleet of motor buses; service began in March.

1925—Residents were complaining as the price of gas had gone up from 5¢ per gallon to 19.9¢.

1925—July 29, *Alfred S. Michaelis*, architect, passed away during an accident at the building of the new memorial hall in Joplin. Alfred and his brother A. C. Michaelis designed many beautiful buildings in the area, including the Methodist Church in Webb City.

1926—April, *C. C. Harris*, elected mayor 1926–1928 (two-year term)

1927—February, the *US 66 Highway Association*, the Main Street of America organization. Held an organizational meeting in Tulsa. Attending were 135 delegates representing thirty-two cities and towns between St. Louis and Albuquerque, New Mexico. The purpose of the organization was to launch a campaign to encourage use of the national highway.

1927—The new West Side School was built, all ground floor level.

1927—June, *Thomas F. Coyne* passed away.

1927—October 27, county commissioners condemned the old Georgia City Bridge after being damaged by a large truck. Improvements will begin immediately at a cost of $350–$500.

1928—Vic Bennett purchased a store from C. H. Baker, a grocery store at 618 West Fourth Street, on the southeast corner. Bennett kept the store until 1934, after a fire; sold to Clarence Martin.

1928—April, *W. H. Tholborn* was elected and served as mayor from 1928–1930.

1928—March, two-story Carl Junction school was destroyed by fire. The twelve classrooms of the 1914 building held all grades from first to twelfth.

1928—A big event for moviegoers as the first talking movies were presented at theaters that could afford to install the special equipment to handle the new movies.

1928—St. Louis Cardinals won the World Series. Webb City was in need to choose a mascot and decided on the Cardinals. The Webb City Cardinals were established!

1929—The *National Honor Society* Webb City Chapter was organized

1929—June, Webb City Bank took over the assets of the First National Bank of Carterville. They reopened July 1, as the Webb City Bank in Carterville.

1930—April, *Walter Ragland* was elected mayor, 1930, and served to 1934 (two terms).

1930—January 13, A. D. Hatten donated land for Hatten Athletic Field on North Madison Street.

1930—October 5, following a parade downtown, the city celebrated the dedication of the new stadium at Hatten Athletic Field with a game between Webb City and Pittsburg High School. There was a 2,500 seating capacity.

1930—The old central school on Webb Street between Church and First Streets was torn down.

1930—December 25, Route 66 is completed from St. Louis to Joplin, except for one mile of road in Arlington, Missouri.

1931—The old mill burned and the Ball & Gunning Milling Company was rebuilt, bigger and better.

1931—The drum corps had cardinals painted on drums, and they performed on Hatten Field for Thanksgiving Day.

1931—The first issue of the *Cardinal notes* was published.

1931—The Blake Theatre burned, 217 West Daugherty. The large crowd that gathered used the post office steps as handy bleacher seats to watch the fire.

1931—May 16, Coyne Hatten, twenty-seven-year-old son of A. D. Hatten, was gunned down behind Morgan Drug Store at Daugherty and Webb. He was the victim of gangster J. E. Creighton, who was initially sentenced to be hanged but was retried and sentenced to life in prison.

1931—The *Joplin Stockyards* opened in August on the southwest corner of Rangeline and Newman Roads. The brick for the building and stockyard had been salvaged from Webb City Baptist College.

1932—Civic pride was credited with rebuilding a theater where the Blake Theatre once stood on Daugherty Street. Due to community efforts, it was named the Civic Theatre.

1932—September 30, *Bonnie and Clyde* robbed the Merchants & Miners Bank in Oronogo.

1933—May, A. D. Hatten deeded land to the city on May 2, to build Hatten Park on College Street (where the Webb City Baptist College had been located). Work began with clearing the college basement to be used for a public swimming pool. A $10,000 grant was received from Public Works Administration in Washington, DC, to fix up the swimming pool.

1933—November, the Civic Club of Webb City raised enough funds to help build the bathhouse at the new pool.

1934—*Clarence Martin* purchased the little store at 618 West Fourth Street from Vic Bennett. They tore down the wood frame store and built a concrete block building. They sold the store to Charlie Highley.

1934—April, *Frank C. Nelson* began term as mayor, 1934–1936.

1934 and 1936—Most severe droughts in American history, creating the Dust Bowl.

1934—September, the first golf tournament was held at the Hatten Farms Club.

1934—September, the central school was demolished. The bricks were used to build the *Smith Shirt Factory* in the same location but facing Liberty Street instead of Webb Street.

1935—Joplin purchased 319 acres west of Webb City on the north side of the Joplin-Webb City Road to develop Joplin Regional Airport.

1935—Officially all passenger streetcars were replaced by buses, although a few streetcars continued to carry passengers through 1938.

1935—It was Lakeside Park's last summer of fun, as it was officially shut down in October.

1935—The first annual *Easter sunrise service* was held at Hatten Farms Golf Course. It was started by the chamber of commerce and the local churches, under the guidance of Harry Hulett.

1935—March, tornado hits airport and Webb City Golf Course.

1935—WPA had fifty men working on the Joplin Airport.

1936—April, *Lee A. Daugherty* elected mayor, 1936–1938.

1936—The opening of the Webb City municipal pool was in July. It was an immediate success, with 10¢ admission fees and a free kiddie swim on Saturday evenings, from 6:00 p.m.–7:00 p.m.

1936—*Betty Browning,* 1928 WCHS graduate and female pilot won the Amelia Earhart Air Race in Los Angeles. She maintained an average speed of 156 mph to win the 25-mile race.

1936—*Broadway Market* opened on Broadway Street.

1937—Easter sunrise services attracted over five thousand spectators. The Easter sunrise services were canceled during the war with plans to revive later, but that didn't happen.

1937—The *Webb City Rotary Club* was established.

1937—July 4, dedication of the Carthage Municipal Park, starting out with 177 acres to expand to 200 acres later.

1938—April, *Dr. M. S. Slaughter*, mayor 1938–1942 (two terms)

1938—July, Pineville selected as the film site for the new Jesse James movie with Tyrone Power as the lead actor.

1938—September, the Joplin Little Theatre was organized at a meeting held in the Connor Hotel.

1938—Opening of Home Beverage

1938—The new Webster school building completed.

1939—The new Franklin School under construction

1939—June 2, the sale of the Southwest Missouri Railroad Company to Joplin Public Service Company was complete with the sale of the Joplin Carthage line for $2,000. The end of an era.

1939—April 16, *Thomas J. Roney* passed away.

1939—June 15, the bell that sits on top of city hall has been removed. No ringing for curfew. The powers that be said that the bell was unsafe due to the weight and damage it was causing to the roof of city hall. It was given to a junk dealer and was never seen again (rumor has it that the bell, in later years, was located and was on display at the fire department at 506 Ellis Street.

1939—August 24, late in the afternoon, a terrific hailstorm occurred with the largest hailstones ever known or heard of by the people of this or any other district. Huge, almost square chunks of ice large enough to fill pint measures and some the size of eggs left gaping holes in the roofs of homes in Joplin, Carthage, Webb City, and other nearby small towns.

1940—*Nance Furniture* store opened in the Masonic building at Nine South Webb Street.

1940—April, a cave-in occurred between Webb City and Carterville, just a mile north of the Missouri Pacific Railroad depot. The cave-in was estimated to be between five hundred and six hundred feet in diameter. It was just in the chats, no danger, except the ground under the railroad track sagged as much as five feet and maybe deeper. A train had just passed through coming from Newport, Arkansas.

1940—May 3, the Southwest Missouri Viaduct between Webb City and Carterville was being dismantled by E. L. Heisten, a Carthage contractor, and twenty men with an audience of several hundred spectators. The viaduct was a 106-foot span of steel and weighed fifty-five tons. The viaduct was being transported to the Grand River Lake near Jay, Oklahoma.

1941—*Huey's Department Store* opened.

1941—*K & H Steak House* was opened at Broadway and Madison (advertised as being located at Wreck Corner.

1941—October, the Newland Hotel was condemned.

1941—December 7, the bombing of *Pearl Harbor*

1942,—January, men began receiving orders from the draft to register and report on February 14–16.

1942—A grove of maple trees south of the Joplin Airport which originally graced the farm home of W. A. Daugherty, one of the early pioneer settlers, were declared a hazard to heavy aircraft and sentenced for removal. Those trees had been in the Daugherty family for more than seventy-five years.

1942—April, mayor terms changed from two years to four years.

1942—April, *Don O. Adamson*, mayor 1942–1946 (one term)

1942—Rationing begins as residents are limited on sugar and gasoline, coffee.

1942—No Christmas lights due to the war.

1942—The Webb City & Carterville Foundry & Machine Works shortened their name to The Webb Corporation. Must easier to say and write.

1942—*August Rodeo* in Webb City draws over six thousand people.

1942—*Smith Shirt Factory* gets contract to make 280,000 shirts for the navy.

1942—December, Webb City observed its first "blackout," as ordered by city council. Mayor Don Adamson and Colonel Ray Watson were authorized to organize wardens, special police, and enforcement to keep a close watch over the city for failure to "outen" the lights in residences, stores, shops, and streets. Failure to comply resulted in a penalty of jail time or a maximum fine of $200.

1943—January, *George Washington Carver* died in Tuskegee, Alabama. He was never sure of his birthday, and it was estimated that he was born around 1864. Six months later, the site near Diamond was declared a place to be used as a memorial to Carver.

1943—January temperatures reached ten degrees below zero.

1943—May, Webb City had floods.

1943—June, The Southwest Missouri Railroad Powerhouse was sold.

1943—November, cases of scarlet Fever were reported in Webb City.

1943—December, Ball & Gunning Mill was sold to Norris Grain Co. of KC.

1944—*Harry S. Truman*, elected vice president of the United States, in 1945, became president, re-elected in the year 1948.

1944—*Webb City Wholesale Grocery Company* was destroyed by fire. Relocated to the old Southwest Missouri Electric Railway powerhouse the next year.

1945—Sam Kallas moved his Coney Island from the southwest corner of Main and Broadway, to the Civic Drive-In Café on Route 66, where Broadway runs into Webb Street from the east.

1945—February, Memorial Park dedication of sign which listed names of Webb City servicemen.

1945—August, President Harry S. Truman announced the end of World War II. A total of 194 Jasper County soldiers lost their lives in the war.

1946—April, *Fred R. Nelson*, mayor 1946–1950 (one term).

1946—June, Free Band Concerts began weekly in Memorial Park.

1946—August, *the Joplin Jalopy*, a B-24 bomber, was put on display at the Joplin Airport, eventually sold for scrap, sat in the Swapper Salvage yard, 517 East Broadway, just east of Webb Corp.

1947—October, Webb City's first operating traffic signal lights were installed in the intersections of Main and Broadway and at Main and Daugherty. They did not last long. Don't know why!

1947—*Herrod's Store* closed after fifty-eight years in business.

1947—Henry Hulett sold his sixty-year-old insurance company to William Waggoner.

1948—The pumps were shut down at the Oronogo Circle, and the mine began to fill with water.

1948—April, *Hal Wise Sr.*, with the *Webb City Sentinel*, passed away.

1948—*Myers Baker Rife and Denham* established and located at 927 West Daugherty.

1949—January 11, the worst ice storm in the history of Webb City to this date. Loss of power, city wells operated by electricity, no water. Wires were down all over town. Beautiful half-century trees were down blocking traffic. Gas pumps cannot operate without electricity. Hospital was without power. The *Sentinel* was published by hand power.

1949—May, Dr. W. J. Stone passed away, veterinarian at Stone's Corner.

1949—The new *Route 66 Drive-In Theatre* by Carthage opened for business.

1949—Minimum wage went from 60¢ to 75¢ an hour.

1950—April, *Robert J. Cummings*, mayor April 1950–November 1951

1950—February 8, A. D. Hatten, prominent pioneer of Webb City, passed away at the age of ninety.

1950—September 1, the beginning of a new company, Cardinal Scales by W. H. Perry.

1951—April, it snowed in April.

1951—Highway 57 routed through Webb City.

1951—July 3, tornado hit Webb City west end.

1951—September, *Margaret Blaine Carney* started a voice studio in her home at 302 South Ball Street.

1951—November, *C. S. Fly* served as mayor pro tem from November 1952 to April 1952.

1951—Western Union and bus station moved from 113 West Broadway to 114 North Webb.

1952—January, Webb City & Joplin Bus service inaugurated.

1952—April, C. S. Fly, mayor 1952–1954; elected mayor to serve out Cummings' term.

1952—The Smith's opened the Webb City Dairy Queen at Fourth and Jefferson.

1952—February, *Williams Chili Seasoning* open its plant in Webb City.

1952—August, Hatten Field dressing rooms and showers for players and public restrooms were built by local volunteers. The rock wall was installed by the WPA.

1953—April, a fierce ice storm hit the area and caused major damage.

1953—June, Webb City Drive-In Theatre open for business.

1953—*The Railway Express Office*, located in the Frisco Depot, closed and consolidated with the Joplin office.

1954—April, *Ed W. Murray*, mayor 1954–1958

1954—July, hot summer, 117 degrees

1954—New businesses in town were: *G&H Redi Mix, Handy Dandy Liquor Store at Madison and Fourth*

1954—The *Royal Furniture Company* expanded with the purchase of the Morris Building next to their store.

1954—*August Hulett* Photography Studio opened at Twenty-Seven South Main.

1955—The *Webb City Casket and Metal Products* opened at 217 North Tom.

1955—October 31, the city had a Halloween costume parade, which ended with a street dance on Main Street. Lots of good clean fun!

1956—The *Webb City American Legion* started a campaign to officially name Webb City as the City of Flags. American Legion Queen candidates sold flags and a door-to-door project to sell flags to the citizens for cost began. Over five hundred were sold.

1956—The *Tuberculosis Hospital* was shut down by court order. Changed into Elmhurst Nursing Home, Webb City.

1956—Monument set at Memorial Park to honor veterans.

1956—February, the Frizzells sold the K & H Steak House, being in business since1941 at the corner of Madison and Broadway.

1956—April, Frisco Church dedicated, Pastor G. K. Rees

1957—July 4, Webb City made the news as the City of Flags, had a mass display of flags waving in almost every home. This event was due to the efforts of the American Legion who started a door-to-door campaign in June 29, reminding residents to fly their flag. The plan was for the citizens of Webb City to proudly display their flags on all holidays.

1957—October, *Dr. Melville Slaughter* was given a reception in honor of fifty years of service.

1958—April, *Dr. Earl Baker*, mayor April 1958–November 1958; Paul Hight, mayor pro tem to 1959.

1958—November, *Paul Hight* served as mayor pro tem from November 1958–April 1959.

1958—*Bob Baker, Bill Myers, Max Myers* opened the MBM Investment Co. where the Civic Drive-In Café used to be located.

1958—May, volunteers built the Assembly of God Church at Church and Webb Streets.

1958—June, *Hal Wise Jr.* with the *Webb City Sentinel* passed away at the age of forty-four.

1958—July, the memorial for veterans was installed in Memorial Park.

1959—April, opening of *Richard's Furniture Inc.*, southeast corner of Main and First.

1959—April, *Don O. Adamson*, elected mayor, 1959–1962, finishing out Dr. Earl Baker's term.

1959—May, fire at the Webb City Iron and Metal Co. on East Broadway.

1959—The *Barbie Doll* hit the shelves, and the first shipment of five hundred thousand dolls sold out immediately

1959—*Radar Hill* was established by the air force in Oronogo across from the Oronogo Circle.

1959—June, *Max Myers and William Myers* purchased the *Webb City Sentinel* and changed the paper to a weekly paper.

1959—The *Hatten Golf Farm* was purchased by Ted Hoffman for a new housing district.

1960—The twist dance was introduced in the fall but did not become a hit until 1961 when Chubby Checker started singing "The Twist."

1960—*Mark Twain School* completed on West Aylor to replace the West End School.

1960—December 25, *Karbe Grocery Store*, Sixteenth and Madison, destroyed by fire.

1960—William Perry opened *Cardinal Castings Inc.*

1961—January, *Claude Hedge* of Hedge Lewis died.

1961—March, the new Karbe Store being rebuilt at 1510 South Madison, same location as previously located before fire.

1962—February, mayhem in Webb City as baseball greats attended the grand opening of *Clete Boyer's Stop and Shop Food Center* on Main Street. About five thousand people came out to meet such famous players as Mickey Mantle, Ken Boyer, Whitey Herzog, Roger Maris, Bill Tuttle, Norm Siebern, Bob Cerv, Bob Allison, Dick Williams, Cal Melish, Hank Bauer, Jerry Lumpe, and Bill Virdon. Big event in a small town!

1962—April, Don O. Adamson, mayor 1962–1966

1962—October, *Wendell's Meat Market* opened for business.

1962—Webb City Bank was building a drive-through bank across the street from the main building.

1962—The color Columbia blue was added to Webb City's school colors of red and white. It was to help differentiate the red and white of Carl Junction during local games.

1963—May, the national guard building (Jamison Building located behind the new Webb City Drive-In Bank) was destroyed by fire.

1963—March, Webb City became the center of attention when *Helen Myers* was named the Missouri Mother of the Year.

1963—Webb City School started their first kindergarten classes.

1963—November, assassination of *John F. Kennedy.*

1964—Part of East Daugherty Street experienced a cave-in.

1964—July, the *Webb City Welfare Office* was closed.

1965—February, *Max Glover's* law office was destroyed by fire.

1965—Grand opening of the Webb City Drive-Through Bank; Pat Orr president of the bank.

1965—November, *Clayton Johnston* of Johnston-Arnce-Simpson Mortuary died in a car accident on Zora Street.

1966—Every other parking meter was removed on Main Street to encourage shoppers.

1966—April, *Robert J. Baker*, mayor, April 1966–October 1969; Mayor Pro Tem Donald Scott served from November 1969–April 1970.

1966—July, three people died due to heat wave.

1966—July 14, explosion at Hercules

1966—August, the city had an option to buy 154 acres around the Sucker Flat area for $25,000 to build a park complex. Close to downtown, a one-time major mining area is a major part of Webb City's historical background. Sucker Flat was never undermined, and only one shaft had to be filled.

1966—September, *Foodtown* announced the building of a new store.

1966—October, the city removed every other parking meter to allow free parking on Main Street.

1966—October, an election for a bond to fund the purchase of land for a proposed park around Sucker Flat was defeated. Bond amount was $310,000.

1967—January 12, the 154 acres of Sucker Flats officially became park property to be used as a public park. Money came from the general fund, advanced to the park board.

1967—The *Webb City Saddle Club* was given a home in King Jack Park. The East-West Road through the center of King Jack Park was built by the Missouri National Guards' weekend projects.

1967—Alba School consolidated with Webb City. Elementary school was still held in Alba, but high school classes were bussed to Webb City. The last graduating class of Alba was the class of '68.

1967—February, a new business, *Ben Franklin Store*, opened on Main Street where the hub was previously.

1967—June, *Matthews Coffee Company* sold to Cain's Coffee.

1968—*June Poyner* submitted winning entry in the Name the Park contest. She beat out fifty entries with *King Jack Park* (the land was known as Sucker Flat before the new name). Runner-up name was Progressive Park.

1968—August, the mayor made the first direct-distance-dialing telephone call from Webb City.

1969—November, *Marion Perry* remodeled the building at Nine South Main and opened *The Empress,* named after the Empress Theatre that occupied that building.

1969—July 12, dedication celebration for King Jack Park

1969—October, the *Pick and Pay Market* on Madison burned down.

1969—November, opening of The Empress.

1969—*Mayor Robert J. Baker* recognized the unpopularity of his decision to purchase the mine land for King Jack Park was having a negative effect on other projects, such as building the new water tower. He resigned in November.

1969—November, *Donald Scott*, mayor pro tem November 1969–April 1970, finishing Baker's term

1970—April, *Robert Patrick*, mayor 1970–1974

1970—August, huge explosion at Ray's Service Station, causes mushroom cloud of smoke in the sky at 1202 South Madison Street.

1970—November, the first *Nic Frising cartoon* appeared in the *Sentinel.*

1971—New Webb City High School, 621 North Madison, construction began.

1971—May 6, tornado wiped out thirty-seven block of Joplin, one death, more than forty injured.

1972—May, the Webb City High School *Class of 1972* was the last class to graduate in the old high school on Broadway.

1973—May 11, tornado struck Joplin at 7:00 a.m.; hundreds injured, three died.

1973—Lewis Burris retired and sold West End Pharmacy after over fifty years of business. Lewis passed away in October of 1973.

1974—Norval M. Matthews book *The Promise Land* was released.

1974—April, Sterling Gant's first term as mayor, from 1974–1976.

1974—April 28, dedication of *Jack Dawson's Praying Hands* statue in King Jack Park, bringing worldwide attention to Webb City.

1974—The old high school on Broadway was torn down.

1974—Dr. Wells-Lee died of a heart attack.

1975—April 24, tornado hit Neosho; killed three, seriously injured three, with numerous other injuries.

1975—March, *Ashley's Department Store* opened in the Kress Building. formerly the Kress Dime Store, on Main Street in Webb City.

1976—Norval M. Matthews' book *An Amazing City* was released.

1976—April, P. D. Crockett, mayor April 1976–Feb. 1985; served two full terms and a partial.

1976—May, open house at new fire station on East Church Street.

1976—Webb City celebrated centennial along with nation's bicentennial. Jack Dawson followed up the Praying Hands with his Kneeling Miner Statue.

1977—Norval Matthews passed away at age eighty-two. Matthews was an author, historian, and business owner.

1978—*Don Roderique* passed away. Roderique was a businessman active in the community.

1978—November 11, the *Connor Hotel*, being prepared for implosion, collapsed prematurely on November 11. The nation tuned in for the frantic search for trapped workers. Amazingly one survived.

1979—*Bob Foos* purchased the *Webb City Sentinel*, along with Marti Attoun from William C. Myers. Long-time employee Merle Lortz became Foos' partner in 1983.

1979—June, Judge Ray E. Watson passed away.

1979—September, Bruner's doubled floor space at 101 West Daugherty.

1980—Completion of the *Cameron Estates* at 324 North Tom. Tallest building in Webb City, fire department had to purchase a new ladder truck to accommodate the building.

1980—April, Webb City got its first Walmart store at Cardinal Drive and Madison Avenue (across from Mount Hope Cemetery) formerly known as Aylor Hill. Atwoods moved into the building later.

1980—September, the first annual Mining Days Celebration organized by Bill Lundstrum to replace the annual fall fiesta. The goal (besides having fun) was to raise money for a community building.

1980—Census report said the population of Webb City was 7,309.

1981—Judge Herbert Casteel and Judge Thomas Elliston announced that Jasper County will no longer be in charge of group care homes. Resulted in the closing of Carthage, Fair Acres, and Webb City Elmhurst. Patients were transferred to privately managed nursing and convalescent homes.

1981—May 10, dedication of the *Pillars of the Past* in front of the high school. Funded by donations. The project was the idea of the student council. The pillars are from the old high school on Broadway which was demolished in 1974.

1981—The new Merchants & Miners Bank opened on Webb Street. The Unity Building, where the Merchants & Miners Bank was previously located, was purchased by Don and Carolyn McGowen and became Pinocchio Preschool and Dance Studio with apartments upstairs.

1981—September, the second Annual Mining Days Celebration featured the *number 60 streetcar* refurbished by Fred Rogers and the Southwest Missouri Streetcar Association. The streetcar offered rides, starting at the depot in King Jack Park going a quarter of a mile toward the Praying Hands, using a tractor to pull. The streetcar stopped at the Praying Hands; the passengers would stand and push the seat backs toward the front of the streetcar and sit facing the back of the streetcar as the tractor pushed the streetcar back to the depot. What an exciting event for the Mining Days Celebration.

1982—Construction of the *Webb City Senior Citizen Building* began by The New Era Construction Company, Pennsylvania and Daugherty Streets.

1982—April 12, *Sunrise Park* was sold to Jim and Arla Parril for $10, 501.

1982—Dedication of the Southwest Missouri Electric Railway Company monument in King Jack Park. Two large ornamental slabs from the famous Connor Hotel flank each side of the monument. The streetcars ran from 1889–1939. Fred (Fritz) Rogers organized this monument.

1982—The third Annual Mining Days Celebration was honored to have the number 60 streetcar operating on its own power as it traveled up to the Praying Hands and back to the depot.

1982—June, the old *Salvation Army Hospital* was razed brick by brick. Corner stone located.

1982—December, fire destroyed the historic *Donehoo Block*, south of the Middlewest Building, home, at that time, of the *Webb City Sentinel*, Cardinal Scales, and the Main Street Bar. The former Empress Building was lost, and the south wall of the Middlewest Building had to be replaced. There had been a fire in the same location one hundred years before.

1982—*Ramey's Grocery* opened at Madison and Broadway in the old Foodtown Building.

1982—The Union Pacific purchased the Missouri Pacific Depot located between Webb City and Carterville.

1983—The Webb City Senior Citizen Building opened on the northwest corner of Pennsylvania and Daugherty Streets. Previous location of the first frame house built by Granville Ashcraft.

1983—June, a book dealing with natural environment of the *George Washington Carver Monument*, written by Webb City's *Ernest J. Palmer*, was published. The book was completed in 1960.

1984—Restoration of Middlewest Building, One South Main, began.

1984—March, a small plane attempting to land at the airport crashed in residential area south of Highway 171. Both men aboard the plane were killed.

1984—September 23, Judge J. Byron Fly died.

1984—September, chamber of commerce directors Dr. Ron Barton, Tom Biesner, Terry Oliver, Mike Bailey, and Bob Foos; Bud Corner committee chairman of the Webb City Preservation Committee.

1984—October, Mayor Pro Tem *Carolyn McGowen*, completed a portion of Mayor P. D. Crockett's term from October 1984–April 1985.

1985—April, *Kathryn Patten* finished out the term for Mayor P. D. Crockett from 1985–1986.

1985—The Carson and Barnes three-ring circus came to town, thanks with the efforts of Bill Lundstrum, park board chairman.

1985—August, YMCA Building sold for $9,500.

1985—September, *Elder's Shirt Factory* announced that after sixty-six years, they were leaving town.

1985—September, *Jeanne's Sweet Shoppe* opened at 10 1/2 South Main.

1986—April, *Bill Lundstrum*, elected mayor 1986–1990 (four-year term).

1986—The *Webb City Nursing Home* moved into their new building behind the old Elmhurst Building, which was destroyed.

1986—September, the seventh Annual Mining Days Celebration were thrilled to have the streetcar association present *Old 60 Streetcar* making a full trip around the loop in King Jack Park. You could now ride the streetcar all the way around without stopping. The streetcar was a big success and the pride of Webb City.

1987—March, Steve Benjamin moved the *Webb City Lumber and Hardware* from East Broadway to 1506 South Madison.

1988—Expansion of a new runway at the airport resulted in the closing of the portion of Carl Junction Road that was located north of the airport. Most of what was left of Carl Junction Road was later renamed Stadium Drive. A short east-west street in the subdivision, north of the American Legion/VFW Hall, is named Carl Junction Road.

1988—In an auction, the fountain at *Bradbury Bishop Drug Store* was sold to the Garland Center in Carthage. A group of businessmen and the Preservation Committee purchased the fountain back before it ever left the building. The Garland Center burned not too long afterward. The fountain would have been destroyed, but it is still in Webb City.

1989—January, the Missouri Pacific Railroad Depot was moved to King Jack Park, east side of Sucker Flat, with a good view of the lake and Praying Hands. Mining Days Committee paid $2,000, and the park board would cover the additional $4,000, to be used as a community center. Due to asbestos, the plans for a community center did not happen.

1989—The Jane Chinn Hospital closed after seventy-nine years of operation.

1989—The last four concrete silos of the Ball & Gunning Mill on Madison were demolished.

1989—After thirty-nine years in business, the Johnson Paint and Farm Supply closed its doors at 111 West Daugherty in November.

1989—The Webb City Cardinals won their first state championship in football versus Sumner in Springfield.

1990—April, *Phil Richardson* was elected mayor, April 1990–October 1992. A controversy involving the police department caused him to leave office early.

1990—April, *Lucinda Hensley* had become the first woman president of the R-7 School Board.

1990—April, election in which *Jeanne Newby* joined the board of education; was the first time since 1927 that two women have served on the school board.

1990—March, the *Ozark Motel* closed, and the new McDonald's opened in that same location in August.

1990—The police recovered three stolen cars from a mine pit between Webb City and Carterville.

1990—June, the first *Cruise Night* on Main Street in Webb City.

1990—The Webb City Dump, in the chats, on Dump Road, was closed because it did not meet state regulations. Dump Road is now called East Road.

1990—The *Cerebral Palsy Center* opened on West Austin in what had been the new addition to Jane Chinn Hospital.

1990—September 8, marked the grand opening of the new McDonald's at 410 South Madison, Webb City. Ronald McDonald was featured in the Mining Days Parade. He also made an appearance at the Mining Days Celebration in King Jack Park.

1991—April, the dump became a tire recycling center, but the owner couldn't handle all the tires, which became an environmental hazard. In April, black smoke rose from the dump, where an estimated seventy thousand tires burned—the *tire fire*.

1991—The Frisco Trail began where abandoned railroad tracks used to be.

1992—The Webb City Mining Days Committee built two shelters at the front of King Jack Park with funds accumulated from the annual city celebrations. No more tents for Mining Days! Later those shelters became the home of the Webb City Farmer's Market.

1992—The badly deteriorated YMCA Building in the one hundred block of West Daugherty was demolished. The trustees of the building were never replaced as they passed away, and no one was responsible to maintain the building.

1992—September, *President George Bush* passed through Webb City as he traveled from the Joplin Airport to Missouri Southern State University.

1992—October, *Sterling Gant* served as mayor, October 1992–April 1994, completing Phil Richardson's term.

1992—November, Webb City Cardinals won their second state championship against Rock Bridge in Columbia.

1993—October, tornado hit the northwest side of town. A lot of citizens were out of town at a Lebanon football game as the tornado hit. No injuries, twenty homes damaged

1993—Hatten Park: volunteers showed up to rake, sweep, clean, and carry off trash.

1993—June, Webb City singers performed at the White House.

1993—November, Webb City Cardinals win their first back-to-back state championship. Third win.

1994—April, Sterling Gant elected mayor, 1994–2002 (two full terms after serving a partial term).

1994—Mural of landmarks along Route 66, by local artist *John Biggs*, was painted on the side of Bruner's Drug Store, along Main Street.

1994—Webb City graduate *Grant Wistrom* signed with Nebraska. After a storied career as a Husker, he played with the Super Bowl champion St. Louis Rams in 2000, and later with the Seattle Seahawks.

1994—Webb City merchants invested in new Christmas decorations, durable long-lasting snowflakes.

1995—The Ramey's Grocery Store that was located in the old Foodtown Building, on Madison and Broadway, built its new store on West MacArthur Boulevard, later became Price Cutters.

1995—A new Lakeside Bridge was built over Center Creek on Old Route 66.

1996—January 12, *Jeanne Evans*, who had recently retired as a popular teacher at Eugene Field School for twenty-five years, died unexpectedly; she was fifty-seven. A memorial tree was planted in front of the Eugene Field Elementary School on March 15, in her honor. Mrs. Evans dreamed of becoming an astronaut. She shared that enthusiasm with her students.

1996—Park board sold 14 acres of King Jack Park (between Paradise Lake and Oronogo Street) for $90,000 to a housing developer. They originally bought 154 acres of King Jack Park land for $25,000, and now sold 14 acres for $90,000. The Alpine Estates had a rough start, and but new owners completed the estates in 2014.

1996—May 31, *Police Chief Emmett McFarland* retired after twenty-three years. Don Richardson, a retired Missouri Highway Patrol officer was hired to take McFarland's place.

1996—The first city engineer had been hired, *Jerry Ruse* from Los Angeles, California.

1996—Citizens of Webb City and Oakland Corners voted to consolidate.

1996—Webb City R-VII added a new auditorium, band room, and practice gym facility to the north side of the high school. The auditorium was named in honor of retired superintendent Ron Barton.

1996—The R-VII school district purchased land on the southeast corner of Highway 96 and D Highway in preparation for the growth of housing in Oronogo. They also purchased property between the high school and Webster Primary Center.

1996—August, a replica of the West End Zinc City sign was installed at the entrance to King Jack Park. The project was spearheaded by Fred Rogers, backed by William Perry II, whose firm built the sign. Rogers was noted as bringing the streetcar back to Webb City. The sign was later taken down for improvements in the park and received damages too severe to be reinstalled.

1997—The old *Dickinson Theatre* on Main Street had been given a reprieve. The building was restored by Rick and Gina Monson. Roof damage had kept the building in bad repair for many years. It eventually became the Route 66 Theater.

1997—June, the 1871 *Georgia City Bridge* was moved to King Jack Park. Paying to relocate the bridge was actually a penalty for the city. An employee attempting to get back at the city administrator Gordon Fish reported to the Missouri Department of Natural Resources that the city had been illegally dumping asbestos floor tile in the chats on the east edge of town. City Attorney Paul Taylor arranged the Georgia City Bridge deal, which became an asset. It is now part of the walking trail though the park.

1997—August, open house for new city hall at Second and Main. The city got a good deal on the purchase of the relatively new building after Empire District Electric closed its office here in town. The building was remodeled and extended with an open room for council meetings and municipal court.

1997—Began new construction of *Harry S. Truman Elementary School* at Highway 96 and Route D.

1997—September 15, new city administrator, John Rogers.

1997—The city's second water tower was built at South Hall Street and Cardinal Drive primarily to serve the nearby Joplin-Webb City Industrial Park.

1997—Webb City Cardinals won their first state championship in boys basketball.

1997—Hometown boy *John Roderique* (WCHS '86), in his first year as coach, led the Webb City Football Cardinals to another state championship.

1998—April, Sterling Gant wins third term as mayor.

1998—Jasper County's first escalator was installed at JC Penney's at the mall.

1998—The Webb City Historical Society had moved into its new location, the old Southwest Missouri Street Car Association Club House, which had been built for the relaxation of streetcar employees.

1998—May, at the close of the school year, the Alba school building was donated to the city of Alba. Elementary students began attending the Harry S. Truman Elementary School.

1998—June 15, Webb City Drive-In Theatre, the outdoor movie theater that provided so many memories (forty-plus years old) demolished. It was on the site of the Webb City Walmart superstore.

1998—August, First year for all-day kindergarten classes in the Webb City School District. No more half-days.

1998—Walmart paid for new traffic light at Thirteenth and Madison.

1998—October, Kathryn Patten, long-time city official, was rightfully named the Webb City Area Chamber of Commerce Champion Booster for 1998.

1999—February 12, Steve Hoenshell sworn in as new postmaster for Webb City.

1999—February, the Consumer store closed its doors, after nineteen years, 1980–1999. Located by the first Walmart store in Webb City. The building became the Big Lots.

1999—March, Webb City received over twelve inches of snow.

1999—March, Walmart became a twenty-four-hour superstore, moved to new location on Madison, site of the old Webb City Drive-In Theatre.

1999—New traffic lights were installed at Madison Street and Seventeenth Street (renamed Fountain Road).

1999—Fifth grade students from Eugene Field and Mark Twain Schools and those former sixth grade students from Sixth Grade Center carried their desks into the new Webb City Middle School.

1999—Addition to the high school completed.

1999—June 5, Grant Wistrom started an annual *Grant Wistrom Football Camp* for local football youngsters.

1999—June 7, American Legion Post 322 dedicated *Barnes Baseball Field* in honor of former Commander Chuck Barnes.

1999—*John Roderique* inducted into the Pittsburg State University Hall of Fame.

1999—July, the police department moved to its new location on Broadway. The new location, dedicated on August 1, was a combination of the old telephone building and the previous water department. Dawson Heritage Furniture Company donated the old telephone building.

1999—The Boys and Girls Club was allowed to use the old city hall for an afterschool program.

1999—Beloved *Bill's Drive-In* served its last footlongs on August 14. It was replaced by Wendy's.

1999—*Ryan McFarland*, a junior on the Cardinals Football team, broke his neck during a football game. He healed, assisted John Roderique at WCHS, and was the football coach at Riverton, Kansas. He then moved on to Seneca as coach.

1999—*Eileen Nichols* selected as the Chamber of Commerce Champion Booster.

1999—November, Broadway Market closed its doors after seventy-five years of business.

1999—New businesses opening on Madison Street: Taco Bell, Arby's, May's Drug Warehouse, Wendy's, Commerce Bank, Walgreen's, Atwoods. New businesses on MacArthur: Arvest Bank. New businesses on Main Street: Hunter's Lane, Rann's Jewelry, Main Street Outlet. The old Dickinson Theatre was opened as Route 66 Music Theater by Rick and Gina Munson.

1999—The Lemmons Charitable Trust gave a $60,000 grant to improve the 119-year-old Webb City Cemetery, including a fence, installed in 2001.

2000—Additional eleven acres added to King Jack Park, just east of the Rodeo grounds to be used as soccer fields. The purchase price was $68,000.

2000—King Jack Park received new walking trails, thanks to a grant from Missouri Department of Transportation. The trail connected Paradise Lake to the front of the park. Along the highway bridges were built and donated by Bill Perry and Cardinal Scales.

2000—City administrator John Rogers' contract was extended.

2000—The city of Webb City approved a mandatory drug testing policy for city employees.

2000—April 18, a portion of Missouri Highway 249 had opened from I-44 to Seventh Street. There were plans to extend the highway north toward Webb City.

2000—A test run for a Farmer's Market in King Jack Park was successful, and manager Eileen Nichols was successful in applying for a grant to improve the market.

2000—March, St. Louis Ram, Grant Wistrom, Webb City's first representative on a Super Bowl champion team, was presented the key to the city.

2000—June 10, Grant Wistrom held his second annual football camp for kids.

2000—July 29, official dedication of the *World War II-era Howitzer* in King Jack Park at Ball Street and MacArthur Boulevard. Robert J. Baker had spotted for howitzers in France, ramrodded the project to always remind everyone of the sacrifices made for peace and freedom. Bob Baker named the howitzer Jeannie.

2000—*Marion* and *Bill Perry Jr.* donated $200,000 to renovate and expand the Webb City Public Library. Their donation spurred a drive to collect $2.1 million. Meanwhile the library made a major move by its card catalog to a database.

2000—The round roof Webb City Junior High School gymnasium on First Street was demolished to make room for a bigger better gymnasium. The high school played games in the demolished gym when it was new.

2000—The big water tower sprung a leak, and the city took advantage of the empty tower to have the interior cleaned. Wouldn't you know it, while the water tower was out of commission, the city experienced a severe drought!

2000—October 16, *Governor Mel Carnahan* died when his private plane crashed while he was campaigning for US senator. The governor had visited and spoke in Webb City in February. He was honored for being the education governor.

2000—October 12, the *Webb City R-VII Hall of Fame* was established with the induction of the first five inductees: Kenny Boyer, W. Alton Jones, Kathy Lewis, W. H. Perry Jr., and Robert L. Teel.

2000—Jerry Fisher was the Chamber of Commerce Champion Booster for 2000.

2000—Webb City Cardinals were state champs again in 2000.

2001—April, William Perry with Cardinal Scales donated two bridges for the new walking trail in King Jack Park.

2001—July 13, a plane crashed in Carterville; six passengers from Louisiana died.

2001—*Skateland* was opened in Webb City by Wes and Marti Brewer, in the old rehabilitated Southwest Missouri Streetcar powerhouse at Broadway and Madison.

2001—Grant Wistrom continues with his annual football camp for kids. One hundred eighty kids participated.

2001—The new gym for the junior high was completed, along with a hallway connecting the gymnasium and annex to the main building.

2001—The R-VII School District had other building reports. Four new classrooms were added to the Carterville Elementary School. An office was added to Webster Primary Center. And a new floor was installed in the High School Cardinal Gym.

2001—*September 11*, the United States was attacked by terrorists. The Twin Towers in New York were destroyed, and thousands perished.

2001—A new addition to the annual Mining Days Celebration was a history bus tour by local historian Jeanne Newby.

2001—December 11, Webb City celebrated its 125th birthday. A ceremony was held in the Ron Barton Theater with many historical artifacts on display.

2001—Renovation of historic bathhouse in Hatten Park

2001—Thanks to the Lemmons Trust $60,000 grant, *Webb City Cemetery* and *Wild Rose Cemetery* both received fencing and gates.

2001—October, inductees to the R-VII School District Hall of Fames for this year were Dick Burdick, Charles Cummins, Lisa Myers, and Judge Ray E. Watson.

2001—Bob Foos was the Chamber of Commerce Champion Booster for 2001.

2001—November, Webb City Cardinals were state champs in 2001. Back-to-back wins!

2001—The price of a first-class stamp went up to 34¢.

2001—Results of the 2000 census showed Webb City's population just two hundred away from ten thousand. Up about 30 percent.

2002—April, *Glenn Dolence* was elected mayor, 2002–2006.

2002—War in the Middle East.

2002—Taige Hou won the statewide math contest. He was honored by Governor Bob Holden. He beat out 3,100 students from Missouri in the competition.

2002—April 13, *Dr. Ron Lankford* received the prestigious Pearce Award from the Missouri Association of School Administrators.

2002—May, for the first time, the Webb City High School Commencement was held at Leggett and Platt Athletic Center at MSSU. It is large enough to accommodate the increased number of attendees to the graduation celebration.

2002—August, the citizens of Webb City approved a one-eight-cent sales tax, mostly for the library.

2002—Thanks to the *Little League* representing the Midwest Region at Little League World Series in Williamsport, Pennsylvania, everyone knew about the town of Webb City.

2002—October, the inductees for the Webb City R-VII School District Hall of Fame were Bob Baker, Clete Boyer, Cloyd Boyer, Frank E. Dale, and Gretchen Myers.

2002—Fritz Rogers was the Chamber of Commerce Champion Booster for 2002.

2002—November 15, new flag by a generous anonymous donor installed next to the Praying Hands. One-hundred-foot pole, 28×40 flag, half-circle wall, brass letters that say, "So Proudly We Hail."

2002—The new Webb City Farmer's Market was chosen as the best farmer's market in the state.

2003—The old Southwest Missouri Railway Clubhouse received a remodel of the first floor, thanks to the Webb City Historical Society. The Clubhouse will be their new location.

2003—May 4, tornado did extensive damage to Carl Junction. Many homes destroyed, many injured and killed two.

2003—Bank robbery of the First State Bank located inside Price Cutter Grocery Store on MacArthur.

2003—September 29, the unexpected firing of city administrator John Rogers created a squabble as to his replacement.

2003—September 30, *Mayor Glenn Dolence* submitted his resignation due to discord at city council. Supporters showed up in his front yard on October 9, to convince him to withdraw his resignation, which he did.

2003—June, dedication of *Wistrom Drive* (part of Crow Street).

2003—Groundbreaking for the new amphitheater and community building in King Jack Park.

2003—*Bob Baker* dubbed as the "Father of our King Jack Park." A road entering King Jack Park from Hall Street was named the R. J. Baker Parkway in his honor.

2003—The new middle school opened.

2003—Southwest Center for Educational Excellence next to Crowder College on South Ellis Street.

2003—Construction of the new fire station on Ellis Street began.

2003—August, the beautifully restored Webb City Bank was completed.

2003—October, the Webb City R-VII Hall of Fame inductees were Larry K. Hayes and Jeremy Rusk.

2003—December 23, *Kathryn Patten* passed away.

2003—December 26, the Webb City Choir left to perform in Florida as part of the Epcot Christmas Candlelight Procession. Returned home on New Year's Eve.

2004—January 19, *Chance Morgan* was the new city administrator. He replaced *John Rogers*.

2004—Gail and Nola Anderson were honored as Webb City's Distinguished Citizen by the Webb City R-VII Schools Foundation.

2004—January 29, grand opening of the new *Mining Days Community Building* (3,200 sq. ft.), and amphitheater (seats 250 with room for 750 on the grass.) Webb City Mining Days Committee donated $125,000 toward the community building, plus the purchase of the kitchen appliances. Grant money paid for the amphitheater and the rest of the community building.

2004—The fire department moved into its new station on Ellis Street.

2004—July 30, Webb City's community director, *Joe Butler*, died in car accident. He was replaced by Joe Cartwright.

2004—New tennis courts were built in King Jack Park, thanks to the generosity of William and Marion Perry.

2004—September, the first Mining Days Celebration to be held at the new Mining Days Community Building and Amphitheater.

2004—*Dollar General* opened in Carterville.

2004—October, Webb City R-VII Hall of Fame inductee was Dale Shellhorn.

2004—December 23, business leader and former mayor Bob Baker passed away; he was eighty-three.

2005—February, open house for the *Webb City Public Library* restoration and expansion.

2005—July, reconstruction of entrance to King Jack Park began. The original Kneeling Miner was removed.

2005—August, *William Perry II* passed away. He was eighty-seven.

2005—The Webb City Mining Days Celebration was combined with the new High School Webbstock, the new high school band festival. There were twenty bands in the parade.

2005—May 25, *Nic Frising* passed away at the age of sixty-two. His cartoons and sense of humor are still missed. His final cartoons in the *Sentinel* warned others not to ignore symptoms of colon cancer.

2005—Summer, the removal of houses began on Madison Street to make room for City Pointe Shopping Center. Beautiful maple trees that graced Madison Street were also removed.

2005—New soccer fields in King Jack Park were ready in August for the fall season.

2005—The southeast entrance to King Jack Park was named *Robert J. Baker* Parkway in honor of the mayor responsible for purchasing the land for King Jack Park.

2005—The Webb City R-VII Foundation recognized and honored Merle Lortz as the Distinguished Citizen of Webb City.

2005—Bob Chancellor was inducted into the Webb City R-VII Hall of Fame.

2006—The Webb City High School Cardinal Pride Marching Band marched in the rain during the Tournament of Roses Parade.

2006—City Pointe Shopping Center opened on Madison Street. The homes it replaced were moved to lots a block west of Madison Street and a block south of Broadway Street.

2006—*John Biggs* was elected to his first term as mayor of Webb City.

2006—The new Kneeling Miner Statue and new entrance to King Jack Park were dedicated in September. This new bronze statue by Constance A. Ernatt, of Wichita, replaced Jack Dawson's 1976 Kneeling Miner Statue.

2006—September, *Aylor Park* was sold to Larry M. Thomas Construction Co. for $37,500.

2006—October, *Phil Walsack* joined the city staff as the new community economic developer, specializing in water and sewer services.

2006—Kathleen Crane was inducted into the Webb City R-VII Hall of Fame.

2006—The R-VII School Foundation honored and recognized Glenn Dolence as the Distinguished Citizen for 2006.

2006—It was the last football season played at the old *Cardinal Stadium*. The concrete block structure was demolished to make room for the higher and wider version.

2006—December, *Carl Francis* was hired to succeed Don Richardson as police chief. Interim Chief Don Melton stayed on as assistant chief and emergency management director.

2006—Year of the drought.

2007—January 14, ice storm

2007—January 15, the roof and west wall of the First Baptist Church collapsed from 3" of ice and snow on the roof.

2007—January 15, former mayor Bill Lundstrum passed away.

2007—March, park board made preliminary plans for water park in King Jack Park, put on hold

2007—April 2, *Steve Garrett* new city administrator. He replaced Chance Morgan.

2007—June 8–12, Webb City had 9.55 inches of rain.

2007—June, Carterville said goodbye to the old Carterville School, 1963–2007.

2007—June, city talked of working with EPA to fill Sucker Flat with area mining wastes. Created lots of controversy among citizens.

2007—September 7, first home game in the new *WCHS Cardinal Stadium*.

2007—Dedication of the Bess Truman Elementary School in Oronogo at the Truman Complex.

2007—Dedication of the new Carterville Elementary School

2007—Bob Nichols was honored as the Distinguished Citizen at the annual Webb City R-VII School's Foundation banquet.

2007—New city clerk *Kim DeMoss* replaced Lorinda Southard, who retired.

2007—EPA cleanup of chat piles between Carterville and Webb City began

2007—October, the Webb City R-VII Hall of Fame inductees were Jack Dawson and Kelli Pryor.

2007—November 3, rededication of Memorial Park with names of seventy-seven Webb City citizens who gave their lives for our country in all of the wars.

2007—*Chuck Surface* (previously a member of the House of Representatives) selected as Webb City director of economic development.

2007—December, ice storm

2007—End of year, 55 inches of precipitation, 9.73 inches above normal.

2008—May 16, the Drury students presented their final study survey of improvement ideas for Webb City. Lots of great ideas.

2008—February 21, The Webb City Mining Days Committee disbanded due to lack of volunteers.

2008—May 1, *Terry James* retired from school board after serving for a record-breaking thirty-five years due to health.

2008—September, Webb City accepted as Dream City. Many changes to take place.

2008—October, the Webb City R-VII Hall of Fame inductees were Harold Conner and Grace Woodward.

2008—November, Webb City Cardinals, state champs for 2008.

2008—The Webb City R-VII School Foundation honored Terry James at the annual banquet as the Webb City Distinguished Citizen for 2008.

2009—April 24, 25, 26, Webb City Lion's Club sponsored the first annual Springtime on Broadway with the theme "Get Your Kicks on Route 66."

2009—October, the Webb City R-VII Hall of Fame inductee was Hugh Hatcher.

2009—Bob Foos was named the Distinguished Citizen of the year at the annual Webb City School's Foundation banquet.

2010—John Biggs re-elected as mayor.

2010—October, the Webb City R-VII Hall of Fame inductees were Mike Copple and Allen L. Hall.

2010—The Webb City School's Foundation honored Ron Lankford as this year's Distinguished Citizen at the annual banquet.

2010—The city council, under the leadership of Mayor John Biggs, purchased 114 acres ($80,000) along East Road from the Aylor family estate, planning to put in Industrial Park, along with 17 acres acquired from EPA.

2010—November, Webb City Cardinals, state champs for 2010.

2011—*Stadium Drive* from Madison Street to Main Street completed. It is located north of the high school campus.

2011—April election, the citizens voted to ban smoking in Webb City restaurants, bars, and other businesses. Contrary to the vote, the city council voted 3–5 against the ban.

2011—May 1, the Heritage Clock on the high school campus was dedicated. A tribute to Webb City educators since 1877, donated by Jim Dawson.

2011—May 22, F5 tornado hit Joplin. It wiped out a big portion of the city, and 162 people were killed and hundreds injured. Devastating!

2011—Summer, a terrible drought and heat wave. Killed lots of trees, plants, and dried up ponds.

2011—October, the Webb City R-VII Hall of Fame inductee was Peggy Wrightsman.

2011—Eileen Nichols was honored as the Distinguished Citizen at the annual Webb City School's Foundation banquet.

2011—November, Bright Futures organized in Webb City.

2011—Webb City Cardinals, state champs for 2011.

2012—February 14, Dr. Ron Barton, retired superintendent, passed away. Services were held in the Ron Barton Theater, named in his honor.

2012—A mine shaft was discovered behind the Elks Club on North Madison. State officials hired a contractor to span the opening with steel beams and cover it with concrete.

2012—October, the Webb City R-VII Hall of Fame inductee was Jane Benson.

2012—Webb City Cardinals, state champs for 2012.

2012—The Webb City School's Foundation banquet honored Jim Dawson as the Distinguished Citizen of the year.

2012—Construction began on the roundabout on Highway 171 and East Road.

2012—Park department remodeled the depot at the park and moved the office there.

2012—Streetcar 60 was given new wheels this year.

2012—Fire chief Ernie Goade retired September 30. Andrew Roughton was appointed as the new fire chief on November 12.

2012—September 26, director of economic development, *Chuck Surface*, died.

2012—The *Minerva Candy Company* had reopened with Tom and Mary Hamsher as the new owners. They did need restoration on the buildings.

2012—A new mural was painted on the north side of the Middlewest Building at Main and Broadway Streets. Donations and grant money paid for the mural. Kyle McKenzie sketched the mural and assisted a multitude of painter in finishing the mural.

2012—December, EPA had begun the task of filling in Sucker Flat in King Jack Park.

2013—The Webb City Roundabout was completed.

2013—October, the Webb City Hall of Fame inductees were Zoe Thralls and Hal Wise Jr.

2013—Webb City Cardinals, state champs for 2013.

2013—The Webb City School's Foundation banquet honored husband and wife *Jim and Karen Latimer* as the Distinguished Citizens for 2013.

2014—April, John Biggs re-elected as mayor for third term.

2014—Gene Mense was honored for his fifteen years of service on the city council.

2014—Webb City King Jack Park hosted its annual Easter egg hunt and attracted six hundred egg hunters this year.

2014—The Webb City Public Library now allowed anyone with a library card to check out books online to be read on a computer, tablet, or phone screens.

2014—October, the Webb City R-VII Hall of Fame inductees were Mark Hughes and Chuck Surface.

2014—October, the Webb City Area Chamber of Commerce honored Richard Crow as this year's Champion Booster.

2014—The Webb City R-VII School Foundation honored *David Collard* as the Distinguished Citizen.

2014—Project graduation sponsored the Webb City Christmas Parade this year. Previously sponsored by the Webb City Area Chamber of Commerce.

2014—The new Carterville Exit was completed.

2014—The Stone's Corner Roundabout was completed.

2014—The Webb City Library had a series of celebrations in honor of their centennial.

2014—July 18, a large portion of downtown Webb City was placed on the National Register of Historic Buildings

2014—March 24, the shopping center on Madison Square was burned due to an intentional fire.

2014—November, Webb City Cardinals, state champs for the thirteenth time, five consecutive wins.

2015—January 20, dome grand opening, ribbon-cutting

2015—Webb City Little League, twelve-year-olds represented Webb City in the Little League Baseball World Series. They became the first American team to receive the Jack Losch World Series Team Sportsmanship Award.

2015—Webb City R-VII Hall of Fame inductees were *Betty Browning*, class of '29; *Kelli Hopkins*, class of '77. Distinguished Citizen—Randy Wilson

2015—October, Hedge-Lewis became Hedge-Lewis-Goodwin.

2016—April, Old 60 Streetcar was back on track after three years of inactivity while the EPA filled in Sucker Flat.

2016—Two additional lakes were added to Paradise Lake in King Jack Park.

2016—Lynn Ragsdale became the new mayor of Webb City after John Biggs resigned to move out of town.

2016—November, Distinguished Citizen—Nancy Spaeth

2017—New turf was put down at the Cardinal Stadium.

2017—King Jack Park, the splash pad and train depot picnic pavilion were added over by the playground and Paradise Lake.

2017—New engine attached to 60 should keep her going for years.

2017—*Jim Steele* honored as the new inductee of the R-VII Hall of Fame at the annual chamber of commerce banquet.

2018—March, *Jeanne Newby* honored as the R-VII Foundation Distinguished Citizen.

2018—April, King Jack Park featured the new splash pad and pavilion by playground.

2018—June, King Jack Park and Paradise Lake featured two new fountains in the main lake.

2018—October, Webb City R-VII Hall of Fame inductees were Dr. David Morris, 1984 graduate and exercise physiologist; and Rex Tabor Jr., a 1968 graduate opera star.

2018—October, the Robert J. Baker Champion Booster for this year was Brad Baker.

2018—October, Webb City's Employee of the Year was Sergeant Michael Larery with the Webb City Police Department.

Bibliography

1883 History of Jasper County.

1899 Webb City Gazette.

A History of the Pleasant Hill United Methodist Church. 1988.

Burk Merker, Rosemond. "1954 Thesis of Webb City's First 25 Years." Graduate of Webb City High School.

Conard, Howard L., ed. *Encyclopedia of the History of Missouri.* 1901.

Crotty, Henrietta, comp. and ed. *A History and Economic Survey of Webb City, Missouri.* Webb City Daily Sentinel, 1937.

Crotty, Henrietta M. *History of the First Presbyterian Church of Webb City, Missouri 1877–1942.* Auspices of the Session of the Church and the Women's Association, 1942.

Hood, Harry C., Sr. *The Southwest Missouri Railroad.* 1976.

Interview with Emmett Hughes plus many other personal interviews over the past thirty-one years.

Interview with Hulda Evelyn Fredrickson Surgi, 1997.

Livingston, Joel T. *A History of Jasper County and Its People*, vols. 1 and 2. Chicago: The Lewis Publishing Company, 1912.

Matthews, Norval M. *An Amazing City* (Webb City Sentinel, 1976).

McGregor, Malcolm G. *The Biographical History of Jasper County, Missouri.* Chicago: Lewis Publishing Company, 1901.

Obituaries on file at the Joplin Public Library, Joplin, Missouri.

"The Heart of the World's Lead and Zinc District." *Webb City Review*, 1909.

The Revised Ordinances of the City of Webb City. 1905.

The Webb City Topic and Mining Journal. 1897.

Webb City High School Annuals. 1908–1955.

Webb City and Jasper County, Missouri Illustrated, 1906–1907. The Webb City Commercial Club.

Webb City Souvenir (January 1900).

About the Author

This book is an expression of the history of a small mining town in Southwest Missouri. After writing about the history of Webb City for a thirty-one-year period, in a local newspaper, many followers asked Jeanne to please share her knowledge in the print of a book, not just the newspaper column. Jeanne has shared her love of history with many organizations, such as the Historical Society, The Genealogy Society, The History Commission, many presentations as a speaker for groups and school classes. That willingness to share her research created this book and more to come. The Missouri House of Representatives presented a resolution that named Jeanne Newby as the local historian of Webb City.

In 2018, Jeanne was honored with the R-VII Distinguished Citizen Award. Previously Jeanne received the honor of being the 2005 Champion Booster of Webb City. Jeanne has served on the Webb City R-VII School Board for over twenty years. Jeanne graduated from Webb City High School in 1969. She served on the city council and many city boards. A strong connection with Webb City and the love of Webb City history created a bond that is now in print.

Printed in the USA
CPSIA information can be obtained
at www.ICGtesting.com
LVHW080033151123
763724LV00008B/569